I0878614

Flaco's Legacy

MUSIC IN AMERICAN LIFE

A list of books in the series appears at the end of this book.

Flaco's Legacy

The Globalization of Conjunto

ERIN E. BAUER

UNIVERSITY OF ILLINOIS PRESS
Urbana, Chicago, and Springfield

This publication was funded in part by grants from the University of Wisconsin Whitewater and the AMS 75 PAYS Fund of the American Musicological Society, supported in part by the National Endowment for the Humanities and the Andrew W. Mellon Foundation.

1 2 3 4 5 C P 5 4 3 2 1
♾ This book is printed on acid-free paper.

Library of Congress Cataloging-in-Publication Data
Names: Bauer, Erin E., 1983– author.
Title: Flaco's legacy: the globalization of conjunto / Erin E. Bauer.
Description: Urbana: University of Illinois Press, 2023. | Series: Music in American life | Includes bibliographical references and index.
Identifiers: LCCN 2022048755 (print) | LCCN 2022048756 (ebook) | ISBN 9780252045028 (hardback) | ISBN 9780252087158 (paperback) | ISBN 9780252054297 (ebook)
Subjects: LCSH: Conjunto music—History and criticism. | Music and globalization. | Jiménez, Flaco.
Classification: LCC ML3476 .B38 2023 (print) | LCC ML3476 (ebook) | DDC 781.64097—dc23/eng/20221104
LC record available at https://lccn.loc.gov/2022048755
LC ebook record available at https://lccn.loc.gov/2022048756

Contents

PART III: THE APPROPRIATION OF CONJUNTO

Acknowledgments

This book stems from three years living and teaching in the Rio Grande Valley of Texas and is indebted to the generosity of the students, colleagues, and friends who welcomed me into their lives and introduced me to the rich musical culture of the region. Years later, with a graduate degree in historical musicology and a shiny new dissertation on sixteenth-century Spanish keyboard music, I couldn't stop thinking about *conjunto* music and its connection to the communities along the Texas border of Mexico. For me, the joy of life in the Valley was an entanglement of friends, food, and music: tasting chili and dancing at the annual Cactus Country Festival in El Sauz, tasting rattlesnake and dancing at the annual Wild Game Dinner and Dance at the Starr County Fairgrounds, and suspending middle school math classes for Friday afternoon dances at Ringgold Middle School. The juxtaposition of this joy in community with the very real economic struggles for the region, the misrepresentations of its people among a national rhetoric, and the politicization of the border outside of any real consideration for the people or the natural environment most affected by these political decisions formed a lasting commitment to bringing outside attention, in some small way, to the music and the culture of South Texas. As a cultural outsider, I filter my analyses through my own lived experiences, which inevitably differ from those most closely connected to the conjunto tradition. I am grateful to those who have shared their experiences with me; the following analyses remain my own, in all their cross-cultural messiness.

In addition to my indebtedness to my students, colleagues, and friends in Rio Grande City and across the Rio Grande Valley, this book would not be possible without the many musicians, fans, organizers, and cultural advocates who have graciously shared their experiences with me. These include (but are certainly not limited to): Betty Barajas, Omar Cadena, Art Campos, Andy Cardenas, Baldomero Cuellar, Rick De La Rosa, Marcus De Leon, Johnny Degollado, Mario Diaz Jr., JD Enmascarados, Linda Escobar, Joel Guzman, Issac Ledesma, Piper LeMoine, Irma Morales, Robert Northrup, Miguel A. Pérez, Sarah Rucker, Frank Sanchez, B. Santa Ana, Sunny Sauceda, Juan Tejeda, Susan Torres, Dwayne Verheyden, and Frutty Villarreal. Special thanks to David Gonzalez and the Guadalupe Cultural Arts Center in San Antonio for providing access to information and materials related to the Tejano Conjunto Festival. I am grateful to my fellow scholars for raising provocative questions at the many conference presentations related to this work and the anonymous reviewers of related articles, this book proposal, and the full manuscript. The work is better for their discerning comments, suggestions, and corrections. Any remaining errors are mine alone. Thanks also to Robin Moore for guiding my early work in this area, to David Garcia for suggesting that I consider incorporating scholarship on genre theory (and directing me to David Brackett's work), Cathy Ragland for ideas and support, and Luis Diaz-Santana Garza for a critical reading of this manuscript. Thanks to Laurie Matheson at the University of Illinois Press for supporting my work and the full production staff for guiding its completion.

Finally, this book would not be possible without the support of my husband, Reed, who has spent countless hours listening to my philosophical musings, responding to my half-baked ideas, and providing the space necessary for thinking, writing, and revision. He has moved with me across the country for academic opportunities, shouldered household responsibilities so I could write, and helped us both to balance pandemic-era parenting with demanding careers. I am forever grateful. And to Will, who won't remember the process, but brings only love and light.

Flaco's Legacy

The Globalization of Conjunto

There are critics out there. I know that. Sometimes those critics say: "Hey, Flaco, how about the beans. You're just eating hamburgers." My answer is, I'll eat a taco, I'll eat a hamburger, I'll eat a pizza, whatever. It makes it more versatile. It's the way I like to make music happen.
—Flaco Jiménez, *Chicago Tribune*

In 2015, Texas-Mexican accordionist Leonardo "Flaco" Jiménez (b. 1939) received a Lifetime Achievement Grammy Award. Displaying a seemingly intentional diversity of sociocultural identities and associated genres on the part of the Recording Academy, that year the musician joined George Harrison, the Bee Gees, the Louvin Brothers, Pierre Boulez, Buddy Guy, and Wayne Shorter to represent "exceptional creators who have made prolific contributions to our culture and history."[1] This description alone sets up one of the primary themes of this book. Flaco serves as a prominent proponent of Texas-Mexican *conjunto* music, a folkloric combination of button accordion with *bajo sexto* (a twelve-string Spanish/Mexican bass guitar) that has historically functioned as a cultural representation of regional working-class identity.[2] However, while Flaco remains well known throughout South Texas—particularly as his global accolades have increased recognition for the local region, his music has perhaps been most popular worldwide among niche audiences initially attracted to the artist's collaborations with artists like Ry Cooder, Bob Dylan, and the Rolling Stones and hybridizations with elements of rock, country, jazz, and the blues.

As such, despite conjunto music's historical connection to Texas-Mexican identity, the Recording Academy describes Flaco's music as representative of "our" culture and history, indicating an adoption of the folkloric music among a commercial audience in the United States, or at least an adoption of the awardee's particular transcultural flavor of conjunto. In this sense,

Texas-Mexican conjunto music has experienced processes of globalization, a word that I invoke to indicate a disconnection—through a diversity of methods that will be explored in detail throughout this book—from the original sociocultural context: geographically, stylistically, and associatively.

This celebratory instance might suggest a multicultural inclusivity indicative of the U.S. American melting-pot narrative, since each of these musical representatives comes from within the United States and therefore is each a member of "our" culture. However, we recall instead a national discourse of ethnic segregation; the historical interpretation of Mexican American as "other," despite frequent cultural appropriations (of food, celebrations, and musical sounds) across hegemonic (well-educated, middle-class, and Anglo-American) circumstances. Is Flaco himself considered by this hegemonic community to be a member of "our" culture? If not, can his music be separated from his sociocultural identity—as determined by this same group—to serve as a disembodied representation of a community to which he does not fully belong? Does the adoption of Flaco's music among a U.S. American commercial audience—as determined by the Recording Academy—suggest a similar adoption for the musician and/or culture, or is this commercialized sense of globalization simply a masked version of appropriation? In addition, if these processes of globalization occur within the United States, are they truly an indication of globalization? Does this term imply a particular distance that a cultural manifestation must travel or does the presence of these processes create an analogous result, regardless of location? I argue that the term globalization remains appropriate across a range of analyses; the process thus produces instances of "globalization" across the diversity of cultures within the United States, despite an intermittent nearness of proximity. As such, this book presents the globalization of conjunto: in Texas, in the United States, in Europe and Asia, and, ultimately, around the world.

Starting in the 1970s, Flaco's music began to travel around the world through a variety of live performances (initially in combination with artists like Cooder but later as the headliner), inter/national distribution of recordings, and transcultural representations in the media. His music has incorporated a number of hybridized elements that shift the aesthetic style beyond its original sonic associations. Strains of his accordion improvisations appear on albums by Cooder, Dwight Yoakam, the Rolling Stones, and more. In addition, international artists like Kenji Katsube from Japan and Dwayne Verheyden from the Netherlands have adopted Flaco's repertory and musical sound, raising questions of sociocultural identity in music removed from its traditional ethnic and socioeconomic heritage.

I structure this book according to these three processes of globalization: media/migration, hybridization, and appropriation. While Flaco is not the only conjunto musician to spread his music among an inter/national audience through these methods, he is the first and most prominent. Together with a few of his generational peers (significantly, Mingo Saldívar, Steve Jordan, and Eva Ybarra), he will thus retain primary consideration throughout the ensuing study, with the understanding that various other regional musicians have pursued similar approaches at slightly later time periods and under the guise of slightly different musical categorizations. At the same time, other regional conjunto musicians have maintained a local prominence and more traditional understanding of the music, indicating that these processes of globalization have been applied intermittently, as distinctive local and global versions of Texas-Mexican accordion music exist simultaneously.

If anything, Flaco's particular style of conjunto exists outside of the regional context, creating a globalized version of the music that functions independently from the local genre. The question of genre then becomes a primary impetus for analysis. What is conjunto—stylistically and socioculturally—and how does this categorization change if either the style or sociocultural context changes? Is it "conjunto" because of a set of fixed musical characteristics or simply due to its performance by Flaco (or other regional musicians)? Does a certain categorization rely on a specific instrumentation, repertory, and sound, or is it more closely connected to a particular ethnic identity? Does the idea of genre change among different populations, i.e., what is conjunto in San Antonio vs. California vs. the Netherlands? How do local genres like Tejano and norteño—stylistically very similar to conjunto but typically considered separately—relate to these concepts of categorization? Finally, how are notions of identity intertwined within these understandings of genre?

Genre is a fluid consideration that arguably holds little meaning outside of awards shows and commercialized marketing. That being said, consideration of musical categorization in these seemingly arbitrary contexts raises interesting questions of social identity. A brief description of Flaco's Grammy Awards will serve as an introduction to some of these questions (which will then be discussed in more detail throughout this book). In addition to the Lifetime Achievement Award in 2015, Flaco has received nine Grammy nominations, winning a total of five awards. Three of these nominations, including one win, came as part of the group the Texas Tornados, while one win came through the supergroup Los Super Seven, both explored in more detail later. In addition, Flaco has participated on a number of other Grammy Award-winning performances, including two nominations with

Dwight Yoakam for "Streets of Bakersfield" from the album *Buenas Noches From a Lonely Room* in 1988, a win with the Rolling Stones for *Voodoo Lounge* in 1994, and an additional win with Max Baca and Los Texmaniacs for the album *Borders Y Bailes* in 2009. A list of each award with the associated categorizations appears below (Tab. 0.1).

Due to a range of generic considerations—including a family history of making conjunto, a consistent instrumentation and repertory related to the most fundamental considerations of the genre, and a sociocultural identity (including location) most closely connected to the historical understanding of the music—Flaco is most typically categorized among local and global fans as a (quintessential) conjunto artist. Yet, the listing of his Grammy Awards suggests the complexities involved with making that particular—or any—generic distinction: despite his most prominent correlation with the conjunto genre, Flaco has received or been nominated for Grammy Awards not only in the categories of Mexican American and Tejano (as would seem expected), but also for country and rock. That being said, the rock nomination is related to the artist's work with the Rolling Stones while the country nominations come through Dwight Yoakam, the Texas Tornados, and a collaboration with Lee Roy Parnell (for "Cat Walk"). This indicates that, while Flaco's performances cross established generic boundaries—at least in a manner determined by the external and hegemonic forces of the Recording Academy and ostensibly tied to some element of sonic structure rather than identity alone—he remains characterized as a "conjunto" artist (if we agree that, for the Recording Academy, Mexican American and Tejano equate to conjunto) unless working together with Anglo-American musicians more typically considered as rock or country artists.

This analysis is further complicated by considering the Tejano Music Awards, a local set of accolades established in San Antonio in 1980 with categories separating Tejano, conjunto, and norteño designations. Flaco received a Lifetime Achievement Award from the organization in 2011 but has not received any awards—in any represented genre—for specific albums or songs. In this regard, it would seem that Flaco and his music inhabit a liminal space between Texas-Mexican and commercialized U.S. American cultures; belonging to both and neither at the same time and thus using processes of globalization to establish an individual genre and sociocultural identity outside of preconceived notions of these categorizations. Interestingly, although Flaco, Saldívar (who received a Lifetime Achievement Award in 2012), Jordan, and Ybarra have not received individual Tejano Music Awards, despite their inarguably prominent positions in Tejano music (broadly defined), Verheyden—a young Dutch accordionist who will also be considered in more

Table 0.1. Grammy Awards (Nominations and Wins) for Flaco Jiménez.

Artist	Category	Year	Result	Song/Album
Flaco Jiménez	Best Mexican-American Performance	1986	Winner	*Ay Te Dejo En San Antonio*
Flaco Jiménez	Best Mexican-American Performance	1988	Nominee	*Flaco's Amigos*
Dwight Yoakam	Best Country Vocal Performance	1988	Nominee	*Buenas Noches From a Lonely Room*
Dwight Yoakam and Buck Owens	Best Country Vocal Collaboration	1988	Nominee	"Streets of Bakersfield"
Texas Tornados	Best Mexican-American Performance	1990	Winner	"Soy De San Luis"
Texas Tornados	Best Country Performance by a Duo or Group with Vocal	1991	Nominee	*Zone of Our Own*
Rolling Stones	Best Rock Album	1994	Winner	*Voodoo Lounge*
Flaco Jiménez	Best Mexican-American/ Tejano Music Performance	1995	Winner	*Flaco Jiménez*
Flaco Jiménez	Best Country Instrumental Performance	1995	Nominee	"Cat Walk"
Texas Tornados	Best Country Performance by a Duo or Group with Vocal	1996	Nominee	"Little Bit Is Better Than Nada"
Flaco Jiménez	Best Tejano Music Performance	1998	Winner	*Said and Done*
Los Super Seven	Best Mexican-American Music Performance	1998	Winner	*Los Super Seven*
Los Texmaniacs	Best Tejano Album	2009	Winner	*Border Y Bailes*
Flaco Jiménez	Lifetime Achievement Award	2015	Winner	Lifetime Achievement Award

detail throughout this book—did receive a Tejano Music Award for Best New Artist (Group) in 2014. Verheyden is influenced by Flaco's aesthetic style. However, while Flaco has not received recognition in this regard, despite his clear sociocultural positionality within the local community, his global successor—idiomatically outside the sociocultural community—has.

Our brief description of Flaco's Grammy Awards also introduces a concise representation of the manifestations of globalization inherent throughout his work. While two of the performances receiving recognition are indicative of a more conservative, regional style (*Ay Te Dejo En San Antonio* and *Said and Done*), most of these recordings instead incorporate outside musicians (Cooder, Parnell, and Peter Rowan, for example, in addition to other members of the Texas Tornados and Los Super Seven, and indicated collaborations with Yoakam, Buck Owens, and the Rolling Stones) and/or hybridized musical characteristics (particularly on *Flaco Jiménez*, explored in detail in Chapter 4). In this way, globalized processes of music making demonstrate an expansion of Texas-Mexican conjunto beyond homologous notions of time and space. Despite persistent scholarly discourse of conjunto music as ethnic identity (by Américo Paredes, Manuel Peña, and Jose E. Limón, most prominently), a cultural artifact that permanently affixes "traditional" musical characteristics to an assumed identity based on heritage and location, Flaco's particular iteration of conjunto—however we define the genre—is not confined to place. Instead, the music travels outside of stereotypical understandings of the Texas-Mexican border, encompassing people, places, and musical traits no longer affiliated with a specific sociocultural identity.

This interpretation is further complicated by the musical interconnections between Texas and Mexico. While Flaco (and others) uses popular songs and musical traits to assert a position at the edge of the U.S. American recording industry, he distances himself from the Mexican origination and continuing influence of his foundational materials. He blends Mexican songs (among others) with popular characteristics to assert a U.S. American identity for the Texas-Mexican music, rather than Mexican. This process obscures the fluidity of culture on the U.S.-Mexico border and reduces the competitive threat to performance opportunities from Mexican musicians. Furthermore, the positionality of artists like Flaco as U.S. American citizens offers travel and performance allowances inaccessible to Mexican musicians. In this regard, while the migration, hybridization, and appropriation of Texas-Mexican conjunto music among a Euro-American hegemony highlights discrepancies of power and ethnic discrimination between Anglo-American and Mexican-American musicians, the continuing but often-invisible reliance of this music on a Mexican repertory, instrumentation, structure, and sound constructs an analogous power differential between musicians on the northern versus the southern side of the U.S.–Mexico border.

Throughout this book, then, I follow scholars like Alejandro Madrid (2008) in writing about borders; in its most obvious manifestation, this analysis encompasses music of the U.S.-Mexico border region, a location and culture misunderstood and frequently misrepresented among the popular discourse. Yet, beyond this initial characterization and transcultural spread, I examine the confrontation of the music of a particular region and associated culture at the border of dramatically different elements of region, heritage, and sonic categorization. I join scholars like Madrid in investigating the borders between "tradition and innovation"; between "different musical genres"; between "the hip" and "the unsophisticated."[3] In so doing, I establish Texas-Mexican conjunto music as a means to examine the implications of globalization across a range of geographic, stylistic, and sociocultural boundaries. Beyond the music itself, I explore identity in music. I consider the continuous flow of space and time that creates new understandings of aesthetic categorization in globally relevant repertories. I thus challenge homologous notions of genre and identity that map one concept onto the other, pushing back against former narratives of Texas-Mexican conjunto as regional, working-class identity to complicate the role of the music among shifting conceptions of the physical and associated epistemological border, its people, and its influence worldwide.

The Processes and Implications of Globalization

This book addresses the globalization of Texas-Mexican conjunto music throughout the United States (in a form of domestic globalization that follows established processes to create a localized view of global implications) and around the world. It identifies former notions of the cultural commodity as representative of regional identity before tracing more recent results of live performances, transcultural media representations, broad distribution of recordings, stylistic combinations of musical elements not typically considered as part of the historic genre, as well as various series of collaboration, participation, appreciation, and appropriation by artists and audiences functioning outside of the stereotypical Texas-Mexican border community. In short, it develops an understanding of globalization through a series of three processes: media/migration, hybridization, and appropriation. The book is then organized according to these three processes. Underlying this primary organization are two fundamental implications of globalization: identity and genre.

The process of globalization is not new, with historic precedent in the cultural clashes—and resulting hybridizations—created by European imperialism. Yet, throughout time, these processes seem to be accelerated by technology: both with the industrial revolution during the nineteenth century and the digital communication capacities starting at the end of the twentieth century. Prominently, Arjun Appadurai (1996) discusses the role of electronic modes of media and transnational mobilization in developing new forms of cultural communities. As Madrid concurs, these technological developments have "propelled the speed, reach, and character of these processes of expansion," with the particular implications of more recent flows of people and ideas making "the current phase of globalization look like a different animal."[4] As such, globalization can be defined as "a continuous process that brings the world closer and closer together."[5] For our purposes, I consider "the world" in its broadest terms, not designated simply by location, but also incorporating a diversity of social practices, aesthetic priorities, linguistic patterns, familial connections, etc.; in short, the entire slippery concept of culture and its interactions with the various manifestations of other cultures, regardless of the distance between associated groups of people. In this way, I consider processes of globalization to function across oceans, but also in more localized communities; particularly in regions of the United States made up of diverse populations in constant conversation with one another, but also around the world.

Across time, globalization has formed the impetus for new forms of musical expression. Intertwined within these shifting forms of expression are shifting concepts of categorization and personal identity. In discussing globalization, I simply add my voice to a wide range of scholars who have considered similar methods of global flow (Turino 1993, Simonett 2001, Edberg 2004, Habell-Pallán 2005, Madrid 2008, and Chávez 2017, to start). Yet, while the global processes in each circumstance are similar, the contexts are different; conjunto is not *banda* or *Nor-tec* or *huapango arribeño* (to name a few), and its primary practitioners are ethnic Mexicans living on the Texas side of the U.S.-Mexico border—not ethnic Mexicans in California or Mexican citizens in Tijuana or Mexican migrants in Texas, respectively. These differences in identity are subtle, but create entirely different circumstances when considering the implications for corresponding processes of globalization. It is therefore these notions of identity, brought about by a continuously globalized form of music and intertwined with complicated distinctions of categorization among all associated parties, that become the most important implications for the musical products and circumstances described in this book.

Scholars like Peña (1985) have described conjunto music as representative of a working-class cultural identity in South Texas. In this way, Texas-Mexican conjunto has been presented as a homologous musical genre that connects culture to category; as David Brackett describes, a "transitory division" in aesthetic style that ostensibly corresponds to a "temporally defined social space," in the same way that so-called "race music" (alternatively relabeled rhythm and blues) has been persistently linked to African-American identity.[6] While, historically, the connection between Texas-Mexican conjunto music and Texas-Mexican identity seems to be an applicable analysis, the genre has been—and continues to be—performed and consumed by individuals outside of the Texas-Mexican community. Meanwhile, although Texas-Mexican people continue to participate in the genre, individual members of the community certainly produce and consume music classified alternatively. In addition, the persistent distinction between conjunto—on the northern side of the geo-political border—and norteño—on the southern side—for artists, audiences, and scholars, despite close similarities in style, repertory, and influence, further complicates peculiarities of genre and its inextricable relationship to identity. Generic classification according to a fixed set of sonic characteristics does not fully describe the range of musical styles either included or not included in this category.

For example, as we will see throughout this book, many performances by artists consistently characterized as conjunto musicians (for our purposes, including, but certainly not limited to Flaco, Jordan, Saldívar, and Ybarra) include elements of other genres: most notably, country, rock, jazz, and the blues. Meanwhile, musicians classified as Tejano, such as Little Joe, and norteño, such as Los Tigres del Norte, display musical elements more consistently aligned with a conjunto categorization. Further complicating matters, a number of inter/national musicians, with presumed sociocultural identities completely disconnected from Texas-Mexican heritage, play music that includes conjunto elements (in varying degrees). Some of these are generally considered to be conjunto musicians (Verheyden and Katsube, for example), while some are not (the Rolling Stones and Rowwen Hèze, as well as more surprising examples like the Texas Tornados). In this way, as will be explored in more detail throughout this book, former understandings of Texas-Mexican conjunto music as regional, working-class, cultural identity do not stand up to modern realities. As more recent scholars like Deborah Vargas (2012) and Alex Chávez (2017) assert, not only do these homologous narratives of genre as identity not represent the current circumstances for Texas-Mexican music, but, in fact, were never entirely appropriate.

Throughout the following chapters, I assert that processes of globalization lead to shifting concepts of genre (and thus, identity). Any generic definition consists, at least in part, of certain stylistic components. For example, for a piece of music to be classified as conjunto, we can argue that it must include certain elements of instrumentation, timbre, structure, rhythm, tempo, language, repertory, etc. Santiago Jiménez Sr.'s recording of "Ay Te Dejo En San Antonio," discussed in detail below, then—consisting of button accordion with bajo sexto, vocal harmonies in thirds, a *ranchera* structure with instrumental introduction and accordion interludes preceding each verse, danceable tempo, the Spanish language, etc.—can most certainly be characterized as conjunto. However, processes of globalization create different interpretations of the piece; how much can the aesthetic traits historically correlated with the genre change for it to still be thought of as conjunto? For that matter, since the elements of conjunto music have varied through time, which temporal moment actually determines a particular definition for the genre?

Brackett raises considerations of "the fleeting quality of genre arrangements and levels at any particular point in time," reminding us that the organization of musical characteristics remains a fluid construct, shifting continuously in time to correspond to the people and places of any given moment.[7] That is, the series of traits associated with the music of the professed father of conjunto, Narciso Martínez, in the 1930s, is not the same as the characteristics of Tony De La Rosa, in the middle of the twentieth century, nor—as we will see—the understanding of conjunto developed through the music of Flaco by the end of the century. Nonetheless, once we do agree on a set of "classic" conjunto characteristics, perhaps determined through Peña's interpretation of the genre as it reached consolidation at the middle of the century, processes of globalization yet again alter this consideration. In this regard, as Chávez notes, those cultural traits considered to be "traditional" are frequently affixed to primordial notions of a particular community, essentializing the music as an "authentic practice of assumed heritage" and thus positioning the associated community as a rigid construct of time and space.[8] In other words, by clinging to homologous notions of music as identity, we lock Texas-Mexican people into a primitivist—and potentially racist—view that defines the border community as old fashioned, folkloric, and outside of modern understandings of U.S. American culture. This seemingly innocent characterization of a community-based genre of music has dangerous implications if projecting primordial notions into the political realm.

In addition, the entire history of conjunto music is built on cultural hybridity. As we will review in more detail below, the music initially developed in the blend of European dance forms with Mexican rhythms (as Madrid notes, "a more syncopated melodic line," among other characteristics); at its core, button accordion with bajo sexto.[9] Over time, stylistic components changed to encompass contemporary circumstances. While the genre fundamentally comprised European polkas, schottisches, and redowas, it later shifted to include Mexican forms like the corrido, huapango, and ranchera, and, even later, inter/national elements like the Cuban bolero, the Colombian cumbia, and—as we see in Flaco's (and others') music—various traits of U.S. American popular music. In this regard, despite scholarly narratives of aesthetic consolidation, conjunto music has never actually achieved stylistic stagnation.

As Madrid attests, "although a characteristic Mexican/Mexican-American style developed as a hybrid of Mexican, border, and European traditions, it did not become a static, fossilized musical practice."[10] Therefore, any argument asserting conjunto music as regional identity does not fully consider the continuous flow of stylistic characteristics emanating from numerous cultural backgrounds throughout time.

The characterization of conjunto in relation to both Mexican norteño and U.S. American popular music constructs and emphasizes systems of power across the global performance space. Following initial German influences, conjunto musicians have built the genre on a Mexican foundation that is often discredited in favor of imagined entries into a more valued arena. Just as U.S. American popular artists use bits of the conjunto sound to construct an exotic invocation of multiculturalism, Texas-Mexican conjunto musicians use Mexican traditions to invoke romanticized elements of the southern region while simultaneously distancing themselves from negative characterizations of the region by also asserting their identification with U.S. American popular culture. In this way, while U.S. American popular artists use conjunto to achieve economic opportunities that remain inaccessible to Texas-Mexican musicians like Flaco, Texas-Mexican musicians like Flaco use a Mexican repertory and sound to pursue global performances that are inaccessible to the Mexican musicians who wrote much of the music and created this sound. Any consideration of conjunto as regional identity and any description of the increasingly globalized nature of these practices must consider the power struggles inherent to its foundation and continuing influences. While scholars like Peña have characterized conjunto according to its origins in resistance to Anglo-American hegemony, the entangled nature of the tradition with Mexico—and the systems of power revealed by this continuing entanglement—is often overlooked.

Furthermore, any designation of a conjunto genre that bars entry of certain aesthetic traits to be analyzed as an authentic representation of the associated cultural community—for example, any dismissal of Flaco's music as outside the domain of "conjunto"—fails to consider the hybridity inherent in the creation and continuation of the music. As Chávez asserts (discussing variants of *son*), in designating certain musical characteristics as indicative of a given genre, all other sounds are necessarily moved "outside the borders of tradition," thus denying "the very hybridity" the music has been built upon.[11] Yet, where is the generic line? If we admit particular stylistic traits through the process of globalization—as we always have—what determines a generic designation of conjunto, rather than any other musical style? Why is Flaco's music overwhelmingly thought of as conjunto, despite sonic characteristics more indicative of alternative musical styles? On the other hand, why are certain manifestations of Tejano and norteño not considered as conjunto? In this regard, it seems that the notion of identity does come into play.

Using this same consideration, the diverse stylistic traits and alternative instrumentation (in particular, a typical lack of button accordion and bajo sexto) used in so-called Tejano music push the genre outside of a primary conjunto designation, despite a corresponding location and ethnic heritage. Meanwhile, despite roughly analogous sonic categorizations for norteño and conjunto—Madrid identifies norteño as the "musical twin sister" of conjunto,[12] while Chávez asserts that cultural outsiders are unable to distinguish between the various associated styles categorized as "regional Mexican"[13]—the understanding of identity most typically aligned with norteño music (that of Mexican and Mexican immigrant, rather than Mexican American) is not accepted within the regional notion of conjunto. Instead, as Limón describes, the type of recent ethno-nationalism observed in the Texas-Mexican community designates the audience for norteño music—northern Mexicans and recent immigrants—as "other" to "native Tejanos."[14] In this view, while "Mexican-Americans are socially and culturally not Mexican immigrants," norteño music threatens the commodification of conjunto, even on U.S. American soil.[15] In this way, Limón asserts, the understanding of identity, as established through Texas-Mexican conjunto, is "forged in a hostile relationship to the presence and music of recent Mexican immigrants."[16] As such, although identity is not directly connected to genre, it certainly plays a role in its analysis.

Brackett refers to genre as a type of "cultural shorthand," simultaneously designating differences between groups of people through associated sonic characteristics while also revealing the arbitrary nature of such distinctions, at once demonstrating "the patterns and contradictions of [categorical] ideology."[17] He further contends that, despite the seemingly indiscriminate nature of sociocultural categorization, generic distinction elucidates a "shared, tacit understanding about which differences [of music and people] are meaningful" and "*how* differences are meaningful."[18] In this way, homologous understandings of musical genre and sociocultural identity are a simultaneously artificial and yet productive construct. Beyond a commercial functionality for musical categorization (and, thus, an associated audience) within the U.S American popular music industry—gatekeeping institutions that "depend on generic intelligibility (at least until a certain level of success has been achieved)" in order to navigate "successful interactions" between artists, record companies, critics, and audiences[19]—and despite an inherent instability of both musical genre and social identity, Brackett suggests that "comparisons between music industry genre assignations . . . and the sound of specific recordings often highlight sociocultural factors in classification precisely because of the lack of an airtight relationship."[20] It is within this context that I pursue analysis of genre, identity, and the social understandings demonstrated by corresponding relationships and contradictions. As Brackett notes, "Beyond the banal level of keeping the wheels of music commerce turning, genres function as ephemeral utterances that provide a clue to the role played by music in the intersubjective social imagination."[21] Examining the categorization of Texas-Mexican conjunto through stylistic traits and sociocultural manifestations of identity then identifies the continuous results of globalization that have shifted understandings of community relationships in a certain temporal moment.

A Brief History of Conjunto

From the initial influence of European salon music and introduction of the button accordion in the second half of the nineteenth century, conjunto music has developed in South Texas over the past hundred years as a unique and popular form of regional dance music. Literally meaning "group," the conjunto genre has come to signify a standard instrumental ensemble consisting of the accordion, the bajo sexto (a Spanish/Mexican bass guitar with twelve strings in six double courses, generally tuned in fourths), an electric bass (previously a *tololoche*, a Mexican upright bass), and drum set. As Peña (1985) has convincingly argued, the conjunto tradition has historically formed a powerful symbol of cultural identity among the rural, working-class Texas-Mexican border community. Yet, in recent years, due to global dissemination of local recordings, casual entertainment platforms such as YouTube, and international performances by popular regional conjunto artists like Flaco, musicians around the world have started to adopt this (formerly) highly localized creative genre, raising contemporary considerations of sociological significance in newly widespread musical repertories. Furthermore, hybrid elements included in certain regional works (although, paradoxically, not typically included in the conjunto offerings of inter/national artists) have simultaneously shifted the understanding of conjunto as cultural identity—if, as scholars like Vargas remind us, the scholarly narratives asserting a musical genre as sociocultural representation have ever truly characterized conjunto within "cultural-nationalist limits of masculinist race and class constructions."[22]

Following its beginnings in the late nineteenth century and a period of stylistic formation corresponding to an initial commercialization from the 1920s through the end of World War II, conjunto music achieved a "classic" era from the late 1940s through about 1970. Although certain regional performers challenged traditional stylistic boundaries, in general, the remaining years of the twentieth century brought "a period of consolidation and decline, as many of the stylistic elements of the classic era—now considered 'the tradition'—were worked and reworked into a less and less dynamic style."[23] From this point forward, the music became, in essence, a "folkloric" tradition, celebrated as a symbol of Texas-Mexican culture and historical struggles, but largely devoid of continuing musical evolution. While many among the regional community took pride in this continued cultural significance, the lack of innovation within the genre failed to attract much of the younger constituency, and the tradition was threatened by the popularity of alternate musical styles.

Although the music stagnated somewhat stylistically in the second half of the twentieth century, a new form of social relevance and national recognition for the working-class cultural tradition came through the intermittent adoption of the regional style by the Chicano Movement in the 1960s and 1970s as a representation of the Mexican-American collective identity. While the traditional music had historically provided a symbol of cultural identity within the local, working-class Texas-Mexican constituency, the representative recognition of the genre among the broader Chicano community served as an important revitalizing force for the contemporary regional sound. As Peña explains, "In this climate of ethnic reaffirmation and reawakened pride in cultural 'roots,' the conjunto was transformed dramatically from cantina trash to cultural treasure."[24] At this point, the working-class music became separated from its humble beginnings, and, corresponding to many of its increasingly upwardly mobile constituents, gained new meaning among an educated, middle-class, Texas-Mexican population.

Beginning with this revitalization of the genre, a number of new musical participants and altered stylistic techniques have shifted the sociocultural symbolism of conjunto and the music itself, indicating that processes of globalization have directly influenced notions of identity and genre. Starting in the last decades of the twentieth century, musicians like Katsube and Verheyden taught themselves to play the button accordion in a conjunto style. Traveling to South Texas, these artists have performed as surrogate members of the Texas-Mexican community. At the same time, listeners worldwide use entertainment platforms like YouTube and other methods of digital communication to participate in the conjunto tradition outside of conventional boundaries of language or location. In addition, just as working-class musicians in South Texas have historically used conjunto as a response to marginalization by Anglo-Americans and "Americanized" Texas Mexicans, the

Dutch rock band Rowwen Hèze sings traditional conjunto tunes in the local Limburgish dialect to respond to the dominant urban culture (and language) of the Netherlands. While the spread of conjunto among an international population might suggest the insertion of global characteristics, artists like Rowwen Hèze, Katsube, and Verheyden actually stay close to the traditional style. In contrast, Texas-Mexican musicians like Flaco regularly incorporate elements of jazz and rock, including blue notes, chromatic runs, and strong accents on the downbeat, within the conventional conjunto sound. These new developments form the primary impetus for this book.

Characteristics of Conjunto: "Ay Te Dejo En San Antonio"

A series of recordings of the classic conjunto tune "Ay Te Dejo En San Antonio" can be used to demonstrate standard characteristics of the Texas-Mexican genre, as well as the participation in contemporary conjunto music by artists outside of the genre's most typical ethnic, geographic, and/or socioeconomic constituency. The song was written by Santiago Jiménez Sr. (1913–1984), a pioneer of the regional sound. Although the song was written and performed much earlier in the musician's career, it was first recorded in San Antonio in 1979 by renowned record producer Chris Strachwitz as part of the artist's final studio recording and released on the Arhoolie label on the album *Don Santiago Jiménez: His First and Last Recordings*. The song was subsequently recorded in 1983 by the East Los Angeles–based roots-rock band Los Lobos, in 1986 by Flaco Jiménez (Santiago Sr.'s son), earning a Grammy for the artist, in 2010 by the young Dutch musician Dwayne Verheyden (b. 1991), and in 2012 by the Texas-Mexican (although originally New Mexico–Mexican) conjunto group Los Texmaniacs, led by acclaimed bajo sexto player Max Baca Jr. (b. 1967).

In the initial recording of "Ay Te Dejo En San Antonio," Santiago Sr. plays the accordion and provides the primary vocals, while Flaco joins his father on bajo sexto and vocal harmonies. As common to the regional sound, the performance maintains a consistent vocal duet, with one voice slightly dominating and the secondary line in parallel thirds. (The typical Texas-Mexican button accordion is strategically arranged so that two adjacent buttons, played together, also produce the interval of a third.) Although Flaco's usual instrument is also the accordion, it is customary within the Texas-Mexican tradition for musicians to master multiple instruments. Juan Viesca plays a traditional type of Mexican acoustic bass known as the *tololoche*, an instrument that is somewhat smaller than the European double bass, but still large enough to provide the requisite low tones more often produced in modern performances by the electric bass. In fact, Santiago Sr. seems to have been the first conjunto musician to incorporate the acoustic bass, including the instrument on his first recording from 1936, while, as Peña attests, "No one else did so until after 1948."[25] Rhythmically, this recording does not include the *tambora de rancho* (a homemade goatskin drum often paired with the accordion through the early 1930s but later criticized as being too noisy) of the early conjunto tradition or the drum set of subsequent performances. According to Carlos Guerra, even after the drums were commonly implemented in live performances during the 1950s, they were often eliminated in recordings since "producers considered them too crude and noisy."[26] The bajo sexto instead provides the necessary rhythmic consistency. In this regard, this recording remains representative of Santiago Sr.'s earlier style. In addition, Santiago Sr. plays the two-row button accordion, customarily retuned to suit his particular vocal register, rather than the three-row instrument of the more contemporary tradition.

The diatonic button accordion used in traditional conjunto music produces one note when the bellows are pulled and another when they are closed. A player's right hand typically manipulates one or more rows of treble keys to create a melodic line, while the left hand plays a series of bass buttons corresponding to single bass notes and triadic chords in major and minor. With each treble row capable of producing a single diatonic scale, multiple rows of buttons (in a three-row instrument, most typically tuned as F-B-E or G-C-F) provide the advantage of playing in different keys, as well as the ability to modulate from one key to another within a single song. While the tradition began with a single-row accordion, later musicians gradually embraced more complex instruments, including multiple-row diatonic accordions as well as—although with limited popularity—chromatic instruments, to aid increasing musical complexity. In modern conjunto practices, musicians often retune or rearrange the reeds of the instrument, sometimes even removing the increasingly abandoned bass reeds, to serve their own creative preferences.

Santiago Sr.'s recording of "Ay Te Dejo En San Antonio" showcases the accordion with an instrumental introduction and subsequent ornamental passage reiterated before each verse and at the conclusion of the piece. During the 1930s, conjunto accordionists like Narciso Martínez started to drop the bass end of the accordion sound and emphasize the right-hand style through intricate, melodic lines. Conversely, Santiago Sr., somewhat removed from the popular trends in the Rio Grande Valley, maintained a more old-fashioned, legato, and straightforward approach. Accordingly, in this recording, the relatively limited accordion ornamentation comprises grace notes and intermittent turn figures (consisting of the note above the principal note, the principal note itself, the note below, and the principal note again) on occasional melodic tones, altered in different instrumental sections to create a sense of constant improvisation, but typically fairly closely connected to the fundamental melodic line and the basic dancelike structure of the polka. The accordion drops out once the voices enter, a conservative regional practice with only singing or playing by the lead performer at any one time.

Originally, the bajo sexto employed six strings (E, A, D, G, C, F), tuned down from the traditional six-string guitar (known as the *guitarra sexta*) and therefore termed the *bajo sexto*, or lower six. By the beginning of the twentieth century, these six strings were doubled at the octave, creating the current twelve-string version of the instrument. Initially, the bajo sexto provided the rhythmic accompaniment for the accordion, along with fills and offbeats. By the 1930s, this chordal accompaniment opened up between verses to include a rapid, fluid musical style with passing tones, scalar runs, and even solo countermelodies, in addition to the consistent rhythmic back beat.[27] In Santiago Sr.'s recording of "Ay Te Dejo En San Antonio," the bajo sexto provides not only the rhythmic background, creating a percussive element that eliminates the need for any additional rhythmic instrument, but also forms a type of duet with the accordion within the instrumental sections through constant motion and an improvisatory style.

Included on *...And a Time to Dance*, Los Lobos's rendition of "Ay Te Dejo En San Antonio" is performed in a slightly higher key (G), corresponding to a contemporary shift to a (typically G-C-F) three-row button accordion, and somewhat faster rendition (130 BPM) than Santiago Sr.'s original recording (125 BPM). In other regards, this later performance remains closely in line with the traditional conjunto style, clearly referencing the customary regional form with few elements of mainstream culture, despite the recording's positionality (at least geographically) outside of the Texas-Mexican community, and despite the band's subsequent use of popular styles. While Flaco's harmonies in his father's original are secondary to the primary voice, Los Lobos emphasizes the close harmonic patterns through a near equivalence of volume between the contrasting vocal lines. The accordion technique in the instrumental passages is slightly more ornamental here than the original, particularly in the section leading into the final verse, but maintains similar methods of embellishment through grace notes and turn figures. This conservatism maintained beyond the original location and socioeconomic circumstances of the genre emphasizes the music's use as cultural folklore, symbolic of the wide-ranging community but, in general, lacking any additional artistic elements to mark the actual external arrangement.

One difference between the Los Lobos recording and Santiago Sr.'s original is the use of the electric bass instead of the more traditional acoustic instrument. This electronic amplification provides greater sonic prominence for the instrument throughout the song while marking the recording as belonging to a later musical practice. This contemporary incorporation of electric instruments within the traditional form separates the music from its old-fashioned roots, but also speaks to a younger and more ethnically diverse audience attracted to U.S. American rock music. From the 1950s, corresponding to economic expansion of the Texas-Mexican middle-class and regular performances in larger venues, regional conjunto music began to consistently use amplification. A single microphone usually served for both voices, while the bajo sexto was adapted to use a pickup, in a similar style as an electric guitar.[28] Around this same time, the traditional *tololoche* began to be replaced by the electric bass. As Peña explains, while in early conjunto practices, the bajo sexto emphasized the bass notes instead of the upbeat strum, with the implementation of the electric bass and its corresponding appropriation of the bass line, "the bajo sexto developed a characteristic emphasis on the upbeat accompanimental strum of the polka that has continued to this day."[29] In addition, although the accordion style by this time typically incorporated Martínez's emphasis on florid, right-hand passagework, with minimal use of the left-hand bass notes, the use of a single microphone to amplify the accordion further necessitated the exclusive use of the right-hand treble keys by most performers.

Flaco's relatively conventional conjunto recording presents a modern instrumentation, including electric amplification and a prevalent use of drums, setting the recording apart from Santiago Sr.'s original offering. Stylistically, Flaco's musical sound is much flashier and more virtuosic than his father's characteristically conservative form, including a type of choppy, staccato technique that is more closely related to performers such as De La Rosa in the middle of the twentieth century than the earlier regional style. Flaco's version begins in a major key (F) slightly lower than either his father's recording (F#, but probably actually played in F on an instrument tuned sharp, as was common at that time) or Los Lobos's rendition (G) and at a slower tempo (118 BPM). The instrumentation is immediately distinguished by the modern drum set, with flashy rolls and intermittent fills beginning at the initial instrumental introduction. The incorporation of the drums provides a rhythmic alternative to the earlier percussive style of the bajo sexto, thus necessitating only basic rhythmic enunciation by the latter instrument and often starkly reducing the characteristic flourishes of the previous bajo sexto technique. In this recording, the bajo sexto line is limited in its improvisatory role as compared to Santiago Sr.'s original recording. With the regional introduction in the middle of the twentieth century of a slow, gliding style of dance called *el tacuachito* (the possum), the tempo of conjunto music slowed somewhat, providing room for additional, showy improvisations by the accordion, as exhibited by Flaco's virtuosic style. In this recording, the slightly slower tempo corresponds to the slower regional style in the second half of the twentieth century, while showcasing Flaco's flashy abilities.

The noticeably ornamental accordion line in this recording is idiosyncratically virtuosic and playfully varied throughout different iterations of the intermediary instrumental interludes, providing alternating staccato and more legato passages, showy turns and scalar runs, and improvisatory-sounding sections. Within conjunto practices of the later twentieth century, these intricate, melodic runs are often called *pisadas*, coming from the Spanish *pisar* (to strike the keys of a piano or pluck a stringed instrument), while the general, improvisational embellishments are typically described as *floreando* (literally, decorating with flowers).[30] Within these ornamental improvisations, Flaco incorporates certain characteristics of mainstream U.S. American popular music. In particular, Flaco frequently integrates the "blue notes," or flattened thirds, fifths, and sevenths, of contemporary U.S. American jazz, blues, and other popular musics by presenting two notes simultaneously (jammed closely together, as T. M. Scruggs illustrates) or through the use of grace notes.[31] Other idiosyncrasies noted throughout Flaco's characteristic style include strong accents on the downbeat and notes sustained for a particularly long duration during a performance with an otherwise fast tempo.[32] This performance of "Ay Te Dejo En San Antonio" illustrates many of these characteristic styles, with blue notes, "jazzy" and chromatic runs, and strong accents on the downbeat. Flaco does not include his characteristic sustained note, but this technique can be found in other performances by the musician and is included on the recording of "Ay Te Dejo En San Antonio" by Verheyden, whose version closely emulates Flaco's model.

Like the Los Lobos recording, the secondary instruments and vocal harmonies in Flaco's performance of "Ay Te Dejo En San Antonio" maintain a greater prominence than Santiago Sr.'s original version of the song, corresponding in part to contemporary advancements in recording technology. As Peña describes, "The best assessment of the conjuntos of the late twentieth century, as compared with those of the golden era, is that advanced recording technologies, such as digital audio technology (DAT), made for a clearer and perhaps cleaner sound."[33] While Flaco's music remains close to his father's traditional form, the younger artist's virtuosic style and modern instrumentation connect the conventional genre to U.S. American rock music, symbolizing an increased interaction with mainstream culture and interest in the regional music among the increasingly Americanized community and an audience beyond the original regional constituency.

Verheyden's recording of "Ay Te Dejo En San Antonio" is even more virtuosic than Flaco's stylistic model. Like Los Lobos's earlier rendition, the song is presented in the key of G and at a tempo slightly faster than the original (130 BPM). The modern drum set and electronic sound are even more prominent and rock based than in previous recordings, and the accordion line includes constant and varied ornamentation through showy melodic riffs, virtuosic scales and turns, and frequent, improvisatory-sounding instrumental passages. Verheyden is clearly in debt to Flaco's style, but takes the idiosyncratic form even further than the earlier recording. The vocal harmonies are sonically equivalent to the primary melodic line, emphasizing the close harmonies of the Texas-Mexican sound. Contrasting earlier versions of the song, Verheyden does not limit the accordion riffs only to instrumental interludes, but plays brief runs between phrases of the verses, increasing as the song continues and even continuing under the vocal line in the latter choruses. This recording represents a continuation of Flaco's earlier style, remaining closely in line with local practices while showcasing the movement of the regional music beyond conventional geographic boundaries and ultimately around the world, thus altering the associated cultural significance.

Los Texmaniacs's recording of "Ay Te Dejo En San Antonio" remains in the key of G but provides a relatively slow tempo (120 BPM), rhythmically closest to Flaco's recording. The accordion introduction displays an ornamental and crisp, staccato style. As in Verheyden's song, this instrumental line is not confined to the interludes, but continues to punctuate each phrase of successive verses, while also remaining under the vocal melody in the choruses. Contrasting Verheyden's recording, these intermittent accordion riffs begin following the first phrase of the first verse and continue throughout the entire track. Throughout the song, the bajo sexto displays a distinct, rhythmically active prominence and greater virtuosity than contemporary recordings, suggesting instead the earlier instrumental practices demonstrated within Santiago Sr.'s original recording, including extended scalar passages and rapid ornamental patterns against the melodic accordion in the interludes, as well as unexpected harmonic fragments and chromatic passages drawn from popular U.S. American musical forms. Uniquely, the second chorus within this recording incorporates English lyrics, demonstrating the group's contemporary appeal to an increasingly broad U.S. American audience and the modern bilingual (and bicultural) nature of the traditional border community.

This range of distinctive iterations are included within typical generic discourse. This designation certainly includes common elements of instrumentation, structure, and sound, particularly in considering the performance of the same song, but also admits certain characteristics of rock, jazz, and the blues, the English language (in the Los Texmaniacs version of the piece), and various sociocultural identities outside of the stereotypical Texas-Mexican community (Los Texmaniacs from New Mexico, Los Lobos from California, and Verheyden from the Netherlands). However, a recording of the piece by the Dutch rock band Rowwen Hèze (explored in more detail in Chapter 8)—employing a keyboard accordion with electric guitar (rather than button accordion with bajo sexto), rewritten lyrics in a Limburgish dialect, a faster tempo, and a sociocultural identity disconnected from typical Texas-Mexican consciousness—is not typically considered within the realm of conjunto. While notions of genre are not rigidly constructed, and while homologous understandings connecting genre directly to identity are not appropriate, there does seem to be a limit to generic inclusion developed along a continuum of musical characteristics and sociocultural identity. Artists like Flaco—directly situated within established conjunto identity—maintain the freedom to push the stylistic boundaries of the genre and still preserve—or be trapped within—conceptions of conjunto. Alternatively, in order to receive generic consideration, artists like Verheyden—notably outside of the ethnic, geographic, and linguistic community—must maintain musical traits established by regional artists like Flaco. Yet, Rowwen Hèze, pushing the boundaries of both identity and style, seemingly goes too far.

Outline of Contents

The following chapters of this book are divided into three sections, based on my understanding of three processes of globalization: media/migration, hybridization, and appropriation. The first part, "The Migration of Conjunto," encompasses the first three chapters. The first chapter of the book, entitled "'*We love you, Flaco!*': *Chicken Skin Music*, 'Mingomania,' and the Inter/national Presentation of Conjunto," discusses the impact of global performances by local artists on the dissemination of conjunto music. It traces inter/national tours and festival participation by Flaco, Saldívar, and Jordan beginning in the 1970s, arguing that global attention to conjunto music was stimulated by these initial presentations. However, while Flaco launched a global career through early collaborations with U.S. American rock stars and Saldívar capitalized on a nationalist impulse to characterize the genre as U.S.

American folklore, Jordan's failed attempts to achieve mainstream success without hegemonic intermediaries ultimately demonstrate the persistence of homologous notions of genre and identity among popular audiences. While Flaco and Saldívar have both accepted a certain understanding of their music—and thus identity—as "other" among U.S. American culture, allowing for elements of exoticization to attract audiences outside of the expected Texas-Mexican community, Jordan's attempts to escape fixed correlations between cultural heritage and aesthetic characteristics (and thus achieve success beyond limited ideas of sociocultural identity) on his own terms have resulted in frustrations, economic limitations, and an ultimate retreat to more comfortable understandings of acceptance for minoritized musicians.

The second chapter, titled "*'Ladies and gentlemen, Dodge presents Flaco Jiménez!'*: Arhoolie Records, KEDA Radio Jalapeño, and the Mediated Dispersal of Conjunto," discusses the role of modern media representations of conjunto on the global dissemination of the genre. It traces the recording history of the genre through small, regional labels like Ideal and Falcón and larger, niche companies like Arhoolie and Arista Texas, contending that, while this method of specialized distribution has disseminated the regional music among a new global fanbase, it has also limited an inter/national understanding of conjunto to Flaco's particular flavor of the genre as interpreted among a bourgeois audience. In addition, this chapter explores the radio presence of conjunto in stations like KEDA in San Antonio, as well as other media outlets (television, print, and online). While these mediated processes of globalization have created a new cultural community outside of traditional understandings of ethnicity, class, language, and location, this diverse audience simultaneously subdues former understandings of genre as identity and dilutes the historic sociocultural significance for the music. In this way, although globalization broadens participation in Texas-Mexican conjunto, it constrains aesthetic traits and community-based meanings among inter/national audiences to what actually receives dissemination through these mediated channels.

The third chapter, entitled "*'From Texas to Washington and across to Michigan and Illinois...'*: Los Cuatro Vientos, Los Texmaniacs, Los Lobos, and the U.S American Spread of Conjunto," explores the performance of conjunto throughout the United States, including musicians emanating from the Midwest, Pacific Northwest, Southwest, and California. Throughout the twentieth and twenty-first centuries, Texas-Mexican workers have followed agricultural and industrial labor throughout the United States, establishing new communities outside of South Texas and spreading cultural practices like conjunto across a broad region. While musicians worldwide often maintain homologous connections to familial heritages, participating in genres of music that correspond to ethnicity and location, nostalgia can help to explain the aesthetic decisions of artists positioned outside of the space and time of primary conjunto practices. In addition, conjunto musicians situated outside of the customary Texas-Mexican identity (in this case, defined primarily through location) tend to retain a more conservative form of the music than artists like Flaco who are solidly established within the local community. As such, as I argue within this chapter, the process of globalization—demonstrated here in the migration of conjunto music throughout the United States—creates hybrid manifestations of the genre (explored in more detail in the next section), but simultaneously maintains a folkloric sensibility among participants outside of the central geographic location.

The second section of this book, "The Hybridization of Conjunto," comprises the next three chapters. Chapter 4, entitled "*'You have to mix it up!'*: 'Seguro Que Hell Yes,' the Texas Tornados, Los Super Seven, and the Cultural Hybridity of Flaco Jiménez," analyzes the global process of hybridity in the music of Flaco, as demonstrated by the artist's solo works and his participation in groups like the Texas Tornados and Los Super Seven. While Texas-Mexican conjunto developed in the nineteenth century as a product of hybridization, the relative standardization of the form in the middle of the twentieth century and subsequent hybridization in the works of Flaco creates a cycle of hybridization (following scholars like Néstor García Canclini) that shifts in time between more and less homogenous aesthetic practices. This process is then further demonstrated by the standardization of many of Flaco's hybridized characteristics in the music of inter/national artists like Baca and Verheyden. In addition, although this process of globalization shifts the musical characteristics of the so-called conjunto genre—at least among certain iterations of performance—it also helps to characterize a bicultural identity for regional performers that better represents the associated constituency than strictly traditional stylistic traits. In this way, Flaco's hybridized pursuits break down former connections between genre and identity while simultaneously forging new correlations. Furthermore, the hybridization of Flaco's music demonstrates an opposite effect to that observed in the preceding chapter: while musicians outside of the most traditional understanding of Texas-Mexican identity (in terms of race, class, language, or location) assert their cultural positionality by remaining closely in line with historic understandings of the music, local artists like Flaco—situated securely within the Texas-Mexican community—characterize the freedom to experiment with alternative formats.

The fifth chapter, entitled "*'I play the jazz accordion!'*: 'Rueda de Fuego (Ring of Fire),' 'My Toot Toot,' and the Country/Zydeco Influences of Mingo Saldívar and Steve Jordan," continues the consideration of hybridization with an analysis of cross-cultural influences in the music of Saldívar and Jordan. Exploring the idea of conjunto as a form of country music and analyzing racialized tensions in genres typically associated with Anglo-American and African-American communities, this chapter further complicates homologous notions of conjunto by inserting alternative identities within the historically Texas-Mexican tradition. Signifying the bicultural identification of certain conjunto performers, works by Saldívar and Jordan seem to maintain balanced elements of at least two distinctive genres (shifting in practice depending on the fundamental stylistic traits of each song). As such, this process of globalization indicates an intentional effort to insert both (or many) generic manifestations into the Texas-Mexican form. In this way, Marco Cervantes argues, Jordan introduces "Blackness" into the regional identity. Yet, this explanation is complicated by the analogous supposition of inserting "whiteness" into Saldívar's performances. Furthermore, the particular cultural combinations employed by each artist ostensibly correspond to noticeable differences in reception for each: Jordan's insertions of stereotypically African-American musical traits have not been fully accepted among either the local community or the more mainstream population, while Saldívar's use of characteristics tied to Anglo-American populations has led to performances at prestigious public events as an ethnic "representative" of the United States.

Chapter 6, entitled "'*It's jealousy...*': Eva Ybarra and the Hybrid Offerings of Women in Conjunto," explores the historical male dominance of Texas-Mexican conjunto, tracing hybrid musical performances of Ybarra as a counterbalance against historiographic narratives of—not only—conjunto as Texas-Mexican identity, but, specifically, conjunto as *male* Texas-Mexican identity. Following scholars like Vargas, this chapter then examines the notion that the lack of female participation in conjunto is—in part—a misconception caused by the exclusion of women from the literature, further dismantling former understandings of genre as sociocultural identity. However, while female artists like Ybarra do pursue processes of globalization, as demonstrated here through hybridized stylistic elements, they function in a similar manner as inter/national musicians situated outside of the primary geographic and sociocultural communities, following artists like Flaco in inserting nontraditional musical characteristics, but rarely pursuing new methods of stylistic innovation. Following analysis of these inter/national practices (as described in Chapters 3 and 8), this interpretation implies that women conjunto musicians also retain close stylistic proximity to more culturally secure artists. In other words, the lack of innovation within female performances (not a lack of hybridization, but rather an overall reluctance to stray too far from accepted practices) suggests that women must likewise assert their positionality within the Texas-Mexican community through relatively close adherence to the globalized pursuits of more prominent male musicians.

The third section of the book, "The Appropriation of Conjunto," comprises the final two chapters. The seventh chapter, titled "'*That's my music!*': Kenji Katsube, Dwayne Verheyden, and the Worldwide Participation in Conjunto," examines the sociocultural significance of international conjunto musicians, arguing that artists outside of the United States "make up" for any lack of "fixed" characteristics of identity (as related to appearance and familial heritage) by maintaining more traditional—or at least pre-established—musical traits. In addition, these artists adopt a performative persona that aligns with traditional Texas-Mexican understandings. This process of globalization then creates a theoretical folk-popular continuum that includes certain variances within a single genre, depending on aesthetic traits but also on sociocultural identities. Furthermore, while these international artists demonstrate a release from historical narratives of conjunto as identity, analysis of individual circumstances does show a significance for the music within each musician's home region. For example, in performing closely within the Texas-Mexican style, Katsube actually demonstrates close adherence to Japanese priorities of mimicry, thus creating a hybridized form of the genre through traditional musical traits and Japanese ideas of performance. Meanwhile, in choosing the accordion to present a descendent of German polka music, Verheyden loosely conforms to aesthetic expectations within his own cultural heritage. In this way, while international musicians do not typically add stylistic elements to pre-established understandings of Texas-Mexican conjunto, they do shift conceptual definitions of the genre via new interpretations of identity.

The eighth and final chapter of the book, entitled "'*¡Esto es globalización!*': Rowwen Hèze, the Rolling Stones, and the Commercialized Appropriation of Conjunto," discusses popular musicians in the United States and abroad who collaborate with local conjunto artists and/or use conjunto influences in their works. These include Dutch rock band Rowwen Hèze and Flaco's collaborations with commercialized rock stars like Cooder, Yoakam, and the Rolling Stones. Depending on circumstance, these musical adoptions can be analyzed as interconnected, exoticized, and/or exploitative. For example, Flaco's early work with mainstream popular artists is considered in parallel with various manifestations of the so-called world music movement, as his music—and presence—is used as an "authentic" representation of simplistic (or primitive) culture; an exotic bit of musical "other" that is inserted by a dominant musician into a dominant artform. However, corresponding to analyses of other manifestations of "world music," such as Paul Simon's

Graceland (1986), the associated minoritized musicians experience a complicated blend of commercial assistance (creating its own elements of discomfort) and exploitation. Alternatively, the wholesale adoption of conjunto songs (albeit with Limburgish lyrics) through Los Lobos into the repertory of Rowwen Hèze represents a worldwide imagined community of musicians drawn from similar aesthetic heritages and sociocultural circumstances. In addition to notions of identity as observed throughout this range of inter/national appropriation, this chapter provides a final consideration of the global classification of conjunto. Throughout the preceding sections of the book, the representative music has maintained a broad categorization of conjunto. As long as the musical adherents remain characterized as "Texas-Mexican" (through "fixed" elements of familial heritage), or the music itself remains closely connected to pre-established tradition (in the case of inter/national musicians like Verheyden and Katsube), this generic classification has fundamentally remained in place, regardless of actual musical traits and despite individual musicians' efforts to maneuver among other classifications. However, commercialized musicians like those considered here are able to navigate a blend of conjunto characteristics amid alternative genres.

A few notes on inclusion: in invoking the term "conjunto," this work details music within the Texas-Mexican tradition that utilizes a core ensemble of button accordion, bajo sexto, bass guitar, and drums. For the most part, it does not include so-called "progressive conjunto," which typically adds keyboard and wind instruments to the standard ensemble (and, as David Harnish notes, enhances the sound "with greater professionalism and virtuosity").[34] Nor does it include the more commercialized genre of *música tejana*—Tejano music (which Cathy Ragland describes as "a modern incarnation of conjunto that sometimes pairs or replaces the accordion with keyboards and the *bajo sexto* with the electric guitar")[35]—despite certain ambiguity of terminology between "Tejano music" as a specific genre and "Tejano musics" as a general term indicating all Texas-Mexican musics (i.e., conjunto, progressive conjunto, *música tejana*, *orquesta tejana*, and such).

In addition, conjunto music, and thus this book in general, is situated on the northern side of the Texas-Mexican border. Despite a close stylistic connection between conjunto—emanating from South Texas—and *música norteña*—from the northern border of Mexico—this work does not detail the historical developments of norteño music (for analysis of the genre and a more detailed distinction between the two styles, see Ragland 2009 and 2012). Much of the following analysis focuses on the Texas region alone—and its worldwide interactions—disregarding the closely related music emanating from the southern side of the border and the messy interconnections of people and culture on both sides of the geo-political boundary. However, the border region is just that—a region; creative influences and sociocultural relationships don't honor this imagined borderline in ways that politicians might expect. As such, in analyzing the U.S.-Mexico border region, it is important to remember that the barrier between Texas and Mexico is a political construct. While the U.S. government might imagine a stark separation between one side of this barrier and the other, the community who lives in the region displays a fluidity of culture and consequent messiness in the tangled interactions caused by the placement of a barrier in the middle of a region.

Finally, this work does not address many of the more conservative manifestations of the Texas-Mexican conjunto tradition continuing to take place among many local communities, instead focusing on performances and stylistic characteristics situated outside of the expected Texas-Mexican constituency. As such, in addition to the development of a folkloric tradition among national and international musicians, the local community itself simultaneously maintains the genre as both a form of cultural folklore (demonstrated through the traditional repertory and sound and performances at community-based events like birthdays and anniversaries) and a more commercialized style of music created through the types of globalization and hybridization analyzed within the following chapters. This project explores the influences, participants, and audiences outside of the traditional cultural community; a globalized atmosphere that creates new understandings of categorization for the traditional music—in its many manifestations—and new sociocultural identities defined therein.

PART I

The Migration of Conjunto

CHAPTER 1

"We love you, Flaco!"

Chicken Skin Music, "Mingomania," and the Inter/national Presentation of Conjunto

In Egypt and Jordan, they liked the huapangos, and in West Africa it was the country songs. The people have a lot of soul there. They really got into the accordion. I ended up writing a corrido (narrative ballad) about my experiences there.
—Mingo Saldívar, *Austin American-Statesman*

By 1990, Flaco Jiménez was enjoying a prominent global touring career. As the culmination of a thirty-three-day European tour, the San Antonio-based accordionist and his band played to a 3,500-person, international crowd at the Montreux Jazz Festival in Switzerland. As journalist Kathleen Hudson notes, the diverse audience "loved it, shouting for more after [Flaco] invited them to join in on 'Volver, Volver.'"[1] Meanwhile, "his encore, 'La Bamba,' left [the audience] dancing."[2] While part of the standard conjunto tradition, these song choices emphasize the "Mexican" folkloric expectations of the international fanbase. Following this more traditional (albeit expectedly folkloric) Texas-Mexican performance, Flaco joined U.S. American roots-rock musician and longtime collaborator Ry Cooder on stage. Later in the evening, Flaco was invited to perform with Bob Dylan. On the subsequent night of the festival, Flaco opened for Van Morrison and John Lee Hooker before finally leaving the lengthy European tour to return home to Texas. While these collaborations with mainstream popular artists will be considered in more detail in Chapter 8, these international performances—through global tours and festivals—demonstrate an initial manifestation of globalization by way of the physical dispersal of conjunto by local musicians like Flaco. Analysis of inter/national performances thus provides an initial understanding of globalization in Texas-Mexican conjunto music via the process of migration.

Likewise, the Carnegie Hall Folk Festival in New York in 1994 presented "a microcosm of nearly the entire history of Texas music," including blues, rockabilly, and a unique blend of country with conjunto.[3] Advertised as "Deep in the Heart of Texas," the program featured Austin blues guitarist T.D. Bell, Sean Mencher (lead guitarist for the Austin rockabilly group High Noon), Austin drummer Lisa Pankratz, Dallas rockabilly singer Ronnie "The Blond Bomber" Dawson, and San Antonio conjunto accordionist Domingo "Mingo" Saldívar (b. 1936) with his band, Los Tremendos Cuatro Espadas. Like Flaco's collaborations with mainstream artists at the Montreux Jazz Festival, this festival showcases Saldívar's interactions with musicians outside of the expected conjunto genre. Yet, Saldívar's participation in the Carnegie Hall Folk Festival also demonstrates the dispersal of conjunto music outside of Texas during the late twentieth century. Flaco's performances spread the genre among mainstream audiences through global music festivals and international concert tours. However, Saldívar more typically performs in nationalist and folk-oriented festivals within the United States, such as Bill Clinton's presidential inauguration in 1993, the Summer Olympic Games in Atlanta in 1996, and the Smithsonian Folklife Festival in Washington, DC, in 2008, among others.

Finally, in 1995, Esteban "Steve" Jordan (1939–2010) and his band, Rio Jordan, opened for the popular Mexican *orquesta tropical* group, Sonora Santanera, in Monterrey, Mexico. Throughout the concert, the two bands alternated sets. Although Sonora Santanera wrapped up around 2 a.m., Jordan continued playing for nearly 1,000 fans until the stage monitors ultimately blew around dawn that next morning (at which point Jordan, upset at the inadequate equipment, launched his accordion some fifteen feet across the stage—effectively ending the performance).[4] While Jordan also disseminated conjunto to an international audience via concert tours in Europe and Japan, the performance antics at this Monterrey concert provide a glimpse into some of the difficulties Jordan faced in achieving mainstream success. However, despite the conclusion of the concert, the performance itself was well received. Davis Bennet notes: "Jordan signed hundreds of autographs that night, and was thrilled with his reception."[5] Despite struggles with popular recognition, Jordan's musicianship is not in question. As a band member from Sonora Santanera illustrates, "Nobody can play like that. [Jordan] must be a devil or a witch."[6] Bennett continues, "People in South Texas, and throughout much of the United States, Europe, and Japan have worshipped [Jordan] with the respect that others gave to Stevie Ray Vaughan, Janis Joplin, and Willie Nelson."

Flaco achieved inter/national success by collaborating with popular artists in a style of roots-rock at the edge of traditional boundaries of Texas-Mexican conjunto (or by "selling out," as Jordan asserts).[7] Saldívar promoted a form of musical folklore by serving as a "feel-good" representation of hegemonic multiculturalism within a nationalist context. In attempting to achieve mainstream success through conjunto itself, Jordan instead confronted the realities for marginalized communities in mainstream society. That being said, Jordan—like Flaco, Saldívar, and various other local artists—did bring the conjunto genre to a widespread audience. In this way, these musicians promoted the initial manifestations of globalization that have stimulated worldwide attention to the Texas-Mexican tradition in the twentieth and twenty-first centuries.

Globalized Inclusions

In considering the cultural effects of contemporary globalization, social science scholars like Arjun Appadurai (1996) outline the dual impact of media and migration on the spread of cultural forms. Accordingly, Appadurai discusses "a theory of rupture that takes media and migration as its two major, and interconnected, diacritics and explores their joint effect on the *work of the imagination* as a constitutive feature of modern subjectivity."[8] Of these two notions, the impact of electronic forms of media in the international dissemination of cultural capital has dramatically altered the landscape of globalization in contemporary society. The effect of media on the transnational dissemination of Texas-Mexican conjunto music will be examined in Chapter 2. Meanwhile, although human movement around the globe is nothing new, the contemporary ease of migration (in combination with "the rapid flow of mass-mediated images") creates new globalized forms of cultural identity, as Appadurai describes, new "diasporic public spheres . . . that are [not] easily bound within local, national, or regional spaces."[9] In the realm of Texas-Mexican conjunto music, international patterns of migration by way of global concert tours and festival participation have produced the first representations of the globalization of the genre in the second half of the twentieth century. In turn, these initial methods of migration have affected the collective imagination to create new forms of cultural identity for the modern Texas-Mexican population.

That being said, beyond this nascent international dissemination and corresponding diversity of cultural identification among non-traditional performers like Flaco, Jordan, and Saldívar, the key musical qualities for much of the conjunto genre—particularly for those musicians remaining in South Texas and performing for a local audience—have remained fundamentally constant. This physical dispersal of Texas-Mexican accordion music results only in the spread of the style of music produced by these non-traditional performers, San Antonio-based artists who frequently insert external musical characteristics (as will be explored in more detail in Chapters 4 and 5) and collaborate with mainstream, popular artists (Chapter 8). While this process of transnational dissemination introduces the conjunto genre to a widespread, cross-cultural population, it simultaneously leads to worldwide misinterpretations of the fundamental (i.e., historical) nature of the artform. International representations of conjunto do not draw from the aesthetic of local musicians performing traditional songs at birthday parties, anniversaries, and quinceañeras ("coming-out" parties; i.e., fifteenth-birthday celebrations), but instead create a new understanding of the musical genre outside of traditional notions of Texas-Mexican culture. In addition, international understandings of the music draw from a Mexican-based repertory and corresponding stereotypes of Mexico as global "other" to imagine a romanticized notion of the Texas artists who use their statuses as U.S. American citizens to sell Mexican music to a global population.

The northern side of the Texas-Mexican border—and its nominal connection to conjunto music—maintains an inextricable relationship with the southern side of the border—and the analogous style of norteño music, two genres separated by a geo-political boundary but fundamentally interconnected in history and interpretation. Despite comparable repertory, instrumentation, and core musical characteristics between the two genres (Cathy Ragland discusses these stylistic distinctions in more detail), many in the region consider the music and associated communities as fundamentally unique.[10] A stark ethno-nationalism (see Limón 2011) in Texas encourages a separation between U.S. American musicians (conjunto and Tejano) and the perception of threatened performance opportunities due to an influx of Mexican immigrants (norteño). In this regard, conjunto and norteño are categorically different and yet profoundly the same. Furthermore, the history of borderlands music is intimately tied to tension between ethnic groups in the region. As such, the interpretation of conjunto music—historically associated with the northern side of the border—is essentially linked to U.S. American sociopolitical concerns. In globalizing conjunto, artists like Flaco use Mexican influences to take advantage of international performing opportunities that remain largely inaccessible to Mexican musicians. As such, systems of power create a complicated hierarchy in which more powerful musicians (mainstream popular artists versus Texas conjunto artists versus Mexican norteño artists) use the music of less powerful musicians to generate more attention, more opportunities, and ultimately more power for themselves.

For our purposes, the globalization of conjunto—here, by way of global performances of local music—is connected to the northern side of the tradition alone (just as considerations of regional practices, more recent innovations, and related genres like progressive conjunto and Tejano remain absent from this analysis in favor of more specific characterizations of a single stylistic classification and time period). This does not eliminate the interrelationship between northern Mexico and southern Texas nor address the necessary interplay between the associated locations, people, music, and cultures. However, throughout this book, the globalization of conjunto treats the migration, hybridization, and appropriation of "Texas" music, as defined by the artists and audiences most closely associated with this classificatory consideration. The Mexican correlations represent a vital, but complex, layer of analysis that will be set aside for now to limit the scope of this work and thus more fully address the interpretation of "conjunto" as it interacts (primarily) with Euro-American hegemony. In many ways, the interactions between Texas and Mexico—like musical innovations situated in South Texas alone—represent local, rather than global, practices. The interconnections between conjunto and norteño music designate complicated regional tensions that are simultaneously analogous and contrasting, too closely connected to be treated separately, and yet too far apart—at least according to the common regional interpretation—to be considered together. I will take up the Texas side of this complexity—lacking an unambiguous appropriateness of generic distinction—and leave further untangling for a later time (and the welcome participation of alternative voices). For now, I will consider the migration of Texas-Mexican conjunto (as historically, stylistically, geographically, and ambiguously defined) outside of the Texas-Mexican region—on both sides of the border. Consideration of Mexican artists and audiences then remains outside the scope of this analysis.

Flaco Jiménez: Inter/national Tours and Popular Festivals

In the early 1970s, Flaco began to collaborate with a series of mainstream artists, including Doug Sahm, Dr. John, Dylan, and, perhaps most significantly, Cooder. A member of the younger Texas-Mexican generation (following conjunto "pioneers" like his father, Santiago Jiménez Sr., who was a key figure in the initial development of the genre), Flaco's previous performances had remained closely within conventional conjunto practices. However, his musical interests embraced elements of U.S. American popular culture, including jazz, country, blues, and rock. While other regional artists had also experimented with various influences of mainstream U.S. American styles, Flaco remains well known for the popularization of these hybridized practices. In 1976, Cooder released *Chicken Skin Music*, an eclectic combination of conjunto, gospel, and slack-key Hawaiian guitar music, featuring Flaco on accordion. Cooder then took Flaco and a band of other Texas-Mexican musicians on a national and international tour, producing widespread recognition and appreciation for the traditional conjunto sound and eventually stimulating a stylistic adoption by a range of Anglo-American, European, and Asian musicians.[11]

In turn, inter/national recognition of the regional form prompted a new sense of cultural pride and attraction to the historical style by a younger, often middle-class community. External interest influenced a "folkloric" understanding of the music and a heightened awareness of the sociocultural significance of the tradition. As Ragland asserts, "Younger musicians who once rejected conjunto and the accordion in the 1970s and 1980s, or those musicians who stopped performing due to lack of interest in conjunto, have since returned to the genre and have been playing before larger, multigenerational audiences."[12] Global attraction to conjunto has not had a significant effect on local practices. However, regional pride in the Texas-Mexican genre and a return to the traditional music came about through the inter/national pursuits of local artists like Flaco.

Flaco's stylistic hybridizations and collaborations with mainstream artists are important components of the globalization of conjunto music; these will be explored a little later. For now, let us examine the impact of Texas-Mexican conjunto performances taking place outside of South Texas (or at least for audiences emanating from outside of Texas). As Ragland notes, conjunto artists like Flaco, Jordan, and Saldívar, and others—those members of the generation following the earlier "pioneers" of the genre—traveled with Texas-Mexican farmworkers and cotton pickers to play at Saturday-night dances along the so-called "taco circuit" throughout the United States.[13] These initial expressions of globalization later spread throughout Europe and Asia. As Ragland describes, musicians like Flaco "have made the music their life's work, as the first 'global' ambassadors of conjunto music and representatives of a people who had once struggled to be counted and recognized for their contributions to the unique culture and music of the region."[14] Of these local artists, Flaco not only led the way, but "has toured the longest and the farthest."[15]

As Flaco himself explains, "At first I started taking this music . . . to England, and then from there we jumped to Australia, we did Japan, we did Holland, Switzerland, Belgium, Spain. And there is many more I cannot

Figure 1.1. Flaco Jiménez (accordion) and Peter Rowan (guitar) on stage at Farnham, UK, in 1985. Photo by Tony Rees. Licensed under CC BY-SA 4.0.

recall. . . . If there's an invitation from any parts of the world, I'll try to be there."[16] For example, following extensive touring with Cooder in the 1970s, by 1991, when Flaco toured Europe with the newly formed Texas Tornados, audiences in the Netherlands already comprised a substantial fanbase for Flaco alone. As bandmember Freddy Fender remembers, "We tore 'em up in Holland the first time we went there. . . . We filled up 1,000- to 2,000-seat places, and Flaco got the biggest applause. They would hold up signs that said, 'We Love You, Flaco.'"[17] That same year, Flaco performed with his own band at the Harbourside Brasserie in Sydney, Australia, the first concert in the musician's first Australian tour.

In 1991, Flaco also performed with the Texas Tornados at the annual South by Southwest Music and Media Conference and Festival (SXSW) in Austin, Texas. Following the initial performance in 1991, Flaco performed as a solo artist in 1994 and 1995. He also performed in 2007 with Augie Meyers, as the Tex-Mex Experience. He performed again with the Texas Tornados in 2010 and 2014 and with Los Super Seven in 2001 and 2014. He also performed as part of a Doug Sahm tribute in 2013. A 2015 performance with Los Texmaniacs was canceled due to the artist's broken hip (the group instead performed without Flaco in 2016). Like Flaco's global tours, these Texas-based performances brought the Texas-Mexican genre to a diverse audience emanating from around the world. SXSW has introduced marginalized genres like conjunto to a popular consciousness and an inter/national audience. This process shifts Flaco's music from folklore into a form of roots-rock. In this regard, generic distinction relies less on actual musical characteristics and more on context. Beyond traditional components of conjunto in Flaco's style, the inclusion of the music in a more mainstream outlet—not as a folkloric representation, but as a full participant in the commercial intent of the festival—suggests interpretation according to more mainstream considerations. Inclusion in a popular context thus creates a popular product, at least for audiences and participants in the festival who assume rock performances at a popular festival. Despite comparable musical elements, performances among folkloric outlets—such as those seen by Saldívar, explored below—create folkloric designations. The context of Flaco's performances instead creates "roots" music, a distinction that allows for commercial inclusion, even if the actual musical elements are largely the same. Although performances by artists like Saldívar at nationalist festivals cement conjunto as a folkloric style, Flaco globalizes—and thus popularizes—the genre through more mainstream performance spaces like SXSW.

By 1994, Flaco was still touring worldwide. As the musician describes, "I was the first to take [conjunto music] to Europe, Australia and Japan. And there's still a lot of roads yet to travel. . . . I feel good about the ambassador role—I feel good knowing I'm opening doors for the young ones who will come after me."[18] Flaco continues, "When I was a kid, I used to look at those geography books, at the pictures of Europe and Japan, and imagine what it would be like to play music for the people there. That all came true, so I don't have any complaints about life."[19] With the release of *Buena Suerte, Señorita,* in 1996, Flaco embarked on a three-week, sixteen-city, major promotional campaign across the Netherlands, Germany, Spain, Switzerland, France, and Austria. As Cameron Randle, vice president of Arista Texas, the record label that produced the album, notes, "How many conjunto records that you know of are sold and toured in Europe first? . . . But he has a big following he has built up after having worked that market in Japan, Europe, Australia, and, particularly, Spain, for years."[20] In this way, Flaco's live performances have brought unprecedented attention to conjunto—in its many manifestations—far beyond the historic region of South Texas.

Following this European tour in 1997, Flaco returned to Texas to play a handful of local concerts, including the Puro Squeeze Box Festival in Freeport. As Flaco emphasizes, "I don't want to lose my touch and feel for my roots. If that means playing at icehouses, in cantinas (bars), or anywhere else people want to hear me, I'll be there. I'm satisfied playing for 150 to 300 people, especially in my hometown."[21] Yet, Nunie Rubio, a young protégé of Flaco who played with the European tour, emphasizes Flaco's international popularity: "I'm still trying to get off the high of singing before 15,000 people in Holland, where Flaco was the sole headliner. We sang in both Spanish and English. But when we sang in Spanish, they knew the words to the songs, sang along and that surprised the heck out of me. Those that didn't know the words just hummed along with the tunes. They seemed to feel honored to have someone like Flaco go back to where the accordion started."[22] That being said, Flaco's music stimulates similar attention in Texas. A 1997 performance at the Tejano Conjunto Festival in San Antonio attracted "13,000 enthusiastic fans who broke the barriers, rushed and stormed the stage for [Flaco's and Rubio's] autograph."[23] In this regard, the globalization of conjunto creates two separate markets. Flaco is popular throughout Europe and Asia, but also maintains a large fanbase in South Texas. The two audiences interact only minimally (when inter/national fans travel to Texas to attend the Tejano Conjunto Festival, for example), and performances in one location do not impact audiences elsewhere.[24]

By 1999, journalists and scholars were drawing attention to Flaco's burgeoning role as a global "ambassador" for conjunto. Ramiro Burr, writing for *Billboard*, noted that the artist "has helped to spread the gospel of conjunto music around the world."[25] At the same time, Manuel Peña explained that Flaco "is the one conjunto performer most responsible for what some music market observers call 'crossing over'—introducing marginal music such as conjunto to a wider audience and thereby increasing their own and the music's exposure."[26] And furthermore, Flaco "became a musical ambassador of sorts; his name is well known in certain pop music circles as the man who brought conjunto music to the attention of Anglo-Americans and even Europeans."[27] Also writing for *Billboard* in 1999, John Lannert emphasized Flaco's "reputation as the ambassador of conjunto" and announced the musician's upcoming annual tour of Europe.[28] Although Flaco received recognition for his role in the globalization of the genre, his performances among an international community were still an anomaly. Flaco pursued a global audience for his work, but the genre as a whole was not directed to a global population. While other conjunto artists have now pursued inter/national audiences, and despite a certain popularity for the genre far outside of South Texas, this is still largely the case. Conjunto is considered a regional, ethnically Texas-Mexican artform, and any participation outside of this tightly constrained consideration is noted among U.S. American journalists and scholars as inconsistent with the historical significance for the music. In this way, cultural products are still thought of as "belonging" to a particular group of people, despite actual practices outside of the original community. Conjunto receives definition as such due to the identity of its primary constituents.

Flaco's early international performances came in coordination with mainstream popular musicians like Cooder. His subsequent global tours brought large performances—akin to stadium concerts—for mainstream international crowds. Meanwhile, by the early 2000s, many of Flaco's national and international performances were included instead in specialized festivals devoted to Latin American cultural representation. This practice is maintained by artists like Saldívar (see below). In this way, although certain Texas-Mexican artists have achieved representation among an international audience, true participation in the mainstream musical culture—especially within the United States—remains limited, at best (as exhibited even more clearly by Jordan; see below). These artists are still generally considered outsiders in popular society worldwide. Texas-Mexican conjunto—at least, when defined as such and closely associated with the Texas-Mexican community—remains largely a folkloric tradition, even when performed across an inter/national space and including musical elements outside of standard historical practices. The genre is still defined according to the sociocultural identities of its performers and principal audience. Despite attempts by artists like Flaco to redefine the music according to popular traits and among a global fanbase, music performed with accordion and by Texas-Mexican artists is characterized as "conjunto"—an exotic bit of folklore and attractive primarily as a cultural curiosity—regardless of interpretation or intent.

For example, in 2004, Flaco headlined the "Mexico on the Potomac" festival in Arlington, Virginia, a free, "seven-hour outdoor celebration of Mexican culture, food, music, visual arts and crafts" that formed part of the city's Neighborhood Day celebration for Cinco de Mayo as part of an ongoing cultural exchange between Arlington and its sister city in Mexico, Coyoacan.[29] It is interesting in this case to note the use of Flaco's music as representative of "Mexico." While the artist identifies according to a Mexican ethnicity, he and his music are fundamentally Texan, based in the United States and distinct from Mexican culture or music. As musicians and fans on both sides of the border will quickly emphasize, Texas-Mexican conjunto and Mexican norteño are fundamentally different. This distinction is partially based on musical elements (according to norteño musician Miguel Luna, the Mexican music is rougher, more emotional, and simpler than its Texas equivalent).[30] However, a largely corresponding instrumentation, structure, and repertory between the two genres indicates that the distinction is even more fundamentally based on identity. As such, Flaco's role here as culturally "Mexican" becomes even more problematic, a clear indication of persistent mischaracterizations among mainstream society of the Texas-Mexican border community as essentially external to the United States. Despite the erroneous cultural association, this depiction pigeonholes Flaco's music as folkloric representation—outside of popular culture, regardless of the artist's attempts to characterize himself and his music as such. A Texas-Mexican musician can easily pass as "Mexican." He struggles to be "American." Meanwhile, Mexican musicians struggle to gain similar performance opportunities among global audiences.

By touring internationally and performing in festivals for a diversity of audiences, Flaco introduced the Texas-Mexican genre to a global population. These initial efforts led to popularity for the genre across a range of contexts, as in the diverse performances by artists like Jordan and Saldívar and the various elements of mediation, collaboration, and hybridization that followed. However, by collaborating with U.S. American rock stars in these initial pursuits and allowing a narrative of folkloric exoticism to permeate his performances—both in his early work with artists like Cooder and later, as a cultural representation of his (or an ostensibly interchangeable) community—Flaco conforms to hegemonic expectations of marginalized identity. Despite global elements in performance, intention, and the music itself, globalized manifestations of Texas-Mexican conjunto remain characterized according to identity. Among popular interpretations, Texas-Mexican musicians create Texas-Mexican music, even when—according to style or location—they do not.

Mingo Saldívar: Nationalist Tours and Folkloric Festivals

Mingo Saldívar was born in Marion, Texas, just outside of San Antonio. Like many Texas-Mexican families, Saldívar's parents supported their eight children by traveling north to pick beans and harvest sweet potatoes. When Saldívar was sixteen, he moved in with a Minnesota farm family to finish school while working as their cook and driver. When he was eighteen, he was an Army paratrooper stationed in Kentucky. Saldívar came from a musical family and taught himself to play the accordion at a young age, but this combination of experiences outside of the local Texas-Mexican community formed the impetus for the artist's later hybridizations of the traditional conjunto style. During the 1950s, Saldívar translated and began performing some of his favorite country-western tunes in Spanish, but with little success in that arena instead returned to the Texas-Mexican circuit and earned a local hit with "Andan Diciendo" in 1957. Remaining in the Texas dancehall circuit and forming his current band, Los Tremendos Cuatro Espadas, in 1975, Saldívar recorded some fourteen albums on regional labels before breaking into the mainstream community in 1992 with a Rounder Records album called *I Love My Freedom, I Love My Texas.* He was nominated for a Grammy Award for that album in 1993 and again for the album *A Taste of Texas* in 2002. He also received a National Endowment for the Arts' Heritage Fellowship award in 2002. Throughout this time, Saldívar has earned a reputation as "The Dancing Cowboy" due to his unique style of dancing with the accordion slung low on his hips as he kneels, spins, and shuffles across the stage, and to his distinctive style of dress with cowboy hat, Western shirt, and boots.

Like Flaco, Saldívar has performed for audiences far outside of the expected South Texas region. Yet, while Flaco's performances have fundamentally comprised—at least initially—large tours throughout Europe and Asia, many of Saldívar's performances have instead centered on folk festivals and other nationalist events in or associated with the United States. Although both artists have developed a following beyond the historic Texas-Mexican community, inter/national audiences frequently look to these non-traditional conjunto artists as musical representations of their home region—exotic elements of cultural capital—rather than global stars (in a more mainstream context). This consideration is twofold. While inter/national conjunto fans appreciate the musical performances of artists like Flaco and Saldívar, this appreciation stops before any recognition of cultural identification for widespread audiences. Inter/national fans enjoy these performances of conjunto, but maintain a fundamental separation between Texas-Mexican artists and global identities. In other words, inter/national fans of conjunto do not consider themselves part of the Texas-Mexican community simply by following the performances of Texas-Mexican artists. Instead, these audiences create a secondary fanbase for the genre, outside of regional interpretations. Similar to the so-called world music movement during the 1980s (see Chapter 8), these widespread audiences instead draw from considerations of elite "worldliness" to mark conjunto music as "exotic" and thus worthy of attention. Identity may certainly play into interpretations for this fanbase, but it is not the identity of the historical regional community in South Texas.

At the same time, the inter/national community listens to the music of these artists as an authentic representation of Texas-Mexican culture, despite the non-traditional nature of these works. As such, musicians like Flaco and Saldívar occupy a liminal space between regional and global communities: attractive as symbolic of the Texas-Mexican community, yet distinctly non-representative of typical Texas-Mexican practices. A hybrid reliance for these artists on both conjunto and popular musical elements (explored in more detail a little later) results in the characterization of the resulting music not as both, but instead as neither. For audiences outside of the traditional conjunto community, the music of Flaco and Saldívar represents the regional culture—and thus, cannot be considered according to mainstream considerations. An emphasis on exoticism cements the music as inherently external. The idiomatic use of the button accordion in combination with the ethnic identity of Texas-Mexican performers means that it is not considered as a popular genre, even if it includes popular elements and despite the artists' attempts to characterize themselves and their music as such. At the same time, audiences associated with South Texas often distance these performances and their performers as outside of standard local concerns. That being said, the performances of Flaco and Saldívar represent different manifestations of similar musical impulses. While Flaco uses popular elements and the patronage of mainstream rock stars to create a space for himself at the edge of commercial practices, Saldívar instead embraces his role as cultural representative, using mainstream elements to forge connections with a mainstream community who then uses his music as proof of multiculturalism. Meanwhile, much of the stylistic foundation and common repertory for the music comes from Mexico, a region left out of these conversations—and resultant economic successes—altogether.

In 1987, Saldívar was still performing for regional audiences, such as at the El Fiesta Ballroom in Seguin, Texas (outside of San Antonio). By 1992, he was headlining the free Harbourfront concert in Toronto, Canada (along with Prairie Oyster—a Toronto-based country group—and Jean Caffeine's All-

Nite Truckstop—an Austin-based, alternative country band). These events preceded Saldívar's performance at Bill Clinton's presidential inauguration in 1993. The inaugural festivities featured two contrasting sets of performances in Washington, DC: a "down home and diverse" daytime festival "invoking roots and heritage" and entitled "America's Reunion on the Mall" and an afternoon concert at the Lincoln Memorial entitled "A Call for Reunion: A Musical Celebration," including popular performers like Michael Jackson, Aretha Franklin, Dylan, Ray Charles, and Michael Bolton and telecast on HBO.[31] The "folklife" concert featured Sioux dancers, Japanese drummers, Louisiana zydeco bands, Memphis soul groups, and more, including Saldívar and Los Tremendos Cuatros Espadas. It was coordinated by the Smithsonian folklife department, with performances in tents on the National Mall and nearby auditoriums in the Smithsonian Institution. As Jon Pareles describes, the festival presented "nationally known performers with connections to ethnic roots" who helped to demonstrate the inclusive society with "a strong regional and ethnic identity and an overarching shared culture."[32]

In this way, while Saldívar did participate in the pre-inauguration festivities, he did so as an outsider to mainstream, popular culture, an "ethnic" element designed to demonstrate cultural inclusivity while remaining purposefully separated from the contrasting popular performances. The sense of globalization inherent in this type of performance is not one of commercialization for conjunto music, but instead, a deeply ingrained sense of folklore for the genre that holds the music—and its associated Texas-Mexican culture—back from achieving any true sense of contemporary relevance among a mainstream population. While still a performance outside of the regional population, this is a very different type of globalization than seen either in Flaco's collaborations with mainstream artists or in his work with his own band in inter/national stadium tours.

A little later in 1993, Saldívar performed again in Washington, DC, for the conclusion of the Folk Masters series (together with zydeco group John Delafose and the Eunice Playboys). In 1994, there was the previously mentioned performance at the Carnegie Hall Folk Festival in New York, while 1995 brought a performance for a Palestinian audience in Jericho as part of an African and Middle Eastern tour (including Ouagadougou, Burkina Faso, and Damascus, Syria) with the United States Information Agency. Despite such performances suggesting multicultural globalization, this tour presents a much different functionality than Flaco's roughly simultaneous tours of Europe, Australia, and Asia. Despite a corresponding sense of exoticism, whereas Flaco performed for large audiences of adoring fans, Saldívar was paraded around by the United States government to unassuming observants as a symbol of U.S. American inclusivity. Stuart Schoffman, an Israeli journalist present for the performance, writes that, despite being "awash in warm, vague, wishful thoughts of commonality and interconnection," and despite the embrace of "an American vision of world peace through Tex-Mex music—joyous sounds so elementally, universally appealing, and so unencumbered by any political weight," relationships between Israelis and Palestinians (and, for that matter, Anglo and Mexican-Americans) "can't be solved by Tex-Mex music."[33]

Following this African and Middle Eastern tour in 1995, Saldívar performed for the Fourth of July at the American Roots concert at the Sylvan Theater on the grounds of the Washington Monument in Washington, DC. The concert was free and featured a variety of folkloric artists, including traditional bluegrass, a Native American women's ensemble, rhythm and blues, and a brass band from New Orleans. Journalist Mike Joyce notes: "Blues, bluegrass, zydeco, conjunto, Cajun, Celtic, brass bands, Puerto Rican, Afro-Latin, American Indian—you name it. They were all part of the split bill of day and evening concerts."[34] Like Flaco, Saldívar performs conjunto across a globalized context. However, he does so as a folkloric representation of U.S. American multiculturalism, rather than a more commercialized manifestation of cultural dissemination.

While Flaco's inter/national performances push the boundaries of what conjunto is and can be, both representationally and stylistically, Saldívar's more nationalist pursuits (frequently under the guise of the United States government) entrench the genre as a form of cultural folklore. The music is played for widespread audiences (outside of South Texas), but—in the case of Saldívar—is used to represent the Texas-Mexican culture as part of the U.S. American ethnic "melting pot" narrative, instead of developing an actual external fanbase for the music (as in the case of Flaco). As Joyce continues, the third annual American Roots concert, "celebrated the rich diversity of American musical experience without regard to the prevailing winds of fashion."[35] Nick Spitzer, artistic director for the concert, notes that the concert tried to "infuse the patriotic images we've all grown up with—the red, white and blue, the patriotic music, all the flag-waving—with a renewed sense of American pluralism. That's what patriotism should be about. The freedom to be culturally and individually different."[36] As nice as that sentiment might sound, the true effect separates marginalized artists like Saldívar from the popular stage and marks performers of music like conjunto—and thus the cultural community as a whole—as "different" from mainstream society. It draws attention to underrepresented cultures, but does so through a lens of exoticism that can be problematic, particularly when promoted by a dominant population, rather than the marginalized community itself.

Also in 1995, Saldívar became suddenly, surprisingly, and overwhelmingly popular in northern Mexico. As Saldívar explains, "I don't know what clicked, . . . but something happened with our music. It's safe to say that most of our bookings are going to be in Mexico while this lasts."[37] The reception for Texas-Mexican conjunto music in northern Mexico has been historically complicated by the popularity for the related norteño genre in the region. In a struggle for limited resources among closely related genres, conjunto and norteño artists have both been quick to discredit the opposing style, leading to limited popularity for conjunto in northern Mexico and vice-versa. As Flaco explains in 2001 (notwithstanding slightly later performances in Mexico), "Of course, I haven't played in Mexico before, so if there's a chance or an invitation I will. But up to now it's been hard for me to penetrate in Mexico, being that I have played all over the world, and being that Mexico is just about two cases [of beer] to get there [implying drinking as related to driving distance]. . . . There is no distribution in Mexico for Flaco Jiménez."[38]

Following Saldívar's Monterrey, Mexico, debut in 1994, "his driving squeezebox and showy stage presence . . . made him a genuine pop star there."[39] As John Morthland explains, Saldívar had only played a few small shows in Mexico before a Monterrey disc jockey made a dance-floor remix of "Rueda de Fuego" ("Ring of Fire"; see Chapter 5). The DJ then booked Saldívar for a 5,000-person performance at the popular Far West Rodeo over the Fourth of July weekend in 1994. Two weeks later, the accordionist appeared on the television show *Orale Primo*, where two teen-aged girls jumped onstage to mimic his dance moves. Subsequently called "Mingomania," those dance moves quickly spread throughout the region. In the dance, as Morthland describes, a teen-aged girl "begins with her head tilted back, staring upward, and her arms in front of her, held apart as if nestling a globe, palms extended; she swivels her hips while moving in a semicircle a few steps to the front, then to the side, and then to the back, her arms always in motion."[40] For the rest of that year, Saldívar performed in Mexico almost every weekend. He played for audiences of some 120,000 people at rallies for both of the Mexican presidential candidates and shared a bill for a 40,000-person crowd at a performance with Grupo Mazz, Emilio Navaira, La Mafia, and Selena. In 1995, the Miami-based Telemundo station filmed Saldívar's Mexican concert at the El Corral ballroom as part of its weekly program. The Telemundo crew also recorded Saldívar's shows in California and Texas. In addition, a film crew from CBS's *Sunday Morning* traveled with Saldívar in 1995, while

Hector Galan's documentary on Tejano music and culture, entitled *Songs of the Homeland*, prominently featured the artist.

Historically, Texas-Mexican conjunto music (and, I would argue, the Texas-Mexican border community in general) has a complicated relationship with Mexico. As mentioned above, Flaco did not achieve prominence in Mexico. Part of this complication is due to constant maneuvering for limited resources: with similar sonic structures, conjunto and norteño musics ostensibly address similar audiences. Promoting one music or the other as quintessentially linked to identity limits attraction to the alternative form, preserving fans and performing spaces among each regional community, respectively. Within this context, Saldívar's music stands out most clearly as external not only among the nationalist spaces in the United States, but also in his own community. Distinct from traditional conjunto performances, Saldívar becomes an oddity among Mexican entertainment spaces, rather than a threat to local artforms like norteño. In this regard, Saldívar—like Flaco and other, non-traditional conjunto artists—occupies a liminal space between Texas and Mexico, between his home community and the rest of the world. He has simultaneously gained success as representative of the regional community (for those unfamiliar with traditional conjunto) and idiosyncratically separate from Texas-Mexican practices (for local audiences and those elsewhere for whom traditional conjunto would threaten their own monetary successes). In gaining access to inter/national spaces, Saldívar has jeopardized local significance, for better or for worse.

By 1996, Saldívar was back to frequent performances at nationally oriented festivals (interspersed with concerts along "the local dancehall circuit that stretches from Lubbock to Seguin to Brownsville" and continuing in Monterrey, Mexico, "at least twice a month to audiences numbering in the thousands").[41] In April of that year, Saldívar and his band headlined a "Sonidos del Sur" (Sounds of the South) performance—featuring a survey of Mexican and Mexican American musical traditions—sponsored by Texas Folklife Resources on the University of Texas campus in Austin. He performed again for the American Roots concert on the Fourth of July at the Sylvan Theater on the grounds of the Washington Monument in Washington, DC. The event also featured country-bluegrass artist Alison Krauss and Union Station, Irish-American fiddler Seamus Egan and Solas, Native American women's a cappella group Ulali, and zydeco performer Boozoo Chavis. This performance (the fourth annual such festival) conveyed the same type of multiethnic inclusivity noted the previous year.

That same year, Saldívar performed at the Summer Olympic Games in Atlanta, Georgia. Entitled "Southern Crossroads" and taking place over two weeks across six stages at Centennial Olympic Park, the festival featured a diversity of musicians from the southern United States (in addition to food, dance, and visual arts). As journalist Steve Dollar illustrates, "Visitors [could] pay to sample various cuisines, learn to two-step and shag, check out the work of indigenous artisans, bone up on the history of recorded music in the region, join a spontaneous Mardi Gras parade and hear continuous live performances by a full spectrum of 130 Southern musicians, from bluegrass legend Ralph Stanley to home-grown hip-hop stars Kris Kross."[42] Free performances brought up to 250,000 members of the public from noon to midnight daily, with a "shifting array of performers" each day.[43] Like many of the festivals that Saldívar has participated in over the years, these performances featured artists based primarily in folkloric practices (or at least willing to be designated as such) emanating from the entire region. In addition to Saldívar, these musicians included Shreveport vocalist Maggie Lewis "playing blues and rock classics . . . with twangy, rockabilly passion," zydeco star Geno Delafose, and Austin-based singer-songwriter Tish Hinojosa.[44] As Dollar notes, "The entertainers reach[ed] from Appalachia, where the inheritors of Scottish ballad traditions presaged country music, to the Mexican border, where conjunto rhythms echo the polka."[45] Organized collaboratively by the Smithsonian Institution, the Southern Arts Federation, and the Atlanta Committee for the Olympic Games, the festival was similar in structure and style to the Smithsonian Folklife Festival (examined below). Despite a geographic location within the United States, and in addition to attendance by regional audiences, the event—as part of the Olympic Games—also attracted numerous visitors from around the world (providing globalization in close proximity).

In 1998, Saldívar played with Tejano vocalist Shelly Lares for a Diez y Seis Celebration (designating September 16, or Mexican Independence Day) at Texas Lutheran University outside of San Antonio. That same year, he participated in the Festival International de Louisiane in Lafayette, Louisiana. This annual festival in the "heart of Cajun country" brings a variety of artists from the French-speaking world (Africa, the Caribbean, Europe, Canada, and Louisiana).[46] As Lafayette tourist official Gerald Breaux emphasizes, "We wanted our kids to be able to see that they weren't alone in speaking French and having French culture. . . . We wanted them to know that there were other people out there who shared the experience of having a hybrid culture. And what better way to bring them into the language than by having them see all these great performers?"[47] Yet, when Saldívar introduced Texas-Mexican conjunto to the festival in 1998, he brought a different type of cultural hybridity.

Over the years, in addition to the traditional lineup of worldwide Francophone musicians, the Festival International de Louisiane began programming artists from outside the primary French heritage. In 1998, the theme was "Our Latin Roots," encompassing a range of Spanish-speaking acts from Texas, Mexico, Puerto Rico, and Cuba. Bringing this theme in line with corresponding themes from the preceding four years demonstrates a perceived connection between French (Cajun) culture and various Latin American musics. This is an interesting correspondence that places Saldívar and his music as representative not just of nationalist, Anglo-American multiculturalism or of his own, Texas-Mexican cultural heritage, but also as a representation of the Latin influence on Louisiana-based Cajun music. Certain connections do exist between conjunto and zydeco (both accordion-based folkloric traditions from minoritized cultures in the southern United States, if nothing else), as also noted in many of the pursuits of Jordan and similarly explored in conjunto-oriented festivals like the Tejano Conjunto Festival in San Antonio. However, Saldívar's participation in the Festival International de Louisiane further solidifies the performer's role throughout the United States as a folkloric symbol of diverse ethnic relationships (regardless of actual cultural affiliations or lingering socio-ethnic inequities).

Continuing in this symbolic role explored primarily through performances at folk festivals throughout the United States—a form of globalization that nonetheless remains largely within the boundaries of the nation-state—Saldívar performed at a "country dance party" for the Lincoln Center Out-of-Doors series in New York City during August 1999.[48] In 2000, he participated in a Latin-American-themed rendition of the annual Open House Arts Festival at the Kennedy Center in Washington, DC., along with nine stages of music and artists like Festa Brazil, Makina Loca, and QuinTango—a Washington, DC-based chamber ensemble devoted to tango music. In 2001, Saldívar performed at the fifteenth annual Lowell Folk Festival in Massachusetts. As journalist Scott Alarik describes, this "most popular free folk festival in the country" brings in "regional and ethnic acts" that perform "traditional" musics of the given cultures, but "also places a premium on showmanship."[49] As such, Saldívar—with his "gyroscopic" dance moves representing "the most expressive approach to conjunto performance ever attempted," his "traditional" performances of regional, ethnic musics, and his enduring role as a cultural representative among folk festivals—seems to be a perfect fit for the type of cultural representation the Lowell Folk Festival (and other, similar events around the country) attempts to convey.[50]

In 2002, Saldívar received a $10,000 National Endowment for the Arts' (NEA) Heritage Fellowship award (as Flaco also would in 2012). These fellowships have been awarded every year since 1982 "to a broad range of traditional artists in recognition of their excellence and their contributions to our nation's diverse heritage."[51] As Jane Chu, chairman of the NEA in 2017, emphasizes, "The artists we honor as part of our NEA National Heritage Fellowship awards are testament to the diversity, ingenuity, and creativity that characterize this nation. . . . We are so grateful for the gifts they have brought to all our lives."[52] While the receipt of this fellowship brought recognition to Saldívar as a valuable musician among a mainstream national audience, it simultaneously demonstrated his role not as representative of his own cultural heritage, but as a symbol of the "nation," a "gift" to the Anglo-American population to use as a representation of multicultural pride. In this way, Saldívar has brought Texas-Mexican conjunto music to a global audience, but has done so not through a worldwide appreciation for the regional culture and not through a popular shift in the music to encompass mainstream, commercial sensibilities, but instead through a sense of cultural folklore that serves the mainstream (heavily Anglo-American) population with little regard for the community—or associated cultural struggles—from which it comes. Following a Capitol Hill ceremony announcing the 2002 NEA Heritage Award Fellowship recipients, the fifteen artists receiving the award, including Saldívar, headlined a free concert in Washington, DC.

In 2004, Saldívar performed a free concert at the Millennium Stage in the Grand Foyer of the Kennedy Center in Washington, DC. Soon after, he performed at Town Hall in New York City as part of a concert billed as "Fiesta Mexicana," also including a mariachi group (Mariachi Los Camperos de Nati Cano), jarocho musicians from Veracruz, Mexico (Jose Gutierrez y Los Hermanos Ochoa), and a group known as Marimba Chiapas. Saldívar then continued with this lineup in a national tour called "Masters of Mexican Music," with the associated musicians demonstrating that (as Steve Kiviat asserts), "traditional approaches can still deliver the fun and romance more often associated with contemporary pop music."[53] Celebrating the heritage of four different regions on both sides of the United States-Mexico border ("the marimba of southern Mexico, the accordion-based conjunto of the Texas-Mexican border, the harp-based jarocho of Veracruz and the mariachi of Jalisco"),[54] the tour traveled—among elsewhere—to the Clarice Smith Center's Dekelboum Concert Hall on the University of Maryland campus just outside of Washington, DC, the College Union Building Ballroom on the Gettysburg College campus in Pennsylvania, the Historic Palace Theatre in Cape Charles, Virginia, and the Capitol Theater in Yakima, Washington (forming the middle of a "four-week West-Coast tour" following a similar tour "by the same groups along the East Coast in March").[55] According to the manager of the tour, Amy Grossman, the purpose of the performances was "to showcase the diversity of Mexico's music" (never mind that Saldívar plays conjunto—from the northern side of the Texas-Mexican border—rather than norteño—from the south).[56] Flaco broadened the conjunto tradition among a worldwide population by inserting popular musical traits and commercializing the genre. Saldívar instead consolidated conjunto as a form of cultural folklore, representative of a broad "Mexican" or "Latin American" (or even just "American") ethnicity, but not truly Texas-Mexican.

In 2008, Saldívar performed at the Texas-themed ("Texas: A Celebration of Music, Food, and Wine") iteration of the Smithsonian Folklife Festival on the National Mall in Washington, DC. Founded in 1967 (as the Festival of American Folklife; renamed in 1998), initial organizers of the event "intended to elicit the admiration and respect of white professional middle-class visitors for the various cultural groups represented."[57] Over the years of the festival, associated themes have brought a handful of Texas-Mexican artists to the event. Numerous scholars have examined the cultural implications of the Smithsonian Folklife Festival. Overall, the event's fundamental theme has remained one of U.S. American nationalism (with Saldívar's participation thus corresponding closely to the musician's other nationalist pursuits). As Emily Satterwhite explains, "During the 1970s, politicians and festival organizers promoted the Festival as a means of 'conserving' folk traditions as national 'resources.'"[58] While this philosophy of national preservation has been maintained, the international tourist industry (and accordingly, international participation) has played an increasingly prominent role in the festival following the name change in 1998.

Yet, as Satterwhite continues, appreciation of other ethnicities has become in itself a form of U.S. American nationalism: "By 2003, . . . some observers went so far as to characterize celebrations of ethnic heritage as 'the American way.'"[59] This observation can be corroborated not only in the various iterations of the Smithsonian Folklife Festival, but also in many of Saldívar's musical pursuits, using his ethnic differences to represent a form of U.S. nationalism among a mainstream, middle-class, and primarily Anglo-American audience. Through a sense of (comfortable) exoticism from mainstream culture, Saldívar brings a notion of "authenticity" that is noted as lacking from popular society. As Satterwhite asserts, "With the embrace of ethnic chic came a renewed interest in groups living supposedly more 'authentic' lives apart from mass society."[60]

This combination of exoticism and folkloric authenticity explains much of Saldívar's appeal as a national symbol of multicultural pride. The music he performs is different (but not too different), while remaining relatable and bringing a sense of nostalgia for simpler times. In this way, Saldívar (and the corresponding mainstream notion of Texas-Mexican culture) provides a national touchpoint while simultaneously diminishing the representative elements of actual ethnic importance (as conjunto music historically represented). Participation by Saldívar in this and other festivals has brought Texas-Mexican conjunto music to a diverse global population, but has limited the style of the genre disseminated (not including many contemporary practices, for example) and turned the music into a national symbol, often leaving out various important characteristics of the minority culture from which it comes. Such performances shift the balance of power for a genre that initially served to create power for its ethnic community. In many ways, Saldívar's performances give the power of conjunto back to the mainstream audience—shifting away from the local Texas-Mexican community. His performances bring attention to himself as a performer, but for the most part do not develop an overall appreciation for the genre among worldwide audiences. In that regard, Flaco's international pursuits achieve similar results.

At the same time, Saldívar embraces the liminality of the border region to simultaneously adopt a Mexican repertory and musical influences, evoke a romanticized stereotype of Mexico, and claim the resulting performative successes for himself, distancing himself from the actual region.

Steve Jordan: Struggles with Mainstream Recognition

Esteban "Steve" Jordan was born in Elsa, Texas, in the Rio Grande Valley. Like Saldívar's, Jordan's parents supported their fifteen children as migrant farmworkers. Jordan was partially blinded as an infant when a midwife rinsed his eyes with a contaminated fluid. Later in life, he was known as "El Parche" (the "Patch") because of the patch he wore over his right eye. During most of the 1950s and 1960s, Jordan lived in California, finally returning to Texas in the 1970s and recording regional hits like "El Corrido de Jhonny el Pachuco," "El Piedrecita," and "Squeeze Box Man." During the 1960s, Jordan toured with Latin percussionist Willie Bobo as a guitarist and immersed himself in the innovative New York jazz scene. During the 1970s, he worked with Carlos Santana and other psychedelic rockers. Jordan appeared in David Byrne's film *True Stories* in 1986, wrote the soundtrack to Cheech Marin's comedy *Born in East L.A.* in 1987, and was nominated for a Grammy Award in 1987 for an RCA album entitled *Turn Me Loose*.

Like Saldívar, Jordan drew from his family heritage and his experiences outside of the Texas-Mexican community to create unique hybridizations of the traditional conjunto style. Jordan's incorporation of electronic developments like the phase shifter, fuzzbox, and Echoplex, along with his psychedelic flamboyance and extravagantly virtuosic accordion technique, earned him nicknames like "The Jimi Hendrix of the Accordion" and "The Accordion Wizard." He's also been compared to bebop artists like Charlie Parker in style, talent, and temperament. Jordan released more than fifty albums for regional labels like Hacienda and Freddie and national labels like Rounder and Arhoolie, but grew frustrated with the lack of royalties. By the last years of his life, he had stopped working with labels altogether. Instead, refusing to let anyone in the industry touch his art, he worked on albums of heavily layered music in which he played every instrument and multitracked his vocals to sing every part. When Jordan died in 2010 due to complications from liver cancer, he left nine full, unreleased albums.

Like Flaco and Saldívar, Jordan spent much of his career disseminating conjunto among a worldwide population. However, while Jordan—at various times during his career—toured internationally (like Flaco) and performed at globally oriented festivals (like Saldívar), he also frequently got frustrated with the realities of the profession and retreated to more comfortable performance spaces in South Texas. For example, in 1977, journalist Ben King Jr. emphasized the inherent unfairness of the music business, noting that, despite Jordan's eminent talent, he was "still touring on the national-Chicano-music circuit and gradually becoming popular with Anglo-university students," but no longer (for a time) touring internationally or pursuing a more mainstream audience.[61] According to John Burnett, by the late 1980s, "it looked like [Jordan's] career was finally taking off."[62] After signing with the RCA record label in 1987, receiving the Grammy nomination (the award went to Flaco instead), and writing the soundtrack for *Born in East L.A.*, Jordan "made a highly successful appearance" at the Berlin Jazz Festival.[63] However, soon after, as James Manheim explains, "seemingly on the verge of mass success, Jordan more or less dropped out of sight."[64] As Jordan himself explains, "I did all those things, like appearing at the Newport Jazz Festival [on the guitar] and I asked myself, 'Is that all there is?' So I decided to come back to my own people and do my own thing."[65] In 1989, Jordan was scheduled to play a "salsa show" with Flaco in Santa Cruz, California, but the event was canceled due to structural damage to performance spaces from the preceding earthquake.[66] By 1990, Milo Miles noted that, while the accordionist's virtuoso playing "deserve[d] a wider audience," Jordan "seem[ed] comfortable just entertaining locals."[67]

Despite a certain acceptance by Flaco and Saldívar to their roles as exotic representations of both Texas-Mexican culture and U.S. American nationalism as a whole, Jordan struggled to achieve mainstream acceptance and consequently returned to the local community. This withdrawal from popular circumstances, particularly on the verge of mainstream success and in contrast to continued pursuits by other regional artists, demonstrates an inhibited interpretation of genre according to persistent stereotypes of identity. Despite hybridized performances across global spaces and frequent attempts to gain classification according to popular considerations, each of these three artists remained fundamentally characterized—at least among global audiences—as quintessentially "conjunto." For Flaco, this generic categorization created exotic insertions into rock tunes by more mainstream artists. Similarly, but with a new result, Saldívar served as a hopeful representation of U.S. American multiculturalism. Unwilling to accept such musical constraints, Jordan removed himself from mainstream consideration entirely. Yet, even among the Texas-Mexican community, Jordan struggled to achieve acceptance for a creative product that was too "conjunto" for mainstream characterization and not "conjunto" enough for consistent local popularity.

In 1992, Jordan performed at the New Orleans Jazz and Heritage Festival. The two-week festival (at the time, at least) emphasizes "roots styles"; as Jimmy Hori asserts, "The whole idea is organic music, the uncut stuff, pretty much unmediated by those modern-day staples: synthesizers, samplers, sequencers."[68] That being said, by 2008, the festival was "one of the largest music events in the world," comprising seven days, twelve stages, and headliners like Sting, Lenny Kravitz, and the Dave Matthews Band—although, according to Helen Regis and Shana Walton, still constructed among producers, participants, and audiences as "authentic, native, and real—in sum, as the folk," in short, "a mechanism for preservation, interpretation, and celebration of the folk."[69] As such, the participation of historically marginalized musicians like Jordan in the festival creates many of the same complexities of interpretation noted in the various festival performances of Saldívar; as Regis and Walton continue, ". . . the same ideological predicaments in how the 'folk' are conceptualized and how culture is (re)produced for public consumption."[70] By 2013, the festival had expanded to attract some 400,000 visitors.

It is in this regard that these festival performances—even within the United States—become a form of globalization. Through national performances that attract a diverse, international audience (in addition to some examples of global touring—albeit less so than in the case of Flaco), artists like Jordan and Saldívar spread the conjunto genre worldwide. In 1992, the New Orleans Jazz and Heritage Festival included only 500 musicians (as compared to some 6,000 in 2013). Jordan performed with New Orleans roots-rock band, The Iguanas (as Flaco also would in 1996), a performance that Hori, writing for *The Beat*, referred to as "one of the best club shows between the two fest weekends," with each group displaying "different but similar kinds of soul and virtuosity."[71] In this way, despite problematic complexities with questions of "heritage" events in general, Jordan's participation in the festival brought the Texas-Mexican conjunto genre to a new population and encouraged innovative connections among related, but separate, repertories.

In 1993, Jordan played a rare concert in Chelsea, in New York City. As Peter Watrous notes, "He's elusive, and would rather be fishing, so this is a rare chance to hear a Texas legend."[72] A week later, Jordan continued his East Coast performances in Washington, DC, backing up his reputation (according to journalist Geoffrey Himes) as "the best accordionist in the world."[73] As Himes continues, this performance by Jordan ("who rarely visits the East Coast") "left the local accordionists in the crowd . . . gaping in astonishment."[74] Few events by Jordan from 1993 to his Mexico performance (described above) in 2001—particularly international events—are well documented (although Abel Salas does note Jordan's ambassadorial experiences "travers[ing] Japan and [holding] court as an underground conjunto cult figure").[75] Michael Corcoran asserts (in 2003) that "accordion players and manufacturers all over the world know about him."[76] Burnett notes that "he has rabid fans in Germany and Japan."[77] In addition, Jordan developed a respectful following in Mexico, a difficult market for conjunto artists to tap (as explored above). As Elijah Wald notes, "In Mexico, Jordan is the only player north of the border that I've ever heard the Mexican players speak of with admiration."[78] Yet, as Jordan's first wife, Virginia Martinez, elucidates, "[Jordan] turned down a tour that would have earned him a million dollars because he didn't want to give an agent his percentage. He said he'd rather have 100 percent of nothing than to give some other man a piece of him."[79]

Conclusions

Each of the conjunto accordionists described above (Flaco, Saldívar, and Jordan) has interacted with mainstream society in various ways. Each has traveled outside of the historic cultural region of South Texas to bring conjunto music to an inter/national population. Yet, these methods of globalization diverge. Flaco used early collaborations with Anglo-American rock stars to launch his own global reception through large stadium tours throughout Europe and Asia. Saldívar emphasized the genre's role as folklore by playing nationalist festivals to inter/national crowds within the United States. Meanwhile, Jordan tried to interact with hegemonic society on his own terms, without the intervention of Anglo-American intermediaries. Becoming frustrated with the difficulties of mainstream success (particularly for traditionally marginalized populations and the associated musical genres), Jordan ultimately retreated to his familial music and his home region.

This process provides some insights into minoritized musics in the United States during the twentieth century. While each of these artists worked at the margins of popular success, and while each played a significant role in disseminating the conjunto genre to a global population, they could not escape an exotic interpretation for their works. Despite the noteworthy impact of migration on the globalization of culturally diverse musics, worldwide dissemination alone (and even positive audience receptions abroad) does not change socioeconomic realities or cultural identities for the historic Texas-Mexican community beyond economic incentives for individual artists and a sense of pride in international recognition (even when superficial) for the genre. Instead, although the conjunto style originated as a counter-hegemonic response to sociocultural discrimination for the Texas-Mexican constituency, the globalization of conjunto produces certain economic successes for musicians like Flaco and Saldívar but does not otherwise impact contemporary Texas-Mexican society. In fact, it frequently removes artistic control from the cultural community itself and places power for the music firmly in the hands of the hegemonic population.

CHAPTER 2

"Ladies and gentlemen, Dodge Presents Flaco Jiménez!"

Arhoolie Records, KEDA Radio Jalapeño, and the Mediated Dispersal of Conjunto

> Some people like to go to Africa and hunt animals. For me, I got that sense of adventure in Texas and the American South looking for extraordinary music.
>
> —Chris Strachwitz, Arhoolie Records

In 2003, the Chrysler automobile corporation launched a television advertisement for the new Dodge Ram 1500 Lone Star Edition, featuring Flaco Jiménez. Specifically aimed at a Mexican American population in Texas, the commercial presents a group of Texas-Mexican men clearing brush, loading their Dodge Ram pickup trucks, unloading large wooden beams, and beginning construction, all to the strains of Flaco's distinctive accordion music. Later completion of the project—highlighted in the sudden headlights of the truck—shows that the men have built a stage. Flaco himself shows up to perform, introduced (in Spanish) with, "Ladies and gentlemen, Dodge presents Flaco Jiménez!"[1]

The mediated inclusion of Flaco is strategically targeted to the emergent buying power of the Texas-Mexican community. The artist and his music thus serve as a cultural representation, encouraging the community to identify with the musical genre, and so also with the proffered product (here, an automobile). As Fred Diaz, senior sales and marketing manager for Chrysler's Southwest Business Center in Dallas, explains, in including conjunto within the commercial, the company decided that Flaco could "help us make a connection with Hispanic buyers and make them say, 'OK, these guys at Dodge understand us, appreciate us and like us.'"[2] This strategic, media-based influence on cultural identity is echoed by the associated advertising agency's vice president and field events director, Jessica Serna: "Music is the driving force for the Hispanic culture. . . . It's an important element on how we get our message out."[3] In this regard, the historical importance of Texas-Mexican accordion music among the associated sociocultural constituency has been appropriated by mainstream U.S. American capitalism and used to sell cars. As Diaz asserts, "Everything about [Flaco], from his music to his demeanor, says Tejano."[4]

Although Texas-Mexican conjunto is historically linked to a working-class population, the participation of Flaco in this commercial indicates that, by the twenty-first century, the genre had moved beyond its socioeconomic roots. It now attracts an increasingly middle-class fanbase who can afford to purchase such products. In this regard, connections between genre and identity shift over time. As cultural identities change, the musical representations tied to former understandings expand to encompass a range of associations. However, it would seem that class-based correspondences are more fluid than those of ethnicity. Contemporary conjunto is not explicitly tied to the working class; yet, it struggles to break free of strict correspondence with a Texas-Mexican heritage. The use of Flaco as an explicit representation of Texas-Mexican culture demonstrates the difficulties the artist has had in breaking free from homologous constraints. In the music of Flaco, conjunto has expanded to encompass a range of external styles, demonstrating a certain hybridity for the music itself, but also among the associated sociocultural community. In this commercial, the Chrysler corporation also exploits this modern hybridization, with Diaz asserting that "[Flaco] can play every genre and is versatile, like our truck."[5] However, the popular perception of Flaco's versatility is limited, as demonstrated in the commercial. Perhaps he can play every genre, but he does not receive consideration as such beyond his Texas-Mexican heritage. For these advertising professionals, the artist quintessentially represents "Tejano," regardless of actual musical characteristics or even a distinction between various Texas-based musics. Flaco is marked as cultural representation due to simplistic, visual traits: an accordion and his complexion. The artist's relationships with his fans in South Texas and around the world create complexities disconnected from historical interpretations of regional identity. His simultaneous disregard for the Mexican artists that created much of his repertory emphasizes the systems of power at play in this music and its role in Texas, in Mexico, and around the world.

This media-based inclusion of Texas-Mexican conjunto music provides just one example of the contemporary dissemination of the genre through radio, television, documentaries, audio recordings, newspaper articles, and online venues.[6] Beyond performances in worldwide tours and inter/national festivals, these methods of mediated dispersal brought attention to the genre outside of more expected associations of class, location, language, and ethnicity. However, these forms of dissemination ultimately produced two distinctive communities for conjunto: one local and one global. Local record labels maintained a folkloric understanding of the genre among a regional audience. Niche record labels (and other media-based dispersals intended for bourgeois audiences) instead introduced the music to a diverse fanbase, but limited the associated understanding of conjunto to the distinctive style created by artists like Flaco. This dissemination of the artform spread a non-traditional form of conjunto based not on common regional practices, but hybridized pursuits of musicians at the border of local and global techniques. It developed new fans for the music but also created an incomplete understanding of the tradition worldwide. It created new opportunities for Texas-based musicians with access to U.S. American systems of dissemination while blocking admittance for Mexican musicians—closely similar in musical style and repertory but lacking the necessary identity for participation—into global performance spaces and economic chances.

Modern media representations of conjunto have effectively created two communities: a local population tied to historical interpretations of the genre and a global fanbase who assume that all Texas-Mexican musicians are fundamentally representative of the Texas-Mexican tradition, despite the unique characteristics of artists like Flaco. Global audiences embody expected cultural identities based on location and heritage, but link the performance of conjunto to stereotypical constructions of class, language, and ethnicity. In this view, Flaco's identity as fundamentally "Texas-Mexican" therefore establishes his music (at least among an unconventional population) as similarly representative of local practices, despite actual musical elements. Although these effects are exhibited in the live performances discussed in the previous chapter, they are most pronounced in the widespread dissemination of conjunto through recordings, radio, television, print media, and online. These methods of dispersal reach an even broader audience than live performance alone, introducing conjunto music to audiences around the world, but also to regional populations historically distanced from the genre due to differences of class, language, or ethnicity. Yet, these distributions spread a very specific style of conjunto, and one that is not truly representative of the local community. In this regard, the globalization of conjunto creates new interpretations of the genre—as defined by musical traits and sociocultural identity—and, perhaps, a new genre entirely (especially if we insist on retaining such homologous associations).

Theoretical Framework: Globalization through Media

Texas-Mexican conjunto music has historically formed an essential component of identity for the associated working-class constituency. Originally, this identity was created via close, physical relationships among local musicians and audiences. Yet, media innovations disseminated the music among a broad population. This process promoted a shared identity for the local, working-class community, but also for the middle-class population in Texas, an ethnic diaspora spread across the United States, and a global fanbase with little connection to the original community.

As Deborah Wheeler demonstrates, cultures around the world define themselves through communication.[7] Unencumbered by the limitations of face-to-face interaction, modern societies develop shared identities through communication via media technologies. They use contemporary mechanisms of mass communication to transmit "shared symbolic forms" and "a sense of group culture" to both a local and global populace.[8] In the case of Texas-Mexican conjunto, musical recordings spread through media venues like radio, television, documentaries, recorded albums, and (more recently) online outlets (in addition to the introduction and access to such recordings disseminated through written texts such as newspaper articles) serve as material symbolism. They generate a widespread sense of cultural identity among a worldwide, imagined community of conjunto enthusiasts and participants. Like the performative dispersals of Chapter 1, these media-based diffusions do not change the meaning for the music among its original community, nor do they take over local characteristics of culture (as often noted in discourses of cultural imperialism in hegemonic, usually Americanized globalizations), but, in introducing Texas-Mexican culture to a fanbase outside of its original intent, the genre itself is shifted—albeit perhaps casually—in interpretation.

For our purposes, the media-based globalization of Texas-Mexican conjunto music will be used to represent simply the worldwide spread of the music throughout the twentieth century through a range of historical and contemporary media platforms. Although such worldwide dissemination leads to an imagined community of conjunto enthusiasts far outside of the traditional constituency, it does not imply global dominance or any sense of cultural imperialism ("Americanization") via this historically marginalized genre. Nor does it eliminate local considerations, either in South Texas or for geographic regions receiving the music outside of its original association. Instead, in the case of conjunto, media-based globalization increases the interconnectivity of the Texas-Mexican community with receptive fans outside of the historic tradition. It introduces the border culture to audiences who may hold cultural misconceptions—or at least little knowledge—of the region and its artistic pursuits. This, in turn, leads to new understandings (and misunderstandings) for the community outside of former considerations.

Recording Conjunto: Regional Labels

Following an initial period of major-label interest in Texas-Mexican conjunto music during the 1920s to 1940s, large U.S. American record companies like RCA and Columbia abandoned the region, leaving, as Peña describes, "a vacuum in the commercial dissemination of such music."[9] Narciso Martínez initially recorded for Bluebird Records, a low-cost subsidiary of RCA Victor specializing in blues and jazz, between 1935 and 1940, while Santiago Jiménez Sr.'s first recordings were for Decca Records in 1936. These major-label companies distributed conjunto beyond the immediate region, leading to interest in the genre in locations like Corpus Christi and Dallas.[10] Yet, this early exposure remained limited, at best. In the years following World War II, a number of small, regional record labels (e.g., Ideal, Falcón, Globe, Corona, El Zarape, and Río Records) filled the gap left by the withdrawal of the major companies. In contrast to the well-financed major labels, these small, regional companies had limited capital resources, inferior equipment and facilities, and "a haphazard system of distribution."[11] The financial difficulties of these local labels generated little exposure for the music outside of South Texas during this time period. As Flaco describes:

> [W]hen my papa played, there weren't record companies out there willing to expose conjunto music. They considered it low class, cantina music, Mexican hillbilly music. . . . The conjunto record companies were all local, independent operations. San Antonio may have been the base of conjunto music but the major labels weren't interested in this scroungy music. It was just among Mexicanos.[12]

This pattern of exposure has continued throughout the twentieth century, as conjunto artists have typically recorded for small, regional labels with strictly local distribution. However, as larger labels have become interested in recording the music, the genre has expanded to new locations.

That being said, recording practices of conjunto music have largely reproduced systems of inequity that emphasize the marginality of the Texas-Mexican genre amid reluctant ties to cultural identity. For example, major-label interest in the genre mirrored dispersal of so-called "race records" by and for southern Black Americans during the same time period. As such, these recordings were promoted as an exotic representation of minoritized practices and aimed primarily at a Texas-Mexican audience. In addition, compensation for the associated musicians was often exploitative. Similarly, as niche labels like Arhoolie and Arista Texas (see below) began to produce and distribute recordings of Texas-Mexican conjunto, the music again served as an exotic representation of the genre. The intended attention turned to more widespread audiences, but the music remained fundamentally considered as "other" outside of the regional community. Distribution of recordings among new locations has therefore expanded interest in the genre and simultaneously limited new interpretations of the music based on stereotypical associations. Meanwhile, the financial difficulties of local record labels have restricted the production value of regional records and largely confined distribution among a nearby fanbase.

Furthermore, these recording practices achieved recognition for the regional music in part by separating it from "Mexico" and stereotypical associations therein. As Flaco describes, major labels considered conjunto as "scroungy" and "Mexican hillbilly music." By instead promoting the music as quintessentially "Texan," disconnected from negative correlations with Mexico—despite cross-border influences and the fluidity of culture throughout the region—niche labels like Arhoolie and Arista Texas brought recognition to conjunto as ethnic folklore, akin to zydeco, the blues, and bluegrass, rather than "Mexican." Doing so paved the way for the nationalistic representations explored in the works of Mingo Saldívar, in particular, but separated U.S. American musicians—and economic opportunities—from Mexican musicians who played a major role in the development of the genre. Texas-based artists used Mexican influences and a romanticized version of Mexican identity (when beneficial and for audiences who didn't know the difference) to take advantage of recording opportunities both dependent on and unattainable for Mexican musicians.

Flaco's first recording was a 1954 single performed with his father for Corona Records, a small, San Antonio-based label specializing in Texas-Mexican music. In 1956, the artist recorded his solo debut with the short-lived, San Antonio-based Río Records. In 1957, he recorded a single for Típico Records that gained local airplay. As Flaco explains, these small labels jump-started his initial musical pursuits: "[T]he local independent recording companies in San Antonio . . . helped me out when I started out."[13] However, distribution for local labels was limited. Flaco describes:

> The local independent labels didn't want to invest or take a chance on exposing it (conjunto) to the big audience. . . . It was just played around the San Antonio area and that was it. I played and recorded on a lot of independent local labels, and I just heard my records around this area. If I went to L.A. or Chicago, there were no records. Nobody knew who Flaco

Jiménez was. And that's sad because there was a lot of lost time, time to let people know what we could do with this music.[14]

As Flaco continues in 1992, with the ultimate release of his first major-label album, *Partners*, "I have never forgotten or abandoned [my roots]. I have been recording for years and years and years on independent labels, but they didn't have the money to be able to expose or promote me to the outside world."[15] By 1975, when Ry Cooder had "discovered" the Texas-Mexican genre, recording with these small labels was still the customary practice for local musicians. As Cooder illustrates, "The records are made on obscure labels in trashy little studios on the Texas-Mexican border, but they still sound great."[16]

In this way, despite Flaco's efforts to receive recognition among the "big audience," he remained constrained by the recording capacity for his music. Recordings made by local labels did not receive mainstream distribution. Widespread distribution of his music came only after attention by mainstream artists like Cooder. Yet, at that point, the music was simultaneously promoted as an "exotic" representation of the Texas-Mexican culture and a hybridized interpretation largely outside of standard regional practices. The artist thus remains characterized according to his sociocultural heritage throughout both local and mainstream recording practices.

Saldívar's first fourteen albums were recorded for regional labels like Hacienda, Joey, and Espada Records. However, *I Love My Freedom, I Love My Texas* (1992), the first of the artist's albums aimed at an Anglo-American audience (including songs like "Ring of Fire," as "Rueda de Fuego," and "Sugartime," as "Lindo Cariñito"; see Chapter 5) was released by Nashville-based Rounder Records and thus received more widespread distribution and broader mainstream success, including a Grammy nomination for Best Mexican-American Album. Likewise, starting in the 1960s, Steve Jordan recorded "more than 100 singles" and "over twenty-five vinyl albums" for small, regional labels like Falcón, Freddie, and Hacienda Records (distributed for a time by RCA).[17] Yet, as Michael Corcoran notes, "His groundbreaking singles for Corpus Christi-based Hacienda Records in the '70s rarely sold more than 1000 copies."[18] However, once Jordan signed with a major record label (RCA Records) in 1985, he also received a Grammy nomination for *Turn Me Loose* (1986)—and recognition in a broader populace.

Recording Conjunto: Arhoolie Records

Following in the ostensible footsteps of the so-called "record men" who toured the southern United States during the early years of the twentieth century, recording African American (and later Mexican American) folk musicians for distribution as "race records," Chris Strachwitz has spent his career recording music in "cotton fields, seedy clubs, and community dance halls" for distribution under his own Arhoolie Records label.[19] However, while earlier "record men" were known for providing small payments (and no royalties) for the musicians involved, Strachwitz has made a point to pay his artists appropriately. Although the Arhoolie label has never made a significant amount of money, Strachwitz has provided royalties and copyright protections for his artists, in addition to widespread exposure that has led to more profitable opportunities. He has refused to sign exclusive contracts with musicians, allowing them to move to larger record labels as appropriate. Strachwitz explains his recording philosophy: "All we are is stewards for the music for a time. . . . But we should not forget the responsibility that comes with it, especially when you are dealing with people who are basically illiterate in the ways of the modern commercial world."[20] He continues, "I wanted to stand up for the beauty of what I believe in. I'm a strong advocate for not only the rights of these artists but also their cultural rights. I do the best I can to be an advocate for the authentic stuff."[21]

Born into an aristocratic family in Germany in 1931, Strachwitz immigrated to the United States with his family in 1947, settling with an aunt in Reno, Nevada. Strachwitz moved to Los Angeles in 1951 to attend Pomona College and served two years in the United States Army before finishing college at the University of California at Berkeley and taking a job as a German teacher at a high school in Los Gatos, near San Jose. While in Reno (and later in California), Strachwitz discovered a number of small, AM local radio stations that played New Orleans jazz and early R&B. As Strachwitz remembers, "I very quickly heard all this amazing music on the radio—hillbilly, polka, jazz."[22] So influenced, he began gathering obscure albums to sell to European record collectors. According to Richard Spottswood, Strachwitz's interest in marginalized artistic forms can perhaps be attributed to his background as an immigrant to the United States:

> [Strachwitz] is probably more American than many of us, but he experienced the music not as something he was born into and took for granted like the air we breathe, but as something rare and delightful, not available to the rest of the world. . . . Coming from another language and culture, he perhaps saw the artistry in this music a little sooner, a little earlier than the rest of us, and his vision of a kaleidoscopic American musical culture, from Tejano to country and Southwestern blues, has helped thwart the single standard the music industry has tried to impose on us over the years.[23]

This is an interesting consideration. Whereas other major labels characterized music of minoritized populations as inherently "other" to the mainstream recording industry (and thus, U.S. American culture as a whole), Strachwitz, emanating from outside of a standard U.S. American cultural heritage (at least according to nationalist interpretations of such), instead embraced the rich diversity of the music he recorded. The reaction to Texas-Mexican (and other) music by a Euro-American fan mirrors the enthusiastic reception of Flaco, in particular, among a European audience. In this regard, the artist's disconnections from homologous characterizations of genre as identity seem to gain a foothold among fans who are similarly disconnected from U.S. American systems of categorization according to complexion. Strachwitz's ability to consider music according to its aesthetic value alone, rather than inextricably entwined with systems of discrimination in the United States, has generated recordings of marginalized musics and distribution among widespread audiences.

At the same time, however, the music he creates often entombs individual interpretations of folkloric styles as uniquely representative of cultural communities. Distribution of such idiosyncratic recordings among a bourgeois audience leads to misunderstandings of broader cultural practices. For example, as in the case of Flaco, individualistic recordings of nontraditional techniques separate listening experiences according to the accessibility of regional or niche record labels, a conspicuously binary choice. Intended for two distinctive audiences, these recording practices create two separate communities: a group of local fans who experience conjunto as a folkloric tradition based on historical techniques and a common repertory and an inter/national fanbase who consider Flaco's unique style to be representative of conjunto as a whole. For subsequent artists to achieve prominence within one group of fans or the other, they must choose to play according to one of these two styles, further entrenching a disconnection in the genre. Meanwhile, Mexican artists—fundamentally connected to local styles—remain detached from either method of U.S. American recording practice and thus unable to participate in such decisions.

Since beginning in 1960, Arhoolie Records has released some 400 albums and more than 6,500 songs,[24] including field recordings from a range of U.S. American roots musics (primarily emanating from Texas, Louisiana, and Mississippi) and a variety of reissues and compilations of small, regional recordings. As journalist Mark Guarino illustrates, in making these field recordings, "Strachwitz would simply show up in town, ask around who some of the local players were, follow some directions and later set up a microphone and press 'record.'"[25] In so doing, Strachwitz brought initial exposure to artists who might otherwise have remained strictly regional performers. As Katherine Bishop asserts, Strachwitz's recordings provided "the first income" many musicians had received from their music, in addition to "exposure outside of their own communities."[26] This process also created a characterization as U.S. American roots music—paving the way for later nationalistic interpretations—for genres like conjunto previously defined alternatively.

Purchasing and listening to Arhoolie records became an educational experience for many consumers—albeit a distinctive community of a middle-class, Anglo-American audience spread throughout the nation. Through Arhoolie albums, folk musics historically at the margins of the dominant culture gained a following. In addition, extensive liner notes (often written by Strachwitz himself) informed these audiences about the recorded artists and associated musical cultures, including information on instruments and tunings. As Bonnie Raitt details, "I would read about the latest releases on Arhoolie in *Sing Out* magazine. . . . Every one of those records was a treasure. . . . Chris became an important figure, a monumental link really, from whom I learned a lot, especially about Cajun and Tex-Mex and zydeco and Hawaiian music."[27] Similarly, Bob Dylan credits Arhoolie records as "where I first heard [blues artists] Blind Lemon Jefferson, Blind Blake, Charlie Patton and Tommy Johnson."[28]

Likewise, Cooder attributes his entire career to a teen-aged encounter with an Arhoolie recording of blues guitarist Big Joe Williams.[29] As Cooder explains, he learned how to play guitar from that recording, ultimately acquiring more such albums and learning from the extensive liner notes, in addition to the music itself: "It started me on a path of living, the path I am still on."[30] In addition, Cooder attributes his discovery of Texas-Mexican conjunto music (leading to his travel to San Antonio to meet and ultimately pursue the *Chicken Skin Music* album and subsequent tour with Flaco, and thus leading to the dissemination of Flaco's music—and the conjunto genre as a whole—outside of the historical South Texas geography) to Strachwitz.[31] As Cooder explains, after hearing the characteristic accordion music on the radio during the 1970s, he called Strachwitz for help in identifying the music.[32] Throughout this activity, as Cooder recalls, "Chris was standing there, saying, 'This is good; this is no good. You'll like this; you won't like that.' And it was always true; he always steers you to the best things."[33]

After exploring blues music during the 1960s, Strachwitz developed a "new passion" for Texas-Mexican conjunto music in the 1970s, resulting in "a deluge of Arhoolie releases" and the documentary film, *Chulas Fronteras*.[34] This interest spread conjunto to a new audience and set the stage for the subsequent inter/national successes of regional artists like Flaco. Strachwitz first discovered conjunto on the radio in Los Angeles during the 1950s, explaining, "I just totally fell in love with [Texas-Mexican music] the first time

I heard it . . . . It's the sound of it, the feel of it, the total authenticity of it."[35] Despite a familial background in a culture with a similar, accordion-based polka element, Strachwitz found a particular attraction to the sound of the accordion in Texas-Mexican conjunto, noting that, "Man, no German can play the accordion like that."[36] Inspired by this "new" style of music, Strachwitz proposed an idea to filmmaker Les Blank to create a documentary addressing the culture and music of the Texas-Mexican border region. This collaboration led to the 1976 release of *Chulas Fronteras*, which follows conjunto musicians like Lydia Mendoza, Martínez, and Flaco (among others) and provided one of the most significant introductions to the music outside of South Texas during the twentieth century.

Following this film project, Strachwitz began recording and releasing a number of Texas-Mexican conjunto albums under the Arhoolie designation, successfully introducing the music to a broad audience outside of the traditional regional community. He also encouraged artists like Flaco to pursue a more innovative (and hybridized) musical style. As Strachwitz explains, while he was initially unsure of the artist's value in singing harmonies, he "loved Jiménez's jazzy accordion playing."[37] As Strachwitz recalls, "Flaco told me, 'Oh you like that? I like to do that too.' . . . I don't think they really appreciated that sort of thing at the dances he played then."[38] The producer's subsequent work with Flaco—and continuing encouragement of the musician's "jazzy" style—ultimately led to the 1985 release of *Ay Te Dejo En San Antonio*, the first Grammy Award-winning album (for Best Mexican-American Performance) for both the artist and the record company. During the 1980s and 1990s, Arhoolie released some four dozen reissues of regional conjunto recordings, further stimulating popularity for the genre outside of its historical audience.

Just as the initial dissemination of Flaco's music in worldwide performance venues came about through the "assistance" of mainstream artists like Cooder and Dylan, it is interesting to note the role of yet another Euro-American figure in the artist's rise to success. In addition to recording and distributing Flaco's music, Strachwitz encouraged the stylistic traits so central to the musician's ultimate success, at least outside of his cultural community. As such, mainstream success for artists from marginalized populations in the United States remains reliant on external support. It is thus Flaco's "fortune" to have connected with Strachwitz and Cooder—based largely on his ability to speak English and his willingness to work across cultural lines, according to Cooder—that allowed for his successes according to (or at least at the edges of) the dominant culture. Texas-Mexican musicians who did not make these connections maintained the more traditional musical techniques popular—and thus necessary for local success—in South Texas. In this way, musicians fundamentally perform according to audience expectation. Musicians in South Texas maintain historical practices of conjunto, while artists like Flaco who were launched into an external community have instead performed according to stylistic expectations of that fanbase (yet ironically remain trapped into considerations according to Texas-Mexican identity).

It is also interesting to note that Flaco gained attention from these Euro-American figures largely due to his minimal successes (at the time) among the regional scene. As a small label, Arhoolie could not attract more prominent Texas-Mexican artists—who were already signed to local labels. Flaco was happy to sign with Arhoolie and willing to play in whatever style these enthusiasts required. As such, he became representative of the Texas-Mexican culture among a bourgeois audience, significantly influential among global conjunto artists, but unrepresentative of local styles and still more prominent among national and international circles than in Texas or Mexico.

By 1995 (the thirty-fifth year of the company), Arhoolie Records was still releasing some twenty-five albums per year. As Strachwitz describes, "A lot of it is reissuing other old 78s . . . and mining a lot of Mexican stuff, and some of it is new."[39] Many of Jordan's—among others'—mainstream releases (before, frustrated with record labels in general, he founded Jordan Records and "quit the label game all together") came through Arhoolie.[40] For example, Elijah Wald, musicologist and longtime roots-music writer for the *Boston Globe*, attributes his own discovery of Jordan's music to a 1993 Arhoolie rerelease of two Jordan albums.[41] Corcoran suggests that readers trace the artist's evolving innovations on the "essential" album, *Many Sounds of Estéban 'Steve' Jordan*, a 1985 compilation by Arhoolie of regional recordings from the 1960s and 1970s.[42] Beyond simply spreading conjunto music to a diverse audience, attention from outside sources such as Arhoolie has brought a certain degree of "validation" to the cultural art form that has long been dismissed as "cantina music." As Strachwitz notes, "I think the artists have enjoyed making the recordings. Most never even asked for anything. For them it was like, 'If this crazy guy comes around and enjoys it, maybe it validates my music.'"[43] While this sense of external validation carries its own problematic interpretations, it is nevertheless an important consideration in the geographic and transcultural dissemination of the Texas-Mexican music.

Recording Conjunto: Arista Texas

Beyond the dissemination of regional recordings of conjunto through California-based Arhoolie Records, the formation of Arista Texas (an Austin-based division of Arista Nashville) in 1993 further expanded the audience for

Texas-Mexican accordion music beyond its original community. Originally intended to find, produce, and market the "best examples of the state's many indigenous forms of music," the label initially focused on Tejano musics, including conjunto.[44] Cameron Randle, a prime impetus in the formation of the Texas Tornados (see Chapter 4), was named as the label's first vice president and general manager. Prior to his time with Arista Texas, Randle also helped with the creation of Flaco's first major-label album, *Partners* (Warner Brothers Records, 1992). As Tim DuBois, head of Arista Nashville, notes, "Cameron's charter [was] to find, develop, and evangelize on behalf of Texas talent in several genres."[45]

In an early press conference, Randle describes his vision for the company as expanding commercial possibilities for Tejano musics while simultaneously maintaining the genre's artistic integrity: "We came to Texas to promote regional music, and we feel Tejano is the most compelling music today. . . . We want to help expand Tejano [by establishing] the commercial integrity of a major-label recording while maintaining the unique and genuine quality of the art form."[46] In addition, Randle cites an objective of moderate expansion for the genre, focusing on the quality of music produced and maintaining the substance of the regional tradition through broad commercialization, rather than concentrating merely on monetary gains. As Randle details:

> For too long, . . . Texas music has been required to meet Nashville, Los Angeles and New York on their terms. There's no reason in the world why Texas can't be met on its own terms. My goal is to make great music that can be successful enough to pay for itself yet not be required to meet gold and platinum standards just to keep its doors open. I want to make records that need to be made.[47]

Despite these presumptive plans for moderate growth, DuBois does emphasize the substantial monetary investment placed in the company: "We are making a serious financial commitment and bringing in the talent and resources of [parent company] BMG and BMG Distribution. I can tell you that we are here to stay."[48]

Early signings to Arista Texas's roster included Flaco and Freddy Fender (also of the Texas Tornados). Following a joint album between Flaco and Fender entitled *A Tejano Country Christmas* (1994), Flaco released a self-titled solo album (*Flaco Jiménez*, 1994). Like the artist's first Arhoolie Records release, *Ay Te Dejo En San Antonio* (and contrasting the many regional recordings earlier in Flaco's career), this first Arista Texas album received a Grammy Award in 1995 for Best Mexican-American/Tejano Music Performance. In all, Flaco has received a total of five Grammy Awards (in addition to a Lifetime Achievement Award in 2015), as well as an additional three nominations. Despite a large proportion of albums produced through small, regional labels, particularly early in the musician's career, each of Flaco's Grammy recognitions comes through a major record label (the relative "largeness" or "mainstream" nature of Arhoolie notwithstanding).

In this regard, the distribution of Texas-Mexican conjunto through large, national record companies has brought recognition to the regional music not feasible through regional recording practices alone. In turn, this circumstance has led to widespread exposure for artists like Flaco who have been picked up by major record labels (and thus, external recognition of Flaco's less traditional style as characteristic of the genre as a whole), while local musicians—and frequently more conservative manifestations of the music itself—have not received widespread dispersal. However, as Juan Tejeda, founder and longtime director of the annual Tejano Conjunto Festival in San Antonio, asserts, this Grammy acknowledgment brings exposure to the genre as a whole: "The exposure gives more recognition to conjunto in general. . . . Flaco is really the first bona fide conjunto artist to get a Grammy."[49] In this way, the entire community conceivably benefits from the cultural introduction produced by major-label interest in certain conjunto artists' works.

By 1998, the Arista Texas division (by that time comprising both Arista Latin and Arista Austin) had been dismantled. Despite early optimism regarding the growing commercial prospects for Tejano musics (stimulated, in part, by the mainstream successes of artists like Selena), yet seemingly contradicting the previously articulated goal of merely moderate growth (as well as the preliminary assertion of full financial support by BMG), the budget for the label was not sufficient to attract an audience that would produce a financially sustainable endeavor.[50] In this regard, while the formation of the Arista Texas record label contributed to the inter/national spread of Texas-Mexican conjunto music (and other Tejano-based genres) for a few years during the 1990s (corresponding to the popular rise of artists like Flaco), its lasting impact in introducing the genre to a broad populace was limited by a lack of commercial interest from that same populace. While musicians like Flaco introduced conjunto to an audience outside of the original constituency, excitement for the music among mainstream culture has remained limited, at best.

The Radio Presence of Conjunto: KEDA

In addition to—and in combination with—the transcultural and inter/national dissemination of Texas-Mexican conjunto music through recordings by companies like Arhoolie Records and Arista Texas, radio presentations of the music have further spread the sociocultural artform among an ever-broadening population. While many of these radio broadcasts have been aimed primarily at a local, Spanish-speaking audience, the transmission of the music into the airwaves has also introduced its sounds to the wider community (who might not encounter conjunto in more traditional, socially constrained venues). In addition, regional radio stations have gradually influenced similar formats in alternate locations with large Mexican-American populations. Furthermore, the promotion of conjunto in a radio outlet has supported the music and allowed it to grow beyond what might be possible through live performances and even recorded albums alone.

During the 1920s and 1930s, radio stations owned and operated by Anglo-American Texans struggled to sell advertising slots during the early morning or late at night. Mexican and Mexican-American radio brokers purchased these less desirable time slots and began broadcasting Spanish-language programs (initially, quiz shows and Mexican radionovelas) aimed at a Mexican-American audience. Like other radio brokers, Manuel Davila used the purchase of time slots on the English-language radio stations in San Antonio to play conjunto music (selling advertising sponsorships to pay for the slots and make a small profit). During this time, most Spanish-language radio segments used hosts and programming (including music) from Mexico and Latin America, instead of local Mexican-American offerings. In this regard, Davila faced prejudice not only from the dominant Anglo-American community, but also from Texas Mexicans who criticized his regional use of the language and the working-class style of music presented. A comment from a listener survey demonstrates this early linguistic criticism: "The complaint is that the American version of Spanish is either too *pocho* (i.e., too intermixed with English words or constructions) or too 'peasanty' (i.e., agricultural terms are used in discussing nonagricultural subjects)."[51]

In 1966, Davila formed his own Spanish-language radio station, KEDA 1540-AM (Radio Jalapeño). Through this format, he continued to push the boundaries of acceptable programming for the region, playing local Texas music (conjunto), rather than more popular Mexican musicians. In this way, Davila is often credited with establishing—or at least popularizing—the contemporary Texas-Mexican sound. As Lisa Cortez Walden notes, "While it is a matter of hot debate whether Tejano music actually originated at KEDA, it is sure that this form of music would not exist were it not for radio stations like KEDA as well as deejays like the Davilas who paid attention to local artists."[52] In fact, Davila was inducted into the Tejano Conjunto Hall of Fame in 1985 (as well as a number of additional awards) for his contributions to the genre.[53] Over the years, KEDA has made a point to program the local and up-and-coming conjunto and Tejano artists that other stations wouldn't play. In doing so, it has also influenced an increasing separation between Texas-based music and Mexican music, with artists jostling for limited broadcast opportunities, despite a similar repertory and sound.

Many local conjunto (and Tejano) musicians got started through the liberal programming practices of KEDA, ultimately becoming successful throughout the region (and even further) by way of this initial, media-based performance opportunity. Nonetheless, Tony DeMars explains, in playing music deemed to be not "appropriate for airplay" by other Spanish-language stations (in contrast to "the more refined music from Mexico City"), KEDA was nicknamed the "cantina station" by other stations, ignored by record labels, and made far less in annual revenue than major-market stations in the area.[54] In addition, despite its significant role in supporting local conjunto music, in more recent years, the station struggled to compete with pan-ethnic media.[55] That being said, by continuing to program local, up-and-coming artists (in addition to African American musicians like James Brown and Aretha Franklin who also weren't programmed on other stations due to their race; since, as Davila's son Ricardo, a longtime DJ for KEDA known as "Güero Polkas" explains, "There was an FCC rule in those days that a station had to broadcast at least ten percent of the programming in English"), KEDA compelled other radio stations to match their program list.[56] As Amanda Lozano asserts, "The Davilas created such a sensation with their brash disregard for racism, which forced other radio stations to play what they were."[57] The family sold the station in 2011.

Beyond a continuing demand for conjunto music on Spanish-language radio stations in Texas, by the 1980s, Mexican music had come to dominate Spanish-language broadcasting throughout the United States. As radio DJ Martín Rosales describes (in an interview with Peña published in 1985), "[B]y executive orders Mexican music reigned supreme in radio stations everywhere in the Southwest except Texas."[58] Similarly, as a 1989 study in *Broadcasting Magazine* asserts, "If you were to switch on any U.S. Spanish-language TV station and guess the origin of the program airing, you would have a better chance of being right saying Mexico or one of a handful of Latin American countries, than the U.S."[59] Yet, while the mid-1970s supported only some thirty to forty Hispanic-format radio stations around the country, by 1989, there were 237 such stations in the United States for a total estimated revenue of more than $150 million.[60] In this way, limited programming availability created tension between Texas and Mexican artists competing for space in media-based distributions of similar musics. Identity-based distinctions between related genres protected opportunities for one group or another by erecting performative barriers.

Even if Mexican-regional music dominated these stations, conjunto and other Tejano musics maintained certain airplay—and thus, media-based dispersal—outside of the primary South Texas region. For example, before ultimately switching to Mexican music, multiple radio stations in the Yakima Valley in Washington (a region with a large population of Texas-Mexican migrants; see Chapter 3) programmed blocks of Texas-Mexican music. Similarly, community advocate Silvestre Durán produced a Spanish-language radio program on WFOB 1430-AM in Fostoria, Ohio, for almost fifty-three years (finally retiring in 2008) that played "Tejano/norteño/conjunto" music for Texas-Mexican migrant families in the region.[61] By the mid-1990s, Tejano music (a more commercialized form of conjunto, with popular appeal and expanded instrumentation) had moved into a position of prominence on radio stations around the country. Writing for *USA Today* in 1995, Edna Gundersen notes that, "Once confined to the Lone Star State, this Tex-Mex polka is the fastest-growing segment of Latin music, dominating U.S. Spanish-language radio stations and generating an estimated $35 million annually in record sales."[62]

Conjunto music also received a national radio boost during this time period, frequently in conjunction with local artists like Flaco and Saldívar who were performing around the country. For example, Saldívar's Fourth of July performance at the American Roots concert on the grounds of the Washington Monument in 1995 was broadcast nationally on NPR and locally on WMZQ and WAMU. That same week, Saldívar appeared on *A Prairie Home Companion*, broadcast nationwide. In 1996, under contract with Arista Texas, Flaco undertook a "radio blitz" with the label, playing for a variety of conjunto, Tejano, and Mexican-regional stations, in addition to so-called triple-A ("adult album alternative") and college outlets. As Randle notes, "That's the beauty of Flaco. . . . Without changing an ounce of who he is, he's the one artist that you can take to Houston and visit an AM conjunto station in the morning, visit a top Tejano station in the afternoon, and take him to a triple-A station that night."[63] Ricardo Davila explains the resurgence of conjunto during this time as "part of a larger movement in pop culture toward an appreciation of roots and world music," emphasizing that, "It used to be a put-down to [play the accordion]. . . . It was thought of as dumb or even sissy, but now it's completely different."[64]

In 2015, corresponding to this continued resurgence of the regional musical form, Rancho Alegre Radio (on KOOP 91.7-FM) started in Austin. This addition followed the closure of the last Tejano music radio station in

2005 and subsequent struggle to reopen KTXZ 1560-AM in 2008, initially simulcast in both AM and FM. This hourlong radio program, hosted by Piper LeMoine and Baldomero "Frank" Cuellar "features Texas roots music and in-depth interviews with musicians," including both Tejano and conjunto music.[65] According to Nancy Flores, the program, which can be streamed online or through the TuneIn radio application, has attracted a following around the country ("from the Pacific Northwest to the Midwest").[66] Like numerous radio formats throughout the twentieth and twenty-first centuries, this modern program thus disseminates a regional tradition among a broader population. As Cuellar emphasizes, the show is intended (in part) to educate listeners among a widespread community: "When people think of Conjunto music, they think of Flaco Jimenez. . . . That's great, but sometimes we only get half the story. There are so many more artists out there, from the Rio Grande Valley to Alice, Texas."[67] LeMoine concurs: "We'll be your (musical) guide, and after listening to the show you'll be able to tell Tejano from Norteno, Conjunto, or banda music."[68] In this regard, modern radio programming not only disseminates a sociocultural tradition to new populations, but also spreads information about that tradition that widespread audiences might not otherwise receive (for example in associating the style of music introduced outside of the regional community by artists like Flaco with the Texas-Mexican tradition as a whole).

Conjunto on Television, in Print Media, and Online

In addition to the widespread dissemination of conjunto music through record labels and radio programming, television has also contributed to the initial globalization of the genre (although to a lesser extent). However, due to its altered socioeconomic considerations, particularly during the early years of the media technology, the adoption of television broadcasting for conjunto has spread the musical form beyond a strictly geographic and cultural dispersal and instead among a new, middle-class audience. As Vicki Mayer explains, during the 1950s, "television ownership and viewing was still a privileged activity; only middle-class Mexican Americans could afford the forty to seventy dollars needed to buy a UHF converter to watch Spanish-language television."[69] With this consideration, media corporations like KCOR-AM/KCOR-TV in San Antonio shared programming between radio and television formats (since, as Mayer describes, the sister stations shared a production studio), presenting locally recorded music for a combined middle-class and working-class audience (one group via television and the other via radio, respectively).[70]

By the 1970s (and certainly by the 1990s), performers such as Flaco, Jordan, and Saldívar were performing on national television outlets (frequently corresponding to live performances outside of the South Texas region by these same artists). For example, Flaco appeared on NBC's *Saturday Night Live* in 1976 with Cooder in promotion of the *Chicken Skin Music* album. In 1979, Jordan performed on the public television concert show *Austin City Limits*, a program also frequented by Flaco (by 1996, "half a dozen times").[71] In 1996, Flaco played with The Mavericks (with the hit song "All You Ever Do Is Bring Me Down") on *The Tonight Show* with Jay Leno. This national media distribution has introduced the local music to a new audience around the United States. As Terry Lickona, producer for *Austin City Limits*, describes, "Every time [Flaco] has appeared on 'Austin City Limits,' we get calls from all over the U.S.—Minnesota, New Hampshire, the Midwest—people who can't even pronounce his name or know what that style of music is called, but they love it.... They want to find out where to find his music."[72] In this way, initial attention to Flaco's music by mainstream artists like Cooder led to recordings by nationally oriented labels like Arhoolie, which led to radio and television distribution across more mainstream platforms like *Prairie Home Companion* and *Austin City Limits*. Each of these platforms has spread Flaco's music beyond his familial community, but simultaneously limited interpretations of conjunto to Flaco's unique style and pigeonholed the artist as quintessentially "conjunto," despite musical elements and attempts to be characterized as something else entirely.

Initiated in 1980, the Tejano Music Awards, held annually in San Antonio, has further disseminated the music among a widespread population. By 1991 (with the Texas Tornados nominated for Most Promising Band, Single of the Year, and Album of the Year Conjunto [Progressive] and Jordan also nominated for Album of the Year Conjunto [Progressive]), the televised program was intended to reach audiences throughout the United States and Mexico.

By 1993, in addition to a sold-out live audience, the awards show was broadcast to "more than thirty television stations in the Southwest."[73] That being said, as examined in more detail in the introduction, artists such as Flaco, Jordan, and Saldívar who have pursued external indicators of success have not received awards for specific albums or songs according to this organization. Instead, the awards show typically honors more commercialized, but also more locally situated "Tejano" artists like Elida Reyna and Michael Salgado, rather than artists like Flaco who remain widely characterized as "conjunto," actual musical elements notwithstanding. Even the winners of the conjunto-specific awards tend to represent local groups such as The Hometown Boys and Los Hermanos Farias who are also frequently characterized as "Tejano" rather than "conjunto." Dwayne Verheyden from the Netherlands has also received an award for Best New Artist from the awards show. These practices demonstrate the political nature of conjunto performances and local recognition. Artists like Flaco struggle at the edge of two separate communities: the local and the global, garnering intermittent recognition in both, but never fully representative of either.

In addition to the *Chulas Fronteras* documentary in 1976 (and its sister project, *Del Mero Corazón*, a short video created from the outtakes of the initial documentary, first released in 1979 and subsequently packaged with *Chulas Fronteras*), a documentary on Texas-Mexican music and culture, entitled *Songs of the Homeland*, premiered on public television in 1995. With narration by Fender and commentary by a number of scholars, the film spread educational details about the music, beyond just the cultural sounds. A somewhat "sloppier" documentary, entitled *Tex-Mex: Music of the Texas-Mexican Borderlands* and created by Jeremy Marre, was released in 1983.[74] In 1991, the British Broadcasting Corporation (BBC) spent ten days in Texas filming concerts and local clubs for a television program on Texas regional musics, further disseminating the music outside of the United States. By 1995, in addition to television inclusion on CBS's *Sunday Morning*, Saldívar had become a hit on the television network Telemundo (see Chapter 1).

In recent years, beyond the inter/national dispersal of Texas-Mexican conjunto through television programming, the genre has spread through print media and, increasingly, through online sources. For example, in correlation with the physical dispersal of regional performances and recordings by conjunto artists like Flaco, Jordan, and Saldívar, newspapers around the world have printed a variety of advertisements and reviews of such performances and recordings (as well as similar offerings for events like the Tejano Conjunto Festival in San Antonio; see Bauer 2019). In addition, starting in the 1990s and targeting middle-class Texas Mexicans, bilingual newspapers like *La Prensa* (San Antonio) and *Que Onda* (Houston) have further disseminated information on conjunto music, thus shifting the primary audience for the genre beyond its working-class roots to instead encompass an ethnic (and multiethnic) community disconnected from former socioeconomic considerations. As Mayer explains, following diversification of the publication's format in the 1990s (and soon imitated by competing works like *Que Onda*), "Marketing materials for [*La Prensa*] aim for a linguistically diverse San Antonio readership, while niche marketing to middle-class Hispanic consumers, such as Spanish teachers and 'Hispanic business people [who want] to polish their knowledge of the Spanish language.'"[75] As I've discussed elsewhere, the last twenty years of the twentieth century also introduced a number of cultural magazines (*Tejano Monthly* and *Latin Times*, for example) that have spread the genre among a worldwide population.[76] Meanwhile, mainstream publications like the *San Antonio Express-News* have played their own role in spreading information about conjunto (for example, beginning in 1982, by sponsoring—together with KEDA Radio—the Tejano Conjunto Festival in San Antonio).[77]

In addition, the rise of the internet during the twenty-first century has opened new media outlets to a diverse population, with a range of websites, YouTube channels, social media, and online radio stations providing new means of cultural dissemination for the Texas-Mexican genre (a phenomenon I've explored in more detail elsewhere; see Bauer 2016 and 2019). As Gheni Platenburg discusses, "The [Texas-Mexican] bands of today also utilize social media and YouTube as a means of getting their names out to the public," while online radio stations have "provided an outlet for Tejano music to continue to thrive."[78] For example, beyond websites like *La Onda Network* and *Tejano Music Home Page* and an online video channel called puroconjunt0210, the "premier website on conjunto music"—*Conjunto is Life*—was created by Martín De Jesús Martínez to disseminate music and information among a diverse community.[79]

Conclusions

In addition to the physical dissemination of Texas-Mexican conjunto music via inter/national performances by artists like Flaco, Jordan, and Saldívar, media-based distributions—in the form of recordings, radio and television broadcasting, print-based publications, and various online dispersals—have created an audience for the regional genre (as posited by Arjun Appadurai) outside of traditional sociocultural considerations of ethnicity, class, language, and location. Whereas historical populations (including working-class Texas Mexicans) shared information—thus developing the notion of "community"—through physical proximity, modern communities are formed through a diverse, media-based range of communicative techniques. In this way, contemporary communities—including the increasingly widespread fanbase for Texas-Mexican conjunto music—do not follow traditional understandings of culture, instead using a variety of musical encounters and corresponding attractions to create an "imagined" community outside of sociocultural boundaries.

That being said, scholars have promoted a phenomenon known as "cultural discount," in which, due to a lack of cultural background and consequent knowledge of a given genre, external audiences value a media-based product less than those within the original community. As Terry Flew and Silvio Waisbord assert, "Even where media technologies and formats are explicitly transnational, . . . considerable adaptation to local and regional languages, cultures, and expectations concerning program genres has been a condition of viability for operating in different countries."[80] For the media-based globalization of Texas-Mexican conjunto, although recordings, radio, television, newspapers, and the internet spread the genre among an increasingly diverse and global population, and although this dissemination has created an external community of conjunto fans (and, to a certain extent, participants), this new community does not maintain the contextual significance for the genre as a form of sociocultural expression. In that way, by gaining a diverse audience (and any corresponding financial incentives for this external enthusiasm), the Texas-Mexican genre in fact loses—or at least reinterprets—much of its original cultural meaning.

CHAPTER 3

"From Texas to Washington and across to Michigan and Illinois..."

Nostalgia and Authenticity in the U.S. American Spread of Conjunto

> The purpose of [the annual Midwest Tejano-Conjunto EXPLOSION] is to expose and showcase the awesome Tejano talent in the Midwest, particularly in Michigan and Ohio.
>
> —Mark Garcia and Mike Avina, M and M Productions

In 1991, a "Fiesta Marketplace Christmas Celebration" brought seven afternoons and evenings of free Latino music and culture to the plaza at the corner of 4th and Spurgeon Streets in downtown Santa Ana, California.[1] The final performance showcased a Texas-Mexican conjunto band from Southern California: Juan Chapa y Su Conjunto. Although the group lives in California, they harbor close ties to the Texas-Mexico border region. For example, bass player Albert Ramon was born in Corpus Christi but moved to California with his family as a young child. He grew up in Azusa and Santa Ana.[2] Visiting his hometown at six years old, Ramon heard Tony De La Rosa perform at a Monday night dance in the town coliseum. As with many of the same generation, Ramon grew up listening to traditional Mexican-American genres and U.S. American popular music. As the musician describes, "I used to buy Beatles albums and stuff . . . but if you played a Tex-Mex record, I'd be right there. It was those records of my dad's [Flaco Jiménez, Beto Villa, De La Rosa, Little Joe and the Latinaires, and Valerio Longoria, among others] that I really liked."[3] In addition, like many regional conjunto musicians, Ramon comes from a family of musicians. He explains: "[My grandfather] used to play accordion back in the old times on the ranches, back when there was no (concrete) around. When I was growing up, he would still always be playing at parties, making the sound of a band all by himself."[4] By the age of nine,

Ramon was playing drums for parties and weddings in Southern California with his uncle's conjunto band. With his own group, Ramon started playing "Top 40 tunes and oldies," in addition to traditional conjunto tunes. However, attributing more mainstream interest in the genre to groups like Los Lobos and the Texas Tornados, he's now "usually able to win an audience just with the Tex-Mex music."[5]

For the 1991 show, Juan Chapa y Su Conjunto played mostly "traditional border tunes," with a few mainstream insertions (influenced by groups like the Texas Tornados) like Freddy Fender's "Before the Next Teardrop Falls."[6] In this regard, these California-based musicians retain a fairly conservative interpretation of the Texas-Mexican tradition. Hybridity in songs and stylistic elements closely follows regional practices by iconoclastic artists like Flaco. However, influenced by artists like Steve Jordan, Chapa (on accordion) is a more innovative performer than international conjunto musicians who fall even further outside of the expected geographic community (see Chapter 7). As journalist Jim Washburn notes, "Though [Chapa] doesn't employ the flamboyant showmanship of some other squeeze box kings, he was all over his three-row button accordions, playing some wild, unpredictable stuff—including occasional car-horn dissonances—that always landed on the *dinero* [money]."[7] The guitar riffs, played by Daniel Flores, meshed with the accordion "in patterns that were full of subtle rhythmic and harmonic accents" and were embellished with "fanciful single-note runs."[8] On bass, Washburn asserts, "Ramon seemed a bit like a conjunto Paul McCartney, playing inventive melodic lines even while singing."[9] Picnic tables and planters set up in front of the stage limited dancing, so one element of standard Texas-Mexican practices was lost. This performance demonstrates just one example of the many conjunto musicians and audiences now scattered across the United States.

During the twentieth and twenty-first centuries, Texas-Mexican workers followed agricultural and industrial labor across California, Oregon, Washington, and the northern Midwest. This emigration spread the Texas-Mexican culture to Mexican-American communities throughout the United States. It created a popularity for conjunto beyond the local constituency. Yet, even when maintaining close familial connections to the Texas-Mexico region, conjunto musicians located outside of the central geography tend to retain a traditional musical style, leaving generic innovations to musicians more closely affiliated with South Texas. As such, national conjunto musicians assert cultural adherence to the Texas-Mexican community by maintaining more conservative stylistic traits than might otherwise be expected. In addition, beyond a heritage-based or aspirational desire to participate within Texas-Mexican culture, conjunto musicians use nostalgia to identify with this form of expression. This chapter explores the spread of conjunto music across the United States (in the Midwest, Pacific Northwest, Southwest, and California) during the twentieth and twenty-first centuries. Like other globalized manifestations of conjunto, many of these national characteristics follow the influence of Flaco (in turn instigated by Anglo-American rock stars like Ry Cooder and Doug Sahm who initially pushed the artist outside of historic regional boundaries). In this way, the dispersal of Texas-Mexican conjunto throughout the United States has created a folkloric sensibility among participants, even as local artists like Flaco pursue alternative endeavors among the mainstream.

Theoretical Framework: Community and Nostalgia

Historically, artists demonstrate close adherence to a cultural community, often corresponding to the ethnic or socioeconomic circumstances of their familial heritage. In the case of Texas-Mexican conjunto music, this adherence has remained particularly pronounced. Since the second half of the twentieth century, the presumed sociological significance of the traditional genre has consolidated the style into a relatively standard instrumentation, repertory, and sound, with regional performers and local audiences often reluctant to change the historical form and corresponding sense of meaning. However, in recent years, a number of musicians outside of the ethnic and geographic community have joined the genre, performing music outside of their strict cultural heritage, in an attempt, in part, to express themselves as part of the Texas-Mexican constituency. Adherence—familial or aspirational—to the expected cultural community is complicated by nostalgia for the traditional genre. Following a winding historical categorization as "a brain malfunction, psychiatric disorder, or variant of depression,"[10] nostalgia is currently defined simply as "a sentimental longing for one's past."[11] For conjunto musicians outside of the central geographic community, nostalgia can explain artists' decisions to express themselves through a genre that is not within their primary cultural, locational, or socioeconomic heritages. The interpretation of Texas-Mexican conjunto is frequently tied to homologous notions of genre as identity; certain musical and demographic traits inextricably linked under a single definition of "conjunto." However, national participation in the genre breaks historical connections between musical elements, the preconceived cultural identity, and the word used to describe such endeavors.

According to psychologists, nostalgia can be used to strengthen social connectedness, provide a sense of belonging or acceptance, and promote creativity (c.f. Sedikides et al., 2008; Wildschut et al., 2010; Routledge et al., 2011; Wijnand et al., 2015). Historically, musicians have demonstrated artistic expression related to a well-defined cultural community, typically through connections of family heritage or, less often, aspirations to join the community (as with international musicians like Dwayne Verheyden and Kenji Katsube). However, in the modern world, historic communities become less defined. In transnational circumstances, traditional connections of class, ethnicity, location, and language no longer determine cultural expression. With easy access to all genres imaginable—Arjun Appadurai's notion of electronic modes of media and transnational mobilization—musicians become free to choose an art form based on personal aesthetics, rather than family history. They sever generic ties between musical traits and cultural identities. Yet this freedom of expression can leave artists adrift, without a clear mode of musicality. In the absence of an expected cultural community, acting on nostalgia can take the place of more traditional methods of expression. Nostalgia can connect contemporary musicians to a familial past that may be disconnected from modern experiences, providing them with a sense of community—shared among performers and a modern audience—that might otherwise be lost.

Artists within the traditional Texas-Mexican constituency maintain community through close proximity and a homogenous population. However, musicians outside of South Texas can regain a valuable sense of social connectedness with nostalgia. In the case of California-based roots-rock group Los Lobos, drummer Louie Pérez notes, "Mexican music was largely just wallpaper for us—it was always in the background, and we never paid much attention to it. We were modern kids who listened to rock and roll. Then when we finally dug up some old records to learn a couple of songs, that was a real revelation to us that this music is actually very complicated and challenging. So at that point we were off and running."[12] As Yossi Maurey explains, "Specific musical styles, genres and textures . . . inevitably evoke a wide range of associated phenomena to which the music originally served as a palpable soundtrack: they conjure up certain political realities, places, and specific social milieux and ethnic backgrounds."[13] It is this social evocation that Los Lobos—and other musicians—accesses through nostalgia for the Texas-Mexican music that formed the "wallpaper" of their and their audience's childhoods.

Conjunto in the Midwest: Jesse Ponce

Mexican and Mexican-American immigration to the Midwestern region of the United States represents a long and diverse process, responding to work on the railroads in the late nineteenth century, new immigration during the Mexican Civil War (1910–1920), labor needs during and immediately after World War I, and increased work opportunities following World War II.[14] In addition, Latinx immigrants from Puerto Rico, other parts of the Caribbean, and Central and South Americas have moved to the Midwest since the 1970s. By the late 1980s, pursuing better opportunities in education and employment, many families of migrant farmworkers had settled in the region year-round, rather than maintaining the so-called agricultural "migrant circuit." As such, David Harnish explains, the Latinx community across the Midwest currently consists of "a mixture of older and newer generations originally (and primarily) from Texas or Mexico but also from countries farther south, other U.S. states, and the Caribbean."[15] With the migration of Texas-Mexican workers came the dispersal of Texas-Mexican culture, including conjunto music.

Relatively disconnected from the geographic border region, the Texas-Mexican diaspora throughout the Midwest maintains a fairly conservative notion of the conjunto genre. The music is used to construct a nostalgic Texas-Mexican community, providing a sense of cultural identity among an older Latinx population who remembers and longs for the music of their youth. In northwestern Ohio, the Farm Labor Organizing Committee (FLOC; founded in 1967 by Baldemar Velásquez) has encouraged musicians to maintain the conjunto style that farmworkers already know—through nostalgia—as a form of "folkloric pride."[16] As Harnish explains, the organization has encouraged "holding onto these roots to provide both unity and identity to the Latino community as a whole."[17] For the diasporic Texas-Mexican community in the Midwest, the traditional form of conjunto music "brought forth ethnic pride . . . and allowed *la Raza* (the people) to claim their rights, identity, and public space."[18] While regional musicians increasingly dissociate historical limitations of genre and identity, Midwestern conjunto artists maintain the most recognizable elements of the genre—a traditional instrumentation, repertory, structure, and sound—in an effort to recognize these same links between musical elements, generic definition, and cultural identity. Midwestern artists and audiences use the traditional genre to assert their own place within Texas-Mexican culture, despite locational insecurities. Homologous interpretations of conjunto then become a necessary tool to connect nostalgic ties to the Texas-Mexican border region with contemporary manifestations of sociocultural positioning in music.

At the middle of the twentieth century, the Texas-Mexican population in Ohio gathered in homes to listen to the traditional music. As a child growing up in the area, Velásquez describes, "We would go to sleep listening to that music. . . . There was one bed for all those kids, and we'd climb up there and sleep in a heap while the music was blaring."[19] In this way, the music became part of the cultural heritage not only for the generation raised in South Texas (who moved to the Midwest for work opportunities), but also for the next generation of children raised outside of the Texas-Mexican region. As Ohio-based conjunto artist Jimmy Bejarano Jr. describes, "Music is a big part of our family heritage and tradition. . . . It was such a big part of being a migrant worker, even when we first came to Ohio."[20] By the 1970s, the music had started to move into clubs and dance halls, as well as weddings, *quinceañeras* (fifteenth-birthday celebrations), and festivals, like the Midwest Tejano-Conjunto Explosion in Sylvania, Ohio. However, community relocation to the Midwest at the middle of the twentieth century effectively halted continuing evolution of conjunto in this region. While musicians in South Texas have altered the genre in an effort to assert their positionality among a national and international population, musicians in the Midwest have instead maintained the most fundamental characteristics of conjunto to assert their place among the Texas-Mexican population.

As Thomas Turino explores, for diasporic communities situated outside of an established cultural region—in his case, rural highlands musicians located in Lima, Peru; here, Texas-Mexican musicians located in the Midwestern United States—"musical performance takes on an even greater importance for signifying identity and social boundaries—because belonging to . . . 'the community,' cannot simply be assumed."[21] Despite the incorporation of musical traits more closely associated with popular genres, Texas-based musicians like Flaco—fundamentally connected to the traditional community through age, ethnicity, location, and socioeconomic status—remain stubbornly characterized in mainstream dialogue as quintessentially "conjunto." Meanwhile, Midwestern musicians achieve "authenticity" within the genre, and thus acceptance within the historical community, by maintaining close correspondence to established traits of the genre. While arguably inappropriate for any true understanding of music or culture, persistent connections between genre and identity demonstrate our societal reliance on the categorization of people—particularly marginalized populations—according to imaginary and irrelevant groupings. These connections simultaneously trap local performers within an identity-based characterization of "other" (limiting local artists' participation in more lucrative generic classifications, regardless of actual musical elements) and allow diasporic performers to assert nostalgic connections to familial heritage through "authentic" musical elements, regardless of identity. In this way, music and identity combine to create complicated notions of the conjunto genre, tied to both and neither at the same time.

One of the most prominent conjunto performers in the Midwest region is Jesse Ponce (although Harnish notes that Ponce's popularity is perhaps most pronounced among the contemporary Anglo-American population in the area who have learned of Ponce through the research projects of scholars like Barbara O'Hagin, Lucy Long, and Harnish himself and thus positioned the musician as a primary representative of the musical style among state agencies—setting him up for awards like the Ohio Heritage Fellowship in 2003—somewhat independently from Latinx acknowledgment in the region).[22] Ponce (1943–2013) grew up in San Antonio as part of a working-class, musical family. His father, Encarnación Ponce, was a violinist and accordion player from Monterrey, Mexico, and Jesse played bajo sexto with the family band from the age of seven. In 1964, Ponce joined Flaco's band on bajo sexto and ultimately went on tour with Flaco and Cooder in 1977. During this time, Ponce developed a number of innovations on the bajo sexto (despite limited enthusiasm for such ventures from many of the more traditional local musicians who "stopped calling him for gigs" and "often asked [him] to play more conventionally").[23] These innovations included exploiting the entire range of the bajo sexto, using amplification in combination with a wah-wah pedal, mastering various Caribbean-derived forms, and learning to solo on the bajo sexto.[24] In this way, Ponce's unusual performance techniques, unappreciated in South Texas, set him up for success working with Flaco and Cooder. In turn, Ponce's work with Flaco established him as an authentic representation of Texas-Mexican practices among the Midwestern community, further emphasizing the distinctive communities developed—via globalization—between musicians staying in Texas, those in Mexico, and those living and performing across the United States and—ultimately—worldwide.

Following this work with Flaco and Cooder, Ponce moved to Toledo, Ohio, in 1979 with an old girlfriend (and eventual new wife), Tila, who was from the area. In Ohio, as Harnish describes, Ponce "found a much smaller, but . . . less-oppressed Latino community and was soon supplementing his income as a plumber by playing bajo sexto with local Latino musicians."[25] However, he struggled to find an accordionist to work with in Ohio who could play at the level he was used to. Ponce notes, "I found some [accordion players] but not the quality I was looking for. It was more headaches than anything else."[26] Instead, the musician learned to play accordion himself (an instrument he would maintain throughout his time in the Midwest). Despite Ponce's innovative work with Flaco in Texas, he maintained a relatively conservative style of music in Ohio. His provenance in San Antonio (the center of conjunto) and work with local musicians like Flaco gave him a certain degree of "authenticity" in Ohio that he leveraged to develop a career in the

Midwest. However, this perception of authenticity meant that the Ohio audience expected a relative conservativeness of performance. Building on the nostalgia of the older generation for authentic Texas-Mexican culture (and disconnected from continuing developments in the border region), Ponce preserved the musical style of his youth (the 1950s–1960s). In this way, he helped to construct an imagined Texas-Mexican community far outside of the historic geographic region (despite close ties to the area for many of the diasporic population). As Harnish asserts, "Northwest Ohio provided a home where Ponce could negotiate, construct the roots of, and build on nostalgia for authentic Tejano culture, the romantic folk heritage desired by the diaspora community."[27] As such, "he and his music's authenticity have become part of the fabric of such institutions as FLOC, the Sofia Quintero [Art and Cultural] Center [in Toledo], and local Latino culture."[28]

In addition to developing a Texas-Mexican sense of identity for the diasporic community within Ohio, Ponce has disseminated the traditional music to the younger generation in his role as teacher in the region. As O'Hagin and Harnish explain, "Jesse loves collaborating, sharing his knowledge and tutoring young musicians."[29] He also performs at events for migrant workers and for inmates at the Toledo jail. While his musical style remains conservative, he has experimented with new arrangements of traditional conjunto tunes and includes a handful of popular songs in performance, such as Woody Guthrie's "This Land Is Your Land" and "Do Re Mi" (also presented in combination with the conjunto standard "Viva Seguin" on *Showtime*, Cooder's 1977 album documenting the international tour for which Ponce played bajo sexto). As Harnish explains, these popular songs are hybridized in a ranchera structure and intended primarily for an Anglo-American audience.[30] While he was encouraged throughout his time in the Midwest (some thirty years) to return to San Antonio, Ponce appreciated his unique position in Ohio. He explains, "I didn't get recognized in Texas, there's so many good musicians. Ohio has given me a lot of recognition."[31] That being said, after recording an album in 2005 in conjunction with the Sofia Quintero Art and Cultural Center and Bowling Green State University, entitled *Playing From the Heart—y Para Siempre*, Ponce did achieve a hit song on KEDA-AM radio in San Antonio with "Mexican Joe." As Ricardo Davila, co-owner and DJ for the station asserts, "It's a good conjunto song. . . . Everybody knows Jesse is a pioneer. You all are very lucky to have him in Ohio."[32] Recording a second album of labor and folk songs with Velásquez (used to "educate the general community in public places about the plight of farmworkers and to advocate for and unify workers on the farms"),[33] Ponce did return to San Antonio to record with Flaco. He finally moved back to Texas for good in 2010 to be closer to family preceding his death in 2013.

Conjunto in the Midwest: Jimmy Bejarano Sr.

Like Ponce, conjunto accordionist Jimmy Bejarano Sr. (b. 1939) was born in South Texas (Brownsville) and ultimately settled in the Midwest. Bejarano Sr.'s family worked as migrant farmworkers, traveling to Nebraska and Montana before settling near the Heinz factory (and plentiful tomato and pickle farms) in Fremont, Ohio, when the musician was still a child. Like many conjunto artists, Bejarano Sr. came from a family of musicians (his father and grandfather also played conjunto music as they traveled the migrant circuit and later, after obtaining jobs at a local steel mill) and began playing at a young age (his father bought him his first accordion when he was just ten years old from a pawn shop in Lima, Ohio).[34] As an adult, Bejarano Sr. worked as a crane operator for Kelsey-Hayes foundry while playing music as a "hobby" with his two sons, Jimmy Jr. on bajo sexto and Ruben on drums (along with Angel Torres on bass), in a band called Los Cuatro Vientos (The Four Winds). Since 1954, Bejarano Sr. has led several bands and performed with a number of other conjunto artists.

Los Cuatro Vientos are one of the few Midwestern conjunto bands to receive recognition outside of the immediate community. The group has performed throughout the Midwest on weekends and made annual tours of Texas and the Southwest. Beginning in 1996, they have also performed consistently at the Tejano Conjunto Festival in San Antonio. The band has recorded eleven albums since 1994 and earned playtime on San Antonio radio stations (holding a record for maintaining the number one position on a local Tejano station for seventeen weeks).[35] In 2011, Bejarano Sr. was inducted into the Tejano Conjunto Hall of Fame through the Guadalupe Cultural Arts Center in San Antonio (at the time, only the second musician out of sixty-five total inductees emanating from outside of Texas).[36] Yet, despite the band's popularity in San Antonio (and despite his son Jimmy's stated desires—before his unexpected death in 2014—to join the musical community in Texas), Bejarano Sr. has been content to remain in Ohio. As Bejarano Sr. states, "It's pretty important to me and the boys to keep it alive. . . . There's not very many bands over here. It's important to keep it up."[37] Bejarano Jr. continues: "We have a lot of fun playing shows and traveling around. You go down [to Texas] and you have some notoriety. We even have a fan club in San Antonio. But it's nice to be able to come back here and lead regular lives."[38] As with Ponce, Los Cuatro Vientos seem to appreciate the development of community and uniqueness of opportunity available outside of Texas. Nonetheless, the group is closely connected to the border region and achieved success based on that community's notion of success. Like Ponce,

Los Cuatro Vientos also maintain a fairly conservative musical style. Despite adding cumbias to the set list in recent years (since "the younger generation likes *cumbias*"), the ensemble maintain "a smooth and traditional sound" based primarily on rancheras and polkas.[39]

Although older conjunto artists like Ponce and Bejarano Sr. maintain a conservative style of the music, younger generations of Mexican-American musicians in the Midwest have (although more slowly than their Texas counterparts) followed some of the more contemporary trends appearing in Texas by the end of the twentieth century. For example, younger musicians and audiences often prefer the so-called "progressive" style of conjunto music (with the addition of guitars, keyboards, and horns) along with new, pan-Latinx genres like cumbia. As Harnish explains, while areas of the Midwest like northwestern Ohio once preserved a traditional form of Texas-Mexican culture, and while an audience for traditional conjunto music certainly still exists, the modern Latinx community in this region has expanded from its working-class, Texas-Mexican roots to encompass a middle-class, pan-Latinx identity. Harnish notes: "Such styles as mariachi and traditional *conjunto* are quaint historic reminders of specific, narrow, folkloric contexts for most Latinos in the area, but are not compelling enough in today's world for widespread consumer support."[40] Conjunto musicians in Texas bring a contemporary relevance to the music through hybridizations and inter/national attention. Meanwhile, conjunto musicians in the Midwest maintain the folkloric genre through adherence to nostalgia, but simultaneously hesitate to speak to those disconnected from this nostalgia. Many in the younger Texas-Mexican generation in the Midwest do not speak Spanish and have never been to Texas or Mexico, identifying instead with mainstream culture and pan-Latinx genres like rap, salsa, and *reggaetón*.

As Jesse Estrada (b. 1976), longtime bassist with Ponce and recent solo artist, recalls, "I remember growing up listening to all different kinds of music and I immersed myself in the Latino culture. . . . Everything from salsa to meringue, Latin jazz, mariachi, creole."[41] Despite spending a large part of his career performing relatively traditional conjunto music with Ponce, this Ohio native (and member of the younger Mexican-American generation) identifies with numerous Latinx genres. In recording his own album, Estrada uses a mixture of conjunto, mariachi, and banda, with cover songs in his own style with "a little twist."[42] In this way, the younger generation of Latinx artists in the Midwest create a new relevance for traditional music with an amalgamation of genres that speaks to a multicultural identity disconnected from former Texas-Mexican understandings. Meanwhile, many members of the younger generation of artists still living in Texas—more closely connected to traditional Texas-Mexican culture—alter conjunto music itself to achieve a sense of bicultural identity with Anglo-American genres (and thus, modern relevance for the traditional music that can still be identified as a form of conjunto). However, these distinctions can perhaps be understood best if tied to notions of genre as identity. Situated outside of the central Texas-Mexican community, artists like Estrada do not acquire a characterization of "conjunto" unless the associated musical traits remain starkly in line with traditional practices. Indeed, it is these specific aesthetic elements that have historically marked diasporic musicians as Texas-Mexican, instead of Mexican-American or Latinx. Yet, Texas-Mexican musicians who routinely incorporate musical elements just as far outside of traditional practices as Estrada remain characterized according to their location—fundamentally "conjunto," regardless of interpretation or intent.

Conjunto in the Pacific Northwest: Santiago Almeida and Joel Guzman

In addition to the agricultural and industrial community of the Midwest, the Yakima Valley in Washington State provides an important center for Texas-Mexican culture. Bajo sexto player Santiago Almeida (1911–1999) was instrumental in the development of the early conjunto genre, recording with accordionist and conjunto pioneer Narciso Martínez during the 1930s (and thus forming the original accordion-bajo sexto pair). Yet, with decreasing popularity for the music during the 1940s, Almeida looked for an alternate method to support his family, traveling north as a migrant farmworker and settling in Sunnyside, Washington, in 1950 to pick apples, cut asparagus, and weed sugar beets.[43] As local journalist Ross Courtney explains, Texas-Mexican migrants from the Rio Grande Valley were the first group of Latinx farmworkers to come to the Yakima Valley.[44] Influenced by the beginning of the Bracero Program during World War II, they were joined by Mexican immigrants. By the 1990s, some twenty-five percent of the region were of Latinx heritage.[45] Almeida continued to play music in Washington, performing for dances and parties in the region and teaching the younger generation how to play in the conjunto style.

Disconnected from continuing innovations in the Rio Grande Valley, Almeida (like Ohio-based musicians like Ponce and Bejarano Sr.) largely maintained the music as a form of cultural folklore. Despite the artist's innovative techniques established with Martínez as the foundation of the genre in the early years of the twentieth century, by the 1990s, Almeida concluded that "modern music [had] passed him by."[46] In this regard, Almeida's movement outside of the central conjunto geography spread the musical genre outside of its home region, but simultaneously halted further innovation and instead established the music (in that region) as a "traditional," folkloric pursuit. "Rediscovered" in the 1980s by a researcher for the Washington State Arts Commission, Almeida was inducted into the Tejano Conjunto Hall of Fame in San Antonio in 1987 and received the Governor's Heritage Award in Washington and an NEA Heritage Fellowship award in 1993, spending the last years of his life receiving awards and accolades for his contributions to the genre.

The child of migrant farmworkers from Texas, accordionist Joel Guzman (b. 1959) grew up next door to Almeida in Sunnyside, Washington. Guzman's father, Guadalupe, was also a musician, and the family performed as a band throughout the migrant circuit—"from Texas to Washington and across to Michigan and Illinois."[47] As Guzman remembers, "We used to take this sound from Texas to Washington, to what they called Little Texas."[48] As the artist explains, the Texas-Mexican community in Washington maintained close connections to Texas during this time: "Tejanos made sure everyone knew they were from the Motherland . . . Texas. . . . They were tough and they weren't afraid to go to school with their tortillas and beans. They were very proud."[49]

In addition, Washington-based conjunto musicians like the Guzmans performed with prominent Texas-based artists like De La Rosa, Paulino Bernal, and Ruben Vela as they toured in the Pacific Northwest. As Guzman illustrates "[W]e made it a point to open up for these groups, or we'd just invited them over to house. All the Texas artists played with us: Manuel Solis, Tony de la Rosa, all of them."[50] He continues: "My dad is a good musician. He sacrificed that by raising us kids in Washington. But we had our own top-notch outfit and we played with the big boys, all the bands that traveled to Washington from Texas."[51] Guzman had written and recorded his first polka ("Puro Tejas") by the age of five. He recorded and ultimately toured with Tejano artist Little Joe in the 1980s, bringing the traditional accordion sound to the commercialized genre. In addition to his later solo pursuits, Guzman has appeared on a number of Tejano albums with artists like Ram Herrera, Grupo Mazz, Ruben Ramos, and Tish Hinojosa. He moved back to Texas in 1983, settling in the Austin area rather than the more expected locations for conjunto of San Antonio or the Rio Grande Valley.

Yet, despite the musician's work with prominent Texas-Mexican stars and relocation to the Texas geography, Guzman—a Washington native—struggles to assert his own authenticity within the Texas-Mexican tradition. As Cathy Ragland notes, the artist "lives on the fringe of the music and the industry he

Figure 3.1. Joel Guzman (accordion). Photo by Eric Perrone. Licensed under CC BY 2.0.

helped promote."[52] As Guzman elaborates, "I mean, I was already an outsider. . . . Even though I had played with Little Joe, when some people found out I was from Washington, they didn't think I knew the music or assumed I couldn't even speak Spanish. But I grew up with Tejano music too and I spent my entire childhood playing and learning conjunto polkas from my father, or other musicians like Mr. Almeida. That's more than some musicians can say now."[53] Throughout his solo repertory, Guzman performs standard conjunto tunes with a conservative style. Emanating from within the expected geography, local conjunto musicians like Flaco, Jordan, and Mingo Saldívar experiment with the traditional genre, secure in their inclusion within the community. Despite close and continuing ties to South Texas, national artists like Guzman instead assert their cultural positionalities by emphasizing "authentic" adherence to the historical genre via relatively conservative elements, rather than any new repertory or techniques.

Conjunto in the Southwest: Max Baca and Los Texmaniacs

Max Baca (b. 1967) was born and raised in Albuquerque, New Mexico. Like the Jiménez family of instrumentalists, his father and grandfather also played the accordion. The younger Baca began learning the instrument at the age of five, drawing particular influence from conjunto legend Narciso Martínez, before ultimately switching to bajo sexto. As Baca explains, "When I was about seven, eight years old, after we saw Flaco [at the Fronterizo dance club in Lubbock, Texas], then, he had a bajo player and his name was Oscar Tellez and I was just drawn to that guy; he was my idol. The minute I saw him and he talked to me, I was just so flabbergasted, 'Man, this guy's great!' and the sound of that instrument, the sound of that bajo sexto, it just really attracted me."[54] After hearing the young musician performing in Albuquerque, Flaco invited Baca to come to San Antonio, learn the traditional techniques of the bajo sexto that many contemporary players had lost, and play in Flaco's band, followed closely by extended performances with the Texas Tornados. As Baca further illustrates, "I learned from the old pioneers. What I want to do is I want to carry on the tradition, but of course now, in a modern way. It's a different era. I want to keep the root of the original pioneers, but modernize it a little bit, to where now you're not just hearing regular *pisadas* or guitar riffs, you're hearing jazzy, bluesier riffs on the accordion and the bajo sexto. And playing rock-n-roll on the bajo sexto. I think that's pretty hip, that sounds pretty cool."[55] Although Baca has continued to perform with Flaco, the Texas Tornados, and Los Super Seven, he formed Los Texmaniacs in 1997 to pursue more progressive forms of the regional music. As Baca describes, the band incorporates "hip music that everybody in the world can relate to, with the traditional conjunto elements."[56] In addition to Baca, the band (rather fluidly) includes David Farías on accordion (changed in 2011 to Josh Baca, Max's nephew), Óscar García on electric bass, and Lorenzo Martínez on drums.

According to Daniel Sheehy, "The musical lives of Los Texmaniacs stand at a major turn in the road in the history of the Texas-Mexican musical tradition. The beginnings of their careers were planted in a time of the music's new social relevance, a creative expansion, and a human and musical diaspora that reached places far beyond the music's home territory in San Antonio and the Rio Grande Valley."[57] Corresponding to the diversity of the band's musical influences, and in addition to Baca's familial roots in New Mexico, the other primary members of the group, with the exception of Farías, similarly emanate from beyond South Texas. García was born and raised in Santa Cruz,

California (although his father was a professional musician originally from McAllen, Texas), while Martínez comes from Southeast Los Angeles and previously marched with César Chávez and performed with Los Perros del Pueblo Nuevo as part of the Chicano Movement. Throughout the twentieth century, Texas-Mexican farmworkers have migrated throughout American agricultural territory, spreading the distinctive musical heritage and settling in diverse locations. The widespread backgrounds of Los Texmaniacs represent this rich history.

Baca explains his implementation within modern practices of the disappearing, virtuosic style of bajo sexto technique:

> I started studying Santiago Almeida, Narciso Martínez's bajo player, who, back then, was a monster, because in those days he was taking the whole load with the bass and the strumming and everything. . . . Nowadays, you don't see bajo sexto players playing like that. They take the top strings off. They just use the bottom three or four strings; they leave out the beauty of the low notes and the rhythm. They just do the "chank," the bottom chank and they don't do the *bajeo*, which is the bass part which makes that instrument so unique. So, when I grew up seeing these guys play, that inspired me, and I said, "Man, that's what I want to do."[58]

In addition to this reliance on Almeida's historic techniques, Los Texmaniacs use the repertory, structure, and instrumentation of the traditional Texas-Mexican genre. As such, emanating from outside of the expected generic geography, they maintain a conservative interpretation of the tradition. However, the group also uses Flaco's more innovative stylistic techniques to attract a modern Texas-Mexican population that identifies with both the traditional regional culture and the U.S. American mainstream. Since 2009, the musicians have recorded three albums for Smithsonian Folkways Recordings, each blending traditional conjunto practices with musical elements more closely connected to U.S. American popular culture.[59] According to Smithsonian, these folkloric albums assert "pride in both their native Mexican culture and U.S. nationhood."[60]

In this way, Baca employs a folkloric consideration of the music drawn simultaneously from the earlier conjunto style and Flaco's subsequent innovations. He thus demonstrates a "cycle of hybridization" (see Chapter 4),[61] wherein Flaco's hybridized elements become expected, homogenous components of the genre and further hybridizations are left to younger generations of musicians. Baca does not integrate new innovations, but incorporates both the "traditional" style and Flaco's hybridized elements into his own understanding of the genre. His methods do not differ in any substantive way from Flaco's example, demonstrating continuing cultural insecurities, even once firmly situated among the local community. National conjunto musicians like Baca assert their own cultural authenticity by remaining closely in line with prior practices. Further innovations are left to local musicians like Flaco, Jordan, and Saldívar, as well as younger musicians like Piñata Protest, who combine conjunto with punk, Sunny Sauceda, who plays conjunto with a heavy-metal twist, and Juanito Castillo, who uses different time signatures to transform conjunto standards. As Turino emphasizes, "more tentative feelings of 'social security'" among musicians situated outside of an expected geographic community and a "higher degree of self-consciousness about identity and tradition" provide "the crucial key to understanding a whole range of [these artists'] social and musical values and practices."[62] In the participation of Texas-Mexican conjunto among nationally oriented musicians, conservative practices are best explained by similar interpretations of cultural self-consciousness, indicating a reluctance to threaten precarious positionalities among an adopted community by straying too far from established musical techniques.

Baca—along with Guzman—also spends time teaching the historic form to younger artists through formal methods of instruction like workshops at the Guadalupe Cultural Arts Center in San Antonio, classes and ensembles at secondary schools and universities (such as Guzman's role as director of the Tex-Mex Conjunto Ensemble at the University of Texas at Austin), and folkloric festival pursuits like the Tejano Conjunto Festival in San Antonio, among others. Baca then demonstrates further adherence to a folkloric understanding of conjunto presentation, rather than continued progression within the traditional form, through what Daniel Margolies describes as part of "a well-articulated effort to teach the attendant culture of the music to a new generation of Mexican-Americans" in South Texas through "increasingly formalized processes . . . outside the norms of traditional community cultural transfer."[63]

As Baca explains, he and his band simultaneously maintain the conservative sounds and repertory of the Texas-Mexican conjunto tradition (despite emanating from outside of South Texas), while also updating the music for a new generation by incorporating characteristics of rock, jazz, and funk. As Sheehy describes, "They go way beyond conjunto, but their mastery of the traditional forms is perfect."[64] Baca maintains the common repertory and older style of bajo sexto playing made popular by performers like Martínez and Almeida (making use of all twelve strings and "adhering to a complex cross-picking style played at a brisk pace"),[65] while also following Flaco's more innovative pursuits in incorporating external musical characteristics

Figure 3.2. Max Baca (bajo sexto) and Los Texmaniacs perform with Texas blues artist Willie J. Laws (electric guitar) in 2013. Licensed under CC BY-ND 2.0.

into the traditional sound. In this way, despite certain innovative techniques and global tours ("touring Russia twice for the State Department; the war zones of Iraq, Afghanistan, Bosnia, and Kosovo for U.S. organizations; and China and Mongolia for the Smithsonian"),[66] Baca maintains the genre as a method of folklore, striving to promote the Texas-Mexican culture among a new audience through adherence to the older sounds—both with Almeida's original and Flaco's subsequent hybridizations. In this regard, Baca's "innovations" are not his own and his primary purpose is to appreciate and maintain, not to innovate further (thus corresponding to the standard adherence to more conservative notions of the genre by musicians emanating from outside of the central conjunto region—and despite Baca's close ties and eventual relocation to South Texas).

Conjunto in California: Conjunto Califas and Conjunto Los Pochos

In addition to Texas-Mexican migration throughout Ohio, Washington, and New Mexico (among others), the movement of Mexican and Mexican-American laborers during the twentieth century has led to a large ethnic community in California (particularly in the Southern California region of East Los Angeles; see Chapter 8). As with other migrant groups throughout the United States, those moving to and growing up in California have struggled to simultaneously maintain strong ethnic heritages and assimilate within their new locations. Beyond Juan Chapa y Su Conjunto and Los Lobos, conjunto ensembles from California include Conjunto Califas (from Visalia in the San Joaquin Valley) and Conjunto Los Pochos (from Los Angeles). As Otono Lujan, the accordion player for Conjunto Los Pochos, notes, "The name of the group, 'Los Pochos,' means Mexican Americans who don't speak the language properly, who are assimilated and not really Mexican. . . . We have embraced the name as a symbol and a title and as proving that we are part of this beautiful (style) that mixes music in a great way."[67] With the adoption of this title and the stylistic traits of the associated music, the group asserts their place within Texas-Mexican culture, despite an external geography.

As with many groups based outside of Texas, these California ensembles maintain close connections with the Texas region. For example, Conjunto Califas co-founder and bajo sexto player, Freddy Saenz, first moved to Visalia from Texas in 1984, having grown up with the traditional genre in the traditional location.[68] Similarly, Lujan explains, "My initial inspiration was from my Mexican grandfather and my Texas grandmother."[69] Furthermore, despite Conjunto Califas's location in California, the band achieved success within the historical context of the Texas-Mexican geography. As drummer and co-founder Andrew Treviño explains, "Nobody in Visalia knows who we are because we're never here. We're always playing somewhere else."[70] That "somewhere else" includes the Central Valley of California, as well as Minnesota, Texas (including the Tejano Conjunto Festival in San Antonio in 2011), and Mexico. The group's most successful song, "El Lowrider," according to Treviño, "hit No. 1 on the music charts for 32 straight weeks in Texas and Mexico."[71] In addition, success within the traditional Texas-Mexican geography is noted as a source of pride and accomplishment. As Ylda Palomino, owner of Palomino's Music and NFL Shop in Visalia (specializing in Tejano music) describes, "Califas have been around for a long time. We support them because they are local and we're proud of them. . . . They performed in San Antonio and they put California on the map because of the way they performed."[72]

Despite the external positionalities of certain participants, Texas-Mexican conjunto thus remains fundamentally a Texas-Mexican practice. In order to achieve acceptance within this community as appropriately "conjunto," those living outside of the region must constantly emphasize their adherence to stylistic norms to "prove" a place within the genre. Identity alone cannot represent a single generic category. However, musicians lacking an assumed identity must maintain a clear correspondence to the stylistic traits most essentially tied to historical interpretations of the music. In the case of conjunto, artists can come from South Texas *or* retain the most traditional elements of instrumentation, repertory, structure, and sound. To do otherwise creates music that can be characterized as Tejano, roots-rock, or simply "Latin"—but does not represent "conjunto," as most fundamentally understood in South Texas and the music industry.

Conjunto in California: Los Lobos

Los Lobos is an East Los Angeles-based roots-rock band formed in 1973 by high-school friends, vocalist/guitarist David Hidalgo and drummer Louie Pérez, and later completed by Cesar Rosas and Conrad Lozano, as well as Steve Berlin in 1984, and in 2012, new drummer Enrique "Bugs" Gonzalez. The group takes influence from a wide variety of sources, including rock, country, folk, blues, and R&B, as well as border musics like Tejano and conjunto, and has been successful among the mainstream musical scene, winning multiple Grammy Awards and recording numerous, commercially recognized albums. Los Lobos's integration of traditional Texas-Mexican music outside of the regional community—both in Southern California and mainstream U.S. American culture—stems largely from a sense of nostalgia for the musical form.[73] As Pérez explains,

> We grew up just like any other kids growing up in the U.S. We were influenced by rock radio. Sure, there was Mexican music played in the house, but we just wanted to homogenize with everybody else. We wanted to play rock 'n' roll. We wanted to listen to rock 'n' roll. We wanted to leave the Mexican music home with our parents. But after we'd been musicians for awhile, we rediscovered Mexican music. . . . We just did it because it felt right.[74]

For Pérez and the other members of the band, the hybridization of Mexican folkloric forms with U.S. American rock "was just the natural way of doing things for guys . . . who didn't fit in completely on either side of the U.S.-Mexico border."[75] Pérez continues: "We were kids playing rock 'n' roll all the way up to 1973. . . . But we became frustrated with what we were hearing and decided to play what we were listening to in the background of our lives."[76] In this way, the hybridity of the group's works represents contemporary cultural realities for Latinx musicians and audiences scattered across the United States and responding to bicultural notions of identity.

The recognition of conjunto music beyond the regional center has resonated with an older Texas-Mexican diaspora in Southern California. However, Los Lobos's eclectic style and incorporation of mainstream rock concurrently speaks to a younger, increasingly Americanized but still culturally connected generation. It further resonates with a broader Mexican-American constituency who has taken the music as a general symbol of cultural strength and solidarity. Traditional conjunto has therefore discovered a newfound appreciation outside of the original location and tightknit sociocultural constituency, while musical hybridizations correspond to contemporary cultural realities. As Richard Pineda notes, "Los Lobos and their music have endured because they represent the history of their community and the identity of being Chicana/o, while moving forward and incorporating diverse influences and musical styles recognizing that music, like identity, does not grow in stasis but thrives through the process of adapting and absorbing elements of the contemporary world."[77] The group has "secured their place in popular culture with a unique *mestizaje* of styles, language, and cultural influences in their music."[78]

Released by Los Lobos in 1983, the extended-play (EP) record *...And a Time to Dance* represents the group's first noteworthy recording effort, receiving critical acclaim despite somewhat limited mainstream sales. The performance remains closely in line with the traditional conjunto style, despite the recording's positionality (at least geographically) outside of the Texas-Mexican community, and despite the band's subsequent use of popular styles. This conservatism emphasizes the music's use as folklore, symbolic of the wide-ranging community but, in general, lacking any additional artistic elements to mark the actual external arrangement. In this regard, the recording establishes the group as part of the traditional community, drawing from pre-established songs and common traits to achieve a social connectedness with the former familial heritage. A review of the album on Amazon.com describes the importance of the band's preliminary offering to the traditional conjunto style: "Los Lobos is a Mexican-American band that mastered every

Figure 3.3. Cesar Rosas (guitar), Conrad Lozano (bass), and Enrique Gonzalez (drums) of Los Lobos perform in Norfolk, VA, in 2017. Licensed under CC BY-SA 4.0.

musical genre south and north of the border and it had two major achievements: 1) it cross-pollinated these traditions and genres, creating a hybrid original style; and, 2) it recorded pure, respectful samples of these Mexican genres, drawing attention to them."

These initial recording efforts influenced recognition of conjunto as symbolic of a general Mexican-American experience. They subsequently created relevance for the traditional music by mimicking the increasing cultural complexities of the youthful ethnic population living outside the local community. As Pineda continues, "The band continues to present traditional forms of rock and roll and Mexican-American folk music to audiences that are drawn to each form of music and yet their music blends and mixes the genres and languages with a fluidity that matches the *mestizaje* of the Chicana/o community."[79] Situated outside of the expected Texas-Mexican geography, Los Lobos's early recording maintains the conservativism necessary to establish the group as an "authentic" representation of the conjunto genre, and thus the associated community. It is interesting to note later shifts in both the group's musical style—now incorporating a range of more mainstream hybridizations—and subsequent categorization not as "conjunto," but instead "roots-rock" (or other methods of classification similarly disconnected from notions of identity).

Participation in the Texas-Mexican tradition by a Los Angeles rock band exemplifies a shift in cultural context for the conjunto genre. Los Lobos has overcome criticism of folkloric insertions in U.S. American culture. Texas-based artists like Flaco have further described reluctance among the conventional constituency to the use of "their" music outside of traditional boundaries. As the regional tradition has traveled beyond its original community, the breadth of participation must be tempered by this criticism of "selling out"; of pandering to the mainstream culture rather than maintaining the music's former, counter-ideological role. The positionality of Los Lobos has introduced the historic conjunto form to a diverse community. However, it has done so by removing the cultural product from its former sociocultural focus. As Pérez explains,

> I have to admit that we've been kind of a tough sell for our own people. We sort of miss both the parents and kids. First-generation Mexican nationals living in the U.S. want to preserve their culture from Mexico. They want to keep things just one way. We don't go over real well with Spanish-speaking people here in the U.S. because they can get the real deal. They have Spanish-language radio. They can buy CDs from rock bands and folk bands who sing solely in Spanish.[80]

Yet, he continues,

> We're hugely respected by Mexican-American kids, the second and third generations, maybe to a fault. They kind of put us on a pedestal for veneration. But at the same time, I don't think they actually listen to our music. They listen to whatever is current and contemporary and exciting for them. . . . I think we've just gotten to a point where we've become heroes to Mexican-Americans for what we've accomplished. . . . But I don't know that our music is particularly popular with the younger Mexican-Americans.[81]

Los Lobos therefore functions primarily as a symbol of diasporic identity in Southern California. Drawing from their own bicultural roots, they speak to an audience of similar backgrounds. Yet, they fail to fully resonate with either the "traditional" community or the younger generation who appreciate the representative capacity of the musicians, but better identify with more mainstream cultural products.

The older Texas-Mexican constituency often express apprehension for new musical traits and widening participation in conjunto. However, many in the younger generation demonstrate pride in more mainstream recognition. For example, a 1985 letter to *Rolling Stone Magazine* illustrates that, "Through their richly textured songs, Los Lobos have captured the spirit of the Mexican-American urban life that I grew up in. Their music gives me yet another reason to be proud of my culture. Viva Los Lobos!"[82] Through these means, the regional genre has also been introduced to a national and international audience, as captured in an Amazon.com review of Los Texmaniacs's *Texas Towns & Tex-Mex Sounds* by a customer in Connecticut: "Ok, I would never have thought I'd 'love' a band so much that had an accordion in it.. but I have a new love for this instrument! It's soulful!" The practices of globalization have produced a widespread interest in traditional conjunto, bringing unprecedented attention and appreciation from unexpected corners of the world and embracing a diverse community beyond historic notions of class, language, and location. In addition, conjunto artists across the United States exhibit many characteristics of nostalgia. These musicians draw from familial connections, but somewhat limited personal experiences, with the ethnic, geographic, and socioeconomic circumstances of the original conjunto constituency. They forge musical connections with a cultural community of their heritage, but not their primary experiences. They further retain cultural connections to more mainstream populations and incorporate elements of this bicultural heritage into the traditional conjunto form. In this regard, national musicians are also closely related to the more mainstream musical pursuits of local musicians like Flaco. Cultural insecurities require them to assert a place within the Texas-Mexican musical community through conservative elements, but identifications across a range of popular genres ultimately create hybrid replications of Flaco's cultural pursuits.

Conclusions

Regional artists like Flaco have played an important role in instigating an inter/national interest in Texas-Mexican conjunto with showy performances and hybridized techniques. Emanating from within the local community, Flaco is fundamentally connected to the musical tradition and its cultural constituency. He maintains clear sociocultural security without the need for nostalgic representations of the traditional music. He thus achieves a freedom to experiment with the historical form, outside of expected musical traits. The combination of button accordion and bajo sexto with the artist's central Texas-Mexican identity establishes him as quintessentially "conjunto," even if closer analysis of the actual music suggests an alternative categorization. That being said, ties to his father's songs create a nostalgic starting point for creative traits beyond the original musical characteristics. As Badia Ahad explains, nostalgia can allow an artist to become more receptive to new ideas, using the characteristic longing for something outside of the present situation to bring about something new.[83]

In addition, while Flaco grew up within the Texas-Mexican constituency, he grew up in San Antonio—connected to the conjunto community but also identifying with more mainstream elements of popular culture. It is perhaps the nostalgia for these early rock experiences that formed the "wallpaper" of Flaco's childhood that the musician draws from in pursuing a creative connection to music beyond more traditional conjunto characteristics. In many ways, this additional sense of nostalgia—similar to that of Los Lobos, but reversed—helps the younger ethnic constituency to create a certain social connectedness with the mainstream culture that they are simultaneously related to and removed from. As Melissa Cain explains, while we often assume that younger generations identify with the culture of their ethnic communities, "current youth culture may be the predominant influence and musics from this [popular] culture may be what [young people] identify with most strongly today."[84] In this regard, Flaco's music uses nostalgia to combine the conjunto heritage with mainstream culture and bring about a new community that relates to the experiences of the contemporary ethnic and geographic population.

However, as seen throughout this chapter, artists outside of the central Texas-Mexican identity—here characterized by geographic locations across the United States—lack the cultural security within the expected conjunto community to pursue similar innovations. Instead, these musicians use traditional characteristics to achieve acceptance within a genre disconnected from their sociocultural circumstances. The use of additional traits either falls closely in line with regional practices (such as those of Flaco) or shifts categorization of the resulting music outside of "conjunto." While artists have historically picked a particular method of musical expression based on a sense of community—familial or aspirational, modern conjunto musicians often add a layer of nostalgia to the choice to play conjunto. Drawing from family ties outside of traditional cultural boundaries, national conjunto musicians leverage childhood experiences to connect to a culture that doesn't fully represent the musicians' modern realities, but better represents society as a whole. The globalization of conjunto then produces either new musical experiences for local musicians like Flaco or new forms of identity for national artists like Ponce, Baca, and Guzman.

PART II

The Hybridization of Conjunto

CHAPTER 4

"You have to mix it up!"

"Seguro Que Hell Yes," the Texas Tornados, Los Super Seven, and the Cultural Hybridity of Flaco Jiménez

> We like to mix it all up. We play the two-steps with the polka beat; we play a little country, country and western; we can play zydeco, Cajun music ... and, say, play some rock 'n' roll, or play some country, and we're at it. Wherever we are, we try to please the people of course.
>
> —Flaco Jiménez

The established terminology used to describe Texas-Mexican accordion music remains vague, at best. The Spanish term *conjunto* simply translates as "ensemble" music; there are musical "conjunto" genres throughout Latin America, none of which retain associations with the Texas-Mexican style. The corresponding Mexican terminology is not clearer; *música norteña* merely refers to music "of the north," i.e., music from the northern border of Mexico with Texas. The term Tejano currently indicates a different style altogether (much more commercialized and with a more modern instrumentation), but does not describe its musical characteristics any better; "Tejano" simply indicates "Texan" (albeit in Spanish, so there is some suggestion of a hybridity therein). Flaco Jiménez notes the terminological vagaries of the Texas-Mexican accordion genre at the same time as he emphasizes its inherent—and continuing—sense of hybridization. Rather than the term conjunto, Flaco advocates for a switch to "Tex-Mex," explaining that, "You will hear people—mostly Mexicans—refer to it as norteño. . . . To me, norteño means 'music of the north'—Texas and the USA. I don't think 'norteño' fits too well because it's not specific. And conjunto is just a group. And if we call it Tejano, then that implies just Texan. For myself, I prefer the term 'Tex-Mex,' because that clearly implies a mixture of styles and cultures. You have to remember it was the Germans and the Poles who brought the accordion to Texas in the first place."[1] Furthermore, he continues, "Tex-Mex is more correct because of our Mexican descent and the fact we were born here in Texas in the US. That's why we call it Tex-Mex."[2] In so representing the genre, Flaco draws attention not only to the hybridity of the music itself, but also to the contemporary biculturality of the Texas-Mexican community as a whole; an important consideration in analyzing the cultural implications of processes of globalization (in this case, hybridization).

As Flaco indicates, Texas-Mexican accordion music (conjunto or Tex-Mex—or even perhaps norteño) came about at the end of the nineteenth century through a process of hybridization; a stylistic mixture between European polka music and Mexican rhythmic characteristics. As Santiago Jiménez Jr. (Flaco's brother and an accomplished—albeit more conservative—accordionist in his own right) describes, "Now if I'm going to play my style [of a traditional German polka] that I'm going to do with the Tex-Mex [conjunto] sound, it would be the same melody, but it's going to be more faster and more wild."[3] Juan Tejeda continues: "When we added then the guitar, or the bajo sexto, as the rhythmic accompaniment to the accordion, then those were the initial beginnings of a new ensemble that departed from its European ensemble counterparts. Then we started, of course, adding Mexican indigenous rhythms like the Wapango [huapango] to the music besides the polkas, sort of like, ta-ta-ta-ta-ta-ta-ta-ta-ta-ta-ta-ta."[4]

In this way, Texas-Mexican conjunto music began in the nineteenth century as a product of hybridization, indicating (following numerous social science scholars) "the processes through which cultural forms become separated from already existing practices and recombine with new forms into new expressions, identities, and practices."[5] Following the standardization of the form by the middle of the twentieth century, conjunto has experienced additional hybridizing processes through the incorporation of mainstream U.S. American rock, jazz, blues, and country. Similarly, using the recurrent hybridization of the Spanish language as an example, Néstor García Canclini describes a "cycles of hybridization" model, in which "we move historically from more heterogeneous forms to other more homogenous ones, and then to other relatively more heterogeneous forms, without any being 'purely' or simply homogeneous."[6] The shift of conjunto in the second half of the twentieth century from a well-established, homogeneous form to encompass new cultural characteristics mimics the initial hybridized development of the genre and thus creates a "cycle of hybridization."

Hybridity can therefore be considered as a constant condition of human society. Cultural products that we consider to be "well-established" (such as conjunto music at the middle of the twentieth century), in fact exist in a state of transition. They continuously shift between more homogenous and more heterogenous forms of expression as the constituency itself explores new understandings of identity. As R. Anderson Sutton asserts, "The notion of cultural purity is demonstrably a myth, as historical analysis of any cultural expression can reveal multiple origins and hybridities that inevitably result from human contact."[7] In this regard, Texas-Mexican culture—and its expression through conjunto music—naturally interacts with numerous influences beyond the regional community, producing not only a historic product of hybridization, but also new manifestations of hybridity, as demonstrated in the works of artists like Flaco.

Texas-Mexican conjunto music has long been a conservative symbol of cultural identity for the working-class border community. Yet, by the last few decades of the twentieth century, local performers like Flaco were combining external genres with the traditional music. Artists outside the traditional conjunto community tend to stick closest to established songs and stylistic traits, thus treating the genre as a form of folklore. Meanwhile, musicians most closely related—geographically, ethnically, and socioeconomically—to the historic constituency often push at the edges of the tradition. Yet, if we concede to Manuel Peña's assertion that conjunto came about through the political and socioeconomic struggles of a particular working-class, ethnic community, why do more recent musicians choose to pursue the tradition using methods and/or elements traditionally external to the class, ethnicity, location, and language of its original constituency? How do such methods of hybridization represent new forms of identity for the cultural community? Who is the intended audience for such works? Flaco provides some of the earliest and most pronounced examples of hybridity between "traditional" conjunto characteristics and elements of U.S. American mainstream music and helps us begin to explore some of these questions of interpretation experienced throughout the "cycles of hybridization" model inherent to contemporary (and historic) conjunto practices.

The Ambassador: Hybridity in the Works of Flaco Jiménez

A substantial component of Flaco's hybrid influences has come through the artist's early collaborations with mainstream U.S. American popular musicians (initially Doug Sahm and Ry Cooder, but also Bob Dylan, Dr. John, Dwight Yoakam, Linda Ronstadt, the Rolling Stones, and many more—explored in more detail in Chapter 8). This process raises interesting considerations, as the products of hybridization in Flaco's music seemingly emerge only through the intervention of Anglo-American hegemony and not through the intent or agency—at least initially—of the Texas-Mexican accordionist himself. This notion is even more complicated by the historic interpretation of conjunto as a counter-hegemonic response to the dominant Anglo-American community. However, for now, and despite any problematic interpretations with the initial impetuses of hybridity in Flaco's works, the artist's independent repertory (without the participation of mainstream rock stars) will provide a good demonstration of the types of cross-cultural manifestations seen in Texas-Mexican conjunto music starting in the second half of the twentieth century.

Despite being born as conjunto royalty (his father, Santiago Jiménez Sr., and grandfather, Patricio, both playing prominent roles in the early development of the genre), and performing with his father's group from a young age (sitting in on the bajo sexto by 1953 at the age of fourteen before switching to accordion and recording with his own group by 1955 at the age of sixteen),[8] Flaco grew up interacting not only with traditional Texas-Mexican culture, but also surrounded by the range of musical cultures in Texas at the time (polka, but also country and the blues, for example) and thus influenced by mainstream, U.S. American popular music. As the artist recalls, "When I was in my teens, I used to tune into American music—to country. I used to listen to rock and roll when rock and roll started. . . . I used to listen to Hank Williams, to Hank Snow, to even Tex Ritter and Gene Autry and all those movie stars that were singing. . . . I started doing some B.B. King on the accordion."[9] Flaco has recorded a huge number of songs, both independently and as a session musician or guest artist on numerous other artists' works. By 1994, he estimated the count at more than sixty albums: "I've sort of lost count, really. I started recording in '54 and have been in the studio ever since. It's around 60 albums, not counting the old 78s (discs which predated modern long-playing phonograph records) on all the little regional labels."[10] These recordings range from traditional conjunto performances to hybrid styles with more mainstream influences, from independent works to collaborations with other musicians. For now, independent recordings with hybrid influences will provide a clear picture of Flaco's contributions to the genre in this regard.

Flaco's self-titled album from 1994 (*Flaco Jiménez*, Arista Records) serves as a good example of the artist's (almost) independent and hybridized recordings. The album won a Grammy Award for Best Mexican-American/Tejano Music Performance in 1996 (Flaco's third of an eventual—to this date—five, following a Grammy in 1986 for Best Mexican-American Performance for "Ay Te Dejo En San Antonio" and an additional award in 1990 with the

Texas Tornados for Best Mexican-American Performance for the song "Soy De San Luis," from their self-titled, debut album). Demonstrating the musician's calculated versatility, his next album, *Buena Suerte, Señorita* (Arista Records, 1996), is far more conservative. As Flaco explains, "I think I have done enough country, rock, and other things with other people. . . . This [new CD] is more hardcore conjunto, you know, more traditional. We're not having any country in it. . . . It is all in Spanish."[11]

In this regard, while, in many of his musical pursuits, Flaco himself responds to hybrid influences experienced by lifelong participation in both Texas-Mexican and the mainstream culture, he also recognizes a need for differentiation of style among his various intended audiences. While certain members of the cultural community (and the more mainstream population) appreciate the biculturality and/or exoticism experienced in the hybridizations of conjunto, others respond better to more traditional musical—and thus cultural—pursuits. Flaco maintains his widespread popularity in part by remembering and responding to both impulses. As Sutton describes (referring to Korean music but applicable around the world), "some cultural forms are recognized as 'pure' and 'authentic,' celebrated as invaluable assets, to be preserved from foreign mixture."[12] This notion seems to also hold truth for Texas-Mexican practices. While some community members—like Flaco and his enthusiasts—recognize the bicultural form of identity demonstrated in hybrid musical works, many members of the ethnic and socioeconomic constituency instead prefer that conjunto (particularly given its meaningful history as a symbol of cultural identity) and the corresponding culture remain pure from outside—especially Anglo-American—influences.

Alternatively (to the subsequent *Buena Suerte, Señorita*), *Flaco Jiménez* is a hybrid work, containing a mixture of Spanish and English lyrics, guest appearances by country artists Lee Roy Parnell, Radney Foster, and Raul Malo of The Mavericks, and effortless shifts between polka and honky-tonk; as Timothy White asserts, the album creates "a pan-cultural transfusion of the first rockin' rank."[13] As Eric Levin notes, the album "cries crossover" (despite a "failure to translate the Spanish lyrics"),[14] indicating the different intended audiences for Flaco's various pursuits. Further demonstrating the work's hybridity and crossover appeal, in addition to the Grammy Award for the album, Flaco received a nomination for "Cat Walk" for Best Country Instrumental Performance. Despite initial marketing by Arista Texas to the Mexican-American market alone, Flaco asserts that the record should also have been aimed at country radio stations: "'They started out promoting the album only for the Spanish-speaking audience. When they asked me if I was comfortable with that, I said no. I told 'em it really belongs (on country radio) too.'"[15]

In this regard, Flaco's manifestations of hybridity seem calculated not only to express his own sense of biculturality in contemporary society, but also to attract a widespread—and aspirationally mainstream—audience. However, not everyone was excited about Flaco's hybridized pursuits. Writing for *Texas Monthly*, Joe Nick Patoski refers to *Flaco Jiménez* as "a big disappointment, for it showed how far Texas's greatest accordionist had strayed," with a sound emulating "Nashville country-pop," rather than "El West Side of San Antonio."[16] Expressing his (and ostensibly others') desire to keep conjunto "pure," Patoski instead praises the more traditional *Buena Suerte, Señorita* as an "exceptional back-to-basics piece of cantina fare—dust, dirty conjunto."[17] As seen throughout the accordionist's career, Flaco's identity as fundamentally Texas-Mexican, despite pursuits across a range of genres, pigeonholes his music as simultaneously not "pure" enough for full consideration as conjunto and also not accepted as anything else.

As Sutton continues, and as demonstrated through the reception of Flaco's musical pursuits, hybrid music "suggests ambiguity from various perspectives, endearing it to some, making it repugnant to others."[18] For those who want conjunto music—as a nostalgic form of cultural identity—to remain "pure" from external influences, hybridizations like those seen in *Flaco Jiménez* create a problematic form of "intentional cultural impurity."[19] This notion helps to explain Patoski's (and ostensibly others') reactions to the two contrasting albums, particularly within the historic conjunto community. That being said, if we subscribe to the "cycles of hybridization" model, over time, these ambivalent reactions to Flaco's cultural mixtures will subside as the new hybrid form becomes the standard (as did "traditional" conjunto at the middle of the twentieth century). Ultimately, further processes of future hybridizations will then continue to alter the genre. As Sutton notes, "What is obviously fusion now, if it persists, becomes a stabilized norm, a genre or set of genres which can later be subject to further hybridizing processes."[20] It is ultimately a community's understanding of historic continuity and musical familiarity that determines which cultural products will be accepted as a form of identity (and when) and which will be rejected as too far outside of cultural "authenticity." As Mervi Tervo notes, "it is the audience which accepts/rejects music's authenticity and credibility."[21] Of course, these interpretations change based on individual experiences and generational standards.

Flaco Jiménez includes ten tracks. Songs like "El Pesudo," "Por Las Parrandas," and "Que Lo Sepa El Mundo" (written by Salome Gutierrez, pioneering conjunto composer, producer, and owner of Del Bravo Record Shop in San Antonio) are relatively traditional conjunto tunes and help to demonstrate the external elements that Flaco adds to the genre through innovative, blues-inflected accordion runs maintained between the vocal lines. "Carolina" and "Por Una Mujer Bonita" have vaguely tropical feels, despite simultaneously maintaining more traditional conjunto elements (form and instrumentation, to start). "Que Problemas" falls more closely into the country side of the album, although it also demonstrates clear hybridity with more traditional conjunto characteristics.

"Seguro Que Hell Yes" is something else entirely, a bilingual party tune produced in collaboration with Raul Malo (the ethnically Cuban lead singer for the Miami, Florida-based Latin/Tex-Mex/country/rockabilly band The Mavericks). As Larry Flick illustrates, the "wonderfully joyful cut" is "impossible to shove into any single category" and "deserves a spin on several radio formats."[22] Furthermore, the song is "so soulful and energetic [it] could make the dead get up and dance,"[23] as the "saucy serving of Tex-Mex revelry . . . pull[s] the listener into its endlessly happy party of galloping beats, fluffy accordion riffs, brassy horns, and bright vocals."[24] The tune was also recorded (in Spanish and English) by country artist Alan Jackson in 2015 (on the album *Genuine: The Alan Jackson Story*). Meanwhile, "Jealous Heart," another bilingual, country-inspired collaboration with singer-songwriter Radney Foster, brings a "wonderfully weepy country ballad" to the album.[25] The classic country tune was written and originally recorded by singer-songwriter Jenny Lou Carson in 1944 and subsequently recorded by a range of artists, including a popular Spanish-language version ("Celoso"), first recorded by the Mexican *trio romántico* Trio Los Panchos in 1966. "Cat Walk," a lyrics-free collaboration with country/blues artist Lee Roy Parnell, showcases a further country/conjunto hybridization, here emphasizing bluesy instrumental riffs between the electric guitar and button accordion. The final track of the album is "Open Up Your Heart," a particularly balanced hybridization between the country genre and more traditional conjunto elements. The song was originally written and recorded by Bakersfield musician Buck Owens in 1966. For our purposes, two songs from *Flaco Jiménez* ("Open Up Your Heart" and "Seguro Que Hell Yes") can be explored in more detail to fully demonstrate Flaco's hybrid techniques. While many of these elements of hybridity come through collaborations with mainstream artists who are external to the Texas-Mexican tradition, the album as a whole seems to maintain an emphasis on Flaco himself, rather than ceding prominence to the more mainstream artists, as explored in the possibly problematic, hybridized pursuits of Chapter 8.

Owens's original version of "Open Up Your Heart" takes a simple verse-refrain form (B1A1 B1A2 B1), beginning with a brief (seven seconds) instrumental introduction, proceeding with a refrain and verse (B1A1), continuing with an additional refrain and verse (B1A2)—this time with a lengthy (twenty-two seconds) instrumental interlude in between, and concluding with a final iteration of the refrain, now with a final repetition of the last two lines in a tag ending (Tab. 4.1). Each of the vocal sections is approximately the same length (twenty-one or twenty-two seconds)—including the instrumental interlude—while the first seven seconds of the introduction and the final seven seconds of the final refrain—corresponding to the tag ending—provide clean bookends to the piece. A moderate tempo of 94 BPM is maintained throughout. While Flaco's version of the song also alternates between verse(s) and refrains (B2B1A1 B2A1), the structure corresponds more closely to a traditional conjunto form, with *ranchera*-like (see below) instrumental interludes between each of the vocal sections. The initial instrumental introduction is longer than any of the vocal sections (twenty-six seconds versus sixteen to eighteen seconds per verse or refrain), while the central interlude clocks in at thirty-four seconds, or two times any of the surrounding vocal sections. Each of the verses and refrains is completed more quickly than in Owens's version of the song, corresponding to Flaco's faster tempo of 117 BPM. The instrumental ending also includes the final repetition of the last two lines of the refrain as noted in Owens's original. Throughout Flaco's recording, the increased emphasis on instrumental passages corresponds to conjunto's fundamental history as an instrumental genre.

Flaco performs a bilingual version of "Open Up Your Heart," shifting the structure and instrumentation to better align with traditional conjunto practices, while maintaining the melody and country-oriented lyrics of the original. Flaco begins with a Spanish-language rendition of the refrain (B2) in loose translation, ending the last two lines in the original English. Subsequent iterations of the refrain alternate between English and Spanish, although the English versions simply repeat the first four lines, rather than including the alternate lyrics of lines 5–6 from the original (B1): "The sun's gonna shine / There'll be blue skies again." While Owens's version provides two verses (A1 and A2), Flaco includes only one (A1). Interestingly, although Flaco sings this single verse in English, he does not maintain the same lyrics as the original. In Owens's first verse (A1), the vocalist reassures his lover that he will not hurt her (as a previous relationship apparently had). For Flaco's version of the verse (A1), the vocalist instead assures his lover that he has "told [her] everything," and thus, she should be ready to love him. While these two versions represent only a subtle alteration of meaning, that Flaco alters the lyrics at all, especially when maintaining the English language, raises questions of interpretation. The newer version seems to place the onus on the male protagonist to convince the female that he is worthy of her love, regardless of previous experiences she may have had, while the original version assumes

Table 4.1. “Open Up Your Heart.” As performed and recorded by Buck Owens. From *Buck Owens All-Time Greatest Hits* (Saguaro Road Records 25828-D, 2010). “Open Up Your Heart.” As performed and recorded by Flaco Jiménez. From *Flaco Jiménez* (Arista Records 18772, 1994).

“Open Up Your Heart” (Structure)					
Owens's Form (Verse-Refrain)	Language (Owens)	Length (Owens)	Jiménez's Form (Verse-Refrain)	Language (Jiménez)	Length (Jiménez)
Instrumental Introduction		0:00–0:07 (0:07)	Instrumental Introduction		0:00–0:26 (0:26)
B1	English	0:07–0:29 (0:22)	B2	Spanish	0:26–0:42 (0:16)
			Instrumental Interlude		0:42–0:55 (0:13)
A1	English	0:29–0:51 (0:22)			
B1	English	0:51–1:12 (0:21)	B1	English	0:55–1:11 (0:16)
Instrumental Interlude		1:12–1:34 (0:22)	Instrumental Interlude		1:11–1:26 (0:15)
A2	English	1:34–1:55 (0:21)	A1	English	1:26–1:43 (0:17)
			Instrumental Interlude		1:43–2:17 (0:34)
B1	English	1:55–2:24 (0:29)	B2	Spanish	2:17–2:34 (0:17)
			Instrumental Interlude		2:34–2:43 (0:09)
			A1	English	2:43–3:01 (0:18)
			Instrumental Ending		3:01–3:21 (0:20)

that she will "open up" to him if only he assures her that he will not hurt her. In this way, while subtle, Flaco's version modernizes the subject matter to give greater autonomy to the (presumably) female lover.

The primary manifestation of country music in Flaco's recording of "Open Up Your Heart" is the song itself, including the English lyrics (with a hint of country-western twang). The hybridization in the recording then comes by way of a recognizable country song performed in a conjunto style, including the alterations to the form discussed above, as well as the standard Texas-Mexican instrumentation. In addition to Flaco's performance on the button accordion, his son, David, plays the drum set, Oscar Tellez plays bajo sexto, and Max Baca participates on bass guitar, together forming the typical four-person ensemble of the standardized genre at the middle of the twentieth century. As typical, the drums emphasize a polka beat, with the bass drum on the beat (1 and 3) and snare drum on beats 2 and 4. Simple, unobtrusive fills fall at the ends of phrases. The drum figures become slightly more prominent during the instrumental interludes, playing against the improvisatory accordion lines. The bajo sexto and bass guitar maintain similar functions as the drums, remaining neatly in the background during vocal sections, but becoming slightly more active during the instrumental interludes, playing against the accordion but never outshining it. Tellez also sings secondary vocals, providing harmonies in thirds, as is common within the conjunto genre. The accordion does not perform during the vocal sections; neither under the vocal lines (as is not typical, but has become more common during the twentieth and twenty-first centuries), nor between phrases (as is much more expected by this time).

The long instrumental interlude in Flaco's recording—preceding the second iteration of the Spanish-language refrain—provides a good demonstration of the types of hybridized figuration, drawing from various external influences, that Flaco inserts within this and other conjunto songs. The section demonstrates a variety of ever-changing rhythms and syncopations, emphasizing a rhythmically improvisatory feel throughout. The ornamentation is primarily scalar in nature, but lends an additional element of improvisation. As such, the passage perhaps relates most closely to a jazz solo, although it largely lacks the harmonic innovations most prevalent within the alternative genre. The artist's characteristic long note appears halfway through the passage, tying this selection to many other instrumental passages within the artist's recorded output. While the section uses the melodic foundation of the Owens original, it inserts unexpected rhythmic shifts and scalar ornamentation to move the passage from its more traditional conjunto roots and further connect Flaco's contemporary interpretation of the genre to a range of external influences.

The title of "Seguro Que Hell Yes" (roughly, "Sure, What the Hell, Yes") alone displays the fundamentally hybrid nature of the song. The simplistic lyrics are in a mix of Spanish and English, with a repetitive refrain appearing between (and as the last line of) each of five verses. As in Flaco's version of "Open Up Your Heart" (and corresponding roughly to the ranchera form common throughout the conjunto genre), instrumental sections separate each of the verses and refrains. Ostensibly directed at a mainstream audience, the lyrics present a simplified form of Spanish, interspersed with English phrases (and Spanish terms like *sangría* and *menudo* that are commonly understood), making a loose interpretation possible even for non-Spanish speakers. In this way, the lyrics seem almost a caricature of Latinx culture (not specifically Texas-Mexican, likely corresponding to the joint participation with Malo, with Cuban heritage), rather than a true representation of the ethnic community. Jackson's 2015 version of the song (certainly intended for a mainstream, country-western audience) maintains the same lyrics as the original, with no English translation. This simplistically bilingual practice corresponds to numerous other "cowboy ballads" and party songs in the country music tradition (i.e., "Meet Me Tonight In Laredo" by Marty Robbins from 1966, "Pancho & Lefty" by Merle Haggard and Willie Nelson from 1983, "I Don't Know What She Said" by Blaine Larsen from 2006, and "Toes" by the Zac Brown Band from 2008), further suggesting the role of "Seguro Que Hell Yes" as a hybrid form of Latinx/conjunto and country-western (like the whole album).

The ranchera structure—consisting of an instrumental introduction, verse and refrain, instrumental interlude, another verse and refrain (and so on), and an instrumental ending—is very common to the conjunto tradition. Flaco's version of "Seguro Que Hell Yes" maintains this general structure, employing an instrumental introduction, followed by the first verse and refrain (A1B), an instrumental interlude, the second verse and refrain (A2B), followed by three more verse and refrain pairs (A3B A4B A5B), each separated by instrumental interludes (Tab. 4.2). The final refrain section is significantly expanded, with the lyrics repeated for more than a minute (1:11) and combined with the previous instrumental material. While this structure designates a Texas-Mexican influence, other aspects of the song do not maintain the typical ranchera characteristics. A general theme of love is common (but certainly not unique) to the ranchera form, as is the major key and moderate tempo (BPM 106). However, the meter is not a polka, and the instrumentation is not the standard four-person ensemble common to conjunto.

Instead, in addition to Flaco's accordion (much less prominent here than in "Open Up Your Heart" and other, more conjunto-oriented recordings)

Table 4.2. "Seguro Que Hell Yes." As performed and recorded by Flaco Jiménez. From *Flaco Jiménez* (Arista Records 18772, 1994).

"Seguro Que Hell Yes" (Structure)		
Original Form (Ranchera)	Language	Length
Instrumental Introduction		0:00–0:20 (0:20)
A1	Spanish/English	0:20–0:29 (0:09)
B	Spanish/English	0:29–0:39 (0:10)
Instrumental Interlude		0:39–0:46 (0:07)
A2	Spanish/English	0:46–0:56 (0:10)
B	Spanish/English	0:56–1:06 (0:10)
Instrumental Interlude		1:06–1:23 (0:17)
A3	Spanish/English	1:23–1:32 (0:09)
B	Spanish/English	1:32–1:42 (0:10)
Instrumental Interlude		1:42–1:49 (0:07)
A4	Spanish/English	1:49–1:59 (0:10)
B	Spanish/English	1:59–2:09 (0:10)
Instrumental Interlude		2:09–2:26 (0:17)
A5	Spanish/English	2:26–2:34 (0:08)
B (Extended)	Spanish/English	2:34–3:45 (1:11)

and Malo's vocals, the performance includes drums, bass guitar, and bajo sexto, in addition to electric guitar, saxophone, trumpet, and keyboards (by conjunto accordionist Joel Guzman). Foster and Parnell join in with additional background vocals. The accordion plays intermittently under the vocals and between phrases, but remains largely in the background throughout. The entire structure of the song can be separated into two larger sections, with a short instrumental interlude (seven seconds) following the first and third verses with refrains (A1B and A3B) and longer interludes (seventeen seconds each) following the second and fourth iterations of the refrain (A2B and A4B). The rather lengthy (twenty seconds) instrumental introduction and final verse with extended refrain (A5B) bookend the entire piece.

Overall, "Seguro Que Hell Yes" fits most closely into a country/pop category, with Latin influences particularly pronounced in the horn lines throughout each of the instrumental sections, as well as the Spanish/English lyrics. In addition to these bilingual lyrics, the conjunto elements come through the ranchera form and Flaco's ornamental accordion interjections throughout. In this way, the song displays almost the opposite style of hybridity as noted in "Open Up Your Heart," with the prominent genre here being country (as opposed to conjunto), albeit with certain conjunto elements (as opposed to country). Taken together with the other tracks, *Flaco Jiménez* thus achieves an overall sense of hybridity, with some songs falling more closely in line with traditional conjunto practices, some songs presenting more country characteristics, and multiple songs lying somewhere in between the two genres (although at various locations along a country-conjunto continuum, as seen in these two examples). As Flaco asserts, "Naturally now you can't stick just with polka and redova and schottisches. You have to play what's going on in the world. Starting with polka, and a little rock-and-roll, or a little cumbia, cha-cha-cha. . . . Because it's pretty hard just to play just polka, polka, polka, or just cumbia, cumbia, cumbia. You have to mix it up."[26]

In this way, by mixing Spanish with English; polka with rock and roll; bajo sexto with saxophone; and so on, Flaco simultaneously localizes his own cultural heritage (notably, in the urban location of San Antonio, rather than the more culturally homogenous—but still emergently bicultural—Rio Grande Valley or more mainstream-oriented urban locations like Los Angeles or Nashville) while using hybrid elements to construct an individual cultural space—for himself and other members of the contemporary constituency (explaining his lasting appeal)—connected to both the "traditional" working-class, Texas-Mexican community and more mainstream practices within the United States. This incorporation of this local heritage with global popularities has allowed many members of the younger Texas-Mexican generations to rediscover conjunto, as its hybrid manifestation connects to the contemporary sense of bicultural identity in a way that more traditional performances of the genre do not. In this regard, "globalization ironically encourages local or 'subaltern' people to rediscover the local," since "hybridization offers an opportunity for local culture to be continued."[27]

Collaborative Hybridity: Texas Tornados

In 1989, influenced by a creative executive at Warner Brothers Records, Flaco teamed up with veteran recording artists Doug Sahm, Augie Meyers, and Freddy Fender to create a Tex-Mex/country/rock amalgamation called the Texas Tornados. Sahm and Meyers were both former members of a Tex-Mex rock band from the 1960s called the Sir Douglas Quintet (imitating a British Invasion pop group; "except we had three Spanish guys, so it was a hard thing to pull off," Meyers notes).[28] Fender (born Baldemar Huerta in the Rio Grande Valley) was a Texas-Mexican country star who had one hit in 1959 with "Wasted Days and Wasted Nights" before a marijuana charge in 1960 and subsequent three-year prison term derailed his career (which would be revitalized in the 1970s with a number of crossover hits, including "Before the Next Teardrop Falls" and a remake of "Wasted Days and Wasted Nights"). Initial reviews of the Texas Tornados referred to the group as "the Mexican Beatles" and "the Traveling Wilburys of Tex-Mex,"[29] indicating the same sort of cross-genre, big-name supergroup as that of Bob Dylan, George Harrison, Jeff Lynne, Roy Orbison, and Tom Petty from 1988–1991. The name of the group seems to be derived from a 1973 album by the "Sir Douglas Band" (one of Sahm's many iterations) entitled *Texas Tornado*, as well as a slightly later album (*Texas Rock for Country Rollers*, 1976) by "Sir Doug & The Texas Tornados." The name provides an evocative representation of the group's Texas-based mixture of conjunto, country, blues, and rock.

The Texas Tornados first performed for Warner Brothers executives at Slim's, a rock and blues nightclub in San Francisco, in 1989. They released their debut album, *Texas Tornados* (in both English and Spanish versions), in 1990 to critical acclaim. From that album, "Soy De San Luis" earned a Grammy Award in 1991. Two more albums, *Zone of Our Own* and *Hangin' On by a Thread*, followed in 1991 and 1992, respectively. Despite continuous support from the alternative country scene and a number of popular songs (at least in live performance), none of the albums achieved gold status (signifying 500,000 albums sold) and none of the songs received substantial radio airplay. Flaco attributes the band's struggles to achieve any lasting mainstream successes to "general confusion over where the Tornados fit in the tightly formatted world of commercial radio."[30] Yet, by 1991, the group had already toured Europe twice and started to develop an international following, thus contributing substantially to the globalization of the conjunto genre (although a very specific style of globalization, since the associated music, while influenced by conjunto, is certainly not of a traditional Texas-Mexican format, but a hybrid form). Flaco's performances around the world with the Texas Tornados ultimately led to greater popularity for his solo repertory (which is more traditionally Texas-Mexican, although still hybridized, as explored above), further influencing the spread of the conjunto genre (in this stylistic manifestation) worldwide. As journalist Chris Heim asserts, by 1992, Flaco was "being heard by more people than ever before thanks to his involvement in the Texas Tornados."[31]

Despite a lack of substantive commercial success, the Texas Tornados "toured and were much loved."[32] As Claudia Perry explains, they "drew large crowds in Texas but existed mainly as a cult band outside the state."[33] In 1991, performing at the first annual Chicago Country Music Festival (with some

42,000 people in attendance), the group "were easily the crowd favorite."[34] That same year, following the release of *Zone of Our Own*, the group presented a "string of sold-out concerts across the country."[35] They made appearances on *Saturday Night Live*, *Austin City Limits*, the *David Letterman Show*, and headlined a national concert tour during the summer of 1992. The group initially split up in 1994 due to "disagreements over song selection and creative control" (as Flaco explains).[36] Yet, Flaco, Meyers, and Fender continued to perform without Sahm (without a name, since "Texas Tornados" was registered to Sahm), such as for the New Year's Eve celebration at the Santa Clara County Fairgrounds in California (including Fender's band and Baca on bajo sexto). As Flaco notes, "You can call us the Three Amigos or whatever. Considering the reputations of me and Freddy and Augie, I think people will recognize the music."[37] This brief hiatus from the formal group actually led to even greater exposure for more traditional conjunto music, since the three remaining artists expanded their performance repertory beyond just Texas Tornados songs, including Flaco's previous (more conjunto-oriented) setlist. As Flaco announces, "We'll be playing all kinds of things, not just Tornados songs. . . . In fact, now that we're not going by that name, we're free to play the whole range of my stuff, Augie's stuff and Freddy's. A 90-minute set is gonna be just too short for us."[38]

Flaco Jiménez, Flaco's solo album discussed in detail above, was produced during this hiatus from the Texas Tornados. The group reunited in 1996 with a new album, *4 Aces*, which achieved some success with radio airplay, particularly with the song "A Little Bit Is Better Than Nada," which was also featured on the 1996 Kevin Costner film, *Tin Cup*. The song "Trying," from that same album, was also included on the 1996 Robin Williams film, *Jack*. After Sahm passed away in 1999 (and Fender in 2006), the group disbanded. Flaco and Meyers joined with Sahm's son, Shawn Sahm, in 2010 for a new iteration of the group, releasing *Esta Bueno*.

Texas Tornados's debut, self-titled album (1990) can serve as an example of the stylistic hybridizations seen throughout the group's work. While the album was released (a few months apart) in English and Spanish versions (identical except for the vocal tracks), the English version will here provide an appropriate representation of the stylistic techniques characteristic of both (and also includes many Spanish-language components). Heim refers to the album as "a spicy Tex-Mex stew filled with tasty bits of conjunto, country, blues and rock."[39] Fender classifies the band's repertory as "Mexican polka, ballad-type music, rock 'n' roll, B.B. King-blues-type stuff."[40] Accordingly, Sahm describes his initial work with the group as "a return to mainstream America,"[41] following a wide range of pursuits comprising a career Jack Hurst refers to as "diverse to the point of the bizarre," with successes in "about every kind of music between techno-pop and opera."[42] While Warner Brothers initially intended to market the group primarily to the "rapidly increasing Hispanic-American population in the U.S.,"[43] as well as within Mexico, the album was played "mostly on country stations" and ultimately reached number 25 on the U.S. *Billboard* Top Country Albums (although David Dishneau asserts that "with a little wider exposure these gracefully aging sons of the Southwest could cut a broad path into the mainstream").[44] Two singles from the album, "Who Were You Thinking Of," and "Adios Mexico," made it on the country and Mexican charts, respectively.[45] By 2013, the song "(Hey Baby) Que Paso" (written by Meyers) had been translated into fourteen different languages and was still being performed internationally.[46] As of this writing, the song is the most popular of the group's tracks on Spotify, followed by "Little Bit Is Better Than Nada," from their 1996 album.

It is important to note the generic interpretation of this album, including Anglo-American artists, in comparison to Flaco's solo pursuits. *Flaco Jiménez* was not programmed on country radio stations, despite Flaco's insistence that it should be and despite a clear country/conjunto hybridity. In contrast, *Texas Tornados* received primary attention within the country realm, including country-radio airplay, despite intended promotion among Latinx and Mexican fans and despite similar country/conjunto features. It is fairly clear to note the difference in categorization between the two albums as a difference of identity. Even with similar musical traits and even with the participation of Flaco and his accordion on both albums, the collaboration with Anglo-American artists in the Texas Tornados alters the characterization of the music as either country or conjunto—not both. Anglo-American musicians "could cut . . . a path into the mainstream"; Texas-Mexican musicians like Flaco—at least when performing alone—are restricted to a Texas-Mexican consideration, regardless of close musical correspondences. In this regard, the music is not what determines the genre.

The participation of more mainstream (or at least Anglo-American) musicians within the Texas Tornados seemingly empowers the incorporation of more traditional conjunto elements than seen in many of Flaco's solo endeavors (while still aimed at a more mainstream audience). While Flaco takes a back seat throughout much of his (slightly later) self-titled album, the accordion—and corresponding conjunto sound—is prominent throughout the *Texas Tornados* album. As the artist himself notes, the group "made a big boost for Tejano, for Tex-Mex, for Conjunto."[47] *Texas Tornados* includes ten songs, for a total playtime of just over thirty minutes. Individual songs combine diverse elements, while the album as a whole is an exercise in hybridity, as the four different artists take the lead on different songs. Meyers brings two of his own songs including "(Hey Baby) Que Paso," originally released as a solo track in 1987 as "Kep Pa So," referring to the musician's time spent in Sweden attempting to communicate phonetically,[48] and "Dinero," ostensibly based on a real-life parking lot encounter with "four dudes who were sitting around wishing they had money to buy gas and some beer and get out of town."[49] Likewise, Sahm contributes his own "Adios Mexico," originally released by the Sir Douglas Quintet (with Meyers) in 1982. Fender's "A Man Can Cry" was originally released in 1960, while Flaco contributes his father's song, "Soy De San Luis," a classic conjunto polka.

These individual inclusions do not vary substantially from their original renditions—some of which already contain certain hybrid elements, thus bringing a general sense of hybridity for the album (in part) through the disparate choices of songs stemming from the collaboration of four distinct recording artists. For example, Meyers (originally from—and stylistically influenced by—San Antonio) already plays a conjunto-inflected accordion line in the earlier version of "Kep Pa So." The lyrics on the English-language version of *Texas Tornados* (and the earlier rendition) for both "(Hey Baby) Que Paso" and "Dinero" include a combination of Spanish and English, as do both the original and new versions of "Adios Mexico." As in the Sir Douglas Quintet original, the *Texas Tornados* version of "Adios Mexico" features Meyers on the organ, rather than a prominent accordion line. Likewise, the new rendition of "A Man Can Cry" does not stray far from Fender's original version. Both versions display the heavy influence of early rock and roll (and country) songs. Meanwhile, the *Texas Tornados* rendition of "Soy De San Luis" maintains a relatively traditional conjunto sound, with a standard Texas-Mexican structure, instrumentation, and vocal harmonization; the only real sense of cross-cultural hybridity occurs in the more rock-oriented production (including a heavy drum beat—albeit still a polka beat), as well as Flaco's blues-inflected ornamental runs.

In addition to these individual contributions by the four different members of the group, the album contains four songs pulled from the archives of classic country-western music. "Who Were You Thinkin' Of" was originally recorded by country music artist Jim Glaser in 1979 and also subsequently released by the Sir Douglas Quintet in 1982. While Glaser's original recording includes Latin-inflected trumpet lines, the subsequent Sir Douglas Quintet version already replaces the trumpets with a conjunto-influenced accordion. With Flaco's participation on *Texas Tornados*, these accordion lines push even further into standard Texas-Mexican technique. In this way, the true sense of conjunto/country hybridity comes with the earlier musical pursuits of Sahm and Meyers; the Texas Tornados maintain these same elements of hybridization, but—in many ways—do not bring new hybrid elements into the previously recorded songs. The full impact of the Texas Tornados then lies in the group's ability to bring the musical style to mainstream consciousness; pushing the hybrid ideas of the Sir Douglas Quintet's previous songs closer to conjunto with the inclusion of Flaco and closer to country with the inclusion of Fender.

Additional country-western songs included on this album contain "If That's What You're Thinking," originally recorded by country singer and songwriter Karen Brooks in 1982. Unlike many of the other recordings on *Texas Tornados*, this song is differentiated on the new album with additional accordion lines in a conjunto style (that do not exist in the original, despite a background accordion part in the Brooks version played by Wayne Goodwin). The lyrics of the original are maintained in the Texas Tornados version, included a brief interlude in Spanish incorporated into both. However, while the English lyrics appear in the new version unchanged from the original (with one additional verse [A3]), the Spanish-language bridge, while maintaining the general meaning in each, does differ slightly in the *Texas Tornados* version. While Brooks simply translates the first two English lines into Spanish for this section (*No me digas que me ames / No quiero oírlo*; Don't tell me that you love me / I don't want to hear it.), the Texas Tornados alter the words (*Ya no quiero que me ames / Ya no quiero saberlo*; I don't want you to love me / I don't want to know it). While the vocalist in the original version just doesn't "want to know" the feelings her lover may have for her and doesn't "want to *hear* it," the (now male) protagonist in the Texas Tornados version now doesn't want his lover to love him at all and here doesn't "want to *know* it." The difference is subtle and the reason for the alteration is unclear (although perhaps stems from the native Spanish speakers participating in the Texas Tornados rendition, rather than the solely Anglo-American musicians in the original).

Structurally, both versions of "If That's What You're Thinking" display a simple verse-refrain, beginning with a brief instrumental introduction and followed by two verses (A1 and A2) and the refrain (B) (Tab. 4.3). Brooks's rendition then moves directly into the Spanish-language bridge (C), while the Texas Tornados version first presents an additional verse (A3) before the bridge (C). Both recordings then present the refrain (B) again, followed by a final repetition of one of the previous verses. The Brooks version uses the first two lines again in a shortened rendition of the first verse (A1), while the Texas Tornados version instead ends with a full iteration of the third, additional verse (A3), expanded by repeating the final two lines. The additional verse

Table 4.3. "If That's What You're Thinking." As performed and recorded by Karen Brooks. From *Walk On* (Warner Bros. Records 1-23676, 1982). "If That's What You're Thinking." As performed and recorded by Texas Tornados. From *Texas Tornados* (Reprise Records 4-26251, 1990).

"If That's What You're Thinking" (Structure)					
Brooks's Form (Verse-Refrain with Bridge)	Language (Brooks)	Length (Brooks)	Texas Tornados' Form (Verse-Refrain with Bridge)	Language (Texas Tornados)	Length (Texas Tornados)
Instrumental Introduction		0:00–0:09 (0:09)	Instrumental Introduction		0:00–0:10 (0:10)
A1	English	0:09–0:33 (0:24)	A1	English	0:10–0:32 (0:22)
A2	English	0:33–0:57 (0:24)	A2	English	0:32–0:55 (0:23)
B	English	0:57–1:49 (0:52)	B	English	0:55–1:40 (0:45)
			A3	English	1:40–2:05 (0:25)
C (Bridge)	Spanish	1:49–2:13 (0:24)	C (Bridge)	Spanish	2:05–2:25 (0:20)
B	English	2:13–3:03 (0:50)	B	English	2:25–3:11 (0:46)
A1 (Shortened)	English	3:03–3:21 (0:18)	A3 (Extended)	English	3:11–3:48 (0:37)

in the Texas Tornados recording does not add much to the overall meaning of the song. The first two lines (Don't say that you want me / To take your love freely) fall closely in line with the analogous portions of the preceding two verses, providing simply another depiction of the fear on the part of the vocalist to express vulnerability in the face of a loving relationship.

The second version of the song is slightly faster than the original (86 BPM versus 80 BPM), which corresponds to the slightly shorter renditions of each analogous section (fifty-two seconds for the refrain (B) in the Brooks version versus only forty-five seconds for the same section as recorded by the Texas Tornados). Each recording provides a brief instrumental expansion preceding the bridge section (C), due to the structural differences presented at the end of the refrain (B) in the original and at the end of the third verse (A3) in the newer version. The Texas Tornados recording of the song does not alter the structure of the original song to better align with standard conjunto practices (turning the form into a ranchera, for example, as noted in many of Flaco's solo recordings of external tunes, as well as those by Saldívar and Jordan, as explored in Chapter 5). However, despite no instrumental interludes between sections (as common to conjunto), the ends of phrases in the Texas Tornados version of "If That's What You're Thinking" are generally expanded with additional accordion runs. This brings the song more closely in line with Texas-Mexican practices and contributes to the overall hybridization of the performance, since the song itself—including the form, meter, and language (with a Western accent)—correlates to the country-western genre.

The two remaining songs on the *Texas Tornados* album include "She Never Spoke Spanish to Me," written by Butch Hancock and originally recorded by Texas country artist Joe Ely in 1977, and "Baby! Heaven Sent Me You," originally recorded by Mississippi-based "swamp pop" (itself a hybrid genre combining New Orleans-style R&B with country-western and traditional French Louisiana influences) artist Jimmy Donley in 1963. Like in "If That's What You're Thinking," the insertion of Flaco's relatively prominent accordion lines into the Texas Tornados version of "She Never Spoke Spanish to Me," while still retaining the general lyrics, language, and structure of the original country song, moves the song solidly into a hybridized manifestation of conjunto and country (as noted in many songs on the album, but not previously explored in Sahm or Meyers's previous works, thus creating the hybridity for this particular group, rather than simply repeating prior hybridizations). Meanwhile, the Texas Tornados version of "Baby! Heaven Sent Me You" does not insert the conjunto-style accordion lines of many of the other songs on this album, instead maintaining the rockabilly feel of the original. However, following English-language iterations of the first two verses, the Texas Tornados recording presents a Spanish-language (loose) translation of the first verse, repeated again following an instrumental interlude and English-language performance of the third verse. In this way, despite a lack of Texas-Mexican structure or instrumentation, the song still conveys a certain country/conjunto hybridity through the insertion of the Spanish lyrics (not present in the original).

As Dal Young Jin and Woongjae Ryoo note, South Korean popular music (K-Pop) does not achieve widespread success within the United States, since its hybrid form makes it sound too much like U.S. American popular music. Instead, U.S. audiences "crave the authentic" and "are not interested in consuming a distilled version of their own pop."[50] In general, Jin and Ryoo assert, "the current form of hybridization in languages and styles—which does not show authentic or locally driven hybrid music—cannot break the largest music market."[51] Similarly, while hybrid groups like the Texas Tornados achieve successes among certain populations (seemingly drawn to a corresponding bicultural identity and/or a sense of exoticism), they show difficulties among a mainstream community for whom the music simultaneously sounds too familiar and yet not familiar enough. At the same time, the music is not "authentic" enough for many members of the historic cultural constituency.

Cultural Preservation: Los Super Seven

In 1998, inspired by a Tex-Mex performance at the South by Southwest festival in Austin in 1997 (via manager Dan Goodman), Flaco joined an additional "supergroup" called Los Super Seven. The group was created (initially) to produce a single, self-titled album and comprised Fender, Ely, country artist Rick Trevino, Tejano musician Ruben Ramos, and David Hidalgo and Cesar Rosas, both from East Los Angeles roots-rock band Los Lobos (see Chapter 3), in addition to Flaco. Aimed at a mainstream market as well as the younger Mexican-American generation, the album comprises traditional Mexican-American border music (with a dedicated intent to preserve these forms of cultural heritage). As Goodman explains, "We decided to do it as a world music project and aim it at the Anglo market as well as at the younger generation of Mexican-Americans who aren't hip to this music."[52] Part of the proceeds from the sale of the album went to the National Council of La Raza, a non-profit organization "dedicated to improving opportunities for Hispanic Americans."[53] In addition to three performances to celebrate the initial release of the album, the group performed on *Late Night with Conan O'Brien* in 1998, thus disseminating the local music to a widespread population. The album also won a Grammy Award for Best Mexican-American Music Performance in 1999. The group returned to the recording studio with a different lineup—and not including Flaco—to release *Canto* in 2001 (comprising musical styles drawn from even further across the Latin diaspora, including Cuban and South American influences). An additional iteration of the group (now including Flaco again) released *Heard It on the X* in 2005.

With an emphasis on preserving regional roots music, the initial Los Super Seven album does not display much of the hybridity seen either in (many of) Flaco's solo albums or in his work with the Texas Tornados. As journalist Richard Harrington notes, "the album itself is a political statement, underscoring the cultural and musical interactions that have been taking place in Texas since the turn of the century, in the process enriching American music."[54] In this regard, the value of the album (and the two subsequent recordings by different iterations of the group) lies in the migratory properties for regional musics like conjunto (instead of the hybridizing effects present in many of Flaco's other works). The group uses well-known artists (many of whom have achieved a certain degree of mainstream success) to present relatively conservative renditions of traditional tunes not only to a mainstream audience, but also to instill an acceptance and sense of pride for the cultural traditions among the younger ethnic community.

In this way, just as Flaco's hybrid pursuits both independently and with the Texas Tornados help the younger cultural generation to express a new form of bicultural identity by modifying traditional conjunto music to better align with contemporary ethnic understandings, his more conservative work with groups like Los Super Seven also helps to develop cultural identification by maintaining and promoting pride in the more traditional culture. Similarly, Nguyen Thi Hien uses the Hùngs Kings temple to illustrate how the U.S. Vietnamese population "are trying to keep traditional culture alive while simultaneously changing and modifying to fit with the culture of their host country."[55] For both populations, cultural identities are established through the preservation of traditional culture, but also as a "dynamic, changeable, creative, and adaptive" response to contemporary situations, such as identification with mainstream U.S. American society.[56] For Nguyen, while "generational differences" often determine such cultural priorities, in general, "Vietnamese [and other diasporic communities in the U.S.] choose to preserve their cultural values, but at the same time they adapt in order to take part in American society while developing their identity as Vietnamese Americans."[57] In contemporary Texas-Mexican culture, Flaco's hybridized performances provide a means for the younger generation to adapt to more mainstream U.S. American culture (while concurrently maintaining their Mexican-American identity). Meanwhile, the artist's more traditional recordings with Los Super Seven (and certain individual works like *Buena Vista, Señorita*) simultaneously reaffirm older and more traditional notions of identity.

Conclusions

Cultural studies scholars have examined the role of hybridity in generating new creative cultures rather than simply oppressing local soundscapes. Cultural hybridization invariably carries a risk in audience reception, since the introduction of external traits into a regional form ostensibly dilutes the role of local characteristics in an important means of community identification. Instead, the uniqueness of the local—in terms of conjunto, the distinctive sound of button accordion with bajo sexto; the idiosyncratic blend of polka rhythms with Latin inflections and the Spanish language—becomes largely subsumed by the homogenizing forces of U.S. American popular culture. That being said, it is important to remember that traditional conjunto is itself a hybridized form, drawing from German polka music and Mexican rhythmic traits to create a new creative culture in the nineteenth-century, cross-cultural expression of the working-class, ethnic community. In that regard, artists like Flaco Jiménez (among others) are repeating past systems of hybridization to alter a style in terms of modern relevance and contemporary cultural expression. Indeed, as Jin and Ryoo explain, "the hybridization of culture must occur as local cultural agents and actors interact and negotiate with global forms, using them as resources through which local people construct their own cultural spaces."[58] Through cross-cultural interactions via physical and increasingly digital processes of migration, modern Texas-Mexican musicians identify not only with their own familial heritage but also with mainstream forms of U.S. American popular culture. These local musicians create their own cultural spaces as an individual negotiation of global forms, using a variety of creative traits that best represent their own interpretations of the contemporary world. They situate and authenticate their music through the sounds of Texas-Mexican conjunto and simultaneously draw connections with other cultural populations to create what is perhaps an aspirational identity more closely tied to the mainstream community.

At the middle of the twentieth century, Texas-Mexican conjunto had reached a well-established but relatively stagnant instrumentation, musical structure, and repertory, serving as a posited symbolic representation of the rural, working-class, ethnic identity. However, beginning with an amalgamation of creative elements at the end of the nineteenth century, this cultural genre has subsequently experienced a "cycle of hybridization," in which the homogeneous, mid-century form gave way to a further hybridization incorporating new characteristics of U.S. American popular music. In addition, nascent processes of migration introduced the regional music to a broader cultural community, creating diverse enthusiasts, participants, and audiences around the world dissociated from conventional political boundaries and traditional conceptions of communities based on race, class, language, and location. This contemporary combination of media/migration and hybridization within the genre has transformed the historic role of conjunto as the symbol of a regional identity, leading to stylistic innovation, national revitalization, and international recognition of the cultural form, demonstrated, in part, through the work of Flaco, but also in the music of Mingo Saldívar and Esteban Jordan (examined subsequently). This cultural manifestation produces a new global community of individuals based on aesthetic interests and personal choice, rather than homologous notions of identity based only on heritage and geographic location.

CHAPTER 5

"I play the jazz accordion!"

"Rueda de Fuego (Ring of Fire)," "My Toot Toot," and the Country/Zydeco Influences of Mingo Saldívar and Steve Jordan

> Charlie Parker just played jazz. I play jazz, but I also play rock, country, salsa, mariachi, cumbias, you name it.
> —Steve Jordan

From 1953 to 1996, a diplomatic project called Arts America, formed by the State Department and under control of the United States Information Agency since 1978, sponsored cultural presentations around the world by more than 10,000 artists.[1] The program started in the shadow of the Cold War. As Tom Teepen quips, "If the Commies were lobbing the Bolshoi Ballet at the world, then by God, we'd launch retaliatory ballet companies of our own."[2] Through the program, Texas-Mexican accordionist Mingo Saldívar toured Africa and the Middle East in 1995. Intended to promote the diversity of U.S. culture abroad, the tour stopped, among other locations, in Jericho. Yet, beyond the transcultural veneer of the venue and audience, the music that Saldívar and his band, Los Tremendos Cuatro Espadas (billed here in English as the Four Tremendous Swords), offered was not the simple Texas-Mexican representation that the organizing team might have expected. Instead, following a few polkas, the musicians "plung[ed] into Latin numbers, country-western [*sic*] tunes by Johnny Cash and Hank Ballard with Spanish lyrics, Cajun music and a touch of rock 'n' roll."[3] Present at the event, Stuart Schoffman describes it as such: "It reflected on the great American mingling of cultures exemplified by Mingo's music—Spanish, Polish, German, Anglo, Cajun—and fantasized about a day when Jews and Arabs, citizens of a multi-cultural society, would clap their hands and stamp their feet side by side in Jerusalem."[4] Beyond the overtly-saccharine nature of this description, and beyond the event's (also significant) representation of globalization through modern transnational mobilization, the mixture of genres in this performance demonstrates some of the practices of hybridization outside of Flaco Jiménez's example observed through the last decades of the twentieth century. However, despite the mixture of musical forms and stylistic traits noted within this performance, Saldívar's music is billed as idiomatically "conjunto," the artist himself a nationalist representation of the U.S American "melting pot" narrative. Despite what music he actually plays and despite the distance his performances have spread beyond the original space and time of the associated genre, Saldívar is fundamentally designated as a Texas-Mexican artist.

Similarly, following Steve Jordan's funeral services at a Catholic church in southside San Antonio in 2010 (the Texas-Mexican accordionist having finally succumbed to his lengthy battle with liver cancer), family, friends, and fans—many one and the same—gathered at Saluté International Bar, a tiny club on the North St. Mary's strip. It was a fitting location, as Jordan had played at the bar, owned by longtime girlfriend, Azeneth Dominguez, every Friday night for the last two years of his life. Eddie Hernandez, known as DJ Plata, devoted his weekly program to the wide range of Jordan's recordings (some fifty-plus albums). Selections included traditional conjunto, in which Jordan "transform[ed] the dumpy diatonic accordion into a light, nimble melody-maker," as in "an early recording of a gorgeous ranchera called 'La Malpagadora.'"[5] They comprised funk, including a "funked-out version of 'Squeezebox Man,'" as well as Latin jazz (including some early recordings on guitar, instead of accordion). The selections included The Righteous Brothers' "You've Lost That Lovin' Feelin'," a "zippy version" of the zydeco tune "My Toot Toot," and a "much-improved" rendition of Blood, Sweat, and Tears' "Spinning Wheel."[6] In addition to Hernandez's program of songs, Bonnie Cisneros read a poem entitled "The Corrido de Esteban y Azeneth." In this poem, Cisneros captures the hybridity exhibited in Jordan's works and noted by those who considered him a musical genius: "South tejas born and bred, Esteban traveled the world on the power of his sound. Mixed genres, reinvented traditions, enraptured listeners, captured cultures, and brought us all to our feet."[7] As in Saldívar's hybridized performance in Jericho, this program represents some of the musical amalgamations within Texas-Mexican conjunto practices in the last decades of the twentieth century. However, regardless of Jordan's significant use of repertory and stylistic traits outside of standard regional understandings, and despite the artist's lifelong attempts to break into a mainstream receptive consciousness, Jordan remains considered according to stereotypical ideas of cultural constraint.

For Saldívar and Jordan, globalization occurs through cross-cultural interactions at the border of Texas-Mexican heritage and migration throughout the United States during the artists' formative years. These interactions have led to a system of hybridization in which the musicians combine traditional conjunto practices with songs and stylistic characteristics from mainstream U.S. American culture, primarily through influences most associated with Anglo-American and African-American cultures, respectively. Robert Holton describes the consequences of globalization, including "the homogenization thesis, in which globalization leads to cultural convergence; the polarization thesis, which posits cultural wars between Western globalization and its opponents; and finally, the hybridization, or syncretism, thesis, in which globalization encourages a blending of the diverse set of cultural repertoires made available through cross-border exchange."[8] While Holton's polarization thesis posits globalization in terms of two conflicting cultural stereotypes, contemporary culture, at least in the case of Texas-Mexican conjunto music, is not that simple. Saldívar's and Jordan's continued identification with familial Texas-Mexican culture does not negate a simultaneous identification with Anglo-American and African-American cultures. In this regard, globalization creates a hybridized cultural product that blends the Texas-Mexican heritage with characteristics of U.S. American popular music. Yet, despite the inclusion of a diversity of stylistic characteristics within their music, artists like Saldívar and Jordan remain confined to the generic classification of "conjunto" (as determined by marketing materials, critical and audience reception, and awards nominations). It would then seem that, at least within a hegemonic system of categorization, sonic traits have less to do with the determination of genre than identity. As David Brackett contends, "the more closely one describes a genre in terms of its stylistic components, the fewer the examples that actually seem to fit."[9]

Mingo Saldívar and "Ring of Fire": The Hybridization of Repertory

Saldívar's songs combine the Texas-Mexican conjunto tradition with country-western, honky-tonk, and rockabilly influences. He has recorded conjunto-inflected versions of "Chantilly Lace," originally by rockabilly star Jiles Peter "The Big Bopper" Richardson, "Sugartime" (as "Lindo Cariñito"), originally made popular by the McGuire Sisters, and "Ring of Fire" (as "Rueda de Fuego"), originally recorded by country star Johnny Cash, among many others. As Saldívar remembers, "I actually began playing popular country and blues songs that I translated into Spanish back in the 1960s. Then I wrote some songs bilingually because the people were listening to English-language music as well as conjunto. Now some of these songs are recognized by English-speaking people, and they like what I do with them."[10] These recordings lie clearly within the conjunto style, with traditional Texas-Mexican instrumentation, structures, and sound. However, in addition to external influences in song choice, they showcase blues-like chord progressions, syncopated, chromatic runs, harmonica-like effects, and even train-whistle sounds.

In terms of transcultural representation, Saldívar's performance of "Ring of Fire" may be one of the more interesting choices of song in the artist's repertory. Written by June Carter and songwriter Merle Kilgore, the song was first recorded by June's sister, Anita Carter, in 1963. Johnny Cash re-recorded the song, adding its iconic, mariachi-style trumpets, and re-released the new recording on his 1963 album, *Ring of Fire: The Best of Johnny Cash* (Columbia). The song, as well as Cash himself, is quintessentially Anglo-American, deriving from a tradition of country music (and relatedly, folk, rockabilly, and rock and roll) in the southern United States. Yet, Cash's version of "Ring of Fire" already includes a component of Mexican culture through the use of mariachi-influenced trumpets. Saldívar's version removes the trumpets, but uses the button accordion to tie this characteristically Anglo-American song to another Mexican-American genre. Diverging somewhat from traditional conjunto practices (but not uncommon in modern renditions), Saldívar maintains an ornamental—and heavily syncopated—accordion line under the vocal part throughout the recording. As John Morthland notes, Saldívar was one of the first performers to "sing and play at the same time," instead of merely "supplying fills and solos between his vocals."[11]

Saldívar's version of "Ring of Fire" ("Rueda de Fuego") is one of several country-music-inflected performances on *I Love My Freedom, I Love My Texas* (1992). The first of Saldívar's recordings to appear on a mainstream label (albeit a label—Rounder Records—specializing in U.S. American roots music), the collection seems aimed at a well-educated, Anglo-American audience. For the album, Carl Finch, co-founder of the Texan polka/dance band Brave Combo, selected thirteen tracks from throughout Saldívar's career. He then re-recorded these tunes with "an all-star band."[12] As such, as seen throughout many of Flaco's works, the hybridity included in Saldívar's music—or at least the hybridity that achieves a lasting effect, in contrast to the artist's individual and largely unsuccessful attempts to hybridize mainstream repertory earlier in his career—is presented through the assistance of a secondary musician emanating from outside of the stereotypical Texas-Mexican community.

In addition, despite the use of country music on the album, and despite the participation of an Anglo-American artist, Saldívar's music—and the Texas-Mexican musician himself—are marketed as idiomatically "conjunto." For example, in a review for *The Beat*, Bob Tarte classifies the album as representing "one of the most instantly engaging musics anywhere," specifically characterizing conjunto and Saldívar's central location within the genre.[13] Yet, Tarte simultaneously acknowledges a contrast between this album and the "redundancy" of more typical conjunto recordings, as well as a hybridity between particular Spanish vocals and the "convincingly cowboy" English-language segments. In addition, and also in parallel with the mainstream circumstances of Flaco's career, *I Love My Freedom, I Love My Texas* earned Saldívar a Grammy nomination—one of two in his career, along with *A Taste of Texas* in 2002—for Best Mexican-American Album. In this way, Saldívar's music has received some popular recognition but only with the incorporation of Anglo-American characteristics and the "assistance" of another Anglo-American artist. Yet, even with these alternate circumstances, Saldívar's music is classified according to his ethnicity; the Grammy assignation of Mexican-American may not help to distinguish between different forms of regional Mexican music, but it certainly characterizes Saldívar as firmly outside of country-western considerations, irrespective of the country-western characteristics in his work.

At the same time, using country-western traits and aiming his music at a U.S. American audience, Saldívar effectively distances himself from negative correlations of "Mexican" in favor of simply "Texan," despite the foundation for conjunto in Mexican influences. This emphasis on Texas (and corresponding exclusion of Mexico) is demonstrated clearly in the titles of the artist's Grammy-nominated albums; aimed at a U.S. American audience, emphasizing the Texas-based ("country") roots of the music, eliminating Mexico from this association, and yet receiving consideration among this purported fanbase as distinctly related to the musician's Mexican heritage. In the United States, Saldívar remains trapped inside a characterization of identity; actual Mexican musicians, however, are not afforded such consideration or performance-based opportunities. For U.S. American audiences (and the Recording Academy)—despite the artist's intent and the dismissal of Mexican musicians, Saldívar serves as an effective representation of Mexico. The artist thus uses Mexican elements to promote a Texas-based sense of nationalism in a sociocultural narrative that simultaneously ignores these Mexican roots and traps Saldívar into external characterization according to a romanticized version of them. The effect is that Saldívar is "othered" according to his ethnic heritage while also "othering" the Mexican musicians responsible for much of conjunto's influences and repertory. Neither group of artists receives the desired recognition, but are all essentialized according to external interpretations of identity.

Saldívar presents his version of "Ring of Fire" ("Rueda de Fuego") with Spanish lyrics, loosely translated from the original, before concluding with an additional verse (the first) and refrain in the original English (and a thick, southern accent) and a final iteration of the initial verse and refrain (A1B) in Spanish. While Cash's original lyrics refer to the "ring of fire" as a state of being produced by love; a place to fall into upon experiencing a "wild desire," Saldívar's translation refers instead to "*your* ring of fire (*tu rueda de fuego*)." Corresponding to "*your* love (*tu amor*)" and "*your* flame (*tu llama*)" in the first verse (A1), the language then seems to indicate a lover's "ring of fire," rather than the "fire" that love itself makes. In that regard, as Saldívar translates Cash's lyrics into Spanish, he reinterprets the lyrical intent, demonstrating that the conjunto version appears not simply as a cover of the original, but a new version of the prototypical material. In this way, Saldívar treats the Anglo-American tune as his own form of cultural expression. He draws from Cash's original but modifies its perceived objective to create a hybridized aesthetic form that represents both sides of the musician's Texas-Mexican heritage.

While Cash's original uses a simple binary form (A1BB A2BB), Saldívar translates the structure of the song into a ranchera, a form typically associated with Mexican mariachi music (and conjunto), further exemplifying the connection between Cash's original—with its mariachi-style brass line—and Saldívar's Texas-Mexican interpretation. As Cash signifies Mexico through these trumpet parts, Saldívar signifies Anglo-American culture through the use of the song itself. As a ranchera, "Rueda de Fuego" consists of an instrumental introduction, verse and refrain (A1B), a brief instrumental interlude (roughly corresponding to material from the verse), a second verse and refrain (A2B), an expanded instrumental interlude (here reiterating material from both the verse and chorus), the first verse and refrain sung in English (A1B), and one more, brief instrumental interlude before a final iteration of the first verse and refrain (A1B) in Spanish, leading into the ending. While this structure is somewhat expanded from a traditional ranchera form (typically alternating between instrumental and vocal sections; comprising an instrumental introduction, verse and refrain, instrumental section repeating the verse, another verse and refrain, and a tag ending), it diverges from the binary form of the original to instead mark the rendition as part of the Mexican-American tradition (Tab. 5.1). Other characteristics of a ranchera

Table 5.1. "Ring of Fire." As performed and recorded by Johnny Cash. From *Ring of Fire: The Best of Johnny Cash* (Columbia CL 2053, 1963). "Rueda de Fuego." As performed and recorded by Mingo Saldívar. From *I Love My Freedom, I Love My Texas* (Rounder Records CD6047, 1992).

"Ring of Fire" / "Rueda de Fuego" (Structure)					
Cash's Form (Binary)	Language (Cash)	Length (Cash)	Saldívar's Form (Ranchera)	Language (Saldívar)	Length (Saldívar)
Instrumental Introduction		0:00–0:09 (0:09)	Instrumental Introduction		0:00–0:45 (0:45)
A1	English	0:09–0:32 (0:23)	A1	Spanish	0:45–1:03 (0:18)
B	English	0:32–0:49 (0:17)	B	Spanish	1:03–1:19 (0:16)
Instrumental Interlude		0:49–1:06 (0:17)	Instrumental Interlude		1:19–1:27 (0:08)
B	English	1:06–1:23 (0:17)			
A2	English	1:23–1:46 (0:23)	A2	Spanish	1:27–1:53 (0:26)
B	English	1:46–2:04 (0:18)	B	Spanish	1:53–2:09 (0:16)
			Instrumental Interlude		2:09–3:03 (0:54)
			A1	English	3:03–3:20 (0:17)
			B	English	3:20–3:36 (0:16)
			Instrumental Interlude		3:36–3:48 (0:12)
			A1	Spanish	3:48–4:06 (0:18)
B (Extended)	English	2:04–2:36 (0:32)	B (Extended)	Spanish	4:06–4:42 (0:36)

observed in this selection include the general theme of love, meter and tempo of a polka, major key, traditional (conjunto) instrumentation, and brief ornamentation (in the accordion) following each line of the lyrics.

Comparing the timing of the two versions demonstrates a reliance on instrumental material in the conjunto recording that only minimally exists in the original (corresponding to conjunto's history as a primarily instrumental genre). While the instrumental introduction and single interlude in Cash's version are nine and seventeen seconds, respectively, Saldívar presents a forty-five-second introduction, followed by three separate instrumental interludes (eight, fifty-four (!), and twelve seconds, respectively). The tempo remains approximately the same for both songs (104 BPM for Cash versus 106 BPM for Saldívar), but the elimination of the mariachi horns and corresponding reduction of time between lines in Saldívar's rendition makes the first verse (each A1) slightly shorter than Cash's example. However, while Cash maintains the same timing for each verse (twenty-three seconds), Saldívar's version of the second verse (A2) is expanded with additional accordion passages between the lines (seventeen to eighteen seconds in the A1 sections versus twenty-six seconds for A2). In this regard, Saldívar's use of a prominent country-western song connects his performance to the mainstream, Anglo-American culture. However, modified structural implications also keep the recording closely within the Texas-Mexican tradition. Saldívar's translation of an Anglo-American song into the conjunto genre turns the hierarchical tables of twentieth-century ethnic hegemonies. While conjunto artists historically asserted sociocultural authority by separating their music from mainstream practices, Saldívar instead claims power over Anglo-American traditions by refashioning Cash's song to fit the Texas-Mexican heritage. At the same time, he distances himself and his music from less highly valued links to Mexico.

That being said, these hybridized practices do not gain entry for the artist into mainstream consciousness. Despite a relatively balanced integration of the two genres—country and conjunto, Saldívar remains neatly characterized according to more primitivist ideas of a "traditional" genre representing the Texas-Mexican identity (rather than acceptance of this popular integration across the range of U.S. American heritage and experiences). Saldívar—and his music—remain "other" to U.S. American commercialism, despite the incorporation of these country-western characteristics. At the same time, this method of hybridization does not change the musical practices, sociocultural identity, or broader understanding of conjunto within the general Texas-Mexican community. Although those living in the contemporary border region display a wide variety of cultural circumstances that cannot be characterized according to any single notion of music as identity, the fact remains that Saldívar's generic mixtures are relatively disconnected from typical conjunto practices demonstrated among more folkloric performances at regional bars, birthday parties, anniversaries, as well as festivals and educational opportunities. As such, Saldívar—and those like him—occupies a liminal space between a Texas-Mexican and a more mainstream U.S. American consciousness; the blend of cultural characteristics in his music correlates to a bicultural sense of identity that is simultaneously both conjunto and country—and thus both Texas-Mexican and Anglo-American—and yet fully characterized according to neither.

Saldívar's methods seem aimed at an audience familiar with both traditions, not simply an inadvertent blending of the artist's own cultural influences. As Tarte notes (with regard to the bilingualism of *I Love My Freedom, I Love My Texas*), "Saldívar is less interested in reaching two different audiences than he is in expounding cultural richness and exploring social tensions."[14] The album is popular among a certain (exclusively) English-speaking audience. However, the artist's hybridity of language and sonic elements seems to place the music within a new understanding of Texas-Mexican identity. Local audiences recognize and identify with both "Mexican" and "American" cultural characteristics. "Rueda de Fuego" emphasizes hybridity in music, but also a bicultural, Texas-Mexican consideration. It speaks to mainstream audiences but represents the local community. That being said, conjunto fans do not always embrace these hybridizations. As Saldívar illustrates, "It took 'em a while to get used to [the music]. They were thinking, 'What is this guy playing, rock and roll or something?'"[15] Saldívar's practices then emphasize—as Helena Simonett interprets—the "individual-centered approach" of contemporary music-making, as well as the continuously shifting taxonomy for a particular genre.[16] The meaning for a certain music in a certain place and time does not remain constant; nor do the associated aesthetic traits. Instead, local musicians appropriate elements of global mass culture—like country-western music—to create individual cultural practices that articulate diverse experiences outside of historical circumstances.[17]

This seemingly intentional method of hybridity also comes through in Saldívar's other versions of Anglo-American popular songs, including "Chantilly Lace" and "Lindo Cariñito" ("Sugartime"), as well as "Swinging Doors" (originally by Merle Haggard), "Cuiden Su Amor" ("I Walk the Line"; also originally by Johnny Cash), "Streets of Bakersfield" (made popular by Buck Owens and Dwight Yoakam), "Burbujitos" ("Tiny Bubbles"; originally written for Lawrence Welk but popularized by Hawaiian singer Don Ho), and many more. Each of these conjunto recordings includes certain elements of popular music, but the most substantial indicators of the external influences are the songs themselves (along with factors like melody, subject matter, structure, and chord progressions that are implicit through these choices of song). Overall, Saldívar presents recognizably Anglo-American songs in a distinctively Texas-Mexican style, thus portraying his own cultural identity as a mix of the two ethnicities. This contradicts the history of conjunto as an ideological response to hegemonic ("white") culture. It emphasizes systems of power in a hierarchical entanglement between Mexico, Texas, and the United States.

In this way, Saldívar's hybridized performances demonstrate a new generic distinction that does not fully conform to preexisting understandings of either country-western or conjunto; as Brackett explains, the "fleeting quality" of genre designations in time and space alter notions of categorization according to specific generic boundaries and lead to synthesized classifications of music as residing within "more than one genre simultaneously."[18] As such, Brackett advocates for the description of a piece of music not as "belonging" to a particular genre, but perhaps only as "participating" in one.[19] Yet, if we—cautiously and perhaps erroneously—associate genre with sociocultural identity, this relegation of mere participation within the mainstream community for minoritized musicians, rather than actual association therein, suggests a fundamental limitation for artists residing outside of the hegemonic U.S. American community to break into mainstream popularity. Regardless of the repertory Saldívar performs, as long as he does so using a ranchera structure or the Spanish language or simply the accordion or perhaps just his own ethnic heritage, he is characterized according to conjunto; thus "participating" within the mainstream culture, but never truly "belonging."

Mingo Saldívar and "La Margarita": The Hybridization of Sonic Elements

Alternatively, comparing Saldívar's renditions of more traditional conjunto selections—such as "La Margarita," appearing on *El Chicano Alegre* (Hacienda Records) in 1995—to "traditional" conjunto recordings displays Saldívar's more prominent use of culturally external characteristics. For example, as compared to Santiago Jiménez Sr.'s version of "Margarita," one of the artist's earliest hits and included (among elsewhere) on the 2016 Smithsonian Folkways Recordings release of *Viva Seguin*, Saldívar's performance contains improvisatory passages, ornamental figuration, chromatic inflections, instrumental countermelodies, rockabilly-style drum patterns and syncopation, and country-western influenced, harmonica-like effects. While Saldívar also employs many of these same sonic elements in his versions of Anglo-American songs, it is within this context of classic conjunto tunes that they stand out from the Texas-Mexican tradition most clearly.

While the instrumental introduction in Santiago Sr.'s earlier version of "Margarita" stays close to the primary melody of the subsequent verse (Ex. 5.1), Saldívar's recording instead uses a contrasting, improvisatory-sounding melodic passage to introduce the classic material (Ex. 5.2). In this way, Saldívar marks the recording as his own from the very beginning. He thus signifies a new interpretation of the traditional tune, rather than a mere cover of the well-known version. This practice is particularly interesting when compared with Saldívar's recording of "Rueda de Fuego," in which Saldívar's instrumental introduction does use the primary melody of the verse and remains closely in line with Cash's original recording. Saldívar claims his recording of the Anglo-American song as his own by using a conjunto style (instrumentation and structure) in conjunction with similar stylistic traits to the original. However, in the traditional conjunto tune, Saldívar instead brings in his own elements by varying the original—since his particular form of instrumentation/structure does not designate the recording as his own within the Texas-Mexican genre.

In addition, while Santiago Sr.'s instrumental introduction includes a few instances of ornamentation and syncopation in the accordion line (a quick turn figure at m. 9 and again at m. 20, a so-called Scotch snap—a short-long rhythm rather than the expected long-short—at m. 10, syncopation and a grace note at m. 14, and additional syncopation at m. 24, all indicated in the transcription below), Saldívar's introduction expands these practices substantially. Saldívar's version provides turn figures starting with the pick-up pattern and continuing in mm. 3, 8, 11, 16, and 23 (indicated in the transcription below). He presents Scotch snaps at mm. 6, 16, and 19. Grace notes appear at mm. 7 and 16. Series of syncopated accents come in at mm. 9, 14, and 19, invoking a harmonica-like effect, particularly as combined with "double-stops" in thirds. Thus, in a mere twenty-four measures, the ornamentation/syncopation is almost continuous. As compared to Santiago Sr.'s recording, Saldívar's rendition is flashy, improvisatory, and virtuosic.

The accordion line does not play under the vocals in Santiago Sr.'s recording (as common throughout the historic tradition). However, Saldívar maintains complicated accordion passagework as a countermelody to the vocal melody throughout his version of "La Margarita." This type of instrumental countermelody in contemporary recordings is not unique to Saldívar's style, but does designate the performer as a member of the younger generation and

Example 5.1. Transcription of "Margarita," mm. 1–27: top melodic line of accordion introduction. As performed and recorded by Santiago Jiménez Sr. From *Viva Seguin* (Arhoolie Records CD 7023, 2001).

Example 5.2. Transcription of "La Margarita," mm. 1–24: top melodic line of accordion introduction. As performed and recorded by Mingo Saldívar. From *25 Golden Hits* (Hacienda Records HAC-8132, 2009).

further separates him from the traditional form of the music as exemplified by the works of Santiago Sr. In addition, while Santiago Sr.'s recording of the song is in a historically common key of G major (consistent with the tuning scheme of G-C-F in the three-row button accordions used in conjunto, as well as the G-C/C-F two-row instruments used by older artists like Santiago Sr.), Saldívar's presentation of the song in D major, while not completely unheard of, does place the more recent recording outside of the most typical Texas-Mexican practices. As common to the historic conjunto style, Santiago Sr. does not include drums within his recording, instead allowing the bajo sexto and *tololoche* to provide the rhythmic foundation. In contrast, Saldívar not only includes a drum set, but takes the rhythmic emphasis even further from the traditional conjunto sound by using a rockabilly beat with heavy backbeat and straight sixteenth notes throughout instead of the more traditional polka style consisting of a bass drum on the beat (1 and 3) and snare drum off the beat (2 and 4). In Saldívar's recording, the drums also play off of the accordion figuration, hitting key rhythms together with the accordion in the introduction (and subsequent instrumental interludes) and aligning sixteenth-note passages with accordion runs.

Following the first verse and refrain (A1A2B1B1) sung in the original Spanish (as performed by Santiago Sr.), Saldívar switches to an English rendition of the second verse and refrain (A2A4B1B2) in loose translation. Like other recordings of the song (including not only conjunto versions, but also performances by Tejano, norteño, and even *banda* artists) Saldívar "mixes and matches" the quatrains of the first two verses, including different pairings and different orders from Santiago Sr.'s original. Thus, Saldívar uses the second quatrain of each of Santiago Sr.'s verses (A1A2; A3A4) to create a new second verse (A2A4). Rather than simply repeating the first quatrain of the refrain (B1B1), he also adds a second quatrain to the English version of the refrain (B1B2). While each verse consists of two quatrains, Santiago Sr. provides one additional quatrain (A5) following the final refrain. As with most other recordings, Saldívar does not include this final verse. Saldívar's translation of the second verse (A2A4) doesn't noticeably change the meaning of the original lyrics. However, he does localize the lyrics of the second half of the verse (A4) by switching from "slippers (*chinelas*)" to "cowboy boots" and from a generalized polka dancing ("*para que baile la polka*") to "riding down to San Benito," in the eastern Rio Grande Valley of Texas. Saldívar also modernizes the lyrics slightly. Instead of the male performer buying shoes and a dress for the female protagonist, as in the original version, Saldívar's version tells Margarita to go and get the boots and dress that she already owns, indicating a bit of feminine independence that does not appear in the original.

Keeping in line with Saldívar's insertion of country-western musical characteristics in the conjunto tradition, the change from "slippers" to "cowboy boots" in this verse signifies a country-western consideration. Likewise, Saldívar's English version of the refrain (B1B2) moves the song closer into the country-western genre. In the original Spanish lyrics, the performer is simply sad to see Margarita crying: "*Qué lástima me da / De ver a Margarita / Que llorando está* (What a pity it gives me / To see Margarita / Who is crying)." We have no indication for the cause of Margarita's tears. However, in Saldívar's English translation, we first learn that Margarita "won't tell [the performer] why" she is crying, and later, that she is, in fact, "crying over [the performer]" himself. This subtle switch of lyrics from the conjunto original shifts the song more closely into the Anglo-American genre, where descriptive stories of heartbreak and love lost make up the standard (beyond the love stories and heroic ballads of conjunto).

Comparing the structure of Saldívar's recording to Santiago Sr.'s earlier example further demonstrates the younger artist's alteration of the Texas-Mexican tradition (Tab. 5.2). Both versions retain the traditional structure of a ranchera. However, as in "Rueda de Fuego," Saldívar provides an additional instrumental emphasis from the original. For example, whereas Santiago Sr. moves directly from the first refrain (B1B1) into the second verse (A3A4), Saldívar instead separates the corresponding sections (B1B1 and A2A4) with a twenty-eight-second instrumental interlude. In addition, while Saldívar's recording of the song is about twenty beats per minute slower than Santiago Sr.'s rendition (138 BPM versus 108 BPM), Saldívar further lengthens each verse with instrumental passages following each quatrain (in particular, after the first section of each verse—A1 and the English version of A2).

In this regard, not only does Saldívar present Anglo-American songs with a conjunto style, he performs traditionally Texas-Mexican songs with a country-western flair. As Geoffrey Himes explains, "Even on his arrangements of traditional Mexican tunes, Saldívar injects the plaintive honky-tonk feel of North American country music—in clear contrast to the bluesier feel of conjunto stars such as Esteban Jordan and Flaco Jiménez."[20] In general, Saldívar's mainstream selections tend to maintain more Texas-Mexican musical traits, while the Texas-Mexican songs contain external musical elements (song choice thus serving as one cultural indicator and aesthetic characteristic as another). Saldívar's recordings present a well-balanced combination of cultural manifestation, with musical characteristics evenly balanced between identification with each of the two communities and continuously shifting to maintain that balance depending on the primary genre of song given.

Table 5.2. "Margarita." As performed and recorded by Santiago Jiménez Sr. From *Viva Seguin* (Arhoolie Records CD 7023, 2001). "La Margarita." As performed and recorded by Mingo Saldívar. From 25 *Golden Hits* (Hacienda Records HAC-8132, 2009).

"Margarita" (Structure)					
Santiago Sr.'s Form (Ranchera)	Language (Santiago Sr.)	Length (Santiago Sr.)	Saldívar's Form (Ranchera)	Language (Saldívar)	Length (Saldívar)
Instrumental Introduction		0:00–0:24 (0:24)	Instrumental Introduction		0:00–0:27 (0:27)
A1	Spanish	0:24–0:37 (0:13)	A1	Spanish	0:27–0:47 (0:20)
A2	Spanish	0:37–0:50 (0:13)	A2	Spanish	0:47–1:02 (0:15)
B1	Spanish	0:50–0:57 (0:07)	B1	Spanish	1:02–1:12 (0:10)
B1	Spanish	0:57–1:07 (0:10)	B1	Spanish	1:12–1:20 (0:08)
			Instrumental Interlude		1:20–1:48 (0:28)
A3	Spanish	1:07–1:20 (0:13)	A2	English	1:48–2:09 (0:21)
A4	Spanish	1:20–1:32 (0:12)	A4	English	2:09–2:24 (0:15)
B1	Spanish	1:32–1:39 (0:07)	B1	English	2:24–2:34 (0:10)
B1	Spanish	1:39–1:49 (0:10)	B2	English	2:34–2:42 (0:08)
A5	Spanish	1:49–2:00 (0:11)			
Instrumental Ending		2:00–2:33 (0:33)	Instrumental Ending		2:42–3:04 (0:22)

That being said, "La Margarita" cannot be designated strictly within the conjunto genre. Beyond Santiago Sr.'s early conjunto recording, one of the most prominent versions of the song is a recording by Little Joe y La Familia generally described (along with the artist) as belonging to a Tejano classification. Appearing (among elsewhere) on *Tu Amigo*, released by Columbia Records in 1990, Little Joe's version of the classic song conforms closely to the language and organization of Santiago Sr.'s example, maintaining the original Spanish lyrics throughout, but later also presenting a bilingual version using Saldívar's English lyrics (on *Nuestra Tradición* in 2007, for example). However, in accordance with the more commercialized generic expectations of Tejano, Little Joe's rendition pushes the song even further into a country-western sound, using a prominent pedal steel guitar, for example. In general, Little Joe has received more mainstream recognition than Saldívar (eight Grammy nominations, including four wins; as compared to two nominations for Saldívar, for example). In this regard, the Tejano musician's interpretation of the same song, with similar—if not further—methods of hybridization, has participated more fully in a popular consciousness than Saldívar's performance. And yet, the processes of hybridization in the two renditions, while related, are not equivalent. Beyond the cultural heritage of the song, the preserved Spanish language (along with descriptive lyrics), and the structure of a ranchera, Little Joe's recording can function relatively neatly within a popular or country-western understanding (the mainstream record label for the Tejano rendition further adding to this consideration).

One surface-level (but important) distinction is that of instrumentation; while the Tejano performance employs a more rock-oriented ensemble of guitar, bass, drum, and horns (derived, in part, from the *orquesta tejana* tradition), Saldívar maintains the button accordion and bajo sexto, creating a distinctive sonic connection to the older conjunto style—and thus, an explicit means for aesthetic interpretation according to a classist and/or primordial characterization. For example, among the Texas-Mexican community, conjunto has historically remained correlated to a working-class constituency. As such, the music continues to be criticized as low-class, "cantina music," with the particular sonic combination of accordion and bajo sexto serving as a signifying element. Furthermore, outside of the stereotypical cultural community, the idiosyncratic sound of accordion with bajo sexto serves as an exotic—and thus precariously primitivist—representation of the music and associated community. Saldívar embraces both sides of his Texas-Mexican heritage in relatively equal balance, here utilizing the structure, Spanish language, repertory, and instrumentation of conjunto in combination with the English language and musical elements of country-western (and elsewhere exchanging a popular repertory for certain conjunto musical traits). The resulting hybridization represents a bicultural identification for a relatively narrow population who accepts the continuing lower-class association of conjunto but also identifies with popular influences. However, the relatively limited recognition for Saldívar's music among the regional community ostensibly speaks to a classist implication, with traditional fans of conjunto turned off by the popular hybridity and middle-class audiences who remain attracted to the more hybridized elements of Tejano, for example, dissuaded by working-class associations of the accordion. At the same time, the indifference for Saldívar's music among the mainstream population suggests an interpretation of conjunto—as characterized by the unique instrumentation and Spanish language, regardless of any actual knowledge of the cultural tradition—as "other" to a popular sense of aesthetic value.

Meanwhile, Little Joe's version of the "La Margarita," maintaining the Spanish language of Santiago Sr.'s original but otherwise recognizable within a popular sonic structure, speaks to a broader audience who can disconnect the music from its class-based and/or primitivist roots. And yet, the Tejano rendition of the song, while still producing certain elements of hybridity, leans away from its conjunto heritage in favor of a more mainstream sound. As such, it dilutes the distinctive representation of the sociocultural community, producing, as Holton defines, a cultural convergence—the "homogenization thesis"—rather than a true hybridization.[21] If the musical genre is then shifted to a corresponding thesis of identity, this interpretation implies a similar convergence of culturally-specific characteristics for much of the Texas-Mexican population. In comparison to Tejano artists like Little Joe, Saldívar does not achieve the same degree of recognition among either a local or a U.S. American fanbase. Yet he maintains the music on his own terms, using processes of globalization to hybridize conjunto and assert an individual manifestation of his own sense of bicultural identity. That being said, while Little Joe is able to receive consideration outside of strictly primitivist interpretations of Texas-Mexican culture, Saldívar, in maintaining more distinctive elements of the traditional musical style, limits himself to homologous notions of conjunto as representative of the regional community. While the Tejano musician's sociocultural identification according to the Texas-Mexican heritage upholds a certain separation from mainstream practices, his relative correspondence to a popular sound allows for his aesthetic consideration outside of strictly regional circumstances. At the same time, even with similar elements, Saldívar is constricted to a stereotypical classification of "conjunto." That being said, neither artist—maintaining the Spanish language, certain Texas-Mexican musical traits, and a stereotypical

Texas-Mexican identity (in heritage and location)—is able to fully break into a mainstream consideration. Despite various country-western (and other) elements, Little Joe remains confined to "Tejano" just as Saldívar is restricted to "conjunto"; for our purposes, merely two sides of the same coin.

Further complicating analysis of this particular manifestation of conjunto, "La Margarita" has also been recorded in a prominent norteño version by Mexican singer and film star Antonio Aguilar, as well as in an additional country-inflected rendition by the Country Roland Band (a South Texas group that consistently blended country with conjunto/norteño). This consideration helps to demonstrate the inherently arbitrary—and restrictively identity-based—nature of genre. The same song, even with similarly hybridized musical traits, is here considered according to a variety of systems of classification. A "norteño" artist (that is, an ethnically Mexican musician emanating from or residing within Mexico) plays norteño music; a "country" artist (most typically, an Anglo-American musician emanating from the southern United States—but not the border with Mexico) plays country; a "conjunto" artist (ethnically Mexican but emanating from or residing within Texas) plays conjunto music, and so on, regardless of song choice or elements of music employed. In this way, as much as Saldívar might like to be characterized according to a country-western sensibility (or at least a bicultural consideration that nonetheless achieves a commercialized prominence), his perceived sociocultural identity limits him to a (precariously primordial) classification according to traditional notions of conjunto; a Texas-Mexican identity thus locked into a stereotypically Texas-Mexican form of music. Meanwhile, the same song performed by alternatively-identified musicians becomes classified as norteño, banda, Tejano, country, etc. It seems that an artist like Alan Jackson—as observed in his "country" recording of Flaco's "Seguro Que Hell Yes" (Chapter 4)—could perform a country-western version of "La Margarita" (or some such), but Saldívar's rendition, regardless of actual sonic elements, remains stubbornly "conjunto."

"Conjunto music, to me, is like country-western...": The Correspondence of Genre

The subject matter and simple lyrics of "Ring of Fire" work equally well in English and Spanish and are equally at home in the rural, storytelling traditions of both conjunto and country-western music. In fact, many of the marked characteristics of country music (such as three basic chords, a relatively simple instrumentation supporting a predominant vocal part with a clear and memorable melody, straightforward structure, and common indicators of authenticity such as the rural setting, family values, relative accessibility of artists, and frequent live performances) also define the conjunto tradition. In that regard, perhaps conjunto can be considered in parallel with country-western; a different manifestation of a similar cultural impetus. Saldívar's use of country within conjunto is then a different form of hybridization than the mixture of two separate genres, such as conjunto and jazz. Saldívar notes the lyrical relationship between conjunto and country-western: "Conjunto music, to me, is like country-western. It's— stories. It's songs about love, trains, trucks, and beer joints and beer drinking, and hardships and happiness, also. But it's something that happens—it'll relate to me or you, or someone else, but it'll relate."[22] In discussing experiences listening to country music as he traveled the United States with his family as a child, Saldívar describes country songs as English-language corridos. He explains: "It's very similar. . . . It's about everyday life."[23] Furthermore, popular country musicians like Gene Autry demonstrate a historic correspondence between country-western and regional Mexican music, as popular recordings take palpable influence—stylistically and linguistically—from Mexican guitar genres. As such, the relationship between country and conjunto is older and perhaps more interconnected than typically considered, with country-western music as a genre—at least within Texas—fundamentally derived from Mexican styles (acknowledging, however, that Texas-Mexican is not—in fact—Mexican, despite a similar reliance on and connection between conjunto and Mexican genres like norteño).

In his work with Ry Cooder, Dwight Yoakam, the Texas Tornados, and others, Flaco also pursues many of the country-conjunto intersections seen in the recordings of Saldívar. In a 1973 interview with Chris Strachwitz, Flaco notes that conjunto and country-western are "almost the same" kind of music.[24] As Strachwitz expands, "They're love songs about women done you bad or something like that?" to which Flaco replies, "Yeah. The I'm going to die drinking, and all that."[25] Flaco continues, "It's just like country music. We have some truck-driving songs or sad songs like [*singing*] 'Your cheating heart,' but still we go more for happiness, to keep people dancing and having a good time. So if there's a sad song, we make it a happy song."[26] This alteration of sad to happy lyrics can be demonstrated in the slightly different interpretation of the indicated situation from the English original in Saldívar's Spanish translation of "Ring of Fire" discussed above, while "Margarita" instead maintains a "sad" correspondence to typical country-western subject matter.

While conjunto itself maintains certain similarities to country-western music, Saldívar's performances among a mainstream population also exaggerate the relationship between the two genres for a widespread audience that experiences conjunto primarily (if not entirely) through non-traditional artists like Saldívar (and Flaco). For example, the *Washington Post*, publicizing a 2004 performance by Saldívar at the Kennedy Center, describes conjunto as "a country-like genre with Mexican American roots." Writing for *Billboard*, Ramiro Burr continues, "Like country music, conjunto's timeless themes of love found, solitude, and redemption speak volumes."[27] And furthermore, "In dozens of dance halls and park pavilions across the American Southwest, couples sashay across the floor to a rhythm and style not unlike that of country." As such, Saldívar's hybridizations of conjunto with country do not create as disparate a mixture as might otherwise be considered. This is particularly true for the mainstream audience who knows conjunto primarily through such external hybridizations, but also for a local audience who sees both traditions as natural extensions of contemporary Texas-Mexican cultural identity. That being said, as a "conjunto" artist, Saldívar is confined to a generic interpretation outside of country-western considerations, regardless of the close musical connections between the two styles. While conjunto is consistently *compared* to country music, it never becomes an actual interpretation of such. As such, external classifications restrict Texas-Mexican artists—according to preconceived notions of ethnicity, location, class, etc., as well as the idiomatic sound of the accordion with bajo sexto—to a homologous understanding of conjunto (and, to a lesser extent, other regional musics like Tejano) as representative of—and thus restrictive to—local musicians.

Steve Jordan and "My Toot Toot": More Hybridization of Repertory

Jordan's songs combine the Texas-Mexican conjunto tradition with jazz, blues, rock, and zydeco. For example, the artist produced conjunto-inflected versions of "My Toot Toot," originally by zydeco musician Sidney "Rockin' Sidney" Simien, "Georgia on My Mind," written by Hoagy Carmichael and often associated with soul musician Ray Charles, and "Yakety Yak," originally recorded by rhythm and blues group The Coasters, among many others. Like Saldívar's music, Jordan's recordings contain a traditional Texas-Mexican instrumentation, structure, and sound, thus remaining within the conjunto style, yet, beyond the external song choices, showcase fast, sophisticated jazzy runs, rock effects like feedback and synthesizers, unusual chord selections, syncopated rhythms and unexpected metric shifts, and virtuosic improvisations related to bebop.

Although lesser known than "Ring of Fire," the song "My Toot Toot" can serve as an illustrative example of Jordan's transcultural interpretations. The song first appeared on Simien's self-produced album, *My Zydeco Shoes Got the Zydeco Blues*, in 1984. Following regional success for the single, Epic Records (a division of Columbia) picked up the song in 1985 to mainstream success. The recording went on to win a Grammy Award in 1986 for Best Ethnic or Traditional Folk Recording. Multiple covers of this song by various artists—each representing a different generic circumstance—display a similar fluidity of categorization as seen in Saldívar's works; the classification of a particular song according to its genre seems less a manifestation of the song itself (or the musical elements included therein), and more an interpretation of identity.

Jordan's version of "My Toot Toot" appears on an album of the same name, released by RCA International in 1985. Jordan presents a mixture of Simien's original English lyrics and a loose Spanish translation. Overall, lyrics in the refrain (B) of "Don't mess with my toot toot" remain in English, while the third line of each refrain ("Now you can have the other woman") is sung in Spanish ("*Puedes hablar con la que queras,*" literally, "You can speak with whomever you want"). In Jordan's version, the verses (A1) are also presented in Spanish. However, while Simien's original presents two different verses (A1 and A2), followed by a reiteration of the first (A1), Jordan maintains the single set of lyrics throughout (A1). Simien's original also provides a lyrical alteration in the refrain of the middle section (B2), while Jordan retains the same refrain throughout. In general, Jordan's lyrics retain the meaning of the original, regardless of language.

The structure of Jordan's version corresponds identically to the original, with an instrumental introduction, refrain-verse-refrain (B1A1B1), instrumental interlude (presenting the music of an additional verse and refrain), refrain-verse-refrain (B1A1B1), a second instrumental section, final refrain-verse-refrain (B1A1B1), and a final instrumental ending (Tab. 5.3). While this structure does not vary from the zydeco original, it can be interpreted (loosely, perhaps) as a Texas-Mexican ranchera, further connecting Jordan's musical interpretation to both the African-American and Mexican-American cultures in the southern United States. Jordan performs the song at approximately the same tempo as the original (86 and 84 BPM, respectively), indicating that the similar lengths for corresponding sections demonstrate similar musical material between the two versions. The only alteration in length appears with a slightly longer instrumental ending in Jordan's rendition of the song.

Like the original, Jordan's version alternates between simple tonic and dominant chords throughout. Like Saldívar's version of "Ring of Fire," Jordan presents a syncopated accordion line under the vocal part throughout, as well as intermittent chromaticism. While these musical characteristics connect the rendition more closely to a popular performing tradition than a traditional conjunto sound, Jordan does not pursue many of the more innovative traits of jazz runs and electronic rock effects seen in some of his other recordings. Instead, the song choice itself marks the performance as outside of the conventional conjunto tradition (while the Spanish language marks what is ostensibly simply a cover song as external to the zydeco—or even more mainstream popular—tradition). As in the case of Saldívar, the performance seems to create an intentional mixture of cultural characteristics, with the African-American choice of song combined with a blatant conjunto structure and instrumentation to draw attention to the hybridization more than a subtle mixture of musical characteristics (especially relatively general traits like thematic material, structure, chord progressions, and syncopation/chromaticism) might achieve.

That being said, while Saldívar's version of "Ring of Fire" is translated into a clear conjunto structure through the alteration from binary form to a ranchera, Jordan's version of "My Toot Toot" stays closer in style to the original. In addition to a structural form that corresponds closely to a ranchera, Simien's instrumentation (lead guitar, keyboard accordion, rhythm guitar, harmonica, bass, and drums—all played by Simien himself) doesn't require much alteration to take the form of a traditional conjunto ensemble. The only real change Jordan makes to the song (itself only minimally mainstream, particularly when compared to the popularity of "Ring of Fire") is the Spanish language translation and a switch from keyboard to button accordion. In this regard, while Saldívar's rendition of "Ring of Fire" demonstrates a balanced and seemingly intentional hybridity between the Anglo- and Mexican-American traditions, Jordan's recording seems to serve instead as a wistful entry into an African-American cultural understanding. Saldívar and Jordan both maintain elements of bicultural representation. However, Jordan's interpretation is tilted more toward African-American sensibilities (through mere maintenance of the original) than Saldívar's more culturally balanced approach. Jordan does perform the song as conjunto, but—unlike Saldívar—he does not go out of his way to insert his cultural heritage in the preexisting tune.

Table 5.3. “My Toot Toot.” As performed and recorded by Rockin’ Sidney. From *My Toot Toot* (Maison De Soul 1009, 1991). “My Toot Toot.” As performed and recorded by Steve Jordan. From *My Toot Toot* (RCA International IL6-7412, 1985).

“My Toot Toot” (Structure)					
Simien’s Form (Ternary)	Language (Simien)	Length (Simien)	Jordan’s Form (Ranchera-ish)	Language (Jordan)	Length (Jordan)
Instrumental Introduction		0:00–0:22 (0:22)	Instrumental Introduction		0:00–0:22 (0:22)
B1	English	0:22–0:33 (0:11)	B1	English/Spanish	0:22–0:33 (0:11)
A1	English	0:33–0:56 (0:23)	A1	Spanish	0:33–0:55 (0:22)
B1	English	0:56–1:08 (0:12)	B1	English/Spanish	0:55–1:07 (0:12)
Instrumental Interlude		1:08–1:31 (0:23)	Instrumental Interlude		1:07–1:28 (0:21)
B1	English	1:31–1:42 (0:11)	B1	English/Spanish	1:28–1:39 (0:11)
A2	English	1:42–2:06 (0:24)	A1	Spanish	1:39–2:02 (0:23)
B2	English	2:06–2:17 (0:11)	B1	English/Spanish	2:02–2:13 (0:11)
Instrumental Interlude		2:17–2:40 (0:23)	Instrumental Interlude		2:13–2:36 (0:23)
B1	English	2:40–2:51 (0:11)	B1	English/Spanish	2:36–2:47 (0:11)
A1	English	2:51–3:14 (0:23)	A1	Spanish	2:47–3:09 (0:22)
B1	English	3:14–3:25 (0:11)	B1	English/Spanish	3:09–3:20 (0:11)
Instrumental Ending		3:25–3:45 (0:22)	Instrumental Ending		3:20–3:48 (0:28)

Steve Jordan and "Grítenme Piedras Del Campo": Further Hybridization of Sonic Elements

While Jordan's renditions of African-American tunes maintain some stylistic correspondence to more traditional conjunto characteristics, his versions of classic Texas-Mexican repertory—such as "Grítenme Piedras Del Campo," appearing (among elsewhere) on *La Bamba*, released by RyN Music in 2017, written by Mexican singer-songwriter Cuco Sánchez, and recorded by various regional artists (Tony De La Rosa, Flaco, Los Dos Gilbertos, Ruben Vela, and more)—showcase additional external traits. For example, when compared to Flaco's rendition of the song, included on the 1986 Grammy-Award-winning album *Ay Te Dejo En San Antonio* (Arhoolie Records), Jordan's performance inserts unexpected rhythmic emphases and shifts in meter, flashy and jazz-inflected figuration, chromatic passages, grating dissonances, and vocal bends.

That being said, this song—as with many adopted by conjunto artists over time—did not originate in Texas. In this regard, the assumption of a Mexican ranchera by conjunto musicians suggests analogies with Saldívar's adoption of "Ring of Fire," Jordan's embrace of "My Toot Toot," and other such hybridizations of repertory. Yet, among the hegemonic ("white") population, the common ethnic heritage for Mexican and Texas-Mexican musicians represents a shared community; the use of Mexican songs by Texas-Mexican artists is accepted/expected, or at least not surprising. Furthermore, just as U.S. American popular musicians have taken bits of the conjunto sound as their own, Texas-based conjunto musicians treat Mexican repertory as a musical buffet. They use Mexican songs as their own, while simultaneously barring entry for Mexican musicians to participate in competitive performance spaces in the United States. The differences in interpretation for these appropriative methods emphasize systems of power between Texas, Mexico, and the United States. The mainstream misinterpretation of the Texas-Mexican community helps to explain the novelty among a popular audience for Saldívar's and Jordan's song choices. Historical hybridizations that comprise the fundamental musical characteristics of conjunto—accordion with bajo sexto, polka with certain Mexican rhythms, and the adoption of Mexican songs—are frequently disregarded in modern depictions of the types of blends seen in the works of Flaco, Saldívar, and Jordan in favor of more unexpected mixtures of cross-cultural identity. However, Texas-Mexican conjunto has always been a hybridized genre.

Hybridization then forms a necessary component of the conjunto genre; a defining factor that establishes a continuing requisite for any contemporary manifestation of the music. In that regard, song choice participates in Néstor García Canclini's "cycle of hybridization," despite a reluctance to consider Mexican elements as external to Texas-Mexican practices. As such, contemporary processes of globalization may travel further—both stylistically and geographically—than preceding circumstances, but the blend of cultural correlations seen in the works considered here is in fact nothing new. What is novel—at least among a popular audience—is the blend of aesthetic characteristics outside of accepted cultural relationships. The incorporation of Mexican characteristics is not remarkable—or perhaps even noticed; there seems to be little distinction made among the hegemonic community between different groups of ethnic Mexicans (or Latinas/os in general, for that matter). Yet, the adoption of stereotypically Anglo- or African-American traits by Mexican-American artists becomes somehow a noteworthy event.

On the surface, Jordan's instrumental passages in "Grítenme Piedras Del Campo" don't stray particularly far from Flaco's example (yet both artists represent a hybridized interpretation of older conjunto practices, and these older practices similarly represent a hybridized repertory of Mexican songs). The instrumental introductions in both convey a similar melody, neither of which is a mere preview of the melody in the subsequent verse (as in Santiago Sr.'s recording of "Margarita," examined above). However, while Flaco's figurations stay nicely in the key of C major (also a common key in traditional conjunto practices), Jordan's patterns drift from his diatonic center of E-flat major (a strange choice in itself for an instrument most typically tuned in G-C-F) to provide chromaticism and dissonances relatively rare for conjunto—although not at all out of place in the jazz practices that Jordan emulates.

For example, while relatively interesting rhythmically, mm. 7–9 in Flaco's rendition is simply a scalar descent from dominant (G) to tonic (C) (Ex. 5.3). Likewise, the figures in mm. 9–11 turn around C, followed by an ornamented, descending C scale in mm. 11–13, and the broken chords in mm. 14–16 outline a C-major triad in inversion, leading to broken octaves on C in the last three measures of this passage. In contrast, while Jordan begins his instrumental introduction by emphasizing the tonic (E-flat), he immediately moves to repeated tones on D-flat, a note lying outside of the diatonic tonality (Ex. 5.4). Mm. 6–8 turn around G, the mediant of the key. Mm. 10–12 outline the tonic triad in inversion, presenting an ornamented scalar descent beginning on E-flat and passing through the lower median (G) before finally landing on the dominant (B-flat). The subsequent pattern (mm. 12–15) also comprises a rhythmically interesting scalar descent from E-flat to G, before the final three measures of the section (mm. 17–19) finally outline a full E-flat major scale descending over two octaves. In addition, while Flaco's version of the song includes brief, ornamental moments (a grace note on the first note and turn figure at the beginning of m. 12), Jordan's version brings additional dissonance through constant ornamentation: turn figures in mm. 7–8, grace notes in mm. 9, 10, and 12, and additional turn patterns throughout the scalar figures in mm. 16–18.

Rhythmically, both instrumental introductions provide some interesting syncopations not normally seen in traditional conjunto practices. However, Jordan's version again expands these innovations somewhat beyond Flaco's corresponding pursuits. For example, while Flaco's recording presents a series of Scotch snaps in mm. 2, 5, and 7–8, the remainder of his passage lies primarily on the expected beats. Jordan's rendition provides a similar sequence of short-long patterns in mm. 10 and 14–15, however this second passage not only shifts the rhythmic intent of the pattern, but also the beat structure as the first note of m. 15 (a sixteenth note) is tied into the previous measure and the first sounding tone of the measure thus occurs just after the downbeat. In addition, while both versions of the song present basic polka-like drum patterns (bass on beat 1 and snare on beat 2) with more flashy fills than typical in more traditional recordings, Jordan's version also accents the first few notes of the song with additional drum hits.

In this way, while both artists take influence from outside musical traditions to bring a popular feel to conjunto, Jordan uses ornamentation, chromaticism, syncopation, and rhythmic emphases to align more closely with jazz than rock and roll. Jordan's unexpected harmonic choices throughout the recording further emphasize this relationship to jazz. As Himes similarly illustrates, describing not this particular recording but a live performance (a situation where Jordan's virtuosity and level of improvisation really shine) in 1993 in Washington, D.C.: "With his long, black hair flowing over his shoulders and a snakeskin patch over his right eye, the 55-year-old Texan manhandled his red Hohner button accordion to send notes speeding off in one direction, only to suddenly slam on the brakes and dart down a harmonic detour before jumping back on the musical expressway."[28] Himes continues by noting the "two extra percussionists" that made "the syncopated rhythms that much more infectious" and Jordan's solos of "rippling runs, rapid-fire bleats, emphatic chords, small doses of echoplex and punctuating pauses—always keeping the improvised melodies moving in unexpected directions."[29] Unfortunately, many of these improvisatory, jazz-oriented performances by Jordan have not been captured in recordings.

Example 5.3. Transcription of "Grítenme Piedras Del Campo," mm. 1–19: top melodic line of accordion introduction. As performed and recorded by Flaco Jiménez. From *The Best of Flaco Jiménez* (Arhoolie Records CD 478, 1999).

Example 5.4. Transcription of "Grítenme Piedras Del Campo," mm. 1–19: top melodic line of accordion introduction. As performed and recorded by Steve Jordan. From *La Bamba* (RyN Music, 2017).

The structure of Jordan's version of "Grítenme Piedras Del Campo" is almost identical to Flaco's example (although itself already a hybridized rendition of the earlier conjunto tradition). Both recordings are presented as rancheras, with an instrumental introduction, verse, and refrain (A1A2B), instrumental interlude, additional verse, and refrain (A3A4B), and instrumental ending (Tab. 5.4). Jordan skips the final quatrain of the second verse (A4) and instead provides an expanded instrumental conclusion; Flaco's version includes only a brief, four-second tag ending at the end of the final refrain. In addition to Flaco's faster tempo for the song (120 BPM versus 110 BPM for Jordan), the earlier recording lengthens each verse with expanded instrumental passages following each line of text. In this regard, while Jordan also provides ornamental figures throughout the recording, Jordan's primary method of hybridization seems to come from an expanded harmonic emphasis (instead of Flaco's accordion figuration). As Don Snowden notes, Jordan's "instrumental style didn't rely strictly on fast, fluid solos and fills. A tart tone, unusual chord selections and unexpected rhythmic shifts were the other components that created a constantly unpredictable sound."[30] As Jordan himself describes, "I play the jazz accordion."[31]

Texas-Mexican conjunto music is, by definition, a hybridized genre, consisting from its inception of European structures (and accordion) with Mexican rhythms and repertory (and bajo sexto). Flaco characteristically extends the conjunto tradition through distinctive hybridizations with mainstream U.S. American culture; however, a comparison of these two performances of "Grítenme Piedras Del Campo" (itself a Mexican song already adopted by older Texas-Mexican musicians) demonstrates that Jordan pushes the transculturalism of the genre further outside of this ethnic purview (and further than the inherent transculturalism of the older tradition). Flaco himself explains: "Steve plays a lot of jazz and rock and roll, which I can do, but his style is more progressive and precise . . . in spite of my knowledge of jazz and rock and roll . . . I am more *rancheron* (rural) and he is more urban."[32] As exhibited through the stereotypically Anglo-American hybridizations of Saldívar, Jordan offers a balanced hybridization between supposed African-American and Texas-Mexican styles, using more conjunto characteristics in jazz, blues, rock, and zydeco songs and more external musical traits in established conjunto selections. The hybridization seems intentional; a means to insert both associations regardless of genre (or actual origin) of song choice.

Drawing from Georgina Born and David Hesmondhalgh, Kirsten Yri argues that musical hybridizations frequently instigate a primitivist discourse, since "the music industry encourages and rewards musicians for staying true to their indigenous styles, whereas collaborations and hybrids have

Table 5.4. "Grítenme Piedras Del Campo." As performed and recorded by Flaco Jiménez. From *The Best of Flaco Jiménez* (Arhoolie Records CD 478, 1999). "Grítenme Piedras Del Campo." As performed and recorded by Steve Jordan. From *La Bamba* (RyN Music, 2017).

"Grítenme Piedras Del Campo" (Structure)					
Flaco's Form (Ranchera)	Language (Flaco)	Length (Flaco)	Jordan's Form (Ranchera)	Language (Jordan)	Length (Jordan)
Instrumental Introduction		0:00-0:19 (0:19)	Instrumental Introduction		0:00-0:19 (0:19)
A1	Spanish	0:19-0:51 (0:32)	A1	Spanish	0:19-0:46 (0:27)
A2	Spanish	0:51-1:21 (0:30)	A2	Spanish	0:46-1:11 (0:25)
B	Spanish	1:21-1:42 (0:21)	B	Spanish	1:11-1:34 (0:23)
Instrumental Interlude		1:42-1:59 (0:17)	Instrumental Interlude		1:34-1:56 (0:22)
A3	Spanish	1:59-2:30 (0:31)	A3	Spanish	1:56-2:21 (0:25)
A4	Spanish	2:30-3:04 (0:34)			
B	Spanish	3:04-3:28 (0:24)	B	Spanish	2:21-2:44 (0:23)
			Instrumental Ending		2:44-3:04 (0:20)

historically been viewed with suspicion."[33] For modern conjunto artists, the oral nature of the tradition, simple, diatonic melodies dictated by the harmonic limitations of the button accordion, and the straightforward, folk-like polka rhythms can stimulate primitivistic associations, particularly for external listeners. While the traditional regional community retains the historically standardized characteristics of Texas-Mexican conjunto and frequently dissuades further hybridization of the style, particularly through inclusion of the hegemonic culture that the music was originally created in response to, and certainly due in part to fear of losing the musical heritage that forms an important piece of cultural identity in the region, mainstream audiences also discourage hybridization of the style by presenting performances by more traditional artists as an epitome of Mexican-American culture in the United States. At the same time, Jordan signifies his own sense of "otherness" within both the local community and mainstream culture by using creative forms designating other marginalized populations, like blues, jazz, and soul, within the traditional style.

As Marco Cervantes has argued, Jordan's incorporation of African-American musical forms like blues, jazz, and soul in conjunto effectively inserts Blackness as a component of Texas-Mexican culture.[34] However, Saldívar's analogous use of Anglo-American forms like rockabilly and country challenges this notion, particularly given conjunto's traditional role counter to Anglo-American society. In considering conjunto as historically representative of the working-class Texas-Mexican community, the incorporation of external characteristics shifts the symbolic affect of the traditional genre. While Jordan's methodology suggests a sociocultural resemblance between the two communities—a similarity of background combining disparate characteristics in a common goal, Saldívar's approach is more problematic. However, relationships between different ethnic communities in Texas have changed since the conjunto genre first came about. If Jordan inserts Blackness into the Texas-Mexican experience, forging cultural connections through a certain commonality of marginalization, perhaps Saldívar does insert whiteness, albeit a whiteness that relates not to the mainstream, hegemonic culture of the early twentieth century, but to a poor, white rurality associated with the mid-century country-western music that Saldívar uses in his work.

"Super Fly" vs. *Ranchera*: The Generic Signification of Clothing

Beyond clear differences in musical style and reception between Saldívar and Jordan, distinction between the two artists can be demonstrated by comparing the clothing choices of the musicians. For example, at the Tejano Conjunto Festival in 2009, Jordan wore "a shiny gold shirt with puffy sleeves, a purple vest, purple bell-bottoms, black boots and his iconic black eye patch."[35] This choice of fashion is common throughout Jordan's performances and mediated images. The cover of *My Toot Toot* (1985) showcases Jordan in a brightly colored, button-down shirt with large, tropical flowers. He wears a chunky turquoise necklace with dangling anchor pendant, oversized rings on four fingers, a gold watch, felt hat, and the ubiquitous eye patch. Lights flash against the backdrop. Analyzing this same image on the cover of *Soy de Tejas* (1979), Cervantes asserts that these lights illustrate "the flash and shine of city life," while the artist's "confident yet slanted pose along with his style of clothing implies separation from strict boundaries."[36] Cervantes discusses the similarities between Jordan's clothing choices of "flashy suits, hats, and boots" and stylistic decisions made by youth of color throughout the Jim Crow and zoot suit eras, noting that "Jordan's extravagant apparel allows him to confront and transcend his marginalized position in the US social structure and demonstrates the ongoing cultural merging between black and Chicana/o subjects in the United States."[37] In this way, Jordan uses not only his music but also his clothing to demonstrate his simultaneous cultural identification with both African-American and Texas-Mexican (albeit in a mid-century, California-inspired *pachuco* sensibility) communities.

Alternatively, while Jordan takes influence from the early twentieth-century zoot suit and what Todd Boyd describes as "Super Fly" African-American styles from the 1970s (both urban trends),[38] Saldívar dresses in a style that simultaneously invokes the country-western tradition in the United States as well as what Cervantes describes as a *ranchera* aesthetic (comprising "cowboy hats, boots, and belt buckles") indicative of rural, working-class Texas-Mexican culture.[39] For example, for a 2004 concert entitled "Masters of Mexican Music" on the University of Maryland campus, Saldívar and his entire band channeled Johnny Cash by dressing all in black.[40] More typically, Saldívar dresses in Western-style shirts, a small black cowboy hat, and cowboy boots. For example, the cover image of *25 Golden Hits* (2009) presents the musician in a brightly colored, Western button-down (with vertical stripes and snaps instead of buttons) and black cowboy hat. The shirt is left open across the chest, with a gold necklace underneath and additional gold rings on at least two fingers. If we agree with Cervantes's assertion that Jordan's gaze away from the camera (and external style of clothing) indicates a self-imposed separation from strict cultural boundaries, Saldívar's direct, forward-facing pose (and Texas-Mexican *ranchera* style of dress) seemingly indicates a closer correspondence with the traditional ethnic community. The close connection between a *ranchera* and country-western style of dress further demonstrates the consideration of conjunto as closely related to country music, indicating an alternative form of hybridity than displayed in two completely separated styles. Nonetheless, this stylistic correspondence helps to showcase Saldívar's simultaneous identification with Texas-Mexican and Anglo-American (or at least Anglo-Texan) communities.

Analysis: Identities of Hybridization

Saldívar and Jordan both mix music from historically male, working-class traditions, and from regions corresponding to their own geographic experiences (Texas and California, respectively). The representative anomaly in each case is simply one of ethnicity. Beginning with the so-called "race records" in the first half of the twentieth century, popular music in the United States has been marketed as "belonging" to a particular ethnic community. While both artists relate to both sides of their hybridizations, the differences in ethnic origin between the genres mark the resultant creative products as cultural amalgamations in a way not noted in the adoption of products from common ethnic heritages (but contrasting classes or locations) like the cumbia—a Colombian folk genre now frequently incorporated within the conjunto tradition. A distinction comes with Saldívar's hybridization of Mexican- and Anglo-American cultures, suggesting a system of colonialization, a merging of the artist's Texas-Mexican heritage with the oppression experienced by the ethnic community in the early years of the twentieth century (when and by which the conjunto tradition came about). In contrast, Jordan's hybridizations of Mexican- and African-American musical cultures produce a combination of ostensibly similar populations. For a general audience, these ethnicities can signify representative cultures: "white" music indicates cultural hegemony, while "Black" music denotes cultural resistance, a simplistic interpretation at best.

Saldívar's use of Anglo-American tunes does not give him any cultural cachet among a mainstream audience, as the music he chooses to employ represents a rural working class not far removed from his own cultural experiences. Similarly, Jordan's use of African-American forms like zydeco—in addition to better-known genres like jazz and funk—draws connections between his (and his community's) socioeconomic struggles and those of other marginalized populations. In addition, while conjunto pioneers created the Texas-Mexican form as a counter-ideological response to the political, economic, and cultural hegemony of the Anglo-American community, as well as the middle-class, upward-aspiring, and increasingly "Americanized"

Texas Mexicans, Saldívar and Jordan created their hybridized conjunto forms during the early years of the Chicano Movement. As such, Saldívar and Jordan came of age in a much different sociocultural atmosphere than their predecessors. While early conjunto artists created a consolidated musical form to strengthen their communal sense of identity against the mainstream culture, artists after the Chicano Movement reclaimed power for the cultural community by incorporating mainstream musics outside of their perceived social heritage within the historic ethnic tradition.

However, these practices still create a complicated dichotomy between artists like Jordan who use stylistic characteristics emanating from marginalized communities and artists like Saldívar who use more highly valued stimuli to derive power from U.S. American hegemonies. Jordan uses African-American influences to challenge systems of power. In turn, he emphasizes his own sense of "otherness" within both Texas-Mexican and U.S. American communities. Meanwhile, Saldívar has achieved popularity through a comfortable sense of exoticism from the mainstream community. By combining "safe," Anglo-American genres like country and rockabilly with distinctive, but still relatable, techniques of Texas-Mexican conjunto, Saldívar achieves an accessible blend of characteristics, allowing the mainstream community to exploit the artist's stereotypically primitivistic tendencies as a self-assured representation of multi-ethnic accomplishment.

So, at the same time that Jordan—combining Mexican-American and African-American characteristics—struggled to sell records, attract audiences, or even pay his rent, Saldívar—by instead combining Mexican-American with Anglo-American traits—was paraded around by the government of the United States through prestigious political events, large performances in culturally elite venues, and as a cultural ambassador in the Middle East and Africa with the United States Information Agency's cultural exchange program. This distinction between the successes of Jordan and Saldívar is equivocal, since, although Jordan was respected as an innovative and incredibly virtuosic musician among elite cultural critics and the local community of musicians, he also spent much of his career mired in drugs and alcohol, playing jazz on the accordion that much of the regional community was not interested in hearing, expressing bitterness that he had not achieved broader successes, and simultaneously refusing to conform to notions of reliability or industry standards. Nonetheless, there is certainly a difference between the artists' respective receptions among the mainstream community and it doesn't seem too far a stretch to attribute at least some of this difference to the particular cultural fusions that each musician chose to exploit. At the same time, the Mexican music at the heart of each of these hybrid impulses remains unacknowledged; lacking in compensation and opportunity as compared to the Texas-based artists who use it to create power for themselves against analogous systems of appropriation. In this regard, hegemonic structures twist and replicate themselves in complicated practices across space and time.

Conclusions: A Continuum of Genre/Identity

Within the Texas-Mexican conjunto tradition, it is very common for musicians to record songs originally written and recorded by other musicians, including other local artists, but also norteño stars, Mexican crooners, and popular musicians like Buck Owens and Johnny Cash. Conjunto artists establish themselves through common songs and expected stylistic characteristics as part of the musical community. New repertory usually makes up only a portion of each musician's output, and successful new numbers are quickly absorbed into the tradition through additional recordings by other regional artists. Songs are not typically considered "owned" by one particular musician, significantly contributing to the contemporary folkloric understanding of the musical genre. Within this context, it is not particularly surprising to see artists like Saldívar and Jordan recording songs originally written by other musicians. What is surprising—at least among a hegemonic audience that doesn't typically recognize Mexican repertory as distinct from Texas-Mexican—is the choice of songs emanating from relatively far outside the sociocultural tradition.

Although the definition of a particular musical genre has historically served to connect a certain audience to stereotypical aesthetic traits (see Frith 1996, for example), Saldívar's and Jordan's music remains marketed either to the original regional constituency or to well-educated, "world-music" patrons (see Chapter 8), rather than broader populations otherwise attracted to the country, rock, jazz, and/or zydeco traits actually included within the music. As such, these artists are locked into homologous understandings of sociocultural identification; no matter what type of music they play, or how it combines to form new conceptions of conjunto, these musicians remain classified according to familial heritage. That being said, the inclusion of accordion throughout these musical representations also seems to designate the fundamental generic characterization of conjunto. For example, despite similar types of cultural hybridity and corresponding social identification (but typically lacking the accordion), musicians like Little Joe remain classified as Tejano artists (in an equally homologous but perhaps slightly less primitivist construction). Meanwhile, Mexican norteño artists maintain the accordion (and many of the same stylistic innovations) as artists like Saldívar and Jordan but, lacking a corresponding admittance of identity among a Texas-Mexican ethno-nationalist sensibility, as noted by Jose E. Limón, fail to achieve recognition within a regional understanding of conjunto.[41] As such, genre becomes an imaginary construct of very specific and seemingly superficial musical characteristics (such as instrumentation), together with a superimposition of identity; a simulacrum-like signification that affixes certain aesthetic traits to certain populations in an unsatisfactory nominal designation that ignores actual circumstance.

This combination of preferred characteristics and externally imposed identification then forms a theorized continuum of acceptance across different combinations of music and identity. Artists like Jordan and Saldívar—closely positioned within the ethnicity, language, and location of the "traditional" conjunto community—remain classified as "conjunto" artists despite alternative musical traits and despite efforts to escape this generic designation. Similarly, Flaco avoids this constrained classification only when working in combination with alternatively situated performers. Inter/national artists who stay closely aligned with "traditional" stylistic practices of conjunto—despite sociocultural positions outside of the most typical designations of Texas-Mexican identity—also maintain generic characterizations of conjunto. Yet, opposing genres like Tejano and norteño represent the limits for these nominal borders. Tejano is generally considered separately from conjunto, notwithstanding corresponding sociocultural identities, while norteño also receives separate treatment than conjunto, irrespective of roughly analogous aesthetic characteristics.

Saldívar and Jordan have both spent their careers merging the traditional music of their familial heritages with the mainstream characteristics they experienced traveling with their families for work throughout the United States (and ultimately, simply experiencing popular culture by living in the United States). Yet, in merging Anglo- and African-American creative forms, respectively, with Texas-Mexican conjunto music, they have produced two distinctive structures, both in hybridized soundscape and in sociocultural significance. It is within these differences that we can begin to explore the inherent consequences of globalization, the contemporary symbolism of cultural forms, and the role of locality in systems of hybridization. Music constitutes an important aspect of cultural identity, and audience reactions to hybrid genres contribute valuable insights into not only an individual artist's identification as a member of a particular community, but also into the modern characteristics of the community as a whole.

Furthermore, as strict ethnic silos—at least with regards to Texas-Mexican conjunto music—at the beginning of the twentieth century gave way to the types of hybridizations described above in the second half of the century, contemporary systems of transculturalism have led modern conjunto artists to write their own songs in an external style. Contemporary bands create rock or punk with a conjunto twist, rather than the other way around, using the alternative style itself to represent contemporary cultural identity, rather than just the songs (and intermittent traits). This process indicates further evolution of ethnic identity in modern-day America, demonstrating that race alone (or class, language, gender, location, etc.) cannot account for cultural representation.

CHAPTER 6

"It's jealousy..."

Eva Ybarra and the Hybrid Offerings of Women in Conjunto

> It's not too easy for me. I struggle a lot because there's a lot of envy. They don't want to see a lady being the leader of the band or making arrangements or making songs. They don't like it.
>
> —Eva Ybarra

Despite alterations in participation and hybridization to the historical understanding of conjunto, the musical community remains overwhelmingly male. Ostensibly stemming from its origins in "uncivilized" venues like cantinas, only a handful of women have ever contributed to the musical genre. Even as the music expands to include artists far outside of a conventional Texas-Mexican identity (ethnically, geographically, linguistically, socioeconomically), the primary performers remain male. This chapter will explore the historic male dominance within Texas-Mexican culture and the continuing lack of women within the musical performance space, even in relationship to the inclusion of male performers emanating from far beyond the local population.

Texas-Mexican culture, particularly among the working-class community, has maintained restrictive notions of gender placement; a context that impacts conjunto music and its continuing constraints on female participation. Despite some changes in recent years, especially as conjunto moves into a more middle-class (and less culturally restrictive) sensibility, very few women have found success within the genre. As Avelardo Valdez and Jeffrey Halley describe, "the statuses of men and women [in conjunto] are rooted in the patriarchal structure of the larger society, qualified significantly by conditions of ethnicity."[1] Throughout time, women have participated in conjunto as fans and organizers, but rarely as musicians. Those who do perform within the genre typically do so as singers—a more culturally acceptable role for women than instrumentalist (and particularly than that of accordionist, the usual leader of an ensemble and, according to Valdez and Halley, considered an "archetypical male instrument").[2]

The historic limitations for women in conjunto music stem from a range of sociocultural considerations. In general, the role of musician within Texas-Mexican culture is not seen as compatible with established gender roles for women. While male musicians frequently dedicate considerable time to developing professional identities as musicians (including touring to perform), women are expected to identify—and maintain associated responsibilities—first and foremost as wives and mothers. Any musical pursuits are therefore secondary, limiting possibilities for success within the genre. In addition, as Valdez and Halley note, "The conjunto scene encourages an episodic lifestyle that may include drinking, drugs, and sexual encounters."[3] In addition to the music historically existing within bars and cantinas (venues deemed unacceptable for female participation), the overall musical culture among performers consists of a stereotypical "boys' club" of gendered relationships equally objectionable—and exclusionary—for women. Furthermore, any inclusion of female musicians within this highly gendered culture creates a threat of sexual disruption for both the women—who are criticized for any perception of impropriety—and the men—who jostle with bandmates for attention from these women and argue with wives and girlfriends suspicious of any such attentions. Finally, the leadership role inherent to the position of conjunto accordionist is not generally considered appropriate (or even possible) for women.

For those women who do decide to pursue conjunto music, a number of obstacles reduce their chances for success. Receiving limited support from family members and the local community, women frequently struggle to find instrumental instruction. Training is traditionally achieved through a mentoring relationship with older family members or established musicians, as in Flaco Jiménez's initial relationship with his father and later mentoring of young musicians like Dwayne Verheyden and Steve Jordan's musical instruction with Valerio Longoria—who learned from Narciso Martínez—and later mentoring of his own sons and younger musicians like Juanito Castillo. That being said, in more recent years, local schools and cultural institutions like the Guadalupe Cultural Arts Center in San Antonio have developed more formalized methods of instrumental instruction, thus providing additional opportunities for women to pursue conjunto. However, as Valdez and Halley describe, so influenced by the sociocultural considerations noted above, those additional opportunities remain limited. For example, in 1993, only fourteen percent of students enrolled in the accordion class at the Guadalupe Center (out of eighty total students) were female.[4] Furthermore, women who have achieved success in the conjunto genre often rely on male family members to be bandmembers and managers. As Valdez and Halley note, "even those women who are successful conjunto musicians rely on the patriarchal system for support."[5]

In addition to the actual sociocultural limitations surrounding female participation in the conjunto genre, Deborah Vargas asserts that the lack of prevalent female musicians is due to a prevailing historiography for the genre (i.e., the perception of limited female participation—particularly in the literature provided by scholars like Manuel Peña and Américo Paredes—may not fully represent reality). As Vargas explains, many of the women who have participated in the conjunto genre do not "easily fit within the heteromasculinized narratives of gender and resistance that are the scholarly legacy of canonical Chicano music studies."[6] Furthermore, Vargas argues that those women who have been included in the scholarly literature display what she calls an "exceptional exemption,"[7] that is, women who are so musically talented that the standard narrative must be momentarily altered to allow for their inclusion (and thus implying that women must achieve at an exceptional level—and a level much higher than men—to be considered "worthy" of mention). Vargas also argues that, since female conjunto musicians do not fit within the standard narrative of working-class masculinity as cultural resistance to Anglo-Texan hegemony, they cannot be analyzed according to the same academic structure. Indeed, Vargas asserts, "Merely adding more women to the scene . . . does little to address gender as a system of social structural power."[8] In this way, analyzing female conjunto musicians according to canonical systems does not describe "the complexity of power in borderlands music," since these musicians do not represent the same notions of cultural code, bodily fit, and working-class labor paradigms.[9]

The preceding chapters of this work mention female participation in conjunto music only minimally, in part due to limited female inclusion in the recent globalization of the genre (and particularly when considering the initial impulses of globalization and hybridization). However, an increasing number of women are participating in the traditional genre, both in local, folkloric pursuits and in the types of globalized processes discussed throughout this work. That being said, the subsequent analysis serves only as a preliminary entry into a long-neglected field of inquiry.

Women in Conjunto: Eva Ybarra

Born in 1945, Eva Ybarra is only slightly younger than the three musicians included most prominently throughout this book (Mingo Saldívar, Flaco, and Jordan, born in 1936, 1939, and 1939, respectively). Ybarra is perhaps the most well-known female accordionist in the history of the genre (others of the same generation include Isabel "Chavela" Salaiza and Lupita Rodela, both discussed in slightly more detail in Valdez and Halley, 1996). Born into a musical family in San Antonio, Ybarra somewhat atypically received encouragement from her family to play music. That being said, her mother still pushed her young daughter to play the piano instead of the more masculine accordion. As Ybarra remembers, "My parents were musicians and my brother played the accordion. I played different instruments from when I was very young, but I cared most about the accordion even though my mom would never let me play."[10] Ybarra recalls her mother's (a composer and singer) objections to the stereotypically male instrument: "Women do not have a strong enough back to play an accordion."[11] The artist continues, "I had a hard time when I started out. . . . They thought the accordion was a man's instrument. Now they accept ladies who play the accordion."[12] After teaching herself to play the accordion—and despite her mother's initial objections, Ybarra's father and brothers ultimately encouraged her to perform the instrument in public, taking her to play at local restaurants and bars from the age of six (and continuing to chaperone her performances at such venues through her late twenties). As Ybarra explains, "Women were not supposed to go into the cantinas—there was nobody in there except drunk men. . . . But I liked playing for the *borrachitos*, the drunk men, because they listened to the music and they cheered."[13] As such, through the support of male relatives, Ybarra has been able to participate as a female accordionist in the male-oriented community of conjunto.

However, as Valdez and Halley explain, Ybarra has struggled throughout her career to schedule enough performances to make a living, instead relying on itinerant performances at various local restaurants (following "a long San Antonio tradition of strolling musicians wandering from cantina to cantina looking for customers").[14] In addition, the artist has struggled to keep a band together, blaming conservative (male) musicians who refuse to take orders from a woman. For example, following a successful performance at the Tejano Conjunto Festival in San Antonio in 1991, her entire (all-male) band quit with no explanation. However, as Ybarra asserts, "It's jealousy. . . . They won't accept a woman getting the applause."[15] In subsequent years, ethnically diverse

Figure 6.1. Eva Ybarra plays Texas conjunto accordion in the Coolidge Auditorium, Library of Congress, on September 13, 2017. Photo by Stephen Winick. Public Domain.

band members and a second female singer (Gloria Garcia Abadia) helped to alleviate these issues. Despite local performance difficulties, Ybarra has found some success at a national level, including national performances at public institutions and a National Endowment for the Arts' Heritage Fellowship award in 2017 (following Saldívar's award in 2002 and Flaco's award in 2012). As Valdez and Halley emphasize, "As a woman, [Ybarra] is not sustained by local networks but is more successful at the publicly funded level."[16] In addition, Ybarra served as an artist-in-residence at the University of Washington in 1998, teaching accordion, bajo sexto, and the *guitarron* for ten months. She teaches accordion at the Guadalupe Cultural Arts Center in San Antonio.

Two major-label (Rounder Records) releases during the 1990s represent Ybarra's most successful entries into a globalized conjunto culture. *A Mi San Antonio* (1993) provides an initial representation of Ybarra's nationally-oriented style, fairly traditional in sound but presenting the artist's original compositions. *Romance Inolvidable* (1996) represents a more innovative offering, encompassing a range of musical structures and various insertions of external styles. As Ybarra describes, "When I play the polkas, I put in a little jazz, a little rock. That's the way I like to do it, . . . [without] getting away from my [musical] tradition."[17] She continues: "I wanted this album to sound different—progressive as well as traditional."[18] In this way, Ybarra displays many of the same characteristics of globalization and hybridization noted throughout this book.

One of the key distinctions between Ybarra's recordings and those of Flaco, Saldívar, and Jordan analyzed in previous chapters (and those of the Texas-Mexican conjunto community as a whole) is the choice of repertory. As explored in previous chapters, Texas-based male artists of the same generation assert their own bicultural identities by inserting hybridity into standard conjunto tunes. They also hybridize U.S. American popular tunes by inserting conjunto instrumentation and structures into established rock and country (among others) selections. Meanwhile, Ybarra writes her own songs, asserting her independence within the historical genre by refusing to conform to expected repertory and simultaneously asserting a role among the U.S. American musical community—outside of Texas—by incorporating jazz harmonies and elements more closely related to popular traditions. As Cathy Ragland asserts, throughout Ybarra's works, the artist "embellishes even the simplest melody with rapid chromatic runs and subtle shifts in tempo with unlikely chord progressions, all indicative of her highly original approach to the tradition."[19] In this way, Ybarra carves out a unique space for herself within the male-dominated tradition, using original songs and hybridized musical elements to speak to her identity outside of the historical conjunto community (due to her gender) but also, like her male counterparts, at the edges of U.S. American musical practices. As such, it is not surprising to see the persistent struggles she has had with reception inside and outside of traditional Texas-Mexican audiences. Nonetheless, as with Saldívar, Ybarra has found her greatest successes as a nationalist emblem of multi-cultural pride; an exotic element presented as a "gift" to mainstream ("white") audiences, but situated outside of functional economic successes according to either Texas-Mexican or U.S. American practices. As with Saldívar, Ybarra's music is simultaneously "too much" and yet "not enough."

In addition to a general comparison between Ybarra and male members of her generation (in particular, Flaco, Saldívar, and Jordan) who have pursued global audiences and hybridized musical traits within their recorded works, it is interesting to consider Ybarra's role within the conjunto community against that of international conjunto musicians like Kenji Katsube and Dwayne Verheyden (see Chapter 7). In general, the further conjunto musicians emanate from the regional conjunto community (in ethnicity, language, and socioeconomic circumstance, in addition to geography), the more closely they tend to adhere to a traditional structure, repertory, and sound. In this way, inter/national musicians create a place for themselves within the local genre, outside of considerations of sociocultural identity. Meanwhile, local (male) artists, secure in their sociocultural positionality, push the stylistic boundaries of the tradition. Combining the conjunto tradition with elements of U.S. American popular culture, they instead declare their positions among mainstream practices. However, female artists like Ybarra, situated inside of the historic Texas-Mexican community in all but gender, present unique identities for local practices.

Positioned firmly inside of the Texas-Mexican community, yet simultaneously outside of a standard conjunto identity, Ybarra does not rely on conservative conjunto characteristics to achieve recognition within the genre. At the same time, she builds hybrid traits into her own songs, rather than relying on preexisting material—either local standards or popular songs—to demonstrate the inherent biculturality seen in the works of her male counterparts. As such, she effectively creates a genre all her own; connected to the historical tradition in instrumentation, structure, and sound, but markedly separate in repertory and hybridized elements of melody and harmony. In this regard, identity directly impacts the manifestation and interpretation of a genre. Situated within the Texas-Mexican community and retaining an expected sound, Ybarra maintains fundamental characterization as "conjunto." Yet, her identity as a woman, historically disconnected from standard conjunto practices and established performance spaces, generates or at least allows for alternative musical traits. At the same time, she struggles to achieve economic success according to standard conjunto considerations (and mainstream practices). In this way, Ybarra functions outside of traditional conjunto considerations, as underscored by her limited recognition according to established local systems but attention from national organizations that create narratives of inclusivity outside of actual circumstances. As with male artists who do not function according to local interpretations of the genre, Ybarra creates a new interpretation of the music that characterizes her own liminality both inside and outside of historic conjunto practices.

Women in Conjunto: Susan Torres

In recent years, following Ybarra's preliminary example, an increasing number of women (although still a minority) have started to participate in Texas-Mexican conjunto music. For example, Susan Torres, born in 1975 in San Marcos, Texas (between San Antonio and Austin), and raised in nearby Kyle, plays accordion with Conjunto Clemencia, also including female drummer Clemencia Zapata (b. 1955). Like Ybarra (and many other conjunto musicians), Torres comes from a family of musicians. As the accordionist explains, "My mom used to play the drums, my grandma played the accordion, and so did my two aunts and my uncle."[20] However, as noted with other female accordionists, her father was not initially supportive. As Soledad Núñez describes, drawing from interviews with the musician, Torres's father "was opposed to her learning & playing the accordion because in his opinion she was a woman and she couldn't do it."[21] However, other family members stepped in to teach Torres the instrument when she was sixteen. The musician explains:

> My uncle . . . taught me and I started off borrowing my aunt's accordion. After my mom saw that I was . . . progressing on the accordion, she gave me the green light to purchase my own accordion. So my grandfather, Fidel, went with me to a pawn shop in Austin. . . . There was a G-tuned accordion and there was an F-tuned accordion and he liked the way the F-tuned accordion sounded, so he said that was the one that I should get.[22]

Participating in the conjunto genre more recently than artists like Ybarra, Torres has not encountered many of the struggles for acceptance observed in older generations (although she does mention a more difficult environment for women participating in the more commercialized Tejano music). Torres explains: "Playing conjunto music, . . . I've always received 'atta girls.' . . . So as far as being a woman playing, I've always felt really welcome. I've never felt like people or that the men were looking down at me."[23] In addition, drawing from former methods of hybridization (as frequently seen in contemporary conjunto artists emanating from South Texas), Torres combines the traditional conjunto sound with a mixture of jazz and blues characteristics, explaining that she tries to emulate accordionists like Jordan: "I've been told that I kind of sound like [Jordan], like some of the stuff that I do. So I guess

Figure 6.2. Susan Torres (accordion). Photo by Lucero Valle Archuleta.

he would be the one that . . . I would aspire to, like his style, the most."[24] In this way, Torres draws from new cycles of hybridization to express her own understanding of the traditional music and her own bicultural identity, while simultaneously pushing the boundaries for participation within the genre as a female musician. In addition, her positionality within the Austin conjunto community (as opposed to the conservative environments of San Antonio or the Rio Grande Valley) has opened doors to performances (and ostensibly, to less traditional gender responsibilities) less accepted elsewhere. As Torres notes:

> Austin's real open to just experimental music. . . . It's not a purist conjunto city like San Antonio and the Valley especially. So, in Austin, . . . we play this one song, "Grazing in the Grass." It's a 1970s song and kind of funky song and we played that in the [Rio Grande] Valley for the Narciso Martinez Conjunto Festival and somebody [in the crowd yelled], "play something we can dance to." . . . In Austin, you can play different stuff, but as soon as you hit San Antonio you better switch gears.[25]

Furthermore, Torres explains, the contemporary audience in Austin (mimicking the spread of the conjunto genre outside of the traditional geographic, ethnic, and socioeconomic community) is diverse:

> In Austin, a lot of the hipster community [are] . . . real interested in conjunto music. . . . There's a place here called the White Horse. . . . There's a lot of hipsters that go there and a lot of the University crowd and it's just all kinds of demographics that go there [to listen to conjunto]. Whereas in San Antonio it's more the kind of *pachuco*, low rider, maybe educated Chicanos that . . . attend those kinds of festivals, not really the Anglo community.[26]

Historically, male conjunto artists have used Texas-Mexican music to assert power for themselves among a hegemonic population. Meanwhile, female conjunto musicians use the genre to assert power within the Texas-Mexican community. Vargas discusses the power of accordion music in South Texas in "regulating economic agency, historical narratives, and constructions of female sexuality."[27] For artists like Ybarra and Torres, conjunto focuses inward, on the local community itself. Alongside certain hybridized elements, these female artists use original repertory and a unique sound to declare independence from expected elements of the male-dominated genre. In doing so, they position themselves within the narrative of conjunto as power, but use that power—developed in individual musical components—to carve out an autonomous space within the musical community. Unique aesthetic elements are separate from male-dominated practices, but authoritative, functioning as statements of female independence in a genre that was historically inaccessible to women. At the same time, positioned outside of the standard musical community, women display only loose connections to historical details of the music. Male conjunto artists remain committed to maintaining certain elements of the standard repertory, structure, and sound, even as they simultaneously assert their biculturality through popular songs and hybrid musical traits. Meanwhile, female conjunto musicians, fundamentally disconnected from such traditions, stray further from established repertories and accepted ideas.

The Globalization of Female Vocalists

Within the male-dominated version of Texas-Mexican conjunto music, the accordion—and, by extension, the accordion player—typically takes a place of prominence as musical and logistical leader of an ensemble. Flaco, Saldívar, and Jordan are all accordion players and thus, serve as frontmen of their bands. Max Baca, on bajo sexto, demonstrates a slight exception to this standard, although he initially played under Flaco before forming his own ensemble. Ybarra asserts her place within the genre by conforming to this rule, playing accordion and leading her band in a position in which women have historically struggled to gain acceptance. Alternatively, many Texas-Mexican women have dismissed the accordion and its representative exclusion, instead using their voices to create power within the musical community. Doing so separates female performers from historical narratives associated with Texas-Mexican musics. As Vargas explains, Texas-Mexican vocalists like Chelo Silva do not easily fit into the scholarly rhetoric.[28]

However, outside of the Texas-Mexican community, reliance on a lead vocalist, instead of the "exoticism" of a lead accordionist, has helped female singers to find a place within U.S. American popular music that has been elusive for male accordionists like Flaco, Saldívar, and Jordan. For example, Silva (1922–1988) signed with Colombia Records in 1955, assuring "international distribution for her recordings,"[29] and toured the United States, Mexico, and South America during the 1980s. Likewise, Rosita Fernández (1918–2006), called "San Antonio's First Lady of Song" by "Lady Bird" Johnson, achieved recognition outside of the historic performance space. As Vargas explains, singing in both Spanish and English and playing to audiences identifying across a range of sociocultural identities, Fernández "used singing and performances to move beyond the conventional racial and class audiences commonly associated with Texas Mexican music."[30] Similarly, singer Lydia

Mendoza (1916–2007) toured across North America and was recognized via national awards like a National Endowment for the Arts' Heritage Fellowship (in 1982) and the National Medal of Arts (in 1999). More recently, Texas-Mexican vocalists like Laura Canales (1954–2005), Tish Hinojosa (b. 1955), and Shelly Lares (b. 1971), among others, have carried forward the accepted tradition of women as singers within the local community, rather than accordionists (and thus, leaders). However, as such, they have also earned accolades and performance spaces outside of traditional Texas-Mexican artistic practices.

Perhaps the clearest representation of the globalization of Texas-Mexican musics through female vocalists can be demonstrated by the career of Selena Quintanilla (1971–1995). Classified as a Tejano artist, rather than conjunto (as are many female musicians, largely due to the lack of accordion, itself often barred from female usage due to the gender constraints discussed above), Selena (as she is best known) brought Texas-Mexican music to the mainstream consciousness in a way that male artists have been unable to do. Simultaneously, as Vargas argues, the figure of Selena "destabilizes heteronormative masculinity in Chicano music."[31] By incorporating musical elements of hip-hop and disco alongside the cumbias and rancheras more expected among a popular audience by the artist's sociocultural identity, Selena used the same types of hybridizations seen in the conjunto recordings of Flaco, Saldívar, and Jordan (among others) to assert her positionality in the local and global communities. Her music gained fans in South Texas, across the United States, and around the world. Her violent death and the popular movie of her life starring Jennifer Lopez brought further attention to the artist and her music. Following Selena's death, Tejano music gained national attention that instigated many of the successful entries into popular culture by artists like Flaco shortly thereafter. As Vargas describes, the circulation of Selena's music outside of an expected sociocultural community "throw[s] for a loop the normative geographic as well as gender registers that uphold the dominant construction of Chicano music."[32] The historical narrative of Texas-Mexican music emphasizes an accordion-based, male-dominated depiction of resistance against the Anglo-American hegemony, generated for, performed by, and directed to a rural, working-class, ethnically and geographically Texas-Mexican population. Female vocalists, especially those achieving recognition outside of the historical community (in a similar manner as male accordionists achieving external recognition), then do not conform to analysis according to traditional understandings of cultural significance.

Conclusions

As Vargas has discussed in more detail, the history and scholarship of Texas-Mexican musics have characterized artistic products as "resistance to systems of white supremacy."[33] At the same time, these traditions and the narratives that have developed to describe them have reinforced "the place of women's sexuality within a gendered hierarchy."[34] Yet, the music of conjunto artists like Ybarra—in existence and powerful in its sonic structure and its interpretation—stands in opposition to historical understandings of female positionality within the conjunto community.

For women outside of standard stereotypes of conjunto performers—rural, working-class, ethnically Mexican, and male, playing the accordion in male-dominated performance spaces asserts power within the Texas-Mexican community. Female accordionists like Ybarra push against historical, gender-based restrictions to participation to present themselves as musical leaders. In doing so, they frequently struggle to achieve acceptance and recognition among the community, even for those like Ybarra who do gain a place in the standard performance spaces. However, Texas-Mexican women occupy a liminal position within the musical community, simultaneously secure in their sociocultural standing but outside of historical understandings of participation. Inter/national conjunto musicians assert their positionality within the sociocultural community by clinging to traditional elements of the music itself. Local male artists combine the standard conjunto repertory, instrumentation, structure, and sound with hybridized elements of U.S. American popular culture—thus asserting a position within mainstream ("white") society. Meanwhile, local female musicians, only loosely affiliated with the historical genre but secure in their cultural positionality, use elements of conjunto to create original repertory and unique traits that lie simultaneously within and independent of standard interpretations of the regional genre. As Ybarra explains,

> I didn't want to copy anyone. I wanted to have my own style. I can copy if I want to, but I wanted to cross over. And I did, because my songs are played in Germany, Australia, Canada. I learned a little bit of music theory—inverted chords, pentatonics, and chromatic scale—that makes me a little bit different. I like to play a little blues. I wrote a huapango called "Huapan-blues," and I have one called "Huapan-jazz." Sometimes people don't like it. They like more traditional. But I'm not that. You don't have to like it. If there are ten people that like it, and one that doesn't like it, I'm winning.[35]

Similarly, Texas-Mexican women have historically used their voices, rather than the stereotypically male-oriented accordion, to carve out a space for themselves within the regional music. As with female accordionists like Ybarra, Texas-Mexican singers function independently from the historical narrative of conjunto as a masculinized, counter-hegemonic response to white supremacy. In part, the participation of women in conjunto music has stimulated hybrid musical elements—in the case of Ybarra, jazz harmonies with original songs—and the attraction of audiences outside of the local community—particularly through female vocalists who remove the accordion from traditional practices. In this way, the globalization of conjunto is stimulated by boundaries originally put in place to exclude women from participation. As with inter/national conjunto artists and accordionists like Flaco, Saldívar, and Jordan who have likewise created music outside of the regional community in audience, song choice, and sonic structure, these global processes function largely outside of regional practices. Although more women have started to participate in the local genre in recent years, female accordionists are still considered to be an anomaly among the traditional population. Although the stereotypically male (and rural, working-class, Spanish-speaking, and ethnically Mexican) identity associated with the historical genre does not fully represent actual practices, it is interesting to note the differences in musical traits within the genre brought about by different sociocultural—in this case, gender—identities. In this case, the identity of a performer creates an alternate interpretation for the historical genre.

PART III

The Appropriation of Conjunto

CHAPTER 7

"That's my music!"

Kenji Katsube, Dwayne Verheyden, and the Worldwide Participation in Conjunto

> I always told myself that I want to be exactly like Flaco Jiménez. I don't want to hear any difference. That was my goal, to keep him alive as long as I live.
>
> —Dwayne Verheyden

The annual Tejano Conjunto Festival in San Antonio, sponsored by the Guadalupe Cultural Arts Center, was created in 1982 as a means to (according to founder and long-time director Juan Tejeda), "celebrate this music, to present the best in the genre, to honor those pioneers who have contributed their lives" to conjunto.[1] Furthermore, it was a way to "educate our own [working-class, Texas-Mexican] people and the whole world about what conjunto music is" and to "dispel those types of [negative] myths and attitudes and perceptions [i.e., its historic perception as 'low-class, cantina music'] about the music."[2] Historically, the festival programmed local conjunto pioneers like Narciso Martínez, Valerio Longoria, and Tony De La Rosa, as well as regional members of the younger generations, such as Flaco Jiménez, Steve Jordan, and Mingo Saldívar, along with up-and-comers (at least originally) like Max Baca, Joel Guzman, and Sunny Sauceda. Yet, in 2000 (in what journalist Ramiro Burr refers to flippantly as "the festival's International Day"), performances at the Tejano Conjunto Festival included a group known as Los Gallos—from France—and another called Los Gatos—from Japan.[3] These performances were not either of the groups' only appearances at the festival. Already in 1992, Tejeda received a request from Kenji Katsube, accordionist for Los Gatos, indicating that the musician was "badly wanting to take part in . . . that very famous conjunto festival."[4] Katsube (with various iterations of his band) got his wish by 1995, performing at the festival in that year, as well as 1996, 1997, 2000, and followed by 2001 and 2002 (before his death from cancer in 2003). Los Gallos performed at the festival in 2000 and again in 2001. In addition, a group called Conjunto San Antonio—from Spain—performed at the festival in 2002, 2003, 2008, and 2014 (with data compiled only through 2014), while a young accordion sensation from the Netherlands named Dwayne Verheyden performed every year from 2010 through 2014 (again with data only through 2014).

While the individual circumstances for each of these international conjunto groups varies somewhat based—in part—on individual geographic origin, each of these musicians cites the worldwide distribution of conjunto recordings and live performances in Europe and/or Asia by Texas-Mexican artists like Flaco and Jordan as the impetus for his attraction to the genre. In addition, following these types of media/migration activities (detailed in Chapters 1 and 2), a number of international fans cite similar attractions to the globalized genre. For example, in 1992, Isao Motegi, a conjunto fan from Ashikaga, Japan, traveled to San Antonio (along with some seven other people from Japan) to attend the festival. Motegi explains that, "I saw Esteban Jordan when he toured Japan in January, but this is much better seeing him here."[5] Furthermore, Motegi notes, "To me, Steve Jordan is greater than Elvis, Sinatra or the Beatles. He is my idol."[6] Similarly, Jo Haigermoser, a visual artist from Germany who, by 1996, had been attending—and producing watercolors at—the festival every year since 1989, first learned of the conjunto genre through "an old Ry Cooder record featuring Flaco Jiménez."[7] As Haigermoser explains, "I just like the sincerity of [conjunto music]."[8] In 2003, a fan named Peter Herzberg from Eindhoven, in the Netherlands, made his third trip (previously, 1997 and 2000) to the festival, together with his wife. As Herzberg explains, he first developed an attraction to the regional genre through Flaco's global performances during the 1980s: "(Jiménez) came to Holland, and I said, 'That's my music.'"[9]

Among the international performers, Katsube first became interested in conjunto after listening to Ry Cooder's *Showtime* (1977), also featuring Flaco. However, the artist became inspired to actually play conjunto music some ten years later when he "found Flaco Jiménez and Steve Jordan on a program for World Music."[10] Similarly, Manolo Gonzalez (born in southern France to Spanish parents), lead singer and bajo sexto player for Los Gallos, describes his own introduction to conjunto music at a 1997 Flaco concert in Paris: "It was like a revelation. My Spanish sensibilities were excited, and I could sense the emotions in the music."[11] Manuel A. Perez, accordionist for Conjunto San Antonio, explains that his group discovered the conjunto genre through traditional recordings by roots-rock group Los Lobos, after which their "curiosity was awakened and then [they] discovered Flaco Jiménez, Steve Jordan, and others."[12] Meanwhile, Verheyden first heard conjunto music through his father's appreciation for Flaco. As the father, William Verheyden, explains, "When my wife got pregnant with Dwayne, she agreed to let me join a shooting club in our village. One of the friends I made in this club introduced me to Flaco's music, and it completely changed my life. So, Dwayne grew up listening to Flaco."[13] As the son continues, following this initial introduction to Flaco's music, "My dad immediately fell in love with Flaco's music and bought his first album the next day. Since that day he played Flaco's music every day at home and in his car. You can probably imagine that I heard Flaco's music even before I was born. So, I can truly say that I grew up with Flaco Jiménez's music."[14] In addition, Verheyden was introduced to Flaco himself in 2008 during a concert tour in the Netherlands. As Amie Victoria Castillo, Flaco's manager at the time, recalls, "We were touring Europe—you know Flaco is an idol over there—and I encouraged him to go hear Dwayne, and eventually to record with him."[15]

Following the global dissemination of conjunto music by regional artists like Flaco, Jordan, and Saldívar in the final decades of the twentieth century, audiences worldwide not only became fans of the Texas-Mexican genre, but also began performing the music for themselves. In this way, international participants in the genre took the cultural product as their own, outside of historic boundaries of ethnic, linguistic, geographic, or socioeconomic heritage. Yet, while regional, non-traditional performers like Flaco, Jordan, and Saldívar have introduced certain external and commercial elements into the traditional form, effectively hybridizing the genre and—in many ways—transforming it into a form of popular music, international participants have maintained close correspondence to pre-established musical characteristics. In this way, even as non-traditional performers spread the genre worldwide, the more recent transnational interest in Texas-Mexican accordion music has simultaneously preserved the tradition as a deeply-ingrained form of cultural folklore, thus establishing the categorization of individual musical pursuits on a representative continuum somewhere between "folkloric" and "popular" understandings.[16]

Over time, conjunto music has incorporated certain external characteristics, but, overall, the commercialization and transnational spread of the style has not altered the creative form in any meaningful way. In fact, any insertion of external elements within the traditional musical form seems to emanate primarily from local musicians, rather than external participants, as might be more logically expected. Instead, as this chapter demonstrates, the international interest and adoption of a highly localized cultural tradition has generated a rather unexpected consolidation of musical style. This process shifts the contemporary understanding of Texas-Mexican music to embrace a fundamentally folkloric interpretation, but it also establishes a conceptual continuum between the original model and more popular pursuits. It simultaneously demonstrates a modern disconnect from homologous notions of genre as identity (if these considerations were ever truly appropriate). Even if we agree that Texas-Mexican conjunto music did once serve as a symbol of sociocultural identity among the regional, working-class population, the recent participation of inter/national artists in the genre—fundamentally separated from such fixed conceptions of identity—removes this interpretation of the music and its associated community in contemporary practices.

Theoretical Framework: The Folk-Popular Continuum and Transnational Personae

Although recent attention to the conjunto genre outside of traditional cultural boundaries might imply a general contemporary incorporation of popular and global characteristics, and although popular elements *are* inserted into certain regional performances, overall, widespread attention to conjunto has had the opposite effect, creating a fundamental and conservative musical style even in listening and participating constituencies far beyond the original working-class community. In fact, international conjunto artists—modern, external performers from Japan, Spain, France, and the Netherlands—often establish their own legitimacy within the genre by maintaining an even more conservative manner than musicians emanating from within the traditional ethnicity and geographic location, separate from commercial considerations and thus suggesting folk music. However, popular musical elements *do* exist within the continuing tradition, and classification as folk music alone cannot fully account for the contemporary range of individual styles. Instead, as Fernando Rios asserts, "[A] folkloric musical representation's sonic resemblance to the rural genre or style it is said to be chiefly derived from can be conceptualized along a continuum."[17] In this regard, any separation of musical genres into distinct categories of "folkloric" and "popular" becomes largely irrelevant.[18] In general, conjunto may lie closer within the realm of folk music, but consideration of a folk-popular continuum more clearly allows for stylistic and commercial deviance within a single genre.

The works of international conjunto artists like Katsube (with Los Gatos), Los Gallos, Conjunto San Antonio, and Verheyden display a form of transnational identity that transcends traditional boundaries of cultural identification as related to elements of heritage; that is, moving beyond historic methods of belonging as related to innate conditions of language, class, ethnicity, and location. As Jane Ferguson notes, although in contemporary practices, the "boundaries between genres are often contested," certain musical genres "often coincide with ideas of national origin and boundary."[19] In the case of Texas-Mexican conjunto music (which also contains certain ambiguities regarding genre, particularly in distinguishing some of the more recent hybridized pursuits from separately-conceived genres like Tejano or so-called progressive conjunto), the genre has historically been considered as closely connected to the cultural identity of the region. This understanding is complicated as international musicians begin to perform the genre as their own. Ferguson also notes the "active creative work that goes into both mimicry and re-signification, potentially giving the copy new meanings not present in the original."[20] In this regard, it is this shift in meaning for conjunto as it spreads to new locations that is most significant, rather than the mere process of appropriation (and corresponding mimicry) observed within the music itself.

In considering the construction of social identity for international performers of conjunto music, it is instructive to consider Philip Auslander's analysis of musical personae in performance practices. In Auslander's view, "What musicians perform first and foremost is not music, but their own identities as musicians, their musical personae."[21] In this regard, musical performance can be considered beyond simply the successful performance of a particular work, but instead as the successful presentation of an artist's identity in terms of setting, appearance, manner, and the actual music performed. Yet, as Auslander asserts, each musical genre creates "a social frame that carries its own particular set of conventions."[22] It is therefore not the performer alone who conveys a certain performative identity, but rather a negotiation between the performer and the audience to conform (or possibly stray from) expectation. In order to achieve success within a genre, the performer must operate within the frame created by the related social group. The setting, appearance, manner, and actual music performed must then align with the musical persona—or cultural identity—the performer asserts, within a well-defined social context.

International conjunto musicians like Katsube, Los Gallos, Conjunto San Antonio, and Verheyden perform among local (Texas-Mexican) audiences, within a conservative framework drawn from traditional practices. As Auslander explains, the frame for a particular genre (such as conjunto) is determined by common understandings among members of a social group. Audience members are therefore deeply invested in the creation of musical personae among performers, using these identities to "fulfill a social function" and thus serving as cocreators of performative identities.[23] In this regard, audiences tend to insist on very conservative manifestations of musical personae. As Auslander asserts, "If one thinks of audiences not just as consumers, but also as the cocreators of the musicians' personae, and as having a substantial investment in those personae and the functions they serve, it is easy to understand why audiences often respond very conservatively (in the literal sense) to musicians' desire to retool their personae."[24] Similarly, a performer "risks being discredited" if all aspects of a performance—setting, appearance, manner, and music—are not consistent with the identity the musician asserts.[25]

Local conjunto artists convey the conjunto frame instinctually—particularly "fixed signs" related to appearance.[26] These local artists then assert certain flexibilities with regard to identity that are not feasible for international artists (who do not naturally represent many of these fixed signs and must therefore maintain close congruence with other aspects of a performance—such as the music itself). Thus, while local performers can "get away" with slight alterations to the music (through hybrid elements discussed in Chapters 4 and 5) and still maintain the local audience's approval within the conception of a traditional, Texas-Mexican identity, international performers—further disconnected from the heritage-oriented aspects of the genre's frame—must maintain more conservative musical elements to "make up" for these aspects of identity that they lack. As Auslander conveys, "There are also many performers whose personae allow their audiences to accept performances that might be perceived as anomalous when executed by other artists operating in the same genre frame."[27]

That being said, even these local musicians receive some criticism for straying too far from the traditional form, sustaining a complicated balance between the hybrid elements popular among global audiences and the more conservative expectations of the local constituency. As Auslander continues, "Any attempt to define (or redefine) the situation depends entirely on the audience's cooperation."[28] Furthermore, individual musicians may change their personae based on different audiences (as seen in Flaco's national collaborations and performances for more mainstream audiences, for example). In addition, performative identities do not necessarily conform to personal personae. In other words, a musician may assert a particular identity to help connect to a given audience, but this persona is not always maintained throughout the rest of the artist's pursuits; musical identity does not necessarily imply a consistent cultural identity. Indeed, according to Auslander, "[T]here is no reason to suppose that musicians perform the same identity when playing music as in their other life routines."[29] This is an important consideration to keep in mind as we analyze the performative pursuits of international conjunto artists. While performers like Katsube, Los Gallos, Conjunto San Antonio, and Verheyden emphasize a Texas-Mexican persona in performances for a local audience (and indeed, their acceptance within the conjunto genre relies on it), these individual musicians may or may not identify with the Texas-Mexican community off the stage and outside of the music itself. Musical persona does not necessarily imply cultural identity. One interesting consideration in analyzing this music is then whether or not—and for whom—this correlation between persona and cultural identity does exist.

Japanese Conjunto: Kenji Katsube

In addition to numerous performances at the Tejano Conjunto Festival in San Antonio, Katsube and Los Gatos produced two albums in the United States (in addition to a demo tape from 1995 including classic conjunto songs like "Viva Seguin," "Cielito Lindo," "Canción Mixteca," and a Japanese version of "El Gato Negro").[30] *Tony De La Rosa Presents Los Gatos de Japon* was released by Hacienda Records in 1996, and *Son Mentiritas*, also with Hacienda Records, was released in 1998. Each album presents a series of classic conjunto tunes, played in a traditional style. In addition to purely instrumental recordings and songs in the original Spanish, each album includes one final tune ("El Mosquito Americano" and "Mujer Paseada," respectively) in Japanese (although each of these tunes is also included in a Spanish version). These recorded performances do not stray from conventional (historical, as established by early- to mid-twentieth-century artists like Santiago Jiménez Sr. and De La Rosa) conjunto practices. As journalist Chito De La Torre notes, "Los Gatos play a nice set of straight-ahead conjunto."[31] It is interesting to consider the classic conjunto repertory included on these albums. While the songs certainly correspond to expected conjunto practices, they fundamentally derive from Mexican composers, adding a layer of complexity to analysis. In using Mexican songs to claim a place in the Texas community, inter/national conjunto artists like Katsube stumble into complex systems of power that do not allow the Mexican musicians who wrote these songs to operate according to the same positionality.

Katsube's first album will serve as an informative representation of the group's musical practices. The album includes ten tracks. The first track begins with a lengthy (1:02) introduction by De La Rosa, a conjunto pioneer. In this introduction (in Spanish until the final sentence or so in English), De La Rosa expresses his pride and sense of honor that Katsube is "carrying forward our music, our culture" and congratulates the group for the "great work" they are doing.[32] The first song itself, included in the same track as the spoken introduction, is "Atotonilco." This instrumental polka originally served as one of De La Rosa's signature tunes. It has been recorded over the years by conjunto pioneers like Santiago Sr., the younger generation of local artists like Flaco, Santiago Jiménez Jr., and Ruben Vela, the subsequent conjunto generation of Baca, Guzman, Sauceda, and more. The second song of the album is "Hasta Cuando," while the third track (another instrumental) is "Querida Lucia." The following song, "El Mosquito Americano," is a fairly common conjunto tune that has been recorded by local artists like Los Dos Gilbertos and Los Fantasmas del Valle. Los Gatos presents the song first in Spanish and then (as track 11) in Japanese. Track 5 is an instrumental polka by the "founding father" of conjunto, Narciso Martínez, also recorded by Jordan, called "Flor de Mexico." The following tune, "Mejor Solo," is another De La Rosa standard. The seventh song on the album, "El Sube Y Baja," has also been recorded by a diverse range of local artists. Next, "Volver, Volver," written by Fernando Maldonado and first released by Mexican crooner Vicente Fernández in 1972, has been recorded by traditional artists like Longoria and Santiago Jr., as well as the Texas Tornados, roots-rock group Los Lobos, the young punk-conjunto band Piñata Protest, and more. The ninth track, "El Circo," is another conjunto classic that has been recorded by a diversity of regional musicians. Preceding the final version of "El Mosquito Americano" in Japanese, the tenth track is a second version of "Hasta Cuando."

Most of the tracks on this first album are relatively well-known conjunto "classics" that had previously been recorded by De La Rosa and/or other local conjunto artists. That being said, many of these songs also retain close connections to Mexican repertory ("Atotonilco" is frequently considered according to the mariachi genre; "Volver, Volver," as a Mexican ranchera, etc.). It is thus important to note that, while the Asian connection to Texas-Mexican practices is a relatively novel circumstance, conjunto is fundamentally a transnational genre, both through an initial European foundation and the later incorporation of Mexican (and other) songs and musical traits. As such, the attention to Katsube's participation within conjunto demonstrates a continued reluctance to both recognize the Mexican (as opposed to Texas-Mexican) influences fundamental to the genre—at least on the part of regional audiences who emphasize an ethno-nationalist separation between Texas and Mexico and the music/musicians emanating from either location—and make any distinction between the Mexican and Texas-Mexican communities—at least on the part of external fans who mischaracterize Mexican/Mexican-American music (and often, culture) as one and the same.

Katsube's alignment with De La Rosa, in particular, stems from international distribution of the local artist's music. According to Linda Escobar, a conjunto singer from Alice, Texas, who achieved widespread success as a child with the song "Frijolitos Pintos" and was Katsube's partner for some ten years once he moved to the United States, the Japanese musician "taught himself the accordion listening to Tony De La Rosa albums."[33] Furthermore, as Escobar asserts, "TONY DE LA ROSA was his GOD! He knew most of his songs and sang like him."[34] Escobar also explains that Katsube met De La Rosa and became friends soon after first performing at the Tejano Conjunto Festival in 1995. His two albums were then recorded with Hacienda Records (a Corpus Christi company who distributed De La Rosa's works for years) under the regional musician's "production and guidance."[35] By aligning himself with a local developer of the genre (and performing very closely within the traditional model, in song choice, but also stylistic characteristics, as discussed below), Katsube helps to assure his own adherence to the historic conjunto "frame" and thus achieve success among the Texas-Mexican audience.

As a Japanese musician, certain "fixed" aspects of Katsube's appearance inevitably lie outside of the genre's framework. By aligning his selections with De La Rosa and maintaining close correspondence to traditional musical characteristics, Katsube presumably "makes up" for the aspects of cultural identity that he unavoidably lacks and instead forges connections with the regional audience through more manageable aspects of setting (within the well-established context of the Tejano Conjunto Festival) and the music itself. Other regional artists maintain their cultural identities even when performing songs (and including hybrid elements) outside of the central conjunto tradition—since they maintain the natural benefit of familial heritage. Meanwhile, international artists like Katsube assert their position within the Texas-Mexican tradition—even as they remain outside of cultural heritage—by maintaining close adherence to more conservative musical elements. In this way, while certain regional musicians insert elements of popular music into the traditional form (through popular songs and/or original repertory, rock/jazz riffs, and commercialized performance practices, for example), international musicians like Katsube consolidate the genre as a folkloric tradition (by using a common, orally-acquired repertory and identifying themselves first and foremost as part of the community, rather than as individualized artists), thus forming a folkloric-popular continuum within a single style.

Furthermore, although Katsube asserts a Texas-Mexican persona primarily through his musical selections, he also ultimately moved to the United States and altered the more "mobile" aspects of his appearance by performing in "Western hats and jeans."[36] As Escobar describes, in addition to his passion for the music itself, Katsube "loved the Hispanic culture."[37] Katsube thus asserts a sociocultural identity that moves beyond the performative persona to instead correlate off the stage and outside of the music alone with the associated Texas-Mexican community. Even in performance, the musician strives to include aspects within the social frame of conjunto—like appearance—that are more easily inserted by artists falling within the historic sociocultural patterns (language, location, ethnicity, and such) of the genre. As such, Katsube develops a form of transnational identity that falls outside of traditional notions of heritage-oriented identification and simultaneously shifts the sense of meaning for the conjunto genre (as its original role as a sociocultural representation of the rural, working-class, Texas-Mexican people does not apply to Katsube's origins outside of this community, despite his expressed connections and adherence to certain aspects of the culture). While local musicians and audiences describe conjunto as a form of cultural representation, for international artists like Katsube, conjunto music is entertainment.

As Mario Diaz Jr., drummer for the Houston-based conjunto group Los Monarcas, explains, "It's a family tradition. Conjunto is the music of the working-class people. To me the music means family, tradition, and a lifestyle. It's something you grow up with. I remember being a kid and heading to my grandpa's on Saturday mornings to listen to his old LPs and 8-tracks so I could learn the history/styles."[38] Meanwhile, Katsube describes, "I love this music, it is music from the heart. . . . This music is pure . . . [and] very earthy."[39] While the Japanese musician displays a passion for the sound of conjunto music, the familial and corresponding representational element of conjunto—for an international artist falling outside the heritage of the tradition—does not exist.

In addition to song selection, the musical characteristics of Katsube's recordings (form, instrumentation, timing, melodies, harmonies, rhythms, and ornamental riffs) closely adhere to the conservative conjunto tradition, as exhibited by De La Rosa's model. Comparison of Katsube's rendition of "Mejor Solo" with De La Rosa's original provides a representative example of the Japanese musician's stylistic adherence to the conjunto tradition. With the exception of one additional refrain presented at the end of the recording, Katsube uses the same (Spanish) lyrics and overall structure as De La Rosa's original (Tab. 7.1). Each rendition employs a simple ranchera form, with instrumental introduction, double-verse and refrain (A1A2B), instrumental interlude, and final verse and refrain (A3B). In addition, Katsube's recording includes an additional instrumental interlude, final repeat of the refrain, and a relatively lengthy (twenty-one seconds) instrumental ending. In addition to the formal instrumental sections in each recording, the middle and end

Table 7.1. “Mejor Solo.” As performed and recorded by Los Gatos de Japon. From *Tony De La Rosa Presents Los Gatos de Japon* (Hacienda Records 7437, 1996). “Mejor Solo.” As performed and recorded by Tony De La Rosa. From *Mejor Solo* (Hacienda Records 7356, 1993).

“Mejor Solo” (Structure)					
De La Rosa’s Form (Ranchera)	Language (De La Rosa)	Length (De La Rosa)	Katsube’s Form (Ranchera)	Language (Katsube)	Length (Katsube)
Instrumental Introduction		0:00–0:18 (0:18)	Instrumental Introduction		0:00–0:19 (0:19)
A1	Spanish	0:18–0:35 (0:17)	A1	Spanish	0:19–0:34 (0:15)
A2	Spanish	0:35–0:50 (0:15)	A2	Spanish	0:34–0:50 (0:16)
B	Spanish	0:50–1:05 (0:15)	B	Spanish	0:50–1:05 (0:15)
Instrumental Interlude		1:05–1:23 (0:18)	Instrumental Interlude		1:05–1:23 (0:18)
A3	Spanish	1:23–1:39 (0:16)	A3	Spanish	1:23–1:39 (0:16)
B	Spanish	1:39–1:58 (0:19)	B	Spanish	1:39–1:54 (0:15)
			Instrumental Interlude		1:54–2:12 (0:18)
			B	Spanish	2:12–2:27 (0:15)
			Instrumental Ending		2:27–2:48 (0:21)

of each verse also include brief instrumental passages. Katsube's recording is just slightly faster than De La Rosa's model (107 BPM versus 101 BPM), but both versions lie within the same general range, as displayed by the almost identical timings for each section of each rendition.

The other elements of the two recordings also demonstrate close correspondence. Each instrumental introduction includes a *grito* (a shout of excitement as the song begins) within the first few seconds. The standard conjunto instrumentation (accordion, bajo sexto, bass guitar, and drums) is used in both renditions, as is a standard polka beat in the drums (with the bass drum on beats 1 and 3 and the snare on beats 2 and 4). De La Rosa plays the accordion throughout the song, including under the lyrics in the verse and refrain sections (rather than just between vocal lines in accordance with somewhat earlier conjunto practices). Katsube maintains this same instrumental practice (although De La Rosa's ornamental passages remain somewhat more active than Katsube's throughout, perhaps denoting a mere difference in technical ability). In addition, Katsube uses almost identical accordion passagework as De La Rosa throughout, as can be demonstrated by comparing the accordion lines for the first (or only) instrumental interludes in each recording. De La Rosa's accordion playing is distinguished (throughout his career) by a crisp, staccato technique (as Manuel Peña describes, De La Rosa's "clean staccato articulation in the performance of the polka became the hallmark of the tejano style") (Ex. 7.1).[40] Katsube's accordion technique in "Mejor Solo" (and throughout his recorded repertory) mimics this clean staccato style (Ex. 7.2).

The instrumental interlude in Katsube's rendition of "Mejor Solo" is remarkably similar to the earlier example, as seen by examining the two corresponding transcriptions. Katsube includes a few more ornamental insertions, as in the triplet arpeggiations in the fifth measure of the excerpt and the repeated sixteenth notes in measures 3 and 7. In measure 9 of each excerpt, where De La Rosa begins the subsequent phrase on a G, Katsube starts (and maintains) the same passage a third higher, beginning on a B. While De La Rosa's transcription ends after measure 13, Katsube's version is extended by three additional measures. De La Rosa includes these measures, with ornamental passagework leading into the following verse, but his version includes a clearer stopping place at measure 13, rather than in Katsube's pause after this additional ornamentation. With the common repertory employed throughout much of the Texas-Mexican conjunto tradition, instrumental passages such as this interlude in "Mejor Solo" provide a good opportunity for artists to put their own stamp on a performance of a well-known song. In this regard, Katsube's close adherence to De La Rosa's example, even in

Example 7.1. Transcription of "Mejor Solo," top melodic line of accordion interlude. As performed and recorded by Tony De La Rosa. From *Mejor Solo* (Hacienda Records 7356, 1993).

Example 7.2. Transcription of "Mejor Solo," top melodic line of accordion interlude. As performed and recorded by Los Gatos de Japon. From *Tony De La Rosa Presents Los Gatos de Japon* (Hacienda Records 7437, 1996).

the passage that could include his own characteristics, demonstrates the Japanese musician's strict imitation of the local model.

Transnationalism and Hybridity in Japanese Conjunto Music

Beyond generalized notions of transcultural identity observed in multiple manifestations of international conjunto practices, it is interesting to consider Katsube's case as a Japanese artist, in particular. Numerous scholars throughout the social sciences have explored what Alison Tokita refers to as "the overwhelming valorization of Western music" in Japanese culture.[41] Shuhei Hosokawa describes the dichotomic Western stereotype of Japanese culture ("mastery of technique vs. depth of feeling . . . expert imitators, but poor innovators"), invoking musicologist Richard Middleton to push back against "the dichotomy between appropriated copy and authentic original" and instead offering "a spectrum between these notions."[42] This perceived dichotomy is clearly demonstrated in the works of Katsube, as the Japanese artist's recordings of conjunto music showcase solid technical performances, but little alteration beyond the traditional genre. Yet, for Japanese society—and thus, Katsube's cultural identity—meaning lies in imitation.

In contemporary scholarship, transculturalism frequently implies hybridity; as different groups of people interact, individual cultural products mix to create new—or at least dramatically altered—styles (as seen in the hybrid works of local artists like Flaco, Saldívar, and Jordan, all explored in depth in Chapters 4 and 5). Léon Tsambu defines the term transculturalism as "the cosmopolitan quality of any person, object or thought into which elements from diverse cultures, civilizations, ethnic groups or countries have been integrated, to such an extent that authenticity of origin may be lost" and furthermore, discusses a form of transnational identity "that is mixed, hybrid or eclectic."[43] This definition suggests that the performance of conjunto music by artists emanating from outside the traditional Texas-Mexican community (in terms of geographic location, language, socioeconomic background, and ethnicity) would create a hybridized style of the genre, incorporating not only expected historic characteristics of the genre, but also elements from the ethnic group newly participating in the artform. In other words, Katsube's performance of conjunto would combine Texas-Mexican characteristics with Japanese idiosyncrasies to create a new—or hybrid—style of the genre.

Instead, Katsube's recordings of conjunto lie entirely within Texas-Mexican conventions, in fact falling more closely in line with the tradition than the works of many contemporary local musicians (which do frequently showcase hybridity with U.S. American popular elements). However, Hosokawa asserts that, for Japanese musicians, the process of appropriation itself actually demonstrates a close adherence to ideals of Japanese culture. For artists like Katsube, the adoption of an external genre in fact creates a certain sense of hybridity, not with a mixture of stylistic elements but through the cultural appropriation itself. In discussing a Japanese salsa band called Orquesta de la Luz, Hosokawa notes that, "This band, because of, rather than in spite of, their seemingly non-Japanese performance, is related more to the cultural conditions of Japan than to those of Latino society," since "simulating is . . . intrinsic to the Japanese sense of self."[44]

The participation of international musicians in the conjunto tradition alters adherence to the historic meaning of the genre. While the working-class, Texas-Mexican community created conjunto as a counter-response to Anglo-American hegemony and continues to use the music as a form of cultural representation for the region, artists like Katsube risk criticism of performing conjunto merely as a parody of tradition, with little understanding or perpetuation of the expressive capabilities of the genre. As Judith Ann Herd asserts, "[M]any critics who evaluate Japanese popular music usually consider it merely a parody of the 'correct' styles that they are accustomed to hearing."[45] Similarly, Hosokawa notes that Orquesta de la Luz "face criticism of merely imitating the sound without grasping the deeper roots of the music,"[46] globalizing salsa "at the cost of eliminating a key element in the original context: ethno-political expression."[47] These concerns may certainly contain elements of truth. Katsube "was in love with this style of music,"[48] explaining that "the sound of the accordion is very warm, exciting,"[49] but never mentioning any deeper sense of sociopolitical meaning for the music itself, the Texas-Mexican culture it has remained so important to, or his own participation within the conjunto community.

That being said, while the sense of meaning that Katsube brings to conjunto music is not the same as the historic interpretation among a rural, working-class, Texas-Mexican population, the Japanese artist does bring meaning to his work. As Ferguson asserts, "it is insufficient to examine processes of appropriation simply in terms of 'sending' and 'receiving' cultures; rather, we need to understand translation that involves a constant symbolic exchange if not interplay, with meanings in constant flow."[50] Different meanings do not necessitate a lack of meaning, and this "translated" interpretation among a new population provides important insights into the contemporary globalization of the genre. Furthermore, while the general conception of musical genre can be helpful in categorizing musical forms and thus informing audience expectation (as Auslander notes, "our social experience of music is radically incomplete if we do not have a sense of what *kind* of music we are experiencing"),[51] these stylistic designations do not hold consistent interpretations as music travels in our globalized society among different groups of people. As Ferguson describes, musical genres "are hardly discrete tapestries that transfer intact from one market to another."[52] In other words, even though Katsube presents music among a local, Texas-Mexican audience and even though the music is similar, the Japanese artist's incorporation of conjunto does not signify an identical transfer of the genre in terms of sociopolitical interpretation. The music holds different meanings for different participants; never mind the early history of the genre.

Although traditional Texas-Mexican conjunto music asserts a sociopolitical interpretation (not through the lyrics, but in the pure act of presenting a low-class form of "cantina music" as a means of cultural representation),

Katsube's interpretation of conjunto music does not maintain this sense of politicism. As Herd explains, Japanese popular music is typically (and ideally) apolitical, and "any hint of controversial ideas will detract from the song's popularity."[53] As such, it makes sense that Katsube, raised in the culture of Japanese popular music, would not go out of his way to maintain any sociocultural sense of meaning for the form, using a performative identity that adopts the music itself (in its imitative entirety) but leaves the historic, sociopolitical interpretation behind.

During the end of the nineteenth century, Japanese culture began to adopt Western music (classical and popular) as the dominant musical system. As Tokita explains, "Japanese people do not need to acquire a Western language to acquire Western musicality . . . because Western music was 'translated' into Japanese culture."[54] Furthermore, "Japan is predominantly a mono-musical culture (meaning in Western or Western-derived music)."[55] In this regard, Western forms of expression, even marginalized genres like Texas-Mexican conjunto, lie closely in line with what the Japanese community consider to be their own cultural expressions. U.S. American musics are not exotic, but familiar, historically suggesting a path to modernization for the region through global alignment with the dominant style. Furthermore, while Western culture has produced "additive" hybridities that combine with a local culture to create transcultural forms, musical culture in Japan has been entirely dominated by Western genres, displacing indigenous forms.[56] That being said, modern Japan is a global, socioeconomic superpower. While adoption of mainstream Western genres is generally accepted and even discussed as a potential form of cultural exploitation on the part of mainstream society, Japanese appropriation of non-dominant forms of music—such as Jamaican reggae and Texas-Mexican conjunto—becomes a potentially exploitative process. As Marvin Sterling notes, members of a lower socioeconomic class "are generally in a weaker position [than hegemonic populations] to weigh in on who consumes their culture and how."[57]

As Hosokawa explains, in contemporary society, "universal" forms of music (rock, pop, jazz, etc.) can be performed across sociocultural boundaries "without raising questions about for whom, of whom and by whom the music is being played."[58] However, musical genres that are closely associated with particular groups (according to geographic location, ethnicity, socioeconomic circumstance, and the like) remain connected to these groups as a form of "local" music. As such, participation outside of historic boundaries can create controversial questions. In Japan, a "niche" culture exists in which domestic artists perform these "local" musics, like salsa, raga, bossa nova, bluegrass, tango, and more. These performances are stimulated by a "modernizing effect posit[ing] Western superiority and Japanese inferiority," beginning from the start of the Meiji era in 1868.[59] The ideal aesthetic within this Japanese niche culture is one of pure imitation. Performers replicate the original model precisely, taking care to distinguish their efforts from mainstream popular genres and thus inserting few—if any—Japanese characteristics.

As Hosokawa continues, this concept of borrowing "is intrinsic to the Japanese sense of self."[60] Within the Japanese traditional arts, strict imitation of past masters is highly valued and thought to lead to technical mastery. This method of instruction is also demonstrated within the Japanese educational system, in which learning is based largely on rote mimicry. In this regard, Katsube's close imitation of the traditional conjunto structure and sound falls closely in line with Japanese niche culture and Japanese instructional practices. Katsube's strict adherence to the conservative style thus produces a form of hybridity that incorporates both traditional Texas-Mexican elements (through the music itself) and Japanese characteristics (through the sheer practice of mimicry). As Hosokawa remarks, "It is a seeming paradox: the better [Japanese niche musicians] play non-Japanese music, the more they become 'Japanese.'"[61]

Furthermore, the importation of Western musics at the expense of indigenous Japanese musics led to a sense of cultural hierarchy for Western music over the Japanese community's own musical roots. As Hosokawa explains, this forced alienation from musical traditions (under a guise of "modernization") leads contemporary listeners and performers to gravitate to global forms of "roots" musics, such as Texas-Mexican conjunto. Niche musicians, according to Hosokawa, "feeling the loss of *their own* folk tradition, search instead for the roots of the Other."[62] Indeed, as Escobar describes, Katsube "loved the way Hispanic families gathered to enjoy music of accordion and bajo sexto and he wanted to be a Hispanic Texan, too. He played the accordion and sang with his entire heart and soul."[63] In adopting the Texas-Mexican conjunto tradition, Katsube adopted not only the music itself, but also the local culture, arguably replacing the Japanese folk traditions suppressed through the Western-inspired processes of modernization with an alternate form of (Western) folklore (and in the process also achieving an alternate style of hybridity drawn from Japanese instructional practices in combination with the Texas-Mexican music).

At the same time, Katsube was welcomed with open arms by the Texas-Mexican community. As Escobar asserts, "The people love him and were in AWE! . . . He was welcomed with OPEN ARMS!"[64] For regional audiences, a Japanese conjunto musician was a novelty that stimulated a sense of pride in the local culture. As Burr explains, describing Katsube's performance at the Tejano Conjunto Festival in 1996, "Of the hundreds packing the pavilion, few danced as most apparently were transfixed by the sight of four Japanese men . . . playing conjunto music."[65] Furthermore, "When the band finished, the crowd let out a roar, demanding an encore."[66] Katsube did not represent a threat to local performers; he existed largely as a novelty act, performing conservative conjunto in prominent venues like the Tejano Conjunto Festival, but not inserting his own musical characteristics or vying for performance outlets against the other regional musicians.[67] Similarly, as Hosokawa notes, "For the Latino, a Japanese band is nothing but 'foreign guests,' and an all-gringo salsa band, if any, would probably be less surprising but more threatening and scandalous than [Orquesta de la Luz]."[68]

Corresponding to Auslander's discussion of musical personae in performance, Japanese musicians are deeply concerned with performative image. As Christine Yano explains, "Image, or the face one presents before the public, is an important part of everyday life in Japan."[69] Japanese performers experiment with different images (following the Buddhist notion of *henshin*, or transformation) to achieve the correct "fit" between the performative persona and audience expectation.[70] Yano agrees with Auslander that a musician is a "chameleon," changing his or her physical identity in accordance with an audience's definition of performative success. In this way, Katsube, presenting conjunto music to a Texas-Mexican audience, creates an image that conforms with local expectation (Western hats and jeans in combination with the standard conjunto instrumentation and a conservative regional sound). He thus achieves success within the genre by creating a cultural identity for himself that not only conforms to the social frame developed among regional audiences, but also mimics his own sense of "Japanese-ness" by conforming to Japanese ideals of image-making (in addition to cultural notions of imitation).

Furthermore, as Herd asserts, Japanese society "values compromise and agreement over strong, individual tastes," awarding performative successes to those artists who best display conformity with the majority.[71] While Western popular musicians achieve success "because of their distinct appearance, talent or personality," Japanese artists who "appear to be like everyone else" and "are not too different or outstanding" instead achieve popularity with local audiences.[72] As such, it makes sense that Katsube, in addition to performing in a relatively precarious position as an outsider to Texas-Mexican culture, would subscribe to Japanese ideals of community by conforming identically to the local majority. In addition, as Yano asserts, whereas popular songs in the United States are typically "critically acclaimed for their originality," Japanese popular music "is valued for its retention of older traits."[73]

In performing conjunto music in a traditional style, Katsube thus (in many ways) conforms not only to Texas-Mexican ideals, but also to his own cultural heritage, creating a new sense of sociocultural hybridity outside of the transnational combination of musical traits alone.

Conjunto in the Netherlands: Dwayne Verheyden

At the time of this writing, Verheyden has released three albums (with a fourth "coming soon," according to the artist's website). The song choices in the first two albums, *Dwayne & the TexMeXplosion in San Antonio* (2010) and *Conjunto Tracks* (2012) correspond relatively closely to classic conjunto repertory (particularly the first album), as performed by local artists like Flaco. However, expanding beyond the one original song ("Janeth") and a handful of hybridized tracks included on the second album, Verheyden's third album, *Desde Holanda* (2015), presents five original songs—written by the artist himself—out of a total of ten tracks on the album. In this regard, while Verheyden began his career by closely imitating the traditional Texas-Mexican style (consolidating the genre as a form of folklore), his later musical pursuits fall more closely in line with popular practices (as original repertory shifts the artist's works along the folk-popular continuum, even though the music itself remains in line with more traditional practices). While Verheyden gained initial acceptance within the genre by strictly adhering to an established repertory and musical sound (therefore "making up" for his own lack of "fixed" characteristics of Texas-Mexican identity related to appearance and familial heritage), once his chosen musical persona achieved success with local audiences, he gained the flexibility to experiment (slightly) with the music itself—as seen with other regional artists—and still maintain acceptance within the Texas-Mexican identity. While Verheyden's first two albums are presented with his band, the TexMeXplosion, his third album is marketed as that of a solo artist, further linking the work to a popular consideration.

While Verheyden's first album more closely adheres to classic conjunto repertory than his second (with almost every track in the first album presenting a well-known conjunto tune or at least a tune by Flaco, including works by the Texas Tornados and Los Super Seven), and his third album includes a much higher percentage of original songs (in combination with some traditional tracks), the second album provides a nice demonstration of Verheyden's balance between the Texas-Mexican tradition, his own Dutch heritage, and elements of more mainstream hybridity (albeit still influenced by Flaco's

Figure 7.1. Dwayne Verheyden (accordion). Courtesy of Dwayne Verheyden.

lead). Of the fifteen songs on the album, maybe five—"Cielito Lindo," "Canción Mixteca," "Prenda Del Alma," "Pollack Polka," and "La Bamba"—can be considered as "conjunto" tunes, although, of these, "Cielito Lindo," "Canción Mixteca," and "La Bamba," were originally (and prominently) Mexican folk tunes. Four more tracks—"Anselma," "Teresa La Panadera," "Voy A Tirarme A Los Vicios," and "Pepita De Mallorca"—present other styles of Latin American culture (Mexican, Colombian, and Paraguayan), although the first three of these songs have also been recorded by roots-rock groups like Los Lobos and Los Super Seven and Tejano acts like Roberto Pulido. The sole original song on the album, "Janeth," is in a loose conjunto style. Four additional tunes—"Wooden Heart," "Blue Spanish Eyes," and the two bonus tracks, "Adios Mi Amor (Bye Bye My Love)" and "Belle Hélène" demonstrate Verheyden's European heritage (and display the close connections between Texas-Mexican and German polka music). Yet, each of these songs also maintains connections to the popular tradition—either within U.S. American culture or European. One additional U.S. American popular song (with close connections to Flaco)—"Stand By Me"—finishes the album. While many of Verheyden's song choices in this second album can still be considered as well within the conservative conjunto tradition (and his musical decisions certainly are, as explored in more detail below), overall, he displays more of the types of stylistic flexibility seen in local artists like Flaco than the strict adherence to tradition seen in the works of Katsube. In this regard, it seems that Verheyden, having "proven" himself as an "authentic" representation of Texas-Mexican cultural identity through his initial forays into the genre (and his early designation as Flaco's stylistic heir), has earned the right to push (although only slightly) at the edges of the tradition, despite not maintaining the same sociocultural heritage and while still achieving acceptance among regional audiences as an appropriate participant in the genre. It is also important to note that Verheyden—emanating from a region with its own accordion heritage (and teachers) and growing up listening to conjunto music—achieved technical mastery at a young age. This technical proficiency helped him to quickly gain support among the Texas-Mexican community. While Katsube—as the first international conjunto artist to participate in regional venues like the Tejano Conjunto Festival—was largely a novelty act due to his cultural heritage, Verheyden was able to overcome the novelty of his own background more quickly (since audiences had seen global conjunto participants before) and bring the focus instead to his musical style. Verheyden then mimics not only the traditional Texas-Mexican style of conjunto, but also the hybridized pursuits of contemporary regional artists like Flaco, Jordan, and Saldívar.

Verheyden, like many other contemporary, local conjunto artists including Flaco, sings in a combination of Spanish and English, depending on the song. The more traditional conjunto tunes included on the album fall closely in line with standard Texas-Mexican practices. However, even the hybridized repertory follows the same musical patterns as Flaco employs throughout his own hybridized pursuits. In this way, Verheyden's conjunto practices are not truly innovative, but simply adhere to the more innovative style explored previously by local artists. On the second album, "Stand By Me" can serve as a good representation of Verherden's musical pursuits, particularly when compared with Flaco's earlier version of the song with Ry Cooder on *Chicken Skin Music*. While Verheyden's version of the song lies closely in line with the preceding Flaco/Cooder recording, it also seems to draw influence from the original Ben E. King performance. Overall, Verheyden's version provides a nice balance between the two earlier recordings, while inserting a handful of structural characteristics that actually bring it somewhat closer within the conjunto tradition than Flaco's example. Cooder alters the lyrics just slightly from King's original ("is" instead of "has" in the first line, elimination of the "nos" at the end of the first verse, elimination of "so darlin,' darlin'" at the beginning of the refrain, "and when" instead of "if" at the beginning of the second verse, and so on). Verheyden seems to be aware of both versions, maintaining many of the original lyrics that Cooder alters, while aligning with some of the secondary changes.

Structurally, King's recording follows a simple verse-refrain pattern (A1B A2B B), with a lengthy instrumental interlude (thirty-two seconds) preceding the final, extended iteration of the refrain (Tab. 7.2). The recording also begins with a relatively lengthy (fifteen seconds) instrumental introduction. Cooder maintains the basic structure of the piece, but repeats the refrain at each iteration and eliminates the instrumental interlude (A1BB A2BB B). Verheyden follows King's original structure more closely than Cooder's, performing each refrain only once and maintaining the instrumental interlude. However, Verheyden also pushes the structure more closely into the standard conjunto style of a ranchera, with brief instrumental passages following each refrain and inserted within the final, extended refrain (in a style of instrumental ending common to the ranchera form). In this way, while Cooder (with Flaco's participation) presents the song with certain conjunto influences (primarily simply through the inclusion of Flaco's accordion lines), Verheyden (free of Cooder's popular participation) manages to insert conjunto characteristics into the song in a manner analogous to that in many of the hybridized pursuits of Flaco, Saldívar, and Jordan. Following a relatively slow introduction in a *rubato* tempo, Verheyden's version of the song maintains

Table 7.2. “Stand By Me.” As performed and recorded by Ben E. King. From *Don’t Play That Song* (Atlantic Records 33-142, 1962). “Stand By Me.” As performed and recorded by Ry Cooder. From *Chicken Skin Music* (Reprise Records MS 2254, 1976). “Stand By Me.” As performed and recorded by Dwayne & the TexMeXplosion. From *Conjunto Tracks* (HKM Records 42533, 2012).

“Stand By Me” (Structure)					
King’s Form (Verse-Refrain)	Length (King)	Cooder’s Form (Verse-Refrain)	Length (Cooder)	Verheyden’s Form (Ranchera-ish)	Length (Verheyden)
Instrumental Introduction	0:00-0:15 (0:15)	Instrumental Introduction	0:00-0:22 (0:22)	Instrumental Introduction	0:00-0:20 (0:20)
A1	0:15-0:47 (0:32)	A1	0:22-1:04 (0:42)	A1	0:20-0:59 (0:39)
B	0:47-1:04 (0:17)	B	1:04-1:22 (0:18)	B	0:59-1:21 (0:22)
		B	1:22-1:41 (0:19)		
A2	1:04-1:35 (0:31)	A2	1:41-2:21 (0:40)	A2	1:21-1:59 (0:38)
B	1:35-1:52 (0:17)	B	2:21-2:39 (0:18)	B	1:59-2:16 (0:17)
		B	2:39-2:58 (0:19)		
Instrumental Interlude	1:52-2:24 (0:32)			Instrumental Interlude	2:16-2:35 (0:19)
B (Extended)	2:24-2:55 (0:31)	B (Extended)	2:58-3:36 (0:38)	B (Extended)	2:35-3:15 (0:40)

Example 7.3. Transcription of "Stand By Me," mm. 1–8: top melodic line of accordion introduction. As performed and recorded by Ry Cooder. From *Chicken Skin Music* (Reprise Records MS 2254, 1976).

Example 7.4. Transcription of "Stand By Me," mm. 1–8: top melodic line of accordion introduction. As performed and recorded by Dwayne & the Tex-MeXplosion. From *Conjunto Tracks* (HKM Records 42533, 2012).

a moderate tempo of 93 BPM. This corresponds closely to Cooder's version of the song, with Flaco similarly providing a *rubato* instrumental introduction before the vocals come in at a more consistent tempo of 85 BPM. Yet, Verheyden's recording again finds a balance between Cooder's version and King's original, which displays a faster tempo of 118 BPM throughout (thus avoiding the *rubato*-feel of Cooder's introduction).

The real similarities between Cooder/Flaco and Verheyden's versions of "Stand By Me" can be demonstrated by comparing the accordion insertions present in both (Ex. 7.3; Ex. 7.4). To start, the instrumental introductions for each recording are almost identical, as seen in the transcriptions of the top accordion line for each. The only difference between the two renditions occurs with the ornamental passagework at the end of each introduction, leading into the first verse. Flaco presents this passagework in triplet figures with large intervallic leaps, while Verheyden instead utilizes sixteenth-note figures, beginning with an octave leap, but then staying within a tighter range.

Likewise, the accordion passagework occurring under each iteration of the refrain is remarkably similar. The following transcription shows the top

Example 7.5. Transcription of "Stand By Me," first repeat of refrain (top melodic lines of vocal and accordion). As performed and recorded by Ry Cooder. From *Chicken Skin Music* (Reprise Records MS 2254, 1976).

Example 7.6. Transcription of "Stand By Me," first refrain (top melodic lines of vocal and accordion). As performed and recorded by Dwayne & the Tex-MeXplosion. From *Conjunto Tracks* (HKM Records 42533, 2012).

melodic line of the accordion figuration (with the primary vocal, for reference) in the first repeat of the refrain in Cooder's recording (in order to include the transition into the subsequent verse) and the first iteration of the refrain in Verheyden's rendition, respectively (Ex. 7.5; Ex. 7.6). While Verheyden alters the vocal melody slightly throughout (particularly in the first two measures of the excerpt and at measure 6—the final vocal phrase), he keeps the underlying accordion figuration closely similar to Flaco's prior example. The most prominent accordion figure, occurring in measure 2 of each excerpt, is identical except for a slight shift in rhythm in the second half of the measure. Verheyden includes an additional measure (m. 7) as he transitions into the subsequent verse, but the final accordion pattern in this excerpt (m. 8), is also identical to Flaco's model (m. 7 in the previous version). In this regard, while Verheyden does insert bits of his own interpretation—particularly in the vocal lines and accordion figuration serving as transitions between sections, he takes close influence throughout from Cooder/Flaco's earlier recording, demonstrating that the hybridity of this song comes entirely from the earlier recording, rather than showing evidence of Verheyden's own innovation.

Transnationalism and Hybridity in Dutch Conjunto Music

As in the case of Katsube, Verheyden's adoption of Texas-Mexican conjunto music can be complicated by examining this aspect of globalization through the specific lens of the artist's Dutch heritage. As Mel van Elteren explains, Dutch popular music (and Dutch popular culture in general) is closely connected to U.S. American popular culture.[74] While country-western music has remained relatively marginal in Dutch society, "older" acts like Emmylou Harris, Johnny Cash, and Willie Nelson and subgenres existing at the edges of "the slick Nashville style [that] is not very popular in Holland"—such as bluegrass and conjunto—do maintain a large following.[75] During the late 1960s, a longing for community in the Netherlands among the youth counter-culture led to an attraction to musical forms with roots in living communities. In country music, according to van Elteren, this process "implied a distanciation from the commercialized Nashville variant and a focus on the more 'authentic' acoustic subgenres," including "an increasing number of Dutch old-time country and bluegrass groups" from around 1970.[76] In addition, unlike newer country stars who can make more money elsewhere, older and more marginal artists often pursue profitable performance opportunities in the Netherlands, rather than in smaller scenes in the United States. As Verheyden notes, "Back in the days, when Flaco was a hit here in the Netherlands, there always were lots of people attending his performances, including the ones he participated in: The Texas Tornados."[77] Understandably, Dutch audiences gravitate to artists who have appeared consistently in the region, rather than those who have not.

Furthermore, the southernmost province of Limburg, in particular (where Verheyden is from), maintains close correspondence with southern German culture, and thus close musical connections with Texas-Mexican conjunto music; both traditions deriving from German polka and brass band music. As van Elteren explains, "The strong resemblance between Tex-Mex music and the musical style of southern Dutch bands as regards the polkalike rhythm may be explained from the Germanic influences both regions underwent in the past."[78] Furthermore, van Elteren asserts that Tex-Mex or conjunto music is simply "an almost natural result of playing up-tempo versions of traditional 'Dutch' accordion music."[79] In this regard, while Verheyden (and other, more rock-oriented groups like Rowwen Hèze and Borderline—see Chapter 8) adopts a musical form that ostensibly lies outside of his own cultural heritage, conjunto music in fact is closely related to the musical style of his home region, as well as popular throughout that region in its own right. As such, in addition to growing up with the genre through his father's affinity for Flaco's recordings, Verheyden's attraction to conjunto does not stray far from the types of music that might be more expected for a young Dutch (and Limburgish, especially) musician to perform. Conjunto is just different enough to make the young artist interesting and unique among local audiences on both sides of the ocean, but not exotic enough—from a Dutch perspective—to designate him as fully outside of his own familial heritage. Yet, as Verheyden explains, playing conjunto—rather than the closely related style of Dutch polka music—enabled him to be "cool" while playing an instrument that was not particularly popular among the younger generation.

Relatedly, while Katsube ultimately moved to the United States and performed primarily in South Texas, Verheyden has remained in the Netherlands, performing in Texas (and elsewhere within the United States) and Mexico, but also touring extensively throughout the Netherlands and Europe. For example, of the twenty-eight tour dates in 2018 listed on the artist's website, one is in Texas (at the Tejano Conjunto Festival), one in Holland, Michigan, six are in Mexico, and the other twenty performances are in Europe (nineteen in the Netherlands and one in Belgium). This is then a very different manifestation of globalization than seen in the performance career of Katsube. While the Japanese artist fully adopted a Texas-Mexican identity and performed as a conjunto musician within the traditional community in Texas, Verheyden—coming after this initial international participation in conjunto music—instead maintains a hybridized classification that draws from his heritage and an imagined Texas-Mexican identity. It is also interesting to note Verheyden's performances in Mexico. While Texas-based musicians have struggled to break into the Mexican market—largely due to sociopolitical conflicts between the two regions and the competitive threat between Texas and Mexican musicians, Verheyden—separated from these cultural clashes—carves out space for himself on both sides of the border. This process emphasizes that generic distinctions between conjunto and norteño have little to do with the music itself.

Similarly, while Katsube imitates De La Rosa, a local artist who did not pursue a global or hybridized career, Verheyden imitates Flaco, a hybrid, inter/national musician who performed throughout the United States and Europe. In this regard, perhaps Verheyden's global performances—like his hybridized recordings—are simply mimicking those of his mentor, rather than demonstrating any personal innovation in style or performance technique. As van Elteren explains, Dutch country groups (and thus related genres like conjunto) are strongly—and often entirely—influenced by U.S. American examples, singing cover songs in the English language and some original tunes in a largely derivative style. As van Elteren notes: "With only very few exceptions, [these groups] still lack originality and a clear identity of their own."[80] Verheyden similarly pushes at the edges of traditional conjunto music, performing hybrid styles related to his own cultural heritage and writing some of his own tunes (albeit in a conventional conjunto style). His music thus suggests a performative identity lying further along the popular side of the theorized folk-popular continuum. However, Verheyden does not stray far from the model of Flaco (in aesthetic style or performance), thus consolidating a form of folklore in accordance with Flaco's more popular lead. As the Dutch accordionist illustrates, from the time he was seven years old, his one goal was "To be as good, and to sound exactly like Flaco Jiménez."[81]

Conclusions: "We sure got some gritos..."

Through the contemporary influences of media and migration, international conjunto musicians like Katsube (with Los Gatos), Los Gallos, Conjunto San Antonio, and Verheyden adopt a style of music that is far outside of expected notions of cultural identity (language, location, ethnicity, and the like). While this external participation might suggest the incorporation of musical styles from these artists' home regions, the actual music produced in fact lies closely in line with traditional Texas-Mexican practices. International conjunto artists thus consolidate the regional form into a style of folklore, maintaining a common repertory, structure, and sound and adopting a musical persona (and often, an entire transnational identity through other aspects of their lives) that aligns with the traditional conjunto community, with little regard for individual artistry.

Alternatively, local conjunto musicians like Flaco, Saldívar, and Jordan shift the conjunto genre into a style of popular music, incorporating hybridized elements, original repertory, and a more commercialized mentality. This process creates a type of folk-popular continuum that encompasses various techniques of globalization within a single, regional genre. However, while these international artists do not typically insert stylistic elements of their own musical cultures, they nonetheless do bring elements of their familial backgrounds into their artistic pursuits, thus creating atypical forms of hybridization related to their varied sociocultural concerns. For example, Katsube draws from his Japanese heritage of close mimicry, a sense of community, and the promotion of Western niche musics, while Verheyden relates his adoption of conjunto to the German style of polka music he heard growing up in southern Limburg. Similarly, Gonzalez explains that his group plays conjunto in part because it relates to French accordion music: "First, the accordion is part of French culture, and the music is simply good roots music, and that music affects us. It is music that makes us respond, it inspires."[82] In addition, Katsube employs the Japanese language in his recordings, while Verheyden includes a handful of his local songs.

By maintaining a relatively traditional conjunto style, these international artists manage to achieve performative successes among the Texas-Mexican community, "making up" for any inevitably lacking "fixed" characteristics related to family heritage by staying closely in line with pre-established musical characteristics. Even a more contemporary musician like Verheyden who does write some of his own music does so within a conservative conjunto consideration. His hybrid repertory, elements of U.S. American popular music, and international performances correspond to methods that Flaco has previously used, eliminating additional innovation from his performative techniques. By maintaining a well-established conjunto sound, these international artists are accepted within the Texas-Mexican community (on both sides of the political border) as non-threatening curiosities (and, in the case of Verheyden—who in 2014 won the Tejano Music Award for Best New Artist—as full-fledged, well-respected members of the community). Verheyden describes, following his first performance at the Tejano Conjunto Festival in 2010: the crowd "applauded and we sure got some *gritos* [shouts of appreciation]. They'd never expect some white *gringos* from Europe play conjunto as good as their own bands do. . . . The fact that people in both Texas and Mexico appreciate that a young guy from the other side of the world plays 'their' [music] is something that I really see and feel … and it feels good, believe me."[83]

It is worth drawing attention to Verheyden's precise language: people from *both* Texas and Mexico. While the regional conjunto/norteño community draws a clear distinction between music—and people—from one side of the border or the other (despite almost identical stylistic elements), this Dutch accordionist, disconnected from the ethno-nationalism separating the two regions, instead classifies the music according to its aesthetic correlations. Beyond local distinctions of identity, Verheyden combines conjunto/norteño considerations to categorize the Texas/Mexican genre through musical elements alone. He is then accepted by audiences on both sides of the border in ways that remain inaccessible for either Texas or Mexican musicians. In this way, international conjunto artists challenge conceptions of heritage as the primary expression of identity, demonstrating that globalization constructs new identities through music.

CHAPTER 8

"¡Esto es globalización!"

Rowwen Hèze, the Rolling Stones, and the Commercialized Appropriation of Conjunto

Let's make a big fiesta. Let's make jamming things between our cultures. I had that feeling that one of these days I would jam with heavy weights and my dreams came true.

—Flaco Jiménez

Beyond Flaco Jiménez's musical hybridizations within the conservative conjunto tradition and his role in disseminating the Texas-Mexican music among a worldwide population, much of the artist's initial involvement in the globalization of the genre comes through his collaborative pursuits with mainstream rock stars. For example, when Flaco was on tour with his band in San Francisco in 1994, he received a phone message from legendary producer Don Was, asking him to come to Los Angeles to record with the Rolling Stones. As Flaco recalls, "I thought somebody was joking with me. In the morning, I called that number and it was Don Was. The Rolling Stones were recording in Hollywood. They picked me up and I didn't know what the hell I was going to record."[1] Along with Max Baca on bajo sexto, the Texas-Mexican artist recorded an accordion part for the song "Sweethearts Together," released on the Rolling Stones' *Voodoo Lounge* album in 1994. The album won a Grammy Award for the band for Best Rock Album in 1995.

As Flaco continues, "I called Don Was and he said, 'Yeah man, we're working on this record, and we're almost finished. But we've got one song that we want you to blend in with on the accordion.' . . . They already had an accordion sound on the part that I did, but it was a synthesizer thing, you know. Don said he thought it sounded good, but he told me they wanted the true sound—the authentic sound of Tex-Mex."[2] This drive for "authenticity," ostensibly gained through the use of folk musics emanating from simple, "unsophisticated" cultures like the Texas-Mexican border community, simultaneously exploited the conjunto tradition as a form of exotic spectacle and helped to spread the music among an international population. It is then important to consider the initial globalization of the sociocultural genre as a manifestation of this sense of exoticism, externally imposed (and by mainstream popular artists—i.e., those emanating from the same dominant culture that the artform was originally created in response to), instead of derived from within the community itself (lacking internal instigation despite local participation).

Similarly, in contrast to direct Texas-Mexican influences in the works of U.S. American rock artists like East Los Angeles group Los Lobos and the works of Dutch conjunto performers like Dwayne Verheyden, inter/national popular artists like the Dutch rock band Rowwen Hèze have developed a style of music incorporating Texas-Mexican conjunto characteristics through a secondary filter of influence (in this case, through the works of Los Lobos). As Jan Brands describes, the 1999 Amsterdam performance of Rowwen Hèze with Los Lobos for the television program *ParadisoLife!* was "one of the most beautiful moments in Dutch pop history."[3] Following individual performances by both bands, Los Lobos and Rowwen Hèze joined together on stage with a bilingual version (Spanish and the regional dialect of Limburgish) of Los Lobos conjunto tune "De Moan" / "Estoy Sentado Aquí." Brands details: "A really great moment, this interplay of men from such different corners of the world. Universal music. Pure happiness."[4]

Following this initial performance, the two bands performed a bilingual interpretation of "Kroenenberg" / "Ay Te Dejo En San Antonio." In this rendition, the Spanish and Limburgish versions of the chorus are sonically almost identical, corresponding to a tongue-in-cheek scenario recounting the failed attempts of a Limburgish narrator to attract a girl in her own language.[5] Accordingly, lead singers Jack Poels and Cesar Rosas sing the chorus together throughout the performance. Tierra Caliente, a group of mariachi musicians from Amsterdam, then joined in to participate on "La Bamba," followed by a joint rendition of "Bestal Mar" / "Anselma." YouTube commenters on these videos excitedly emphasize the ethnically and geographically inclusive performances.[6]

> Fantastic. Makes me glad to be alive!
> *¡Esto es globalización!* [This is globalization!]
> See we are all of one world. Love this song. Love this band.
> I don't care what anyone thinks about how music "should be." This is just joy joy joy.

This secondary Texas-Mexican influence of Los Lobos on the Dutch rock group Rowwen Hèze denotes a further manifestation of the globalization of conjunto, ultimately indicating that shared sociological experiences, despite differing regions, ethnicities, languages, and the like, can create a unified combination of creative characteristics.

While these performances demonstrate a wide range of inter/national musicians using the influences of Texas-Mexican conjunto music (with and without participation by local artists), they also demonstrate the globalization of the genre, not only in its spread to external populations, but also in its adoption—in various forms—among a global community. While each of these performances showcases the adoption—and adaption—of conjunto by artists falling outside of not only the primary culture and location of the Texas-Mexican tradition, but also outside of the primary conjunto genre (as opposed to international conjunto artists like Kenji Katsube and Verheyden), the individual manifestation of these cross-cultural pursuits varies based on the sociocultural positionality of the external artists themselves. This allows us to consider the appropriation of conjunto as a process of interconnection, exoticism, or exploitation.

"World Music" and a Framework of Exoticism

The initial globalization of the Texas-Mexican conjunto genre—noted at first in Flaco's musical collaborations during the 1970s with Anglo-American rock stars like Doug Sahm and Ry Cooder—falls closely in line with the so-called "world music" efforts of the 1980s by artists like Paul Simon and David Byrne. These exoticized pursuits follow earlier Orientalist practices like the use of the sitar and participation by Ravi Shankar (with the Beatles) in rock music of the 1960s and stem from even earlier manifestations of Orientalism in the Western art music of the nineteenth century. As Aaron van Klyton notes, "the early success of world music was based on differences situated through discourses of exoticism, discovery, authenticity, othering/difference, and a sense of place."[7] It is these simultaneous discourses of exoticism and authenticity that initiated the first external interest in conjunto music and led to collaborative pursuits, but also to the hybridizations and international attention explored previously. The globalization of the genre through the intervention by hegemonic figures like Cooder suggests exoticism and exploitation, particularly for a music fundamentally created in response to just such sociocultural hegemonies.

The "world music" movement of the 1980s was created by a group of record executives in 1987 as a marketing category used to describe cultural appropriations of non-Western musics by elite Western performers, as well as international genres presented to a middle-class, Western audience.[8] Works like Simon's *Graceland* have arguably generated profitable forays for the minoritized artists (here, Black South Africans) into mainstream musical successes, as well as certain degrees of respect, recognition, and validation for marginalized musical styles. However, they have also received criticism of cultural imperialism, since—notwithstanding monetary compensation but largely disregarding actual musical contributions—the music produced inevitably belongs to the elite artist only, replicating global power structures through the inherent inequity of the music industry. As Steven Feld explains, these collaborative practices "are asymmetrical, specifically assuming that 'taking without asking' is a musical right of the owners of technology, copyrights, and distribution networks."[9] Furthermore, as Louise Meintjes reminds us, in *Graceland*, "Simon profits financially from the project over and above everyone else."[10]

Invocation of the sociocultural "other" has appeared in earnest in musical practices since at least nineteenth-century Orientalism. Inserting exotic elements into familiar creative styles does not typically imply any serious knowledge of the appropriated culture (although, in the case of world music, it can), but instead brings a sense of drama and excitement in the unknown—new flavors—to the expected musical works. Yet, participation by minority musicians in the resulting, exoticized works, as in world music pursuits like *Graceland* and Flaco's various cross-cultural collaborations, adds a layer of "authenticity" to the stylistic appropriations. That being said, these notions of authenticity—used as a marketing tool among commercial culture—also denote a sense of primitivism, marking (and encouraging) the contemporary minority other to remain "frozen in the past."[11]

Flaco Jiménez: Consideration of Collaboration as Exoticism and/or Exploitation

A member of one of the most—if not *the* most—prominent and influential families in the conjunto genre, Flaco grew up deeply ingrained in the traditional Texas-Mexican style. However, growing up in San Antonio, he also experienced a variety of other musical sounds. Yet, his initial participation in mainstream musical culture came about only through the intervention of Anglo-American rock stars. In 1972, San Antonio singer-songwriter Doug Sahm brought Flaco on board to play studio sessions with Bob Dylan and Dr. John. Actual mainstream recognition began with Flaco's participation on Ry Cooder's album *Chicken Skin Music* (1976) and the subsequent international tour.[12] As Flaco notes, "Even though Doug was the first to line me up Dylan and Dr. John, I don't think it was time yet for my instrument to really come into its own. It was there, barely. . . . I think it was Ry who really did it for me."[13] He continues, "I always give credit to Ry . . . because he really was the one who opened the doors for me to record for a major label and expose my solo stuff."[14] That being said, Flaco's first major-label solo album didn't come out until 1992 with *Partners*, another collaborative pursuit presenting a series of duets with Flaco and mainstream country-western stars.

Following Flaco's mainstream "discovery" through his work with Sahm and Cooder, the Texas-Mexican artist came to be in high demand as a studio musician, recording with acts like Peter Rowan, Willie Nelson, The Clash, Santana, and Bryan Ferry, among many others. As concert promoter Lucy Peña asserts, "Anybody that's anybody in the music industry has worked with Flaco Jiménez."[15] However, while Flaco's work with mainstream artists has brought a certain degree of global recognition to both the artist and the musical community he represents, he has also received criticism of "selling-out," distancing himself from his home culture, and/or being exploited by the dominant industry.

Analogous to Simon's *Graceland* and other "world music" collaborations, the minority participant (in this case, Flaco) is paid fairly throughout these works as a studio musician (i.e., as a wage laborer rather than a major contract artist, as the music industry dictates). His work with prominent recording artists has led to greater recognition and more profitable opportunities—record contracts, concert tours, etc.—for Flaco and (to a certain extent) for the entire Texas-Mexican community (as *Graceland* paved the way for later successes in the West for Ladysmith Black Mambazo and Black South African music in general). Flaco attributes much of his later success to these cross-cultural collaborations, noting that, "Some time ago, people would say, 'Oh, the accordion, that's what grandpa liked, to play Lady of Spain or O Sole Mio, you know?' Now it's changed—the accordion is a groovy instrument. It's a rockin' instrument!"[16] And furthermore, "I like combining different cultures in English and Spanish—which we did—because it opens more roads for Tex-Mex."[17]

Just as the Black South African community appreciates *Graceland* for the "international exposure it offers" and the "prestige and popularity it brings at home,"[18] Flaco articulates a general appreciation for mainstream recording artists in bringing attention to Texas-Mexican music: "Besides Doug, I recorded with Buck Owens, Dwight Yoakam, Linda Ronstadt, the Rolling Stones—so many—so many, it would take two days. I really appreciate their help, to make people understand that there are channels among cultures."[19]

Furthermore, Flaco attributes his success not to his own stylistic preferences, but to mainstream artists like Cooder and Sahm: "Doug told me: you're not supposed to play just that simple, traditional conjunto music. There are so many players who stayed in the same crater like my papa did. Doug showed me there were other worlds out there."[20]

However, despite Flaco's (and Ladysmith Black Mambazo's) own appreciation for the benefits produced by his work with hegemonic artists, it is difficult to consider these creative products without also noting the power differentials in such appropriations between elite artists like Simon, Cooder, and the Rolling Stones and more marginalized performers. Carol Silverman discusses this distinction between appropriations by the powerful and by the marginal, asserting that, "When the powerful appropriate, the marginal often lose in the process because they cannot fight back in terms of ownership or copyright."[21] Regardless of certain benefits gained for artists like Flaco in these types of collaborations, the economic rewards from the final product are greater for the more powerful musicians. As Feld describes, musical appropriation "is a melody of admiration, even homage and respect; a fundamental source of connectedness, creativity, and innovation." However, it "is harmonized by a counter-melody of power, even control and domination; a fundamental source of maintaining asymmetries in ownership and commodification of musical works."[22] In addition, it is disconcerting (Feld uses "arrogant") to assume (or even simply notice) that recognition of marginalized artists like Flaco must come through the "assistance" of Anglo-American rock stars. In considering the actual contributions of marginalized performers as compared to the elite musicians, the elements of "exoticism" brought about through the minority participation often seem to bring more to the final creative products than the rock stars' efforts alone. As Feld notes, in *Graceland*, "the actual musical contribution—the structure and performance of the song materials—seems to owe much more to the bands [here Los Lobos and zydeco group Dopsie and Company] than to Simon."[23] Analysis of Flaco's actual musical contributions on his various cross-cultural collaborations demonstrates similar results.

Flaco Jiménez: Socio-Musical Analysis of Cross-Cultural Collaborations

Two of Flaco's most prominent collaborations include his work with the Rolling Stones on "Sweethearts Together" and with Dwight Yoakam and Buck Owens on "Streets of Bakersfield." Flaco's most noticeable contribution to "Sweethearts Together" (the tenth track on the *Voodoo Lounge* album

Table 8.1. "Sweethearts Together." As performed and recorded by the Rolling Stones. From *Voodoo Lounge* (Virgin CDV 2750, 1994).

"Sweethearts Together" (Structure)		
Original Form (Ranchera-ish)	Language	Length
Instrumental Introduction		0:00–0:16 (0:16)
B1	English	0:16–0:40 (0:24)
Instrumental Interlude		0:40–0:46 (0:06)
A1	English	0:46–1:10 (0:24)
B2	English	1:10–1:34 (0:24)
Instrumental Interlude		1:34–1:39 (0:05)
A2	English	1:39–2:02 (0:23)
B3	English	2:02–2:25 (0:23)
Instrumental Interlude		2:25–3:01 (0:36)
A3	English	3:01–3:25 (0:24)
B3	English	3:25–3:48 (0:23)
Instrumental Ending		3:48–4:41 (1:00)

from 1994) appears in the lengthy (thirty-six seconds) instrumental interlude following the third iteration of the refrain (B3). The structure of the song takes the form of a Texas-Mexican ranchera, beginning and ending with instrumental passages, and presenting a series of verse-refrain pairs (A1B2, A2B3, and A3B3) separated by brief (each only five to six seconds, other than the section following the third refrain) instrumental interludes (albeit also including extended vocal patterns) (Tab. 8.1). The lyrics of each refrain are altered briefly with each iteration. In addition to Flaco's prominent participation in the lengthy interlude, he also provides subtle accordion patterns underneath and between successive lines of lyrics, beginning with the second refrain and increasing in prominence through the rest of the recording.

Yet, despite Flaco's inclusion on a mainstream rock album, he does not incorporate the hybridized characteristics from Western popular music noted in the instrumental passagework of many of his later solo pursuits. Instead, his instrumental contribution remains very conservative, arguably indistinguishable from the types of accordion passagework any number of Texas-Mexican conjunto performers before him might have inserted into a similar work. In this regard, Flaco fulfills the expected role within world music practices of the marginalized musician as exotic element. He provides an "authentic" insertion of conservative characteristics for mainstream consumption. Throughout the artist's work with various Anglo-American rock stars, the mainstream media refers to Flaco's contributions as some sort of south-of-the-border cultural (and frequently culinary) stereotype.

For example, writing for *Rolling Stone* in 1992, Don McLeese asserts that "Jiménez has provided the hot sauce on recordings by Ry Cooder, Dwight Yoakam and Linda Ronstadt."[24] Writing for *USA Today* in 1992, David Zimmerman suggests that Flaco's country-western "partners" on his album of the same name "seem to get extra zip from Jiménez's insistent, spicy rhythms."[25] Writing for *Billboard* in 1996, Ramiro Burr notes that "Jiménez's three-row button accordion has long spiced the works of a diverse group of artists."[26] Writing for *The Beat* in 1998, Bob Tarte describes the artist's "tasty accordion solo" on Jimmy Sturr's "big polka orchestra" album, *Dance With Me*.[27] Numerous journalists also describe the Texas-Mexican "flavor" provided by Flaco's accordion passages on more mainstream works. In this way, as van Klyton notes, "World music was commercialized in Western markets through discourses of 'Otherness' and exoticism."[28] While Texas-Mexican conjunto music emanates from within the United States, and hence is not truly "world music" in a strict, geographic sense, it maintains many of the same sociocultural characteristics related to minoritized communities exploited throughout other world music pursuits and can be considered in the same analysis. As Feld asserts, "the situation [involving the relationship between the colonizing and the colonized] would have been little different had world music been more bluntly termed *third world music*."[29]

In addition, according to van Klyton, "authenticity formed a key component of early marketing strategies [of world music]."[30] This desire for authenticity—inherent in the associated mainstream discourse but also in the conservative nature of resulting products like "Sweethearts Together"—is also observed throughout Flaco's cross-cultural collaborations. For example, at the beginning of Cooder's work with Flaco in 1975, the mainstream artist describes his desire for "purity" in music, present in "old songs" and "Tex-Mex music." As Cooder explains, "I listen to that kind of music [conjunto] all the time now. . . . Of course, the music was even better back in the '50s, before commercialism started affecting everything, but it's still some of the best stuff I've heard."[31] Interestingly, although the artist pursues certain hybridizations on albums like *Chicken Skin Music*, he expresses disdain for hybridizations in minority musics like conjunto in favor of the "authentic" musical elements. He notes: "To me . . . when you mix things up, you lose the power of the original. That's why I like the Depression music and the regional stuff. When music starts getting hybrid, it starts getting weaker. And when people start mixing styles, when they start getting very conscious and then self-conscious about what they're doing, they start to ruin it."[32] Apparently it is acceptable for Cooder himself to hybridize any musical forms he desires, but the source material should remain "pure."

Furthermore, despite Flaco's insistence that his first major-label solo album (*Partners*) conveys his own stylistic preferences and unique manner of cross-cultural hybridization, with individual song choices by the participating artists, the album is read in the mainstream media as an "authentic" contribution to commercial culture. Writing for the *Chicago Tribune* in 1992, Chris Heim asserts that the "partners" on the album "seem to know and respect the music and chose songs and a style of presentation that remain true [ostensibly to traditional Texas-Mexican culture, regardless of Flaco's actual hybridized style or intent]."[33] Similarly, reviewing Flaco's single "Jealous Heart" (an additional collaboration with country singer Radney Foster) for *Billboard* magazine in 1995, Larry Flick praises the "fleet-fingered accordion work" that "adds a little grit to the proceeding," in contrast to "the slick production that currently dominates the country music mainstream."[34] This positive citation of "grit" further demonstrates the mainstream desire to keep minority artists like Flaco in a primitive "box," separated from the dominant musical practices like the "slick production" of the mainstream. In the same way, in describing Flaco's participation on the soundtrack for *Happy, Texas* in 1999, Dean Buckley notes that the musician's contributions positively "inject color [exoticism] without detracting from the album's overall homey feel [authenticity]."[35] By 2000, John Kelly, writing for *The Irish Times*, argues that the sound of Flaco's accordion is "essential for anyone who wants to create a Tex-Mex essence."[36]

Furthermore, despite certain elements of the standard Texas-Mexican conjunto structure present in "Sweethearts Together," Flaco did not control any aspects of the recording beyond his own instrumental passages. As the musician explains, upon arrival at the studio, he listened to the almost-finished song and then played along as he thought best (in what he assumed was only a trial run):

> When I got to the studio, Keith and Mick were there. It was straight to the recording booth. Mick said: check out the song and we'll give you a few passes. I heard the song. It was simple. It wasn't that hard rock thing these crazy guys do. After one pass, I told Jagger to play it again so I could get the feeling of the song. He told me to simply play along. I tried to blend what the song was about. Then I got secure as to what I was going to do. I told Mick I was set to go. He says: why? It had been a dry run for me but that sneaky guy had punched me in and the track was already recorded. . . . There were no takes at all.[37]

Flaco's own opinion of the song as "simple," in addition to the minimal expectations for any sort of preparation (or preference on the part of the mainstream artists) of musical material or technique provides a clear demonstration of the type of simplistic instrumental passagework desired by the band for the track. Flaco brought a Texas-Mexican "flavor" to the work, but any further sense of musicality—despite the artist's virtuosic abilities—was not necessary for the bit of exoticism desired. Rosas of Los Lobos describes a similar process in working with Simon on the *Graceland* album (for "All Around the World or The Myth of Fingerprints"):

> We expected [Simon] to have a song for us to interpret when we met him in Los Angeles, but he said, "You guys just play," and we said "Play what?" We just worked up a bunch of stuff that he eventually got a song out of, and that was it. . . . We felt a little detached from the finished piece, we didn't have any real involvement in it.[38]

In both cases, the elite artist wants a certain, exotic sound, but doesn't seem to be concerned with the specific musical elements needed or even a particularly high level of musicianship. In addition, while neither minority artist fully participates in the overall production of the song, the elite artist simply expects Flaco and Los Lobos, respectively, to come up with the musical material with little—if any—preparation. Yet, once the final product is released, the elite artist takes primary credit (and primary economic benefit) for the exotic insertion—and thus the song as a whole.

Flaco's work with Yoakam and Owens on "Streets of Bakersfield," on Yoakam's 1988 album, *Buenas Noches From a Lonely Room*, demonstrates similar circumstances as in his other collaborative works, although here Flaco's contribution is more prominent and more closely in line with traditional conjunto practices. As in the previous example, the structure of the song takes the form of a ranchera, with an instrumental introduction, interlude, and ending (incorporated into the extension of the final refrain) (Tab. 8.2). Verse-refrain pairs (A1B and A2B) appear between each instrumental section, with one additional repetition of the refrain (B) at the end of the recording. Throughout the performance, Flaco provides accordion passagework in much the same way as he does within the conjunto tradition, performing between lines of lyrics and as part of each instrumental section. However, while standard conjunto practices give the lead instrumental line consistently to the accordion, here Flaco alternates instrumental passages with the lead guitar and fiddle (much as Yoakam and Owens alternate lead vocals throughout). The accordion contributions remain conservative throughout, but the work seems much more collaborative in nature than the Rolling Stones song, providing

Table 8.2. "Streets of Bakersfield." As performed and recorded by Dwight Yoakam. From *Buenas Noches From a Lonely Room* (Reprise Records 25749, 1988).

"Streets of Bakersfield" (Structure)		
Original Form (Ranchera)	Language	Length
Instrumental Introduction		0:00–0:09 (0:09)
A1	English	0:09–0:45 (0:36)
B	English	0:45–1:03 (0:18)
Instrumental Interlude		1:03–1:21 (0:18)
A2	English	1:21–1:56 (0:35)
B	English	1:56–2:14 (0:18)
B (Extended)	English	2:14–2:46 (0:32)

a true sense of hybridity (and seemingly more equal musical contributions), rather than mere exoticism. The country-western style and rhythmic emphasis also relate more closely to the conjunto tradition than rock practices, demonstrating a more consistent sense of creative alliance throughout. In this way, while cross-cultural partnerships between minoritized musicians and elite popular artists can raise issues of exoticism and exploitation, the mere act of collaboration does not necessitate cultural imperialism. Individual circumstances are dictated by the individuals involved.

The Dutch/Mexican "Oompah-Rock" Connection between Rowwen Hèze and Los Lobos

By 1999, Rowwen Hèze had achieved regional successes with versions of Los Lobos-inspired conjunto tunes like "Anselma" (as "Bestel Mar"), "Ay Te Dejo En San Antonio" (as "Kroenenberg"), and "Estoy Sentado Aquí" (as "De Moan"). After starting as an English cover band, Rowwen Hèze gained initial prominence by singing "party music" in a regional, Limburgish dialect. When the group discovered Los Lobos, they created a distinctive sound combining characteristics of Texas-Mexican accordion music, U.S. American rock, and the regional brass band. Rowwen Hèze's characteristic approach and eventual success can be traced to the group's early assimilation of Los Lobos's musical style. As Poels, lead singer and songwriter for the group, illustrates, "When we first heard [Los Lobos's] album . . . *And a Time to Dance*, it was like a sledgehammer. It was like falling in love for the first time. In our own way, we have further embroidered on the music. Playing a lot, writing many songs, and eventually you get like Los Lobos, with your own sound."[39] In the Netherlands, Los Lobos is often referred to as "the Latin American equivalent of Rowwen Hèze,"[40] while Rowwen Hèze is called "Los Limbos," a reference to the regional community and the group's primary musical influence.[41] This relationship between seemingly disconnected cultural communities demonstrates the effect of common socioeconomic background on modern musical globalization, as will be discussed in detail below.

Looking deeper into the seemingly unexpected musical relationship between the Limburg region of the Netherlands and the Mexican-American community of East Los Angeles, certain similarities of background become clear, creating what George Lipsitz calls a "family of resemblance," in which seemingly disparate cultural groups draw from parallel life experiences to cultivate a cohesive understanding from individual elements; in Marshall Berman's words, a "unity of disunity."[42] In addition, while the concept of "Americanization" generally promotes a certain ambivalence and even animosity among communities overrun by the external culture, this Dutch absorption of Mexican-American musical characteristics instead generates a common stylistic "family" among ethnically and socioeconomically marginalized populations. In contrast to more exploitative understandings of cross-cultural assimilation between U.S. American rock stars and global roots-rock bands, common social backgrounds among poor, ethnically diverse, and typically marginalized communities—regardless of extreme geographic and cultural distances—instead create metaphorically collaborative groups that transcend perceived positional boundaries. In this way, modern musical globalization shifts any sense of cultural unification from historical groupings of race, language, and location to instead encompass individual identification based on socioeconomic background and personal association. In our modern, interconnected society, global cultures become more about economic positionality—rich versus poor; mainstream versus minority—than Europe (or other geographic locations) versus America.

Los Lobos emanates from the historically poor, primarily Mexican-American region of East Los Angeles. From the second half of the twentieth century (following the migration of Mexican laborers at the beginning of the century), the community has struggled to achieve equal opportunities of education, employment, and political representation as the surrounding (Anglo-American) neighborhoods. Similarly, although geographically distant, Rowwen Hèze comes from the village of America (!) in the southern Dutch province of Limburg, a rural community in the impoverished De

Peel region of the province, best known economically for the extraction of peat for fuel. As Mel van Elteren explains, "The area is extremely poor, and its culture is marginal vis-à-vis the Randstad [the urban center of the Netherlands including Amsterdam, The Hague, Rotterdam, and Utrecht]."[43] In addition, while the broader Los Angeles community maintains a certain multiculturalism, sophistication, and affluence, the province of Limburg, situated between Germany, Belgium, and the Netherlands, shows a similar globalization and economic advantage, especially as compared to the more financially downtrodden De Peel. East Los Angeles and the De Peel region of the Netherlands can thus be seen as analogous communities in more expansive, richer, and cosmopolitan areas.

Related to each group's positionality within a broader cultural community, Rowwen Hèze and Los Lobos are each associated with a secondary language or dialect within the regional form of communication. While the principal language of Southern California is English, particularly within the mainstream rock community (as well as the more influential political, economic, and educational arenas), Los Lobos sings in English, Spanish, or a localized mixture of Spanish and English. By maintaining this culturally evocative dialect outside of the original community (as the band's popularity has spread, particularly in recent years, beyond the confines of East Los Angeles and even beyond the primary Chicanx fan base), Los Lobos preserves an explicit connection to the band members' cultural roots and helps to legitimize a minoritized heritage among wide-reaching geographic and socioeconomic contexts. They establish a counter-hegemonic response (albeit understated) to the mainstream, heavily Anglicized, rock community.

Similarly, Rowwen Hèze has upheld a distinctively provocative resolution to sing in the band members' own, regional Limburgish dialect. When Poels first joined the group in 1985, he did so under the stipulation that the local dialect was used in performance. This decision to sing in a language only really understood by a closely localized population designated the group as a symbolic representation of the marginalized community, forming a deeply loyal fan base and also establishing a certain counter-hegemonic response against the mainstream, primarily urban (and also largely Anglicized), Dutch culture. Louis Peter Grijp is quick to note that the symbolic element for Rowwen Hèze and other regional, "dialect" bands creates a sense of personal identification and broader, inter-province unification through a powerful rural-versus-urban dichotomy, but does not provide a particular regional identity, in the sense of one rural province versus another. As Grijp explains, "[N]one of the singers to our knowledge has ever mentioned regional identity as the motivation behind his or her decision to sing in dialect. . . . Regional rivalry is barely—if ever—an issue for . . . dialect singers. The contrast between countryside and city . . . does play a key role, however. [Dialect bands] have given the countryside a voice."[44]

While Rowwen Hèze has developed a certain creative significance beyond the local De Peel population, as with Los Lobos, the persistent use of the Limburgish language serves as a vivid reminder that the group's roots and continuing ties remain within their own community (although, ironically, this shared sense of local belonging and commitment to the personal language has in turn created an alternative cultural community for the two bands). Through the personal uses of the local form of the Spanish language by Los Lobos and this individual, regional Limburgish dialect by Rowwen Hèze, the preservation of intimately cultural practices throughout musical performances intended, at least in part, for more ethnically and socioeconomically diverse audiences establishes a deliberate, minority response to the dominant popular culture.

Both Los Lobos and Rowwen Hèze draw from a wide variety of cultural influences, but a primary creative basis for each group is Texas-Mexican conjunto music with elements of U.S. American rock to create an amalgamation of European polka and Western popular music. According to the band's website, the name "Los Lobos" ("the wolves") was inspired by a National Geographic article about real wolves in the wild, creating parallels with the group's struggle to "gain mainstream rock success while maintaining their Mexican roots."[45] At the *ParadisoLife!* performance in 1999, David Hidalgo describes the background of the group: "Our music is a mix of everything. We come from the east of Los Angeles, the Mexican area of the city. There you can taste as a child from many cultural and musical influences. In our youth radio brought a lot of rhythm and blues and soul music. In addition, you had the English music, like the Beatles, and of course, Mexican music, on our mothers' morning radio. All this together is Los Lobos."[46] Meanwhile, the name "Rowwen Hèze" (indicating "rough" or "crude") refers to Christiaan Hesen, a nineteenth-century resident of De Peel, who, as van Elteren describes, was "a legendary freak, . . . famous as a faith healer."[47] By invoking the legendary regional character of Christiaan Hesen, the band not only maintain a close connection to the location and cultural background, but also create a lasting association with the regional, working-class community.

Moving beyond the cheerful "party" repertory, the band have increasingly introduced a melancholic aspect to their music, using their own dialect to describe everyday life and ordinary people from within their own, often marginalized community. The local understanding of Christiaan Hesen as an unconventional, uncivilized individual, deviating drastically from accepted societal practices, outside of the community, yet the first to come to the aid of his community, helps to establish the band among regional audiences as an encouraging indication of cultural solidarity against contemporary threats of urbanization and globalization from the mainstream, "Americanized" population. In this sense, Rowwen Hèze paradoxically uses "America," through the marginalized music of Los Lobos, to counteract the "America" of the heavily Anglicized popular culture of the Netherlands. In addition, the dichotomous personality and cultural symbolism of Christiaan Hesen seemingly mimic the band's contrasting reputation for playing wild, party music and deeper, melancholic tunes, as well as the bifocality of the musicians within an urban-rural, rich-poor, mainstream-marginalized duality, and in a sense, through the unexpected Dutch-Mexican connection between Limburg and East Los Angeles.

Cultural Assimilation in the Works of Rowwen Hèze

As van Elteren illustrates in more detail (1994; 1996; 1997), following the Second World War, Dutch musical practices became largely dependent on Anglo-American popular styles. While this assimilative tendency is true for much of the world during the second half of the twentieth century, the propensity seems particularly pronounced in the Netherlands. Indeed, as Grijp attests, "there is not even a typically Dutch style, in either classical, popular, or folk music."[48] In this regard, the mainstream, urban culture that Rowwen Hèze ostensibly responds against is the same U.S. American culture counteracted by the minoritized elements of Los Lobos. Indeed, as van Elteren emphasizes, "[F]or the generations who grew up in Holland after the Second World War, the Anglo-American pop/rock music was often part of their collective life history too!"[49]

In recent years, a historically prevalent use of a number of distinctive regional dialects in the Netherlands has given way to a certain linguistic standardization due to a growing decline in the number of local speakers with each generation, the increasing use of standard Dutch, and a blending of local dialects into sprawling "regiolects."[50] However, a number of rural musicians have recently started to perform in these regional dialects. In addition to a sense of marginalization for provincial communities due to humble occupations and meager economic opportunities, the characteristic languages of the farming population of the Netherlands mark its inhabitants as a downtrodden, minority community in comparison to the "sophisticated" urban center of the country.

Describing the experiences of lead singer Bennie Jolink of Normaal, one of the first and most successful of the current "dialect bands," as a student chasing the artistic community in Amsterdam, Grijp writes, "He may have looked pretty hip, but as soon as he opened his mouth, his Achterhoeks [a region in the eastern part of the country] accent exposed him as a 'peasant' and people lost interest. The suffering inflicted by these incidents would have far-reaching artistic consequences."[51] As Grijp explains, for Normaal, Rowwen Hèze, and other contemporary Dutch groups who sing in their own regional dialects, the significance of these lingual practices for the general rural community of the Netherlands is less about the specific language or individual province, but instead about personal expression and cultural pride in the entire marginalized population outside of the urban mainstream. In this regard, the "family of resemblance" formed through the common sociological backgrounds and corresponding musical characteristics of Rowwen Hèze and Los Lobos can be reasonably expanded to also encompass other dialect bands such as Normaal. According to Grijp, "What also came across was the all-important message—the fact that dialect was used instead of standard Dutch or English. The Achterhoeks spoken by Normaal therefore represents the 'language of farmers' in general. The contrast that Jolink and his kind liked to exploit is that of city versus country, of Randstad versus province."[52]

In categorizing Los Lobos as an "authentic" Mexican-American band, using ethnic characteristics to counteract the mainstream musical sound, while simultaneously responding to Anglo-American creative dominance by reclaiming certain hegemonic elements as part of their own cultural heritage, Dave Marsh compares the group to Menudo, a commercially successful Puerto Rican boy band, active especially during the 1980s. As Marsh explains, Menudo has "consolidated a Latin-tinged Europop sound that has made them as popular in Mexico City as in New York or San Juan," conquering the more limited Latin market and ultimately pursuing widespread American success.[53] Yet, quoting *New York Times* columnist Stephen Holden, Marsh emphasizes that "Menudo is really nothing more than a Latin version of the Osmonds or the Partridge Family and will have the same lasting impact: none." In contrast, rather than pandering to the mainstream, commercial public, Los Lobos maintains their own socioculturally significant, hybridized sound.

For both Rowwen Hèze and Los Lobos, a common heritage of local marginalization has stimulated a geographically diverse, creative unification through the use of Texas-Mexican accordion music. By combining elements of their own ethnic and socioeconomic heritages with other marginalized forms, the groups have produced a single, imagined community standing against the mainstream, heavily Americanized and Anglicized national and international cultures. Similarly, by taking popular characteristics from dominant musical practices as their own, these musicians create a counter-response to the typical hegemony of mainstream musical practices. In contrast to more exploitative practices of cultural appropriation by U.S. American rock stars like the Rolling Stones, these groups thus create a new significance for historical musics, outside of more limited boundaries based on class, location, language, and ethnicity. That being said, doing so pigeonholes these groups into more marginalized characterizations outside of popular practices. Unlike Texas-Mexican artists like Flaco, these groups are not classified as "conjunto." Nonetheless, in using Texas-Mexican elements in coordination with marginalized, albeit not specifically Texas-Mexican identities, these groups are typically characterized as some form of "roots-rock," unlike the pure "rock" classification of groups like the Rolling Stones who combine certain Texas-Mexican elements with a mainstream, Euro-American identity. As such, while "conjunto" is certainly not a fundamentally negative characterization, these generic groupings remain fundamentally connected to notions of identity, despite musical characteristics, interpretations, or intent.

Musical Influences in the Works of Rowwen Hèze

The traditional musical characteristics for the Texas-Mexican border community and the Dutch province of Limburg draw heavily from German polka music (as also seen in the music of Verheyden). In this regard, Rowwen Hèze's stylistic reliance on Los Lobos should be framed not as a simple cultural appropriation, but rather as a contemporary re-appropriation of a style of music that actually originated in the band's own backyard (and was similarly appropriated from Germany years before by both regions). However, Rowwen Hèze (following Los Lobos) also adopts the conjunto and rock characteristics that the genre gained through the twentieth century.

While Rowwen Hèze implements musical characteristics emanating from the primary style of Los Lobos (and thus conjunto music in general) among a variety of performances, three Dutch recordings ("Bestel Mar," "Kroenenberg," and "De Moan," all originally appearing on *Boem*, 1991) connect most precisely with songs from the Los Angeles band (as "Anselma" and "Ay Te Dejo En San Antonio," from *...And a Time to Dance*, 1983, and "Estoy Sentado Aquí," from *La Pistola y el Corazón*, 1988, respectively) and can thus provide

Figure 8.1. William "Tren" van Enckevort (accordion) and Jack Poels (guitar) of Rowwen Hèze perform at TEDxRoermond (The Netherlands) in 2013. Licensed under CC BY 2.0.

a representative stylistic correspondence. Although the comparative melodies, instrumentation, and performance style in these recordings are almost identical, the lyrics in each language are surprisingly distinct. For example, while the Spanish version of "Anselma" describes the threatening, tyrannical actions of unrequited love, the Limburgish rendition of "Bestel Mar" relates a comfortable evening spent at the local pub. In particular, the Los Lobos chorus of "*Anselma, Anselma, Anselma* (representing a girl's name)" becomes Rowwen Hèze's "*Bestel mar, bestel mar, bestel mar* (repeated requests to 'order more')," while the last lines of the corresponding first verses (A1) invoke the narrator's willingness to go to jail for shooting Anselma's new husband and the gently shining "redeeming light" of the neighborhood bar, respectively. Similarly, while the Spanish version of "Ay Te Dejo En San Antonio" relates the experiences of a cheating lover, the Limburgish rendition of "Kroenenberg" attempts to attract a (presumably) Spanish-speaking girl by mimicking the Spanish lyrics of the original in the refrain (and describing such failed attempts in Limburgish in the verses). In this regard, while Rowwen Hèze maintains a lyrical connection to the Los Lobos original, the interpretation of the song is still altered substantially. Finally, while the Spanish version of "Estoy Sentado Aquí" conveys a sentimental musing on love lost, the Limburgish version of "De Moan" presents a similar impression but uses a completely different scenario. For example, while the singer in the Spanish rendition is sitting, drinking tequila, and feeling sad, the Limburgish narrator recalls "the last time [the moon] was smiling" as he waited for his lost love.

In addition, the Limburgish versions of the songs are consistently faster than their Spanish counterparts (160 vs. 145 BPM for "Bestel Mar" / "Anselma"; 95 vs. 90 BPM for "De Moan" / "Estoy Sentado Aquí"; and 160 vs. 130 BPM for "Kroenenberg" / "Ay Te Dejo En San Antonio"). However, despite these differences in meaning (although without a decent command of both languages, the typical listener would not likely pick up the contrasting translations) and tempo, as well as subtle changes in musicality attributable to individual idiosyncrasies of performance, the corresponding recordings lie within the same musical classification. Even the consistently faster tempos in Rowwen Hèze's renditions do not mark the Dutch band's performances as outside of the U.S. American style, but only as a slightly different rhythmic interpretation of the continuing Texas-Mexican tradition. For example, earlier versions of "Ay Te Dejo En San Antonio" also exhibit contrasting tempos, including the original recording by conjunto pioneer Santiago Jiménez Sr. (125 BPM), on *Don Santiago Jiménez: His First and Last Recordings* from 1980 (representing a late recording at the end of the musician's life of a significantly earlier musical style), as well as his son Flaco's version at 118 BPM (from *Ay*

Te Dejo En San Antonio, 1986). In this regard, Los Lobos already plays a faster version of Santiago Sr.'s original.

Comparing the overall structure and timing for each recording further demonstrates the close similarities between the musical style of Los Lobos (and thus, the Texas-Mexican tradition as a whole) and Rowwen Hèze. The Los Lobos version of "Anselma" received a Grammy Award in 1984 (at the time of this writing, the first of an eventual eleven nominations and three wins for the band) for Best Mexican/Mexican-American Performance. Verheyden includes a recording of the song (as "Anselma," thus maintaining the original Spanish) on the album *Conjunto Tracks* in 2012. The structure of Rowwen Hèze's rendition of "Bestel Mar" / "Anselma" is almost identical to Los Lobos's earlier model (Tab. 8.3). Whereas Los Lobos presents a second iteration of the second verse (A2), Rowwen Hèze provides an actual third verse (A3). Whereas Los Lobos plays a brief instrumental ending, Rowwen Hèze presents an additional iteration of the refrain (B). Otherwise, the two structures are the same, conforming to a standard ranchera style (including brief instrumental passages between each verse and refrain—A1B, A2B, A3B—and longer instrumental sections following each refrain). In this regard, while Rowwen Hèze changes the lyrics to better represent the experiences—and language—of their own community, they maintain the fundamental musical sound of the original, thus (as with other international conjunto artists like Verheyden) asserting their own "authenticity" within the world of conjunto by staying even more closely aligned with a traditional model than many local musicians (i.e., by using Los Lobos as a direct example, rather than inserting any external characteristics beyond the alternate language and lyrical interpretation or any innovations outside of the established Texas-Mexican style).

Similarly, the two recordings of "Kroenenberg" / "Ay Te Dejo En San Antonio" maintain close structural similarity (Tab. 8.4). The Spanish-language original of the song, "Ay Te Dejo En San Antonio," is a conjunto standard that was written by Santiago Sr. and recorded by a range of Texas-Mexican artists, including Flaco, Santiago Jiménez Jr., Max Baca, and the Texas Tornados, as well as Verheyden. Rowwen Hèze's version of the song maintains the original form until the conclusion, when this Dutch version presents additional iterations of the refrain in place of Los Lobos's instrumental ending. The Rowwen Hèze version also includes additional trumpet lines (presumably emanating from the Dutch brass band tradition but also closely corresponding to Mexican mariachi music) on top of the expected accordion. It should also probably be noted that, while the standard Texas-Mexican instrument is the diatonic button accordion, Rowwen Hèze instead maintains the piano accordion typical of German-influenced polka bands (as opposed to Verheyden, who

Table 8.3. "Anselma." As performed and recorded by Los Lobos. From ...*And a Time to Dance* (Slash Records 1-23963, 1983). "Bestel Mar." As performed and recorded by Rowwen Hèze. From *Boem* (HKM 656.737-2, 1991).

"Bestel Mar" / "Anselma" (Structure)					
Los Lobos's Form (Ranchera)	Language (Los Lobos)	Length (Los Lobos)	Rowwen Hèze's Form (Ranchera)	Language (Rowwen Hèze)	Length (Rowwen Hèze)
Instrumental Introduction		0:00–0:17 (0:17)	Instrumental Introduction		0:00–0:16 (0:16)
A1	Spanish	0:17–0:42 (0:25)	A1	Limburgish	0:16–0:39 (0:23)
Instrumental Interlude		0:42–0:48 (0:06)	Instrumental Interlude		0:39–0:44 (0:05)
B	Spanish	0:48–1:01 (0:13)	B	Limburgish	0:44–0:56 (0:12)
Instrumental Interlude		1:01–1:18 (0:17)	Instrumental Interlude		0:56–1:12 (0:16)
A2	Spanish	1:18–1:43 (0:25)	A2	Limburgish	1:12–1:35 (0:23)
Instrumental Interlude		1:43–1:48 (0:05)	Instrumental Interlude		1:35–1:39 (0:04)
B	Spanish	1:48–2:01 (0:13)	B	Limburgish	1:39–1:51 (0:12)
Instrumental Interlude		2:01–2:18 (0:17)	Instrumental Interlude		1:51–2:08 (0:17)
A2	Spanish	2:18–2:42 (0:24)	A3	Limburgish	2:08–2:31 (0:23)
Instrumental Interlude		2:42–2:48 (0:06)	Instrumental Interlude		2:31–2:35 (0:04)
B	Spanish	2:48–3:00 (0:12)	B	Limburgish	2:35–2:47 (0:12)
Instrumental Ending		3:00–3:05 (0:05)	B	Limburgish	2:47–3:02 (0:15)

Table 8.4. “Ay Te Dejo En San Antonio.” As performed and recorded by Los Lobos. From *...And a Time to Dance* (Slash Records 1-23963, 1983). “Kroenenberg.” As performed and recorded by Rowwen Hèze. From *Boem* (HKM 656.737-2, 1991).

“Kroenenberg”/“Ay Te Dejo En San Antonio” (Structure)					
Los Lobos’s Form (Ranchera)	Language (Los Lobos)	Length (Los Lobos)	Rowwen Hèze’s Form (Ranchera)	Language (Rowwen Hèze)	Length (Rowwen Hèze)
Instrumental Introduction		0:00–0:23 (0:23)	Instrumental Introduction		0:00–0:17 (0:17)
A1	Spanish	0:23–0:37 (0:14)	A1	Limburgish	0:17–0:30 (0:13)
B	Spanish	0:37–0:44 (0:07)	B	Spanish–ish	0:30–0:36 (0:06)
Instrumental Interlude		0:44–1:07 (0:23)	Instrumental Interlude		0:36–0:54 (0:18)
A2	Spanish	1:07–1:22 (0:15)	A2	Limburgish	0:54–1:06 (0:12)
B	Spanish	1:22–1:29 (0:07)	B	Spanish–ish	1:06–1:12 (0:06)
Instrumental Interlude		1:29–1:52 (0:23)	Instrumental Interlude		1:12–1:32 (0:20)
A3	Spanish	1:52–2:06 (0:14)	A3	Limburgish	1:32–1:45 (0:13)
B	Spanish	2:06–2:14 (0:08)	B	Spanish-ish	1:45–1:51 (0:06)
			B	Spanish-ish	1:51–1:57 (0:06)
Instrumental Ending		2:14–2:32 (0:18)	Instrumental Interlude		1:57–2:03 (0:06)
			B	Spanish-ish	2:03–2:10 (0:07)
			B	Spanish-ish	2:10–2:19 (0:09)

Table 8.5. “Estoy Sentado Aquí.” As performed and recorded by Los Lobos. From *La Pistola y el Corazón* (Slash 9 25790-1, 1988). “De Moan.” As performed and recorded by Rowwen Hèze. From *Boem* (HKM 656.737-2, 1991).

“De Moan” / “Estoy Sentado Aquí” (Structure)					
Los Lobos’s Form (Strophic)	Language (Los Lobos)	Length (Los Lobos)	Rowwen Hèze’s Form (Strophic)	Language (Rowwen Hèze)	Length (Rowwen Hèze)
Instrumental Introduction		0:00–0:20 (0:20)	Instrumental Introduction		0:00–0:19 (0:19)
A1	Spanish	0:20–0:51 (0:31)	A1	Limburgish	0:19–0:50 (0:31)
A2	Spanish	0:51–1:21 (0:30)	A2	Limburgish	0:50–1:19 (0:29)
Instrumental Interlude		1:21–1:40 (0:19)	Instrumental Interlude		1:19–1:38 (0:19)
A2 (Extended)	Spanish	1:40–2:23 (0:43)	A2 (Extended)	Limburgish	1:38–2:18 (0:40)

ultimately shifts to a button accordion to better represent the Texas-Mexican style). Finally, a comparison of the two recordings of "De Moan" / "Estoy Sentado Aquí" further showcases the close similarities in structure between the works of Rowwen Hèze and those of Los Lobos (Tab. 8.5). Both bands use guitar passages in addition to the respective accordions, and Rowwen Hèze also employs the trumpets of the previous analysis.

Musically (i.e., sonically, instrumentally, harmonically, and rhythmically), and beyond the differences in language and location, the two bands thus take part in the same creative community, effectively forming a single, unified artistic style drawn from a common background of socioeconomic marginalization, as well as a corresponding regional heritage of polka rhythms, Western rock characteristics, and European accordion music. Given this similarity of historical and sociocultural experience, it is not particularly surprising that the De Peel region of the Netherlands and the Mexican-American community of East Los Angeles join together musically, at least within these specific Texas-Mexican numbers, to form a shared artistic culture beyond traditional hereditary and locational boundaries. It is interesting to compare this single musical community forged outside of expected lines with the otherwise distinctive communities surrounding Texas-Mexican traditions based on local and global audiences. Artists like Flaco, emanating from the historical regional community according to expected notions of class, heritage, and location, aim hybridized performances at contrasting audiences, simultaneously addressing local and global populations while gaining full acceptance according to neither. Meanwhile, mainstream artists like the Rolling Stones incorporate elements of conjunto, aimed strictly at a mainstream audience, while never receiving categorization according to anything other than rock. In contrast, groups like Los Lobos and Rowwen Hèze, marginalized but more closely connected to mainstream interpretations of genre and location, manage to form a new community, distinctive from local heritage and popular practices, but significant worldwide.

"Families of Resemblance" between Marginalized Cultures

The modern world introduces an overwhelming arrangement of cultural possibilities. In our media-based, global society, intimately linked through more and more effortless forms of mass communication and transnational mobilization, individual artists become free to choose a personal identity from any number of disparate backgrounds, regardless of ethnicity, class, language, or location. However, within this dizzying assortment of creative decisions, the more historically comfortable consideration of local community and clear cultural identification disappears, leaving much of the global population longing "desperately for something solid to cling to."[54] Faced with too many cultural possibilities in the chaos of modern life, musicians around the world are often drawn to what is familiar, although perhaps not historically typical, to form a personal sense of belonging outside of traditional positional boundaries. In the case of Rowwen Hèze, the socioeconomic background, counter-hegemonic symbolism, and accordion-based musical characteristics of Los Lobos create a familiar sense of cultural community, despite dramatic differences of geographic circumstance. The sociocultural background of the Limburg band does not fit into mainstream European culture. In this regard, the group does not reject its Dutch heritage, since it does not form a part of this dominant majority (and since the popular mainstream is actually comprised of fundamentally Anglo-American musical characteristics), but instead incorporates cultural resonances from halfway around the world, drawing from common social experiences to create its own interpretation of creative community outside of traditional understandings of heritage-oriented boundaries.

As John Tomlinson explains, the discourse related to the concept of "Americanization," typically referring to a type of cultural imperialism, "treat[s] the issue as one of domination of national culture by national culture. But this conceptualization can only be strictly coherent where we can speak of a unified national cultural identity in the supposedly 'invaded' culture. Where we cannot—where, for example, there is a struggle between ethnic or regional cultures within a nation—this discourse of cultural domination will be compromised."[55] In the case of Los Lobos and Rowwen Hèze, commonalities of socioeconomic background and minority-based (ethnic and rural, respectively) marginalization connect the geographically distant bands more than traditional considerations of cultural imperialism between the United States and Europe draw them apart. Similar uses of personal, locally secondary languages, corresponding musical experiences in the form of German accordion music and Western rock characteristics, as well as analogous understandings of counter-hegemonic responses to dominant global communities through the adoption of mainstream characteristics and the celebration of culturally evocative, regional idiosyncrasies instead combine to create a unified and unexpected collaboration of style.

In this way, it seems that, in the cultural chaos of the modern world, conjunto music can help to rearticulate a sense of meaning for marginalized communities through unprecedented, worldwide connections of similar economic positionalities, feelings of cultural discrimination, and corresponding sonic characteristics in regional experiences. Social distinctions of wealth and poverty travel across huge geographic distances to redefine traditional notions of culture based on the boundaries of the nation-state. As a Spanish-speaking fan describes a bilingual YouTube recording of "Estoy Sentado Aquí"/"De Moan," "It's a Dutch cover of a Los Lobos adaptation of a traditional norteño [the style of conjunto music emanating from northern Mexico rather than South Texas] song. It is then, I think, a Dutch local global style.[56] Indeed, for any meaningful musical understanding within popular culture in the contemporary, complicated, and highly interconnected world, a "local global style" drawn from widespread commonalities of socioeconomic background and familiar, although often unexpected, heritage seems to create a more appropriate cultural community than notions of common language, ethnicity, and location alone.

Conclusions

This chapter denotes a wide range of manifestations of the globalized influences of conjunto music, including some of the many cross-cultural collaborations of Flaco with mainstream rock stars and the international adoption of conjunto influences by the Limburgish rock group Rowwen Hèze (through the secondary influence of Los Angeles roots-rock group Los Lobos). While each circumstance provides a divergent analytical opportunity—encompassing elements of authenticity, exoticism, and exploitation, as well as notions of connection between corresponding communities, even miles apart—each demonstrates at least one of the many ways the products of globalization take on lives of their own, traveling beyond the original sociocultural significance in which they emerged to provide new forms of meaning among new and changing populations.

Discussing the diversification of the Nor-Tec fan base across a variety of ethnic, class-based, and geographic experiences, Alejandro Madrid notes that the music "came to mean different things for the different communities that embraced it."[57] As with Texas-Mexican conjunto music, this re-signification of a cultural product according to new circumstances alters the interpretation of a genre according to new audiences—both at home and around the world. As Helena Simonett concurs, "the meaning of a text escapes the intentions of its author: as a text passes from one cultural or historical context to another, new meanings may be drawn from it—meanings that were never intended or anticipated by its author or contemporary audience."[58] Texas-Mexican conjunto music was created in the beginning of the twentieth century as a counter-hegemonic response to the dominant community. As the genre has traveled through time and space, it has gathered new musical characteristics, new audiences, new participants, and new meanings. Yet, what is perhaps the most interesting part of this analysis is the characterization of these new meanings among diverse populations.

As noted throughout previous chapters, local conjunto artists like Flaco, Steve Jordan, Mingo Saldívar, and Eva Ybarra have inserted a range of hybridized characteristics into the traditional conjunto sound. Through live performances and other inter/national events, they have introduced the music to new fans around the world. Through mainstream recordings and diverse media distributions, they have opened the genre to increasingly widespread attention. However, these artists occupy a liminal space between the historical regional community and more mainstream attention. Among the regional population, they are often criticized as "selling-out," and thus, not truly "conjunto." Among inter/national and more mainstream audiences, they are instead characterized as fundamentally representative of the Texas-Mexican region, despite the actual musical traits employed and attempts to "break in" to a popular consideration.

Meanwhile, artists outside of the historical Texas-Mexican class, location, or ethnicity, such as Verheyden and Joel Guzman, often struggle to achieve local recognition as "conjunto," in spite of conservative, regional elements. Yet, rock musicians like the Rolling Stones, Yoakam, and Rowwen Hèze, outside of the primary conjunto community and inserting only some elements of the genre, maintain characterization according to their own identities: not fully conjunto, but also capable of consideration among a more popular realm. For these artists, the genre allows for bits of exoticism that do not alter interpretation according to identity alone. As such, groups like the Rolling Stones—the epitome of Euro-American wealth and privilege—achieve what Flaco never could: the use of the traditional music in a mainstream genre without boundaries of interpretation according to complexion. It is painfully poignant that Flaco himself created the accordion line—but not the credit—that gave the Rolling Stones consideration as such.

CONCLUSION

Continuing Considerations

Campaigning for President of the United States in 2015, Donald Trump visited Laredo, Texas, asserting that to do so was to put his life at risk, alluding to a perception of the high rate of crime in the border city: "I may never see you again, but we're going to do it."[1] Yet, according to the FBI's Uniform Crime Reporting Program, the rate of violent crime in the city at the time was "well below the state and national average."[2] This sentiment of looming danger echoes General Barry McCaffrey's militaristic appraisal of the U.S.-Mexico border in 2011 as "tantamount to living in a war zone" and Attorney General Jeff Sessions's later characterization of El Paso as "ground zero" and a "beachhead against the cartels."[3] Similarly, during a 2019 visit to McAllen, Texas, Trump declared a crisis of "thousands of illegal immigrants trying to enter our country."[4]

However, according to the McAllen police chief, Victor Rodriguez, the city's crime rate in 2018 was the lowest it had been in thirty-four years.[5] At the time, Henry Cuellar, United States Representative for the region, also noted that the border cities typically maintained lower crime rates than other metropolitan areas in the country. As Cuellar asserts, "Portraying the southwest border as unsafe only serves to systematically hamper our region's economic and community development. . . . There is no national emergency at the U.S.-Mexico border—the data is proof that the area is safe and open for business."[6] Likewise, Christopher Wilson, deputy director of the Wilson Center's Mexico Institute, reports that FBI statistics between 2011 and 2015 demonstrate that "all but one of the twenty-three U.S. counties along the border had violent-crime rates lower than the national average for similar counties."[7] While (as of 2018), polls indicate that most U.S. Americans believe that the U.S.-Mexico border is not secure, the number of Border Patrol agents has increased by more than 400% since the early 1990s.[8] Although Trump is technically correct in his characterization of "thousands of immigrants" entering the country, the 300,000 people apprehended for crossing the border illegally in 2017 was the lowest recorded number since 1971,[9] and far fewer than the 1.6 million people apprehended in 2000.[10]

This rhetoric of danger and violence (and open racism) surrounding the Texas-Mexican border region is nothing new. Anglo-American newcomers to Texas in the nineteenth century labeled Texas Mexicans as "a racial abomination," declaring that "the intermingling of Indian, European, and African bloodlines result[ed] in a human depravity."[11] During the same time, requesting aid from the United States against the Mexican government, Stephen F. Austin asserted that, "A war of extermination is raging in Texas—a war of barbarism and of despotic principles, waged by the mongrel Spanish-Indian and Negro race, against civilization and the Anglo-American race."[12] Leading a charge against the Mexican army, Sam Houston proclaimed that whites would never "mix with the phlegm of the indolent Mexicans, no matter how long we live among them."[13] Following the successful conclusion of the Mexican-American War, United States Secretary of State James Buchanan expressed concern in granting U.S. American citizenship to the Texas Mexicans who were now living on conquered lands, referring to them as "an inferior, indolent, mongrel race."[14] As Michelle García attests, the latest fears and atrocities directed at the Texas-Mexican border represent the "progeny" of these earlier "white conquerors," who echo their forefathers "in the warnings that 'animals' are crossing the border and threatening to 'infest' the nation."[15] While Mexican-American citizens experience hateful rhetoric and diminished opportunities due to this legacy of racism in the United States, Mexican citizens are often disparaged and mischaracterized as "other" among even Mexican Americans.

The greatest crisis at the U.S.-Mexico border may be one of misconception. Responding to the president's visit to the Rio Grande Valley in 2019, McAllen mayor Jim Darling notes that he hoped Trump would experience the same sense of surprise most people feel when first visiting the region, indicating that most people "don't realize what a dynamic place it is."[16] In an editorial for the *Washington Post* in 2018, college student Victoria Ochoa describes her hope of dispelling some of these continuing misconceptions by convincing people to actually visit the region:

> I wonder what will finally placate the fearful people 1,500 miles away who sent those border agents and National Guard troops to the borderlands.

More checkpoints, more families detained, vaster tent cities? Maybe the wall they dream of? For most people, or most open-minded people, a simple visit might be enough to be reassured that this is not a scary place.[17]

That being said, numerous border residents express concerns that the politicians who do visit the area frequently fail to gain a true picture of the region and its rich cultural heritage. Describing Trump's visit to McAllen in 2019, Hidalgo County Judge Richard Cortez notes that little was accomplished through the visit: "President Trump came here with an agenda. . . . The whole trip was orchestrated to hear what he wanted to hear and he didn't meet with any local officials that I know of. As far as the president was concerned, the whole trip was a photo op."[18] Darling shares a similar response (implicating both political factions), while also indicating the negative results of such misconceptions to the Texas-Mexican community as a whole:

> So the Republicans are going to come down and they'd go on a gunboat or a helicopter and they take photo ops in front of those. Then the Democrats come down, go to the detention center, get some photo ops with the kids. . . . Both do press conferences before they leave and go to Washington and not talk to each other. But those images are both negative to us.[19]

Likewise, following the same presidential visit, R. David Guerra, a retired bank president from McAllen, explains, "I appreciate any president that would come down to the border. . . . What I cannot accept is any president or high-ranking official believing in all the misconceptions of the border and then writing that narrative for themselves as a basis for support from their core."[20]

In actuality, the Texas-Mexican border is relatively safe, with residents living "normal" lives (in a manner very similar to people throughout the rest of the United States and Mexico) and enjoying a rich biculturality that can be experienced—among other traditions—through the music of the region.[21] As Monica Stewart, a longtime resident of McAllen, attests, "I don't like my city being portrayed as if there's a crisis and unrest, when the reality is we're one of the safest cities in the U.S."[22] Joaquin Zamora, a McAllen city commissioner and Hidalgo County prosecutor concurs: "We're a wholesome community. . . . We're an American city that's on the border. What we don't want is the perception that we're a dusty border town with burros and carts, AK-47s being fired every 30 minutes and Molotov cocktails being thrown. Because that's not what's happening in McAllen."[23] Despite this political rhetoric, perhaps the first step to truly understand and appreciate the U.S.–Mexico border region is to examine its music, particularly as this music has become increasingly relevant to audiences throughout the country and around the world.

Inclusions and What Remains

This book only begins to address the many manifestations of Texas-Mexican conjunto music—especially as it moves beyond traditional notions of repertory, structure, sound, and sociocultural identity—during the second half of the twentieth century. It explores the performance of conjunto beyond South Texas by a handful of Texas-based artists. It examines the hybridized characteristics and repertory of these same musicians. It considers the adoption of the traditional genre by musicians emanating from outside of the historical community—through location and heritage. It notes the appropriation of the traditional genre by popular musicians in the United States and the Netherlands. Each of these representations is directly connected to the group of male Texas-Mexican accordionists most prominent during the 1960s-1990s: Flaco Jiménez, Steve Jordan, and Mingo Saldívar. The role of women within these circumstances is also briefly discussed, as demonstrated by Eva Ybarra. Yet, local and more recent considerations of the genre are not addressed. In addition, this analysis draws a strict line at "conjunto," leaving out all music (norteño, Tejano, and even progressive conjunto) that is closely related in musical elements or sociocultural association, but characterized—for many reasons—alternatively. As such, this book represents a preliminary treatment of the contemporary genre as it interacts with worldwide fans.

In addition to the processes of globalization discussed throughout the preceding chapters, contemporary conjunto music among inter/national participants and certain members of the local constituency has been consolidated into a more traditional form of cultural folklore. For example, beyond the global performances and dissemination of major-label recordings by regional artists like Flaco, Jordan, and Saldívar and the continuing stylistic innovations of more recent musicians, many local conjunto artists perform in traditional venues with a traditional repertory, instrumentation, and sound. In addition, the music has received support from festival performances and educational institutions. These processes create two styles of contemporary conjunto. The more commercialized form of the music displays external musical traits, innovative performance techniques, and original (or external) repertory. It is aimed at a diverse audience often disconnected from the traditional sociocultural community. A more folkloric form of the music maintains (often as a matter of principle) the historical genre for local audiences. In general, this book explores the more commercialized form of conjunto—through processes of globalization. However, these corresponding folkloric practices are important and remain to be fully analyzed.

Beyond my analysis of the folkloric implications of the Tejano Conjunto Festival (Bauer 2019), historian Daniel Margolies works on some of the methods of sustainability present within recent conjunto practices. As Margolies explains, "The development of a sustainable system in which conjunto music has thrived has been carefully crafted in Texas by a diverse array of committed individual musicians, activists, and others in the community through festivals such as the Tejano Conjunto Festival en San Antonio, apprenticeship programs, and organizations like the Conjunto Heritage Taller in San Antonio."[24] Margolies further examines a number of conjunto ensemble programs recently included in public schools and universities, including La Joya Independent School District (ISD), Edcouch/Elsa ISD, San Benito ISD, Los Fresnos High School, and Roma High School, in addition to established programs at the University of Texas at Austin (overseen by ethnomusicologist Robin Moore and taught by Joel Guzman) and Palo Alto College (directed by Juan Tejeda and including instruction by musicians like Ybarra and bajo sexto player Jesús "Chucho" Perales).[25] With these types of analysis—in addition to the analysis within this book of the globalization of conjunto—we can begin to move beyond historic interpretations of the Texas-Mexican genre as a representation of the working-class identity and instead develop new understandings of the music (and its associated culture) as it interacts with the modern world.

Furthermore, although a number of inter/national musicians and certain local artists have consolidated the genre as a form of cultural folklore, more recent local artists have followed the examples of Flaco, Jordan, and Saldívar to push the conjunto even further from its stylistic and sociocultural roots. In recent years, musicians like Juanito Castillo, Los Nahuatlatos, and Piñata Protest, among others, have increasingly altered the traditional musical style through the incorporation of elements of punk, ska, and heavy metal, in addition to jazz, blues, and rock. In effect, these performers have strategically established themselves at the edge of a musical tradition that is itself already at the margins of U.S. American popular culture. In so doing, these innovative and—for some—iconoclastic artists have reinterpreted the music to reflect their sense of (bi)cultural identity in the modern world. The omnivorous nature of these styles contrasts with the traditional working-class format, where regional musicians are typically expected to maintain the conservative genre as a cultural representation of the creative community. In using external elements, these artists mirror more socioeconomically privileged musicians, who take influence from any form they desire.

While conventional conjunto was established in the early twentieth century as a symbolic representation of the rural, working-class ethnic identity, in recent years, the musical practice has been adopted by international artists like Kenji Katsube and Dwayne Verheyden, incorporated by national and international popular musicians like Girl in a Coma, The Iguanas, Rowwen Hèze, and Los Lobos, and served as a stylistic foundation for external mixtures by local artists such as Castillo, Los Nahuatlatos, and Piñata Protest. While many artists ethnically and socioeconomically positioned closer within the mainstream of U.S. American society typically take any number of global and cultural elements as their own, omnivorous inspiration, the use of external characteristics within a musical genre historically situated at the margins of popular society showcases a dramatic shift in the cultural position of traditional Texas-Mexican musicians. While these progressive ensembles remain at the margins of the local community, their fluent incorporation of external elements demonstrates the dichotomous background of the younger ethnic generation within both the traditional cultural heritage and popular culture in the United States. Furthermore, the ability of these bands to take influence from mainstream society shows that the cultural population is increasingly moving to a more central sociological location in the contemporary U.S. American atmosphere. By asserting their cultural identities at the margins of the already marginal musical tradition, these new musicians effectively shift the creative genre closer to mainstream practices, establishing an acceptance for their dichotomous backgrounds within modern society in a way that wasn't possible in historical conjunto practices.

This book explores the globalization of conjunto, as defined by the artists and audiences who produce and consume the music. Certain elements distinguish the genre—button accordion with bajo sexto, polka rhythms, a ranchera structure, and the Spanish language, to start—but, as we've seen throughout this book, generic distinctions are slippery and rely on more than just musical elements alone. Nonetheless, in describing the globalization of conjunto, I have maintained the generic boundary line, as typically employed by artists and audiences. I have thus not addressed genres like norteño, Tejano, and progressive conjunto which display similar traits and similar sociocultural interpretations. There is certainly still work to be done in theorizing the complicated relationships between these alternative genres, the communities who are characterized according to them, and the continuing processes of globalization inherent among them. Considering the seemingly arbitrary distinctions between genres of music that sound fundamentally similar but are characterized separately—conjunto and norteño, for example, which use an analogous instrumentation, repertory, structure, and sound—demonstrates the continued reliance on notions of identity to classify music according to one genre or another. Yet, these ideas are intertwined, since genres of music like conjunto and Tejano which remain associated with similar sociocultural identities, in addition to certain analogous elements, are also characterized separately. Connected to these analyses are complex considerations regarding the interplay between Texas and Mexico. The complicated connections between Texas-Mexican musicians and Mexico and Texas-Mexican musicians and the United States should also be noted.

Instead, this book considers the external characterization of a single genre of music as it travels outside of its historical interpretation—both in fundamental traits and in sociocultural identity. It traces a path of globalization through unexpected performance spaces, unprecedented hybridizations, and cross-cultural imaginings. It addresses altered interpretations of a meaningful cultural commodity as it moves beyond the original understanding. In doing so, it does not provide a complete interpretation of Texas-Mexican conjunto music in the waning years of the twentieth century (or beyond). It largely leaves out local practices in favor of global influences. It also neglects similar genres (and thus, in essence, the southern side of the U.S.-Mexico border) in favor of conjunto alone. There is still work to be done. However, in characterizing the genre outside of South Texas, we can begin to understand the interconnections between Texas-Mexican accordionists, the popular recording industry, and global enthusiasts. We can then start to understand the lingering prejudices and misrepresentations of Texas-Mexican people among external populations.

Considerations of Genre

As Charles Briggs and Richard Bauman explore, in the realm of linguistic anthropology, "[A]ll of us know intuitively that generic classifications never quite work: an empirical residue that does not fit any clearly defined category—or, even worse, that falls into too many—is always left over."[26] As demonstrated throughout this book, the genre of Texas-Mexican conjunto music falls into similar interpretations. "Conjunto" encompasses certain musical traits. Yet, music with analogous elements—Tejano and norteño, to start, as well as the popular genres that have used bits of Texas accordion music as exotic or nostalgic or imagined features—is characterized alternatively. In contrast, with the appropriate performative identity, the conjunto genre expands to incorporate a repertory and musical traits emanating from far outside of expected practices. In this way, the classification of conjunto as such is simultaneously too broad and too narrow. For artists hoping to break free of stereotypical considerations as fundamentally Texas-Mexican (and thus outside of the economic rewards of mainstream success), "conjunto" represents a restrictive categorization; the sound of button accordion with bajo sexto locks local musicians into external characterizations as quintessentially conjunto, regardless of actual aesthetic elements or intent. Yet, artists from outside of the expected community—in location or heritage—struggle to achieve acceptance as "conjunto" without strict adherence to stereotypical musical elements. As such, generic interpretation is established largely by audience (indicating fans and the industry itself).

Despite the ineffectiveness of generic categorization—Briggs and Bauman use "fuzzy"—the process of classification remains stubbornly affixed to musical interpretations.[27] As David Brackett asserts, despite "internal inconsistencies" of classification, these labels provide a method of "symbolic communication"; a means of characterizing the relationships between groups of people and the power structures underlying the system of commodification in the contemporary recording industry.[28] As Brackett continues, what is important in examining the use of musical genres is not the label itself or the aesthetic traits housed under any single label, but rather the "social functions" of such classification; the consideration of "why these labels seem so important despite their rather transparent malleability."[29] In the case of conjunto, the question becomes less which musical traits are accepted within regional categorization, but by whom? In genres outside of conjunto, does the accordion fundamentally designate exoticism? If so, the distinctions between exotic elements used on the mainstream, Grammy Award–winning *Voodoo Lounge* (for Best Rock Album) and the fundamental exoticism of the peripheral, Grammy Award–winning *Flaco Jiménez* (for Best Mexican-American/Tejano Music Performance) comes down to a difference in sociocultural identity. The blends of conjunto and rock/country on each album demonstrate the power structures at play in the contemporary industry. The more highly valued genre maintains a barrier of entry only accessible from within the expected sociocultural community. Texas-Mexican artists may participate within that genre under the patronage of a more highly valued musician, but remain characterized as fundamentally "other" elsewhere, regardless of close similarities between the hybridizations used in "Sweethearts Together" and "Seguro Que Hell Yes," for example.

In this context, the generic characterization of each song tells us more about the societal power of each titular musician than the actual musical result. In the same way, inter/national artists gain entry into the conjunto genre only through strict imitation of the expected regional style (or, in some cases, the patronage of established local musicians). Musical genres set up a hierarchical structure of economic and social rewards that replicate systems of power in sociocultural circumstances. Highly valued musical genres represent communities in power; the valuation of genres like rock and country simultaneously demonstrate which communities hold social power at any given time and function to retain the power for the associated artists and audiences. Unsurprisingly, communities in power structure the economic rewards for highly valued genres in ways that consolidate their own power and create barriers to external participation. As Briggs and Bauman note, invocation of a certain genre signifies "negotiations of identity and power"; in the case of music, artists use genre to assert the necessary authority to "decontextualize discourse" as it relates to certain historical significance and to "recontextualize it in the current discursive setting."[30] In other words, musicians use genre to link new offerings to a different place or time. They invoke unexpected generic connections to tie new creative products to different groups of people. They use highly valued categories of music to reinterpret historical social structures and assert power for themselves. They assert power over groups of people by assuming different musical genres as their own. In doing so, they break ties between music and its context, using established connections to develop new meanings and new systems of power across altered circumstances.

In the case of conjunto, local musicians and national artists claiming a Texas-Mexican cultural heritage use generic implications of space and time to simultaneously form connections with a traditional past, assert their own authority within that tradition, and create a new significance for the music outside of traditional constraints. Similarly, international conjunto musicians, fundamentally disconnected from the traditional community, invoke the genre to tie themselves to an imagined group of conjunto enthusiasts. Meanwhile, popular musicians like Dwight Yoakam and the Rolling Stones assert power over minoritized musicians by using the music outside of its historical context; lacking cultural authority within the genre, they instead simply assume desirable musical characteristics as their own. Likewise, globally-oriented musicians like Flaco invoke highly valued genres like rock and country to assert power within a popular space. At the same time, they minimize the Mexican influences in their music, failing to acknowledge their indebtedness to a Mexican repertory, structure, instrumentation, and sound and instead distancing themselves from the associated perceptions of poor rurality endemic to global stereotypes of Mexico. In this way, just as popular musicians assert power over minoritized artists by inserting elements of "exoticism" within their recordings, Texas-based conjunto artists assert power over Mexican musicians by minimizing their impact to the genre.

Brackett notes the characterization of a musical text as "participating" within a certain genre, even if it does not fully "belong" to that same genre.[31]

In this regard, certain musical elements do designate one genre or another, despite a certain fluidity of classification based on external considerations. These invocations of one genre in the context of another—participation outside of possession—create a complex system of signification; a persistent implication of power and identity in the inclusion of one trait over another and the interconnections between parts of the whole. In the case of conjunto, musical elements hold meaning. The use of popular songs in a conjunto structure designates participation within mainstream society. The use of the button accordion and bajo sexto in a popular context indicates power over the conjunto genre—and its primary constituents—through hegemonic claims on the distinctive regional sound. The careful use of standard elements of the Texas-Mexican tradition outside of expected cultural associations suggests participation within the conjunto community; preexisting power structures and the proportion of associative elements determine whether and for whom participation turns into belonging. A classification of "conjunto," then, implies the use of certain musical traits, but categorization is by no means strictly based on standard elements—or their lack—alone. Instead, the understanding of musical genre intermingles with complexities of social power and sociocultural identity to comment on the structure of society in South Texas and around the world. In this way, the consideration of genre—and its fluidity over time—emphasizes the capricious nature of human relations, the instability of sociocultural identities, and the shifting boundaries of idiosyncratic inclusion—in both aesthetic elements and among groups of people. As Brackett continues, in contrast to a standard generic evocation of "stasis and spatiality," "[T]o describe a text as 'participating' in, rather than 'belonging' to, a genre emphasizes temporality."[32]

The globalization of conjunto demonstrates inter/national adherence to a genre of music outside of historical associations of ethnicity, class, or location. It emphasizes the continuing hybrid impulses of performance. It designates systems of power among performers and audiences worldwide. Yet, perhaps even more clearly, it accentuates the temporality of genre. The characterization of conjunto as it traveled around the world with Flaco during the 1970s, as it joined the global jazz scene with Jordan in the 1980s and formed the basis for "Mingomania" in the 1990s, as it mixed and intermingled with elements of rock, country, and jazz—both in performance and interpretation, as it was taken up by Dwight Yoakam and the Rolling Stones: all of these indicate a specific time and place. The definition of conjunto in the Rio Grande Valley at the beginning of the twentieth century is not the same as that in San Antonio in the 1950s and does not designate the continuing path of the genre by the end of the twentieth century. Historic interpretations of the music coexist with modern characteristics, particularly in functional performance spaces across South Texas and for (inter/national) musicians striving to achieve acceptance according to local considerations of identity. If anything, local adherence to folkloric practices is more surprising than contemporary shifts in inclusion and interpretation. Yet, global considerations of the genre, as demonstrated here by the twentieth-century performances and recordings of artists like Flaco, Jordan, Saldívar, and Ybarra, as well as the concurrent adoptions of the music by a range of musicians disconnected from traditional understandings of Texas-Mexican identity, demonstrate the fluidity of genre through space and time. Conjunto cannot be defined by one single set of musical elements, one single performative identity, despite a standardization of the genre for a moment during the middle of the twentieth century (and continued adherence to that moment among certain performers). The genre ebbs and flows over time to characterize new moments, new participation, new interpretations, and new identities.

Final Thoughts: The Globalization of Conjunto

In characterizing the worldwide path of Texas-Mexican conjunto music, a single, historically-based definition of "conjunto"—button accordion with bajo sexto, polka rhythms, a well-established repertory—does not fully represent the music as it has moved outside of the expected community. Local audiences frequently insist on traditional performances in functional venues (dance halls, cantinas, and for birthdays and anniversaries, for example) and a standard repertory, instrumentation, structure, and sound. Yet, more globally-oriented musicians like Flaco, Jordan, and Saldívar instead play popular songs in a conjunto style and incorporate elements of rock, country, and jazz into the historical conjunto sound. In doing so, they aim the music at a global audience, disconnected from traditional interpretations of conjunto as response to twentieth-century U.S. American hegemonies. Meanwhile, inter/national musicians, fundamentally outside of the traditional Texas-Mexican community (in location, class, language, and/or ethnicity) mimic traditional conjunto. They closely align their performances with an expected ideal—or at least the interpretation of such, based on performances by global artists like Flaco—to assert their positionality within Texas-Mexican practices as an "imagined community" of interpretation outside of former connections of identity (see Anderson 1983). As such, the genre is not characterized by strict adherence to musical traits. Instead, like generic interpretations across space and time, it is tied to homologous notions of sociocultural identity—

music as ethno-racial representation, even as it travels outside of the original circumstances and is performed by and for people no longer connected to the original community. Local artists are classified as "conjunto," regardless of actual musical elements or intent. Yet, to achieve a similar inclusion, artists from outside of the expected community maintain strict adherence to stereotypical traits.

Throughout its history, Texas-Mexican conjunto music has been frequently characterized as low-class, "cantina music"; representative of a working-class rurality that has been looked down on and essentialized as fundamentally characteristic of the entire region. There are two problems within this narrative: the negative characterization of working-class rurality and the essentialization of the region. In tracing the global path of conjunto through the twentieth century, I in no way intend to criticize the working-class association of the genre or its local practitioners. I also do not intend to imply that global attention to the genre negates or in any way supersedes regional practices. Texas-Mexican conjunto in its "traditional" form and among its historical constituency is alive and well. Attempts by artists like Flaco to gain recognition among popular and international audiences do not imply that all musicians strive for external successes or that economic successes in this regard would counteract regional performances. However, for artists who do choose to peddle their music within the mainstream industry, essentialized considerations of the community limit their characterization outside of local, ethno-racial stereotypes.

The characterization—both inside and outside the local community—of conjunto music as inherently working-class; as negatively derived from performances at bars and therefore fundamentally simplistic, old-fashioned, and disreputable extends to external considerations of the community as a whole. It tells us more about continuing relationships between the ethno-racial constituency and hegemonic ("white" and wealthy) populations who adopt the "exotic" sound of the button accordion within their own works but disallow entrance into popular considerations for anyone classified as "conjunto" than actual characteristics—or value—of the music itself. As sociologists like Bethany Bryson have hypothesized, within high-status genres like rock, "Individuals use cultural taste to reinforce symbolic boundaries between themselves and categories of people they dislike."[33] In this regard, elite cultures exclude minoritized artists under the guise of "taste" but actual suppression of material resources like recording contracts, performance spaces, and audience attention. As Bryson continues, "high-status individuals see other cultural forms as crude, vulgar, or dishonorable."[34] For conjunto—characterized from the start as fundamentally low-class and disconnected in this way from economic opportunities across South Texas and, later, in the United States and around the world—elite culture has adopted the sound of conjunto as exotic "flavor" and yet reinforced a boundary around actual participation by Texas-Mexican musicians in mainstream practices. The sound of the accordion creates a symbolic barrier to popular acceptance: inherently "other," despite song choices and musical elements that strive for consideration as rock, country, or jazz. The sociocultural identities of the associated musicians—stereotypically poor, rural, and ethnically Mexican—are likewise excluded from acceptance as anything but "conjunto." Misinterpretations of the Texas-Mexican border community—in music, culture, diversity, and politics—lead to essentialized notions of people and priorities. In turn, such stereotypical understandings generate barriers to participation outside of the region in music, but also in education, politics, and economic opportunity.

South Texas represents a vibrant and diverse community. Conjunto music is just one manifestation of the rich cultural heritage present and thriving across the region. The music connects people to familial traditions, provides the soundtrack for celebrations and important events, and represents the community and its struggles for power against a hegemonic society. However, from the middle of the twentieth century, this music has also traveled outside of the Texas-Mexican community, generating new audiences, new participants, hybridized traits, and new meanings across inter/national spaces. These new representations don't affect traditional interpretations of the music among the original community, but expand consideration of genre and identity in an increasingly globalized society. Further analysis of conjunto in South Texas and in connection with genres like Tejano and norteño is necessary to fully understand the significance of the music in its home region from the second half of the twentieth century. Yet, analysis of conjunto outside this region demonstrates the need for honest relationships between the hegemonic community and artists from the U.S-Mexico border. Lacking these connections, the music and the people most closely affiliated with it remain excluded from consideration according to U.S. American notions of "success," meaning that economic opportunities in the recording industry are constrained.

Furthermore, stereotypical limitations of identity based on musical "taste" link the characterization of a specific genre—in this case, conjunto—to a preconceived understanding of the people who create it, perform it, and enjoy it. All too often, adherence to a certain genre designates primitivist representations of the listener's sociocultural identity, while knowledge of a performer's geographic location or familial heritage ties classification of the musical result to these same essentialist understandings. In fact, artists use musical genres like conjunto to construct a complex system of power and identity, drawn from historical associations but fundamentally representing their own ways of experiencing the world. This does not signify any one circumstance or creative result, but represents a broad range of people, locations, languages, and musical characteristics. The globalization of conjunto thus demonstrates the breadth of human experience, even emanating from a single community, and the connections among us all.

Notes

Introduction

Epigraph: Chris Heim, "Texas Tornado Flaco Jiménez Whips Up a Tex-Mex Storm," *Chicago Tribune*, Aug. 7, 1992.

1. Nancy Flores, "Flaco Jiménez to Receive Lifetime Achievement Grammy Award," *Austin American-Statesman*, Sept. 26, 2016.

2. Throughout this work, in order to avoid confusion between the many conjunto-oriented members of the Jiménez family, I refer to each family member by his first name; thus, Patricio, Santiago Sr., Flaco, Santiago Jr., and David. While doing so raises concerns of a general disrespect for these artists, particularly when taking socioeconomic discrepancies into account (and considering that I do refer to all other scholars and musicians by last name alone), the decision increases clarity throughout. It also maintains consistency with my previous works on conjunto, as well as those of scholars like Cathy Ragland.

3. Madrid, *Nor-tec Rifa!*, 3.

4. Ibid., 20.

5. Ibid.

6. Brackett, "Questions of Genre in Black Popular Music," 75.

7. Ibid., 76.

8. Chávez, *Sounds of Crossing*, 69.

9. Madrid, *Nor-tec Rifa!*, 57.

10. Ibid., 58.

11. Chávez, *Sounds of Crossing*, 69.

12. Madrid, *Nor-tec Rifa!*, 56.

13. Chávez, Sounds of Crossing, 216.

14. Limón, "'This Is Our *Música*, Guy!,'" 120.

15. Ibid., 121.

16. Ibid., 122.

17. Brackett, "Black or White," 171.

18. Ibid.

19. Brackett, "Questions of Genre in Black Popular Music," 77.

20. Ibid., 80.

21. Ibid., 89.

22. Vargas, *Dissonant Divas in Chicana Music*, 53.

23. Peña, *Musica Tejana*, 105.

24. Ibid., 115.

25. Peña, "The Emergence of Conjunto Music," 17.

26. Guerra, "The Unofficial Conjunto Primer," 8.

27. Ragland, *Música Norteña*, 53.

28. Scruggs, "'Ay, Te Dejo en San Antonio,'" 22.

29. Peña, "The Emergence of Conjunto Music," 20.

30. Scruggs, "'Ay, Te Dejo en San Antonio,'" 30.

31. Ibid., 56.

32. Ibid., 54.

33. Peña, *Musica Tejana*, 109.

34. Harnish, "Tejano Music in the Urbanizing Midwest," 204.

35. Ragland, "Tejano and Proud," 91.

Chapter 1. *"We love you, Flaco!"*

Epigraph: Cathy Ragland, "Conjunto Cowboy Has It All; Saldivar Delights Worldwide Audiences with Classic Blend of Styles," *Austin American-Statesman*, Apr. 11, 1996.

1. Kathleen Hudson, "Swiss Festival-Goers Love Tex-Mex," *The Kerrville Times* (TX), July 20, 1990.

2. Ibid.

3. John T. Davis, "Dawson, Saldivar a Pair; Unlikely Match to Offer," *The Austin American-Statesman*, May 12, 1994.

4. Davis Bennett, "Squeezemaster: But Will Steve Jordan Ever Change? Naaah," *Current*, May 9, 2001.

5. Ibid.

6. Ibid.

7. Ibid.

8. Appadurai, *Modernity at Large*, 3.

9. Ibid., 4.

10. Ragland, *Música Norteña*.

11. For more information on Flaco Jiménez's work with Ry Cooder on *Chicken Skin Music*, see Bauer 2014. For more information on the adoption of conjunto by international musicians, see Bauer 2016.

12. Ragland, "Tejano and Proud," 99.

13. Ibid., 88.

14. Ibid.

15. Ramiro Burr, "El Premio Billboard: Flaco Jiménez," *Billboard*, Apr. 24, 1999.

16. Flaco Jiménez, "Oral History," interview by *American Roots Music*, PBS, audio transcription, https://www.pbs.org/ americanrootsmusic/pbs_arm_oralh_flaco jimenez.html.

17. Jack Hurst, "Not Just Miles Apart: Folky vs. Country's the Difference, Nikki Nelson Says of Paulette Carlson," *Chicago Tribune*, Aug. 15, 1991.

18. David Plotnikoff, "The Three Amigos Texas, Si," *San Jose Mercury News*, Dec. 30, 1994.

19. Ibid.

20. Burr, "Jimenez returns to Conjunto on Arista-Texas set," *Billboard*, May 18, 1996.

21. Ramon Hernandez, "Triple Grammy Award Winner Flaco Jimenez Goes Back to His Roots," *La Prensa*, Nov. 9, 1997.

22. Hernandez, "Flaco Jimenez: Mentor/Nunie Rubio; Protege Make Winning Conjunto Music Combination," *La Prensa*, Nov. 16, 1997.

23. Ibid.

24. For more information on international audiences attending the Tejano Conjunto Festival, see Bauer 2019.

25. Burr, "El Premio Billboard: Flaco Jiménez."

26. Peña, *Musica Tejana*, 107.

27. Ibid.

28. John Lannert, "El Premio for Jimenez," *Billboard*, Feb. 20, 1999.

29. Marianne Meyer, "Live!; What: 'Mexico on the Potomac Outdoor Festival When: Noon Saturday Where: Gateway Park, Arlington," *The Washington Post*, May 6, 2004.

30. Ragland, *Música Norteña*, 3.

31. Jon Pareles, "The Inauguration: A Musical Smorgasbord; 2 Concerts Gel Sounds of America," *The New York Times*, Jan. 19, 1993.

32. Ibid.

33. Stuart Schoffman, "In Sunny Jericho, a Texas Two-Step with Palestinians," *MetroWest Jewish News* (East Orange, NJ), May 4, 1995.

34. Mike Joyce, "All on the Mall. A Day of Diverse Music and So Fourth," *The Washington Post*, July 5, 1995.

35. Ibid.

36. Ibid.

37. John Morthland, "Magic Fingers," *Texas Monthly* 23, no. 7 (July 1995): 81–82.

38. Jiménez, "Oral History."

39. Morthland, "Magic Fingers."

40. Ibid.

41. Ragland, "Conjunto Cowboy Has It All."

42. Steve Dollar, "Olympic Arts Festival/Southern Crossroads; Festival Lineup Features a Regional Who's Who," *The Atlanta Journal and Constitution*, May 26, 1996.

43. Ibid.

44. Dollar, "Atlanta Games; Special Section; Day 15; City; Culture; Crossroads Finds a Niche; Visitors Discover Sounds of South Cover Broad Area," *The Atlanta Journal and Constitution*, Aug. 2, 1996.

45. Ibid.

46. Gene Scaramuzzo, "Festival International de Louisiane Lafayette, LA April 24–26," *The Beat* 17, No. 5 (1998), 50.

47. Ibid.

48. Ben Sisario, "Summer Festivals: Pop/Jazz; An Abundance of Performing Arts Nationwide," *The New York Times*, May 9, 1999.

49. Scott Alarik, "Lowell Folk Festival Is Note Perfect," *Boston Globe*, July 30, 2001.

50. Peña, *Musica Tejana*, 108.

51. "50th Anniversary 1967–2017: Spotlight on American Folk Masters," Smithsonian Institution, https://festival.si.edu/2017/50th-anniversary/spotlight-on-american-masters/smithsonian.

52. Ibid.

53. Steve Kiviat, "A Tex-Mex Night to Marimba," *The Washington Post,* Mar. 18, 2004.

54. Ibid.

55. Cal Blethen, "Musical greats bring their region's specialty Sunday to Yakima's Capitol Theatre," *Yakima Herald-Republic* (WA), Nov. 5, 2004.

56. Ibid.

57. Satterwhite, "Imagining Home, Nation, World," 11.

58. Ibid., 16.

59. Ibid., 19.

60. Ibid.

61. Ben King Jr., "The Genius of Squeeze Box Magic: Esteban Jordan Accordionist," *San Antonio Express*, Sept. 30, 1977.

62. John Burnett, "The Corrido of the 'World's Best Accordionist,'" *All Things Considered*, NPR, June 2, 2009.

63. James M. Manheim, "Esteban Jordan," *Contemporary Musicians* 49 (2005): 108.

64. Ibid.

65. King Jr., "The Genius of Squeeze Box Magic."

66. Erin Blair, "Weekend Events Have Been Canceled," *Santa Cruz Sentinel* (CA), Oct. 20, 1989.

67. Milo Miles, "Home Entertainment/Recordings: Soundings; Rough-Hewn Melodies from Texas Romantics," *The New York Times*, Apr. 15, 1990.

68. Jimmy Hori, "Summer Festivals," *The Beat* 11, no. 5 (1992), 54.

69. Regis and Walton, "Producing the Folk at the New Orleans Jazz and Heritage Festival," 400.

70. Ibid., 401.

71. Hori, "Summer Festivals," 54.

72. Peter Watrous, "Sounds Around Town," *The New York Times*, July 16, 1993.

73. Geoffrey Himes, "Esteban 'Steve' Jordan," *The Washington Post*, July 26, 1993.

74. Ibid.

75. Abel Salas, "Last Words: A Conjunto Pilgrimage; Or, Confessions of an Accordion Fiend," *Current*, May 30, 2001.

76. Corcoran, "The Invisible Genius," 4.

77. Burnett, "The Corrido of the 'World's Best Accordionist.'"

78. Callie Enlow, "'El Parche' Slips Away," *Current*, Aug. 8, 2010.

79. Corcoran, "The Invisible Genius," 5.

Chapter 2. "Ladies and gentlemen, Dodge Presents Flaco Jiménez!"

Epigraph: Meagan Roberts, "Chris Strachwitz Gets Sense of Adventure from Recording Extraordinary Music," *Stock Watch*, Oct. 17, 2014.

1. "Chrysler Breaks Campaign Targeting Texas Hispanics: GlobalHue Spots Feature Tejano Music Star Flaco Jimenez," *Adweek*, Mar. 31, 2003.

2. Ibid.

3. Ibid.

4. Ibid.

5. Ibid.

6. Media are often defined according to three categories: print media (newspapers and magazines), broadcast media (radio and television), and the internet. While audio recordings are not consistently included within this definition, for our circumstances, they invoke a corresponding analysis. In the case of conjunto, widespread dissemination of the music has been achieved through print media, broadcast media, the internet, and musical recordings. As such, the history of conjunto recordings, the labels producing these products, and the resulting global impacts will be considered alongside more standard definitions of media. A broader interpretation of media as mass communication certainly lends credence to this inclusion.

7. Wheeler, "New Media, Globalization and Kuwaiti National Identity," 432.

8. Ibid.

9. Peña, *The Texas-Mexican Conjunto*, 71.

10. Jiménez, "Oral History."

11. Peña, *The Texas-Mexican Conjunto*, 71.

12. Jiménez, "Flaco Jiménez Talks with Aaron Howard about Fame and Music on the Texas Border," interview by Aaron Howard, *RootsWorld: Listening to the Planet*, 2000, http://www.rootsworld.com/interview/flaco.html.

13. Hernandez, "Triple Grammy Award Winner Flaco Jimenez Goes Back to his Roots."

14. Heim, "Texas Tornado Flaco Jimenez Whips Up a Tex-Mex Storm."

15. Lannert, "Rock/Country Acts 'Partner' Up with Jimenez on Tex-Mex Set," *Billboard*, Sept. 5, 1992.

16. Lynn Van Matre, "Cooder's Bootleneck Conjures up the Dust Bowl Decade," *Chicago Tribune*, Feb. 16, 1975.

17. Tony Russell, "Obituary: Esteban 'Steve' Jordan: Hailed as 'the Hendrix of the Accordion,'" *The Guardian*, Sept. 22, 2010. Hernandez, "Esteban Jordan: El Sabio del Acordeon," Aug. 14, 2010, http://www.ramiroburr.com/true/site/index.php?option=com_content&view=article&id=729:esteban-jordan-el-sabio-del-acordeon-&catid=3:newsflash.

18. Corcoran, "The Invisible Genius," 4.

19. Katherine Bishop, "A One-Man Company Records Ethnic Musicians," *The New York Times*, Aug. 6, 1988.

20. Ibid.

21. Morthland, "Unsung," *Texas Monthly*, Oct. 2000.

22. Jim Harrington, "Arhoolie Records Founder Chris Strachwitz Celebrating 50 Years of Preserving American Roots Music," *San Jose Mercury News*, Jan. 30, 2011.

23. Larry Rohter, "Keeper and Protector of the Down-Home Sound; Born a German Count, Enthralled by Music Rooted in America," *International Herald Tribune*, Dec. 2, 2010.

24. Harrington, "Arhoolie Records Founder Chris Strachwitz Celebrating 50 Years of Preserving American Roots Music."

25. Mark Guarino, "Arhoolie at 40: Boxed Set a Melting Pot of American Music," *Daily Herald* (Arlington Heights, IL), Nov. 17, 2000.

26. Bishop, "A One-Man Company Records Ethnic Musicians."

27. Rohter, "Keeper and Protector of the Down-Home Sound."

28. Ibid.

29. Harrington, "Arhoolie Records Founder Chris Strachwitz Celebrating 50 Years of Preserving American Roots Music."

30. Mac McDonald, "Arhoolie Records Releases Book, CDs Celebrating 50-Plus Years of Music," *Monterey County Herald* (CA), Jan. 25, 2013.

31. For more information on *Chicken Skin Music*, see Bauer 2014.

32. Barry Mazor, "Music: Five Decades of Arhoolie," *Wall Street Journal*, Feb. 5, 2013.

33. Ibid.

34. Edward L. Stratemeyer, "From Cotton Fields to Dance Halls, an Outsider's Journey; At 40, Arhoolie Records, the Brainchild of Chris Strachwitz, Remains a Repository of Vernacular Music; Blues, Zydeco, Sacred Steel—You Name It," *The New York Times*, Oct. 8, 2000.

35. Harrington, "Arhoolie Records Founder Chris Strachwitz Celebrating 50 Years of Preserving American Roots Music."

36. Ibid.

37. Morthland, "Unsung."

38. Ibid.

39. Chris Morris, "Arhoolie Records Owner Justly Honored," *Billboard*, Apr. 22, 1995.

40. Callie Enlow, "'El Parche' Slips Away."

41. Ibid.

42. Corcoran, "The Invisible Genius."

43. Bishop, "A One-Man Company Records Ethnic Musicians."

44. "Record Label Looking for Texas Talent," *The Paris News* (Paris, TX), Dec. 5, 1993.

45. Ibid.

46. Burr, "Arista Commits to Tejano's Growth," *Billboard*, Feb. 12, 1994.

47. "Record Label Looking for Texas Talent."

48. Burr, "Arista Commits to Tejano's Growth."

49. Burr, "The Crowned Heads of the Conjunto Sound," *Billboard*, Aug. 3, 1996.

50. Salas, "Record Label Abandons Tejano Experiment," *Hispanic*, Sept. 1998.

51. Mayer, "From Segmented to Fragmented," 295.

52. DeMars, "Buying Time to Start Spanish-Language Radio in San Antonio," 79.

53. For a list of awards, see DeMars (2005), p. 78.

54. DeMars, "Buying Time to Start Spanish-Language Radio in San Antonio," 80.

55. Mayer, "From Segmented to Fragmented," 296.

56. Angela Covo, "The End of an Era, for Now," *La Prensa*, Aug. 21, 2011.

57. Amanda Lozano, "Güero Polkas: The Man that Shaped Tejano," *La Prensa*, Mar. 17, 2013.

58. Peña, *The Texas-Mexican Conjunto*, 71.

59. "Hispanic Broadcasting Comes of Age," *Broadcasting*, Apr. 3, 1989.

60. Ibid.

61. Margarita De León, "Durán Retires after 53 Years as Spanish Radio DJ, Promoter," *La Prensa* (Toledo, OH), Sept. 5, 2008.

62. Edna Gundersen, "Taking Tejano beyond Texas," *USA Today*, Apr. 6, 1995.

63. Burr, "Jimenez Returns to Conjunto on Arista-Texas Set."

64. Burr, "The Crowned Heads of the Conjunto Sound."

65. Flores, "Tejano, Conjunto Back on FM Radio," *Austin American Statesman*, Aug. 24, 2015.

66. Ibid.

67. Ibid.

68. Ibid.

69. Mayer, "From Segmented to Fragmented," 295.

70. Ibid.

71. Burr, "Jimenez Returns to Conjunto on Arista-Texas Set."

72. Ibid.

73. Patoski, "The Sound of Musica," *Texas Monthly*, Jan. 1, 1993.

74. For a review of all four films, see Scruggs 1999.

75. Mayer, "From Segmented to Fragmented," 299.

76. Bauer, "Beyond the Border," 44.

77. Bauer, "Blurring Boundaries in Rosedale Park," 177.

78. Gheni Platenburg, "Popularity of Tejano Music Wanes, Conjunto, Other Re-

gional Mexican Music Takes Over," *McClatchy-Tribune Business News* (Tacoma, WA), Oct. 16, 2011.

79. Hernandez, "Conjunto is Life for El Padrino of Los Padrinos," *La Prensa*, June 2, 2010.

80. Flew and Waisbord, "The Ongoing Significance of National Media Systems in the Context of Media Globalization," 627.

Chapter 3. "From Texas to Washington and across to Michigan and Illinois..."

Epigraph: "M and M is Back," *La Prensa* (Toledo, OH), Aug. 31, 2005.

1. Jim Washburn, "Pop Music Review: Chapa Ends Fiesta Series on a Spicy Note," *Los Angeles Times*, Dec. 24, 1991.

2. Washburn, "Melting Pot of Music O.C. Festival: Albert Ramon y Su Tierra Chicana, a Tex-Mex Band with German and Blues Influences, Takes its Sounds to Santa Ana Streets at Marketplace Christmas Celebration," *Los Angeles Times*, Dec. 12, 1991.

3. Ibid.

4. Ibid.

5. Ibid.

6. Washburn, "Pop Music Review."

7. Ibid.

8. Ibid.

9. Ibid.

10. Wijnand, et al., "The Mnemonic Muse," 2.

11. Sedikides, et al., "Nostalgia," 305.

12. Los Lobos official website, http://www.loslobos.org/site/band.shtml.

13. Maurey, "Dana International and the Politics of Nostalgia," 85.

14. Harnish, "Tejano Music in the Urbanizing Midwest," 207.

15. Ibid., 208.

16. Ibid., 204.

17. Ibid., 205.

18. Ibid., 214.

19. Rod Lockwood, "Hitting the High Notes: Collection of Distinctive Sounds Keep Toledo Tuned in Musically," *The Blade* (Toledo, OH), May 20, 2007.

20. Kevin Milliken, "Conjunto Crossroads: Ohioan Jimmy Bejarano Sr. Inducted in Texas," *La Prensa* (Toledo, OH), May 20, 2011.

21. Turino, *Moving Away from Silence*, 199.

22. See Harnish et al., 2002, O'Hagin and Harnish 2006, and Harnish 2009.

23. Tahree Lane, "'I Have Music in My Blood'; Versatile Toledo Performer Jesse Ponce Immerses Listeners in Hispanic Heritage," *The Blade* (Toledo, OH), July 5, 2006. Harnish, "Tejano Music in the Urbanizing Midwest," 198.

24. Harnish, "Tejano Music in the Urbanizing Midwest," 216.

25. Ibid., 199.

26. Lane, "'I Have Music in My Blood.'"

27. Harnish, "Tejano Music in the Urbanizing Midwest," 217.

28. Ibid.

29. O'Hagin and Harnish, "Music as Cultural Identity," 63.

30. Harnish, "Tejano Music in the Urbanizing Midwest," 213.

31. Lane, "'I Have Music in my Blood.'"

32. Ibid.

33. Harnish, "Tejano Music in the Urbanizing Midwest," 200.

34. Milliken, "Conjunto Crossroads."

35. O'Hagin and Harnish, "Music as Cultural Identity," 64.

36. Milliken, "Conjunto Crossroads."

37. Ibid.

38. Jack Buehrer, "Our Neighbor," *The News-Messenger* (Fremont, OH), July 5, 2004.

39. O'Hagin and Harnish, "Music as Cultural Identity," 61.

40. Harnish, "Tejano Music in the Urbanizing Midwest," 206.

41. Milliken, "Latino Profiles: Jacob Estrada Recording 2nd CD," *La Prensa* (Toledo, OH), May 11, 2018.

42. Ibid.

43. Nicholas K. Geranios, "Star of 'Conjunto' Music Wary of Limelight After Long Years of Obscurity," *Los Angeles Times*, Oct. 24, 1993.

44. Courtney, "Tejano-Music Group Raising Money to Fund Radio Station."

45. Geranios, "Star of 'Conjunto' Music Wary of Limelight After Long Years of Obscurity."

46. Ibid.

47. Ragland, "Let His Fingers Do the Walking; From Washington State to Austin, Joel Guzman has Brought the Accordion Back to Tejano Prominence," *Austin American Statesman*, Jan. 25, 1996.

48. Chito De La Torre, "Tejano's Youngest Legend: Joel Guzman," *La Prensa*, Nov. 17, 1995.

49. Ragland, "Let His Fingers Do the Walking."

50. De La Torre, "Tejano's Youngest Legend."

51. Ragland, "Let His Fingers Do the Walking."

52. Ibid.

53. Ibid.

54. "Hearth Music Interview with Max Baca of Los Texmaniacs," *Hearth Music Blog*, www.hearthmusic.com, Feb. 2, 2013.

55. Erin Eggers, "No Limits for Bajo Sexto," *San Antonio Express-News*, Apr. 18, 2012.

56. "Borders y Bailes: Los Texmaniacs," *Smithsonian Folkways*, http://www.folkways.si.edu.

57. Ibid.

58. "Hearth Music Interview."

59. *Borders y Bailes* (2009), *Texas Town & Tex-Mex Sounds* (2012), and *Cruzando Borders* (2018).

60. "Los Texmaniacs," *Smithsonian Folkways*, https://folkways.si.edu/artists/los-texmaniacs.

61. García Canclini, *Hybrid Cultures*.

62. Turino, *Moving Away from Silence*, 194.

63. Margolies, "Voz de Pueblo Chicano," 37.

64. "Performer: Los Texmaniacs," *Lowell Sun* (MA), July 26, 2017.

65. Ragland, "Reviewed Work," 218.

66. Patoski, "Conjunto Ambassadors Los Texmaniacs on the Magic of 'Musica Alegre,'" *Texas Highways*, May 2019.

67. John Farrell, "Mexican Cocktail with a Squeeze of Accordion," *Daily Breeze* (Torrance, CA), Oct. 4, 2010.

68. Juan Villa, "Visalia Tejano Band Seeks Local Recognition," *Visalia Times* (CA), Sept. 24, 2011.

69. Farrell, "Mexican Cocktail with a Squeeze of Accordion."

70. Villa, "Visalia Tejano Band Seeks Local Recognition."

71. Ibid.

72. Ibid.

73. For a detailed history of Los Lobos's musical career, see Morris 2015.

74. Radley Balko, "How the Wolves Survive," *Reason* 39, no. 1 (2007): 53–57.

75. John Rogers, "Chicano Rock Pioneers Los Lobos Marking 40 Years," *Associated Press*, Dec. 15, 2012.

76. Leila Cobo, "El Premio Billboard Award: Los Lobos—Just Another Band from East L.A. Impacts the World of Mexican-American Music," *Billboard*, Apr. 28, 2001.

77. Pineda, "Will They See Me Coming?," 185.

78. Ibid.

79. Ibid., 197.

80. Balko, "How the Wolves Survive."

81. Ibid.

82. Andrew Keeler, "Los Lobos Fame Grows, but They Retain Roots," *Evening Tribune* (San Diego), June 28, 1985.

83. Ahad, "Post-Blackness and Culinary Nostalgia in Marcus Samuelsson's *Yes, Chef*," 7.

84. Cain, "Musics of 'The Other,'" 72.

Chapter 4. "You have to mix it up!"

Epigraph: Adrian Jackson, "Tex-Mex-Mix," *Sydney Morning Herald*, Feb. 21, 1991.

1. Plotnikoff, "The Three Amigos Texas, Si."

2. John Kelly, "Squeezing Life from Music," *The Irish Times*, May 27, 2000.

3. Paul Brown, "Tex-Mex Accordionists Inspired by Polka Created Conjunto Music," *Morning Edition*, NPR, Aug. 22, 2003.

4. Ibid.

5. Vestel, "Limits of Hybridity Versus Limits of Tradition?," 466.

6. García Canclini, *Hybrid Cultures*, xxv.

7. Sutton, "'Fusion' and Questions of Korean Cultural Identity in Music," 4.

8. Timothy White, "Flaco Jimenez's Tex-Mex triumph," *Billboard*, Oct. 22, 1994.

9. Jiménez, "Oral History."

10. Plotnikoff, "The Three Amigos Texas, Si."

11. Burr, "Jimenez Returns to Conjunto on Arista-Texas Set."

12. Sutton, "'Fusion' and Questions of Korean Cultural Identity in Music," 4.

13. White, "Flaco Jimenez's Tex-Mex triumph."

14. Eric Levin, "Flaco Jimenez," *People* 43, no. 5 (1995): 26.

15. Plotnikoff, "The Three Amigos Texas, Si."

16. Patoski, "Hot Box," *Texas Monthly* 24, no. 6 (1996): 22.

17. Ibid.

18. Sutton, "'Fusion' and Questions of Korean Cultural Identity in Music," 12.

19. Ibid., 4.

20. Ibid., 12.

21. Tervo, "From Appropriation to Translation," 176.

22. Larry Flick, "Single reviews: AC," *Billboard* 106, no. 45 (1994): 95.

23. J.D. Considine, "A Pervasive Sense of Desperation," *St. Louis Post-Dispatch*, Dec. 29, 1994.

24. Flick, "Single reviews: AC."

25. Considine, "A Pervasive Sense of Desperation."

26. Jiménez, "Flaco Jiménez Interview," interview by Chris Strachwitz, *The Arhoolie Foundation*, 1973, audio transcription, https://arhoolie.org/flaco-jimenez-interview/.

27. Jin and Ryoo, "Critical Interpretation of Hybrid K-Pop," 115.

28. Greg Kot, "A Timeless Format: New Zealand's Verlains Finally May Be Ready for a Career in Rock," *Chicago Tribune*, Apr. 2, 1992.

29. "Tornados have Tex-Mex Blend," *Kenosha News* (WI), Apr. 3–10, 1992. Chris Dafoe, "Tornados Put New Twist in Texans' Careers," *The Toronto Star*, Sept. 21, 1990.

30. Plotnikoff, "The Three Amigos Texas, Si."

31. Heim, "Texas Tornado Flaco Jimenez Whips Up a Tex-Mex Storm."

32. Claudia Perry, "Tex-Mex Twister: The Tornados Are Back and Riding High in the Saddle," *San Jose Mercury News*, July 26, 1996.

33. Ibid.

34. Dan Kening, "Everything Fine at Festival Except for its Location," *Chicago Tribune*, July 22, 1991.

35. "Tornados have Tex-Mex Blend."

36. Plotnikoff, "The Three Amigos Texas, Si."

37. Ibid.

38. Ibid.

39. Heim, "Latest from Was (Not Was) is more than 'Okay': New Albums," *Chicago Tribune*, July 27, 1990.

40. Joe Edwards, "Tornados Whip Up Quick Success: Freddy Fender Makes Comeback," *Leader-Telegram* (Eau Claire, WI), Mar. 31, 1991.

41. Dafoe, "Tornados Put New Twist in Texans' Careers."

42. Hurst, "Sahm Brainstorm: Doug's Tornados Are Blowing in Country's Door," *Chicago Tribune*," July 29, 1990.

43. Hurst, "Winds of Change: Texas Tornados Give Fender Another Turn in the Spotlight," *Chicago Tribune*, July 19, 1991.

44. David Dishneau, "Music Review: Tex-Mex Hot," *The Janesville Gazette* (Janesville, WI), Oct. 9, 1990.

45. Perry, "Tex-Mex Twister: The Tornados are Back and Riding High in the Saddle."

46. Lozano, "Augie Meyers: A Living Musical Legend," *La Prensa*, Dec. 1, 2013.

47. Jiménez, "Oral History."

48. Margaret Moser, "Three Stories about Three Augie Meyers Songs," *Austin Chronicle*, Oct. 30, 2009.

49. Randy Lewis, "Tornados Whippin' It Up: The Tex-Mex Rockers Who'll Blow into O.C., Are a Hot Ticket," *Los Angeles Times*, June 27, 1991.

50. Jin and Ryoo, "Critical Interpretation of Hybrid K-Pop," 127.

51. Ibid.

52. Chet Flippo, "RCA To Debut Los Super Seven: Mexican-American 'Supergroup' Does One-Time Project," *Billboard*, Aug. 22, 1998.

53. James Reindl, "Los Super Seven," *The Janesville Gazette* (Janesville, WI), Sept. 24, 1998.

54. Richard Harrington, "Magnificent Seven: Ole! To the Music of Mexico," *The Washington Post*, Feb. 3, 1999.

55. Nguyen, "Cultural Adaptation, Tradition, and Identity of Diasporic Vietnamese People," 441.

56. Ibid., 444.

57. Ibid., 448.

58. Jin and Ryoo, "Critical Interpretation of Hybrid K-Pop," 116.

Chapter 5. "I play the jazz accordion!"

Epigraph: Corcoran, "The Invisible Genius."

1. Michael O'Sullivan, "The Shrinking of American Cultural Diplomacy," *The Washington Post*, Sept. 23, 1996.

2. Tom Teepen, "U.S. Culture Gets Grounded," *The Atlanta Journal and Constitution*, Sept. 17, 1996.

3. Schoffman, "In Sunny Jericho, a Texas Two-Step with Palestinians."

4. Ibid.

5. Enlow, "Plata," *Current*, Aug. 25, 2010.

6. Ibid.

7. "@Salute International Bar- Bonnie Cisneros poet," https://youtu.be/6tI_jkSmmsc, uploaded June 18, 2011.

8. Holton, "Globalization's Cultural Consequences," 141.

9. Brackett, "Questions of Genre in Black Popular Music," 76.

10. Ragland, "Conjunto Cowboy Has it All."

11. Morthland, "Magic Fingers."

12. Himes, "Saldivar: Conjunto With Country," *The Washington Post*, Apr. 9, 1993.

13. Bob Tarte, "Jean-Paul, Georges et Rigo," *The Beat* 11, no. 5 (1992): 21.

14. Ibid.

15. Morthland, "Magic Fingers."

16. Simonett, *Banda*, 14.

17. Ibid., 48.

18. Brackett, "Questions of Genre in Black Popular Music," 76.

19. Ibid.

20. Himes, "Saldivar."

21. Holton, "Globalization's Cultural Consequences," 141.

22. "From Head to Toe: Growing Popularity of Conjunto Music and its Musicians," CBS News Transcripts, Jan. 28, 1996.

23. Alejandro Perez, "Conjunto Dreams; Guadalupe Festival Glides into its 24th Year with a Forward-Looking Roots Celebration," *Current*, May 5, 2005.

24. Jiménez, "Flaco Jiménez Interview."

25. Ibid.

26. Jiménez, "Oral History."

27. Burr, "The Crowned Heads of the Conjunto Sound."

28. Himes, "Esteban 'Steve' Jordan."

29. Ibid.

30. Don Snowden, "Jordan Lives Up to His Colorful Rep," *Los Angeles Times*, July 10, 1991.

31. Katy Vine, "The Apprentice," *Texas Monthly*, June 2011.

32. Hernandez, "Esteban Jordan."

33. Yri, "Medievalism and Exoticism in the Music of Dead Can Dance," 56.

34. Cervantes, "Squeezebox Poetics," 836.

35. Steve Jordan, "The Corrido of the 'World's Best Accordionist,'" interview by *All Things Considered*, NPR, June 2, 2009.

36. Cervantes, "Squeezebox Poetics," 869.

37. Ibid., 871.

38. Boyd, *The Notorious Ph.D.'s Guide to the Super Fly '70s*.

39. Cervantes, "Squeezebox Poetics," 869.

40. Kiviat, "A Tex-Mex Night to Marimba."

41. Limón, "'This Is Our *Música*, Guy!'"

Chapter 6. "It's jealousy..."

Epigraph: "Eva Ybarra, the Accordion Queen, Was Born to Play," *Texas Highways*, Sept. 19, 2017.

1. Valdez and Halley, "Gender in the Culture of Mexican American Conjunto Music," 148.

2. Ibid., 151.

3. Ibid., 153.

4. Ibid., 152.

5. Ibid., 164.

6. Vargas, "Borderland Bolerista," 188.

7. Vargas, "Resounding Chicana Music," 113.

8. Vargas, *Dissonant Divas in Chicana Music*, 111.

9. Ibid., 113.

10. Lea Thompson, "'La Reina del Acordeón' Celebrated at Guadalupe," *La Prensa*, Mar. 18, 2015.

11. Valdez and Halley, "Gender in the Culture of Mexican American Conjunto Music," 155.

12. Fernando Del Valle, "Women of Conjunto Taking Center Stage," *McClatchy-Tribune Business News* (Tacoma, WA), Oct. 20, 2011.

13. Morthland, "Eva, Diva: Meet San Antonio Accordionist Eva Ybarra, Conjunto's Main Squeeze," *Texas Monthly* 24, no. 7 (1996).

14. Valdez and Halley, "Gender in the Culture of Mexican American Conjunto Music," 155.

15. Morthland, "Eva, Diva."

16. Valdez and Halley, "Gender in the Culture of Mexican American Conjunto Music," 155.

17. Silja J.A. Talvi, "La Reina de Acordeón: Silja J.A. Talvi Talks with Accordion Queen Eva Ybarra," *RootsWorld: Listening to the Planet*. http://www.rootsworld.com/rw/feature/ybarra.html.

18. Morthland, "Eva, Diva."

19. Ragland, "Ybarra, Eva," *Grove Music Online*, s.v, November 26, 2013, www.oxfordmusiconline.com.

20. Liliana Valenzuela, "Torres Says, 'Play What's in Your Heart,'" *Austin American Statesman*, May 9, 2013.

21. Núñez, "Sin Las Mujeres No Hay Conjunto," 23.

22. Susan Torres, interview with author, June 11, 2014.

23. Ibid.

24. Ibid.

25. Ibid.

26. Ibid.

27. Vargas, *Dissonant Divas in Chicana Music*, 111.

28. Vargas, "Borderland Bolerista," 188.

29. John Koegel, "Silva, Chelo," *Grove Music Online*, s.v, November 26, 2013, www.oxfordmusiconline.com.

30. Vargas, *Dissonant Divas in Chicana Music*, 35.

31. Ibid., 186.

32. Ibid., 202.

33. Vargas, "Borderland Bolerista," 188.

34. Ibid.

35. "Eva Ybarra, the Accordion Queen, Was Born to Play."

Chapter 7. "That's my music!"

Epigraph: Hector Saldaña, "Conjunto Sensation Makes Saluté Debut," *San Antonio Express-News*, May 17, 2012.

1. Juan Tejeda, interview with author, Apr. 26, 2014.

2. Tejeda, interview with author, Apr. 26, 2014. For a detailed analysis of the Tejano Conjunto Festival, see Bauer 2019.

3. Burr, "Conjunto Talent Comes from Across 2 Oceans—S.A. Festival Includes Bands from France, Japan," *San Antonio Express-News*, May 14, 2000.

4. Carlos Guerra, "Tex-Mex Music Catches on Around the World," *Austin American Statesman*, May 1, 1992.

5. Bennett, "Conjunto Festival Draws Worldwide Fans," *San Antonio Express-News*, May 16, 1992.

6. Ibid.

7. "German artist captures flavor of Conjunto Festival, West Side," *San Antonio Express-News*, May 12, 1996.

8. Ibid.

9. Kate Hunger, "Fans Bring Fans to Conjunto Festival—They Love the Show, but It's Hot and Humid in Those Seats," *San Antonio Express-News*, May 11, 2003.

10. De La Torre, "Los Gatos: An Itchy Conjunto Taco," *La Prensa*, May 19, 1995.

11. Burr, "Parlez-Vous Conjunto?—It's Our Roots, Too, Says French Group," *San Antonio Express-News*, May 11, 2001.

12. " . . . se despertó en nosotros la curiosidad y después descubrimos Flaco Jiménez, Steve Jordan y otros." Manuel A. Perez, interview with author, Jan. 28, 2014.

13. Bryan Rindfuss, "Dutch Tejano?" *Current*, May 26, 2010.

14. Dwayne Verheyden, interview with author, Apr. 30, 2013.

15. Rindfuss, "Dutch Tejano?" For additional analysis regarding the international participation in conjunto music, including a more in-depth study of Verheyden's works, see Bauer 2016.

16. In general, I use the term "folkloric" here to refer to music that maintains a common repertory among a wide range of musical participants, is passed from generation to generation through oral transmission, consistently considers individual songs as belonging to the community rather than a single, creative artist (when the initial composer is even known), and/or does not address a national, mainstream

audience or use monetary incentive as a primary method of stylistic continuation. In contrast, the term "popular" indicates music that produces new and original repertory, stylistic distinctions between individual artists, consideration of songs as "belonging" to the original composer rather than the group as a whole, and/or intended association with an inter/national, mainstream, or money-oriented audience (regardless of actual participation with the mainstream community or total money earned).

17. Rios, "The Andean *Conjunto*, Bolivian *Sikureada* and the Folkloric Musical Representation Continuum," 6.

18. While Rios's (2012) analysis includes what he terms "folkloric musical representations," indicating presentational versions of musical practices that are often directly connected to aspirant pursuits of nationalism, rather than my understanding of "folkloric" vs. "popular" musical practices (defined above), I believe that his conception of an analytical continuum, although not an identical situation, still aids in a deeper understanding of the globalization of Texas-Mexican conjunto explored throughout my work. In both scenarios, as Rios notes, "folkloric representations range widely in their degree of sonic faithfulness" (2012, 7).

19. Ferguson, "I Was Cool When My Country Wasn't," 116.

20. Ibid., 117.

21. Auslander, "Musical Personae," 102.

22. Ibid., 117.

23. Ibid., 115.

24. Ibid.

25. Ibid., 113.

26. Ibid., 109.

27. Ibid., 113.

28. Ibid., 108.

29. Ibid., 104.

30. De La Torre, "Los Gatos."

31. Ibid.

32. "Están llevando adelante nuestra música, nuestra cultura. . . . te va felicitar por tu gran trabajo que estás haciendo tú y tus muchachos Los Gatos." Los Gatos de Japón, "Atotonilco," from *Tony De La Rosa Presents Los Gatos de Japon* (1996).

33. Linda Escobar, interview with author, June 11, 2013.

34. Ibid.

35. Ibid.

36. Burr, "Band from Japan Plays Conjunto with Heart," *San Antonio Express-News*, May 14, 1996.

37. Escobar, interview with author.

38. Mario Diaz Jr., interview with author, June 4, 2014.

39. Burr, "Japanese Band Has a Yen for Conjunto," *San Antonio Express-News*, May 10, 1996.

40. Peña, *Musica Tejana*, 100.

41. Tokita, "Bi-Musicality in Modern Japanese Culture," 167.

42. Hosokawa, "'Salsa No Tiene Frontera,'" 511.

43. Tsambu, "Transnationalism and Transculturalism as Seen in Congolese Music Videograms," 53.

44. Hosokawa, "'Salsa No Tiene Frontera,'" 527.

45. Herd, "Trends and Taste in Japanese Popular Music," 75.

46. Hosokawa, "'Salsa No Tiene Frontera,'" 510.

47. Ibid., 514.

48. Escobar, interview with author.

49. De La Torre, "Los Gatos."

50. Ferguson, "I Was Cool When My Country Wasn't," 116.

51. Auslander, "Musical Personae," 105.

52. Ferguson, "I Was Cool When My Country Wasn't," 116.

53. Herd, "Trends and Taste in Japanese Popular Music," 95.

54. Tokita, "Bi-musicality in modern Japanese Culture," 161.

55. Ibid., 161.

56. Ibid., 172.

57. Sterling, "Between National Subjectivity and Global Artistry," 349.

58. Hosokawa, "'Salsa No Tiene Frontera,'" 519.

59. Ibid.

60. Ibid., 524.

61. Ibid., 527.

62. Ibid., 520.

63. Escobar, interview with author.

64. Ibid.

65. Burr, "Band from Japan Plays Conjunto with Heart."

66. Ibid.

67. For additional analysis along these lines, see Bauer 2016.

68. Hosokawa, "'Salsa No Tiene Frontera,'" 519.

69. Yano, "Inventing Selves," 115.

70. Ibid., 121.

71. Herd, "Trends and Taste in Japanese Popular Music," 91.

72. Ibid., 95.

73. Yano, "Inventing Selves," 118.

74. van Elteren, "Country Music in the Netherlands," 53.

75. van Elteren, "Dutch Country Music," 95.

76. Ibid., 93.

77. Verheyden, interview with author.

78. van Elteren, "Country Music in the Netherlands," 56.

79. Ibid.

80. van Elteren, "Dutch Country Music," 99.

81. Verheyden, interview with author.

82. Burr, "Parlez-Vous Conjunto?"

83. Verheyden, interview with author.

Chapter 8. "*¡Esto es globalización!*"

Epigraph: Jiménez, "Flaco Jiménez Talks with Aaron Howard About Fame and Music on the Texas Border."

1. Ibid.

2. Paul A. Harris, "For True Tex-Mex, Just Call on Flaco; Jimenez has Added Tejano Sound to a Ton of Albums," *St. Louis Post-Dispatch*, July 22, 1994.

3. Jan Brands, "Een moment van puur geluk (2)," in *Boem* 30, November 1999, http://www.rowwenheze.nl/band/verder-naar-vroeger. "*Een van de allermooiste momenten uit de Nederlandse popgeschiedenis.*"

4. Ibid. "Echt een heel groot moment, dit samenspel van mannen uit zo verschillende uithoeken van de wereld. Universele muziek. Puur geluk."

5. Special thanks to Barbara Beckers and Leonie Cornips (Maastricht University) for providing Dutch translations of "Bestal Mar," "De Moan," and "Kroenenberg." The English translations from the Dutch are my own.

6. http://youtu.be/pa0_WRlwsx8, http://youtu.be/i01zlclNBVU, and http://youtu.be/UrXWknnGzGg or http://youtu.be/61rjvGFJot0, respectively.

7. van Klyton, "Space and Place in World Music Production," 101.

8. For a deeper analysis of Ry Cooder's work with Flaco Jiménez and this early connection to the world music movement, see Bauer 2014.

9. Feld, "Pygmy POP," 15.

10. Meintjes, "Paul Simon's Graceland, South Africa, and the Mediation of Musical Meaning," 47.

11. Yri, "Medievalism and Exoticism in the Music of Dean Can Dance," 54.

12. See Bauer 2014.

13. Plotnikoff, "The Three Amigos Texas, Si."

14. White, "Flaco Jimenez's Tex-Mex triumph."

15. "Jimenez to Perform at Tejano Festival," *The Facts* (Clute, TX), Aug. 1, 1997.

16. Jackson, "Tex-Mex-Mix."

17. Lannert, "Rock/Country Acts 'Partner' up with Jimenez on Tex-Mex Set."

18. Meintjes, "Paul Simon's Graceland, South Africa, and the Mediation of Musical Meaning," 61–62.

19. Jiménez, "Oral History."

20. Jiménez, "Flaco Jiménez Talks with Aaron Howard About Fame and Music on the Texas Border."

21. Silverman, "Gypsy/Klezmer Dialectics," 175.

22. Feld, "Notes on World Beat," 31.

23. Ibid.

24. Don McLeese, "Country & Western," *Rolling Stone*, Aug. 20, 1992.

25. David Zimmerman, "Musicians Band Together for Albums from the Heart // 'Partners' in Tex-Mex Sound," *USA Today*, July 15, 1992.

26. Burr, "Jimenez Returns to Conjunto on Arista-Texas Set."

27. Tarte, "Missouri Loves Company," *The Beat* 17, no. 6 (1998).

28. van Klyton, "All the Way From . . . ," 106.

29. Feld, "A Sweet Lullaby for World Music," 147.

30. van Klyton, "All the Way From . . . ," 106.

31. Van Matre, "Cooder's Bottleneck Conjures up the Dust Bowl Decade."

32. Ibid.

33. Heim, "Flaco Jimenez Partners," *Chicago Tribune*, Aug. 20, 1992.

34. Flick, "Country," *Billboard*, Mar. 11, 1995.

35. Dean Buckley, "The Gay Movie Beat: Three New Soundtrack CDs Pop Out of the Closet and onto the Turntable," *The Advocate*, Oct. 26, 1999.

36. Kelly, "Squeezing Life from Music."

37. Jiménez, "Flaco Jiménez Talks with Aaron Howard About Fame and Music on the Texas Border."

38. Meintjes, "Paul Simon's Graceland, South Africa, and the Mediation of Musical Meaning," 41.

39. Jan Brands, "Een moment van puur geluk (2)." "Toen wij voor het eerst hun plaat 'And a time to dance' opzetten, kwam dat aan als een moker. Dat was als voor de eerste keer verliefd worden. Op onze eigen manier hebben we op die muziek verder geborduurd. Veel spelen, veel liedjes schrijven, en dan krijg je, net als Los Lobos, op den duur een eigen geluid."

40. Peter Knieriem, "CD Review: Los Lobos—Disconnected in New York City," in *Muziek.NL Magazine*, December 12, 2013, http://www.muziek.nl/cd-reviews/cd-revew-los-lobos-disconnected-in-new-york-city.

41. It is interesting to note, although outside the scope of this study, that Rowwen Hèze is also often nicknamed "The Pogues of De Peel," referring to the group's further musical inspiration from the popular Celtic punk band from London.

42. Lipsitz, *Time Passages*, 136.

43. van Elteren, "Rocking and Rapping in the Dutch Welfare State," 62.

44. Grijp, "Singing in Dutch Dialects," 241–42.

45. http://www.loslobos.org/site/band.shtml.

46. Quoted by Brands, "Een moment van puur geluk (2)." "Onze muziek is een mix van van alles. We komen uit het Oosten van Los Angelos, uit de Mexicaanse buurt van de stad. Daar proef je als kind van heel wat culturele en muzikale invloeden. In onze jeugd bracht de radio veel rhytm and blues en soulmusic. Daarnaast had je de Engelse muziek, zoals die van de Beatles, en natuurlijk de Mexicaanse muziek, 's morgens op moeders radio. Dat alles bij elkaar is Los Lobos."

47. van Elteren, "Rocking and Rapping in the Dutch Welfare State," 181.

48. Grijp, "Singing in Dutch Dialects," 235.

49. van Elteren, *Imagining America*, 181.

50. Grijp, "Singing in Dutch Dialects," 226.

51. Ibid., 227.

52. Ibid., 229.

53. Marsh, "Rock & Roll's Latin Tinge," 111.

54. Berman, *All That Is Solid Melts into Air*, 18.

55. Tomlinson, *Cultural Imperialism*, 73.

56. http://youtu.be/f2Q3Uht-s_w. "Es un cover holandés de una adaptación de los lobos de una canción tradicional norteña. Es, entonces, pienso yo, estilo holandés local global."

57. Madrid, *Nor-Tec Rifa!*, 7.

58. Simonett, *Banda*, 15.

Conclusion

1. Erica Grieder, "Trump Knows Nothing About Texas, and That's Hurting the Country," *Houston Chronicle*, Jan. 22, 2019.

2. Ibid.

3. Christopher Wilson, "5 Myths About U.S.-Mexico Border," *Newsday*, May 26, 2018.

4. Carlos Sanchez, "'They Don't Realize What a Dynamic Place It Is': Locals Raise Their Voices Amid Border Fight," *Texas Monthly*, Jan. 10, 2019.

5. Ibid.

6. Ibid.

7. Wilson, "5 Myths About U.S.-Mexico Border."

8. Ibid.

9. Ibid.

10. Sanchez, "'They Don't Realize What a Dynamic Place It Is.'"

11. Michelle García, "The Border and the American Imagination," *The Baffler*, July 2, 2018.

12. Ibid.

13. Ibid.

14. Ibid.

15. Ibid.

16. Sanchez, "'They Don't Realize What a Dynamic Place It Is.'"

17. García, "Border Theater," *The Baffler*, Sept. 14, 2018.

18. Sanchez, "'They Don't Realize What a Dynamic Place It Is.'"

19. Ibid.

20. Ibid.

21. Conjunto music, and thus this book in general, is situated on the northern side of the Texas-Mexican border. As such, much of the preceding analysis focuses on the Texas region alone—and its worldwide interactions, disregarding the closely related music (norteño) emanating from the southern side of the border and the messy interconnections of people and culture on both sides of the geo-political boundary. However, the border region is just that—a region; creative influences and socio-cultural relationships don't honor this imagined borderline in ways that politicians might expect. As such, in analyzing the U.S.-Mexico border region, it is important to remember that the barrier between Texas and Mexico is a political construct. While the U.S. government might imagine a stark separation between one side of this bar-

rier and the other, the community who live in the region display a fluidity of culture and consequent messiness in the tangled interactions caused by the placement of a barrier in the middle of a region.

22. Mitchell Ferman and Manny Fernandez, "In Texas, Trump's Visit Offers Two Views of a Border," *The New York Times*, Jan. 10, 2019.

23. Ibid.

24. Margolies, "Conjunto Sustainability and the Schools."

25. Margolies, "Transmission of Texas-Mexican *Conjunto* Music in the 21st Century."

26. Briggs and Bauman, "Genre, Intertextuality, and Social Power," 132.

27. Ibid.

28. Brackett, "Questions of Genre in Black Popular Music," 89.

29. Ibid.

30. Briggs and Bauman, "Genre, Intertextuality, and Social Power," 148.

31. Brackett, "Questions of Genre in Black Popular Music," 76.

32. Ibid., 77.

33. Bryson, "'Anything but Heavy Metal,'" 885.

34. Ibid., 884.

Discography

Brooks, Karen. *Walk On*. Warner Brothers Records 1–23676, 1982.

Cash, Johnny. *Ring of Fire: The Best of Johnny Cash*. Columbia CL 2053, 1963.

Cooder, Ry. *Chicken Skin Music*. Reprise Records MS 2254, 1976.

———. *Showtime*. Warner Brothers Records BS 3059, 1977.

De La Rosa, Tony. *Mejor Solo*. Hacienda Records 7356, 1993.

Jackson, Alan. *Genuine: The Alan Jackson Story*. Legacy 88725406392, 2015.

Jiménez, Flaco. *Ay Te Dejo En San Antonio*. Arhoolie Records 3021, 1986.

———. *Buena Suerte, Señorita*. Arista Records 18816, 1996.

———. *Flaco Jiménez*. Arista Texas 18772, 1994.

———. *Flaco's Amigos*. Arhoolie Records, 1988.

———. *Partners*. Reprise Records 26822, 1992.

———. *Said and Done*. Virgin Records 46530B, 1998.

———. *The Best of Flaco Jiménez*. Arhoolie Records CD 478, 1999.

Jiménez, Sr., Santiago. *Don Santiago Jimenez: His First and Last Recordings*. Arhoolie Records CD 414, 1980.

———. *Viva Seguin*. Arhoolie Records CD 7023, 2001.

Jordan, Steve. *La Bamba*. RyN Music, 2017.

———. *Many Sounds of Estéban 'Steve' Jordan*. Arhoolie Records CD 319, 1985.

———. *My Toot Toot*. RCA International IL6–7412, 1985.

———. *Soy de Tejas*. Hacienda Records LP-7905, 1979.

King, Ben E. *Don't Play That Song*. Atlantic Records 33–142, 1962.

Little Joe y la Familia. *Nuestra Tradición*. Sony Music Distribution 711841, 2007.

———. *Tu Amigo*. Columbia Records 46229, 1990.

Los Gatos de Japon. *Son Mentiritas*. Hacienda Records 7454, 1998.

———. *Tony De La Rosa Presents Los Gatos de Japon*. Hacienda Records 7437, 1996.

Los Lobos. *...And a Time to Dance*. Slash Records 1–23963, 1983.

———. *La Pistola y el Corazón*. Slash 9 25790–1, 1988.

Los Super Seven. *Canto*. Legacy 61429, 2001.
———. *Heard It on the X*. Telarc Distribution CD 83623, 2005.
———. *Los Super Seven*. RCA Nashville 07863-67689-2, 1998.
Los Texmaniacs. *Borders y Bailes*. Smithsonian Folkways SFW40555, 2009.
———. *Texas Towns & Tex-Mex Sounds*. Smithsonian Folkways SFW40565, 2012.
Owens, Buck. *Buck Owens All-Time Greatest Hits*. Saguaro Road Records 25828-D, 2010.
Ponce, Jesse. *Playing from the Heart—y Para Siempre*, 2005.
Rockin' Sidney. *My Toot Toot*. Maison De Soul 1009, 1991.
———. *My Zydeco Shoes Got the Zydeco Blues*, Maison De Soul LP-1009, 1984.
Rowwen Hèze. *Boem*. HKM 656.737-2, 1991.
Saldívar, Mingo. *25 Golden Hits*. Hacienda Records HAC-8132, 2009.
———. *El Chicano Alegre*. Hacienda Records 7305, 1995.
———. *I Love My Freedom, I Love My Texas*. Rounder Records CD6047, 1992.
Texas Tornados. *4 Aces*. Reprise Records 9 46197-2, 1996.
———. *Esta Bueno*. Proper Records PRPCD060, 2010.
———. *Texas Tornados*. Reprise Records 4-26251, 1990.
———. *Zone of Our Own*. Reprise Records 9 26683-2, 1991.
The Rolling Stones. *Voodoo Lounge*. Virgin CDV 2750, 1994.
Verheyden, Dwayne. *Conjunto Tracks*. HKM Records 42533, 2012.
———. *Desde Holanda*. HKM Records, 2015.
———. *Dwayne & The TexMeXplosion in San Antonio*. T2 Entertainment, 2010.
Ybarra, Eva. *A Mi San Antonio*. Rounder Records CD 6056, 1993.
———. *Romance Inolvidable*. Rounder Records CD 6062, 1996.
Yoakam, Dwight. *Buenas Noches from a Lonely Room*. Reprise Records 25749, 1988.

Works Cited

Ahad, Badia. "Post-Blackness and Culinary Nostalgia in Marcus Samuelsson's *Yes, Chef.*" *American Studies* 54, no. 4 (2016): 5–26.

Anderson, Benedict. *Imagined Communities: Reflections on the Origin and Spread of Nationalism*. New York: Verso, 1983.

Appadurai, Arjun. *Modernity at Large: Cultural Dimensions of Globalization*. Minneapolis: University of Minnesota Press, 1996.

Auslander, Philip. "Musical Personae." *TDR: The Drama Review* 50, no. 1 (2006): 100–119.

Bauer, Erin. "Beyond the Border: Meaning and Authenticity in the Adoption of Texas-Mexican Conjunto Music by International Artists." *Latin American Music Review* 37, no. 1 (2016): 34–64.

———. "Blurring Boundaries in Rosedale Park: The Importance of the Tejano Conjunto Festival on the Transnational Dissemination of Traditional Texas-Mexican Accordion Music." *Latino Studies* 17, no. 2 (2019): 164–186.

———. "Cross-Cultural, 'Oompah-Rock' Identities: Stylistic Unification and Common Background in the Music of Rowwen Hèze and Los Lobos." In *Het dorp en de wereld:dertig jaar Rowwen Hèze*, ed. Barbara Beckers and Leonie Cornips, 172–179. Nijmegen, Netherlands: Vantilt Publishers, 2015.

———. "The Participation of Flaco Jiménez on Ry Cooder's *Chicken Skin Music*: Cross-Cultural Collaboration and the (Inter)national Discovery of Texas-Mexican Accordion Music." *Rock Music Studies* 1, no. 2 (2014): 148–169.

Berman, Marshall. *All That Is Solid Melts into Air*. New York: Simon and Schuster, 1982.

Boyd, Todd. *The Notorious Ph.D.'s Guide to the Super Fly '70s: A Connoisseur's Journey through the Fabulous Flix, Hip Sounds, and Cool Vibes That Defined a Decade*. New York: Harlem Moon, 2007.

Brackett, David. "Black or White? Michael Jackson and the Idea of Crossover." *Popular Music and Society* 35, no. 2 (2012): 169–185.

———. "Questions of Genre in Black Popular Music." *Black Music Research Journal* 25, no. 1–2 (2005): 73–92.

Briggs, Charles L., and Richard Bauman. "Genre, Intertextuality, and Social Power." *Journal of Linguistic Anthropology* 2, no. 2 (1992): 131–172.

Bryson, Bethany. "'Anything but Heavy Metal': Symbolic Exclusion and Musical Dislikes." *American Sociological Review* 61, no. 5 (1996): 884–899.

Cain, Melissa. "Musics of 'The Other': Creating Musical Identities and Overcoming Cultural Boundaries in Australian Music Education." *British Journal of Music Education* 32, no. 1 (2015): 71–86.

Cervantes, Marco. "Squeezebox Poetics: Locating *Afromestizaje* in Esteban Jordan's Texas *Conjunto* Performance." *American Quarterly* 65, no. 4 (2013): 853–876.

Chávez, Alex. *Sounds of Crossing: Music, Migration, and the Aural Poetics of Huapango Arribeño*. Durham, NC: Duke University Press, 2017.

Corcoran, Michael. "The Invisible Genius: Steve Jordan," *Journal of Texas Music History* 3, no. 1 (2003): 1–5.

DeMars, Tony R. "Buying Time to Start Spanish-Language Radio in San Antonio: Manuel Davila and the Beginning of Tejano Programming." *Journal of Radio Studies* 12, no. 1 (2005): 74–84.

Feld, Steven. "A Sweet Lullaby for World Music." *Public Culture* 12, no. 1 (2000): 145–171.

———. "Notes on World Beat." *Public Culture Bulletin* 1, no. 1 (1988): 31–37.

———. "Pygmy POP. A Genealogy of Schizophonic Mimesis." *Yearbook for Traditional Music* 28 (1996): 1–35.

Ferguson, Jane M. "I Was Cool When My Country Wasn't: 'Mao' and 'Deng' Making Transnational Music in the Golden Triangle." *Asian Music* 47, no. 2 (2016): 114–137.

Flew, Terry, and Silvio Waisbord, "The Ongoing Significance of National Media Systems in the Context of Media Globalization." *Media, Culture & Society* 37, no. 4 (2015): 620–636.

García Canclini, Néstor. *Hybrid Cultures: Strategies for Entering and Leaving Modernity*. Translated by Christopher L. Chiappari and Silvia L. López. Minneapolis, MN: University of Minnesota Press, 1989 (2005).

Grijp, Louis Peter. "Singing in Dutch Dialects: Language Choice in Music and the Dialect Renaissance." In *Reframing Dutch Culture: Between Otherness and Authenticity*, ed. Peter Jan Margry and Herman Roodenburg, 225–244. Hampshire, England: Ashgate, 2007.

Guerra, Carlos. "The Unofficial Conjunto Primer." In *Puro Conjunto: An Album in Words and Pictures*, ed. Juan Tejeda and Avelardo Valdez, 3–9. Austin, TX: CMAS Books / San Antonio, TX: Guadalupe Cultural Arts Center, 2001.

Harnish, David. "Tejano Music in the Urbanizing Midwest: The Musical Story of *Conjunto* Master Jesse Ponce." *Journal of the Society for American Music* 3, no. 2 (2009): 195–219.

———, Lucy Long, and Barbara O'Hagin. *A Celebration of Latino Music Culture in Toledo, Ohio*. Bowling Green, Ohio: Partnerships for Community Action, 2002.

Herd, Judith Ann. "Trends and Taste in Japanese Popular Music: A Case-Study of the 1982 Yamaha World Music Popular Music Festival." *Popular Music* 4 (1984): 75–96.

Holton, Robert. "Globalization's Cultural Consequences." *The Annals of the American Academy of Political and Social Science* 570 (2000): 140–152.

Hosokawa, Shuhei. "'Salsa No Tiene Frontera': Orquesta de la Luz and the Globalization of Popular Music." *Cultural Studies* 13, no. 3 (1999): 509–534.

Jin, Dal Yong, and Woongjae Ryoo. "Critical Interpretation of Hybrid K-Pop: The Global-Local Paradigm of English Mixing in Lyrics." *Popular Music and Society* 37, no. 2 (2014): 113–131.

Limón, José E. "'This Is Our *Música*, Guy!': Tejanos and Ethno/Regional Musical Nationalism." In *Transnational Encounters: Music and Performance at the U.S.-Mexico Border*, ed. Alejandro L. Madrid, 111–126. Oxford: Oxford University Press, 2011.

Lipsitz, George. *Time Passages: Collective Memory and American Popular Culture.* Minneapolis: University of Minnesota Press, 1990.

Madrid, Alejandro. *Nor-Tec Rifa!: Electronic Music from Tijuana to the World.* New York: Oxford University Press, 2008.

Margolies, Daniel S. "Transmission of Texas-Mexican *Conjunto* Music in the 21st Century." *International Journal of Intangible Heritage* 6 (2011): 26–33.

———. "*Voz de Pueblo Chicano*: Sustainability, Teaching, and Intangible Cultural Transfer in Conjunto Music." *The Journal of American Culture* 34, no. 1 (2011): 36–48.

Marsh, Dave. "Rock & Roll's Latin Tinge." In *The First Rock & Roll Confidential Report*, ed. Dave Marsh, 110–112. New York: Pantheon Books, 1985.

Maurey, Yossi. "Dana International and the Politics of Nostalgia." *Popular Music* 28, no. 1 (2009): 85–103.

Mayer, Vicki. "From Segmented to Fragmented: Latino Media in San Antonio, Texas." *Journalism and Mass Communication Quarterly* 78, no. 2 (2001): 291–306.

Meintjes, Louise. "Paul Simon's Graceland, South Africa, and the Mediation of Musical Meaning." *Ethnomusicology* 34, no. 1 (1990): 37–73.

Morris, Chris. *Los Lobos: Dream in Blue.* Austin: University of Texas Press, 2015.

Nguyen, Thi Hien. "Cultural Adaptation, Tradition, and Identity of Diasporic Vietnamese People: A Case Study in Silicon Valley, California, USA." *Asian Ethnology* 75, no. 2 (2016): 441–459.

Núñez, Soledad A. "Sin Las Mujeres No Hay Conjunto: Mapping Chicana Feminisms in the Performances of Susan Torres, Clemencia Zapata, & Ruby Franco." Master's thesis, University of Texas at San Antonio, 2014.

O'Hagin, Isabel Barbara, and David Harnish. "Music as Cultural Identity: A Case Study of Latino Musicians Negotiating Tradition and Innovation in Northwest Ohio." *International Journal of Music Education* 24, no. 1 (2006): 56–70.

Peña, Manuel. *Musica Tejana: The Cultural Economy of Artistic Transformation.* College Station, TX: Texas A&M University Press, 1999.

———. "The Emergence of Conjunto Music, 1935–1955." In *Puro Conjunto: An Album in Words and Pictures*, ed. Juan Tejeda and Avelardo Valdez, 13–30. Austin, TX: CMASBooks / San Antonio, TX: Guadalupe Cultural Arts Center, 2001.

———. *The Texas-Mexican Conjunto: History of a Working-Class Music*. Austin: University of Texas Press, 1985.

Pineda, Richard D. "Will They See Me Coming? Do They Know I'm Running? Los Lobos and the Performance of *Mestizaje* Identity through Journey." *Text and Performance Quarterly* 29, no. 2 (2009): 183–200.

Ragland, Cathy. *Música Norteña: Mexican Migrants Creating a Nation between Nations*. Philadelphia: Temple University Press, 2009.

———. "Reviewed Work: Border y Bailes by Daniel E. Sheehy, Max Baca and Carolina Santamaría Delgado." *Yearbook for Traditional Music* 42 (2010): 218–219.

———. "Tejano and Proud: Regional Accordion Traditions of South Texas and the Border Region." In *The Accordion in the Americas: Klezmer, Polka, Tango, Zydeco, and More!*, ed. Helena Simonett, 87–111. Urbana: University of Illinois Press, 2012.

Regis, Helen A., and Shana Walton. "Producing the Folk at the New Orleans Jazz and Heritage Festival." *The Journal of American Folklore* 121, no. 484 (2008): 400–440.

Rios, Fernando. "The Andean *Conjunto*, Bolivian *Sikureada* and the Folkloric Musical Representation Continuum." *Ethnomusicology Forum* 21, no. 1 (2012): 5–29.

Routledge, Clay, Jamie Arndt, Tim Wildschut, Constantine Sedikides, Claire M. Hart, Jacob Johl, Ad J. J. M. Vingerhoets, Wolff Scholtz. "The Past Makes the Present Meaningful: Nostalgia as an Existential Resource." *Journal of Personality and Social Psychology* 101, no. 3 (2011): 638–652.

Satterwhite, Emily. "Imagining Home, Nation, World: Appalachia on the Mall." *The Journal of American Folklore* 121, no. 479 (2008): 10–34.

Scruggs, T. M. "'Ay, Te Dejo en San Antonio': Conjunto, Anglos, and the Jimenez Family of San Antonio." Master's thesis, University of Texas at Austin, 1985.

———. "Film and Video Reviews: 'Chulas Fronteras,' 'Del Mero Corazón,' 'Tex-Mex: Music of the Texas-Mexican Borderlands,' and 'Songs of the Homeland.'" *Ethnomusicology* 43, no. 3 (1999): 572–578.

Sedikides, Constantine, Tim Wildschut, Jamie Arndt, and Clay Routledge. "Nostalgia: Past, Present, and Future." *Current Directions in Psychological Science* 17, no. 5 (2008): 304–307.

Silverman, Carol. "Gypsy/Klezmer Dialectics: Jewish and Romani Traces and Erasures in Contemporary European World Music." *Ethnomusicology Forum* 24, no. 2 (2015): 159–180.

Simonett, Helena. *Banda: Mexican Musical Life Across Borders*. Middletown, CT: Wesleyan University Press, 2001.

Sterling, Marvin D. "Between National Subjectivity and Global Artistry: Ethnography, Afro-Asia, and Jamaican Music in Japan." *Popular Music and Society* 39, no. 3 (2016): 346–358.

Sutton, R. Anderson. "'Fusion' and Questions of Korean Cultural Identity in Music." *Korean Studies* 35 (2011): 4–24.

Tervo, Mervi. "From Appropriation to Translation: Localizing Rap Music to Finland." *Popular Music and Society* 37, no. 2 (2014): 169–186.

Tokita, Alison. "Bi-Musicality in Modern Japanese Culture." *International Journal of Bilingualism* 18, no. 2 (2014): 159–174.

Tomlinson, John. *Cultural Imperialism: A Critical Introduction*. London: Pinter, 1991.
Tsambu, Léon. "Transnationalism and Transculturalism as Seen in Congolese Music Videograms." *Journal of African Media Studies* 7, no. 1 (2015): 51–67.
Turino, Thomas. *Moving Away from Silence: Music of the Peruvian Altiplano and the Experience of Urban Migration*. Chicago: University of Chicago Press, 1993.
Valdez, Avelardo, and Jeffrey A. Halley. "Gender in the Culture of Mexican American Conjunto Music." *Gender and Society* 10, no. 2 (1996): 148–167.
van Elteren, Mel. "Country Music in the Netherlands: Why Is It Still Marginal?" *Popular Music and Society* 20, no. 3 (1996): 53–93.
———. "Dutch Country Music: Between Creative Appropriation and Mere Epigonism." *Popular Music and Society* 22, no. 1 (1998): 91–113.
———. *Imagining America: Dutch Youth and Its Sense of Place*. Tilburg, Netherlands: Tilburg University Press, 1994.
———. "Rocking and Rapping in the Dutch Welfare State." In *European Readings of American Popular Culture*, ed. John Dean and Jean-Paul Gabilliet, 55–68. Westport, Connecticut: Greenwood Press, 1996.
van Klyton, Aaron C. "All the Way From … Authenticity and Distance in World Music Production." *Cultural Studies* 30, no. 1 (2016): 106–128.
———. "Space and Place in World Music Production," *City, Culture and Society* 6 (2015): 101–108.
Vargas, Deborah R. "Borderland Bolerista: The Licentious Lyricism of Chelo Silva." *Feminist Studies* 34, no. 1/2 (2008): 173–197.
———. *Dissonant Divas in Chicana Music: The Limits of La Onda*. Minneapolis: University of Minnesota Press, 2012.
———. "Resounding Chicana Music: Listening to Eva Garza." *Women & Music* 16, no. 1 (2012): 113–132.
Vestel, Viggo. "Limits of Hybridity Versus Limits of Tradition?: A Semiotics of Cultural Reproduction, Creativity, and Ambivalence among Multicultural Youth in Rudenga, East Side Oslo." *Ethos* 37, no. 4 (2009): 466–488.
Wheeler, Deborah. "New Media, Globalization and Kuwaiti National Identity." *Middle East Journal* 53, no. 3 (2000): 432–444.
Wijnand, A.P. van Tilburg, Constantine Sedikides, and Tim Wildschut. "The Mnemonic Muse: Nostalgia Fosters Creativity through Openness to Experience." *Journal of Experimental Social Psychology* 59 (2015): 1–7.
Wildschut, Tim, Constantine Sedikides, Clay Routledge, Jamie Arndt, and Filippo Cordaro. "Nostalgia as a Repository of Social Connectedness: The Role of Attachment-Related Avoidance." *Journal of Personality and Social Psychology* 98, no. 4 (2010): 573–586.
Yano, Christine. "Inventing Selves: Images and Image-Making in a Japanese Popular Music Genre." *Journal of Popular Culture* 31, no. 2 (1997): 115–129.
Yri, Kirsten. "Medievalism and Exoticism in the Music of Dead Can Dance." *Current Musicology* 85 (2008): 53–72.

Index

Page numbers followed by *t* refer to tables and *f* refer to figures.

ERIN E. BAUER is chair of the Music Department and an associate professor of musicology at Muskingum University.

Music in American Life

Only a Miner: Studies in Recorded Coal-Mining Songs *Archie Green*
Great Day Coming: Folk Music and the American Left *R. Serge Denisoff*
John Philip Sousa: A Descriptive Catalog of His Works *Paul E. Bierley*
The Hell-Bound Train: A Cowboy Songbook *Glenn Ohrlin*
Oh, Didn't He Ramble: The Life Story of Lee Collins, as Told to Mary Collins *Edited by Frank J. Gillis and John W. Miner*
American Labor Songs of the Nineteenth Century *Philip S. Foner*
Stars of Country Music: Uncle Dave Macon to Johnny Rodriguez *Edited by Bill C. Malone and Judith McCulloh*
Git Along, Little Dogies: Songs and Songmakers of the American West *John I. White*
A Texas-Mexican *Cancionero*: Folksongs of the Lower Border *Américo Paredes*
San Antonio Rose: The Life and Music of Bob Wills *Charles R. Townsend*
Early Downhome Blues: A Musical and Cultural Analysis *Jeff Todd Titon*
An Ives Celebration: Papers and Panels of the Charles Ives Centennial Festival-Conference *Edited by H. Wiley Hitchcock and Vivian Perlis*
Sinful Tunes and Spirituals: Black Folk Music to the Civil War *Dena J. Epstein*
Joe Scott, the Woodsman-Songmaker *Edward D. Ives*
Jimmie Rodgers: The Life and Times of America's Blue Yodeler *Nolan Porterfield*
Early American Music Engraving and Printing: A History of Music Publishing in America from 1787 to 1825, with Commentary on Earlier and Later Practices *Richard J. Wolfe*
Sing a Sad Song: The Life of Hank Williams *Roger M. Williams*
Long Steel Rail: The Railroad in American Folksong *Norm Cohen*
Resources of American Music History: A Directory of Source Materials from Colonial Times to World War II *D. W. Krummel, Jean Geil, Doris J. Dyen, and Deane L. Root*
Tenement Songs: The Popular Music of the Jewish Immigrants *Mark Slobin*
Ozark Folksongs *Vance Randolph; edited and abridged by Norm Cohen*
Oscar Sonneck and American Music *Edited by William Lichtenwanger*
Bluegrass Breakdown: The Making of the Old Southern Sound *Robert Cantwell*
Bluegrass: A History *Neil V. Rosenberg*
Music at the White House: A History of the American Spirit *Elise K. Kirk*
Red River Blues: The Blues Tradition in the Southeast *Bruce Bastin*
Good Friends and Bad Enemies: Robert Winslow Gordon and the Study of American Folksong *Debora Kodish*
Fiddlin' Georgia Crazy: Fiddlin' John Carson, His Real World, and the World of His Songs *Gene Wiggins*
America's Music: From the Pilgrims to the Present (rev. 3d ed.) *Gilbert Chase*
Secular Music in Colonial Annapolis: The Tuesday Club, 1745–56 *John Barry Talley*

Bibliographical Handbook of American Music *D. W. Krummel*
Goin' to Kansas City *Nathan W. Pearson Jr.*
"Susanna," "Jeanie," and "The Old Folks at Home": The Songs of Stephen C. Foster from His Time to Ours (2d ed.) *William W. Austin*
Songprints: The Musical Experience of Five Shoshone Women *Judith Vander*
"Happy in the Service of the Lord": Afro-American Gospel Quartets in Memphis *Kip Lornell*
Paul Hindemith in the United States *Luther Noss*
"My Song Is My Weapon": People's Songs, American Communism, and the Politics of Culture, 1930–50 *Robbie Lieberman*
Chosen Voices: The Story of the American Cantorate *Mark Slobin*
Theodore Thomas: America's Conductor and Builder of Orchestras, 1835–1905 *Ezra Schabas*
"The Whorehouse Bells Were Ringing" and Other Songs Cowboys Sing *Collected and Edited by Guy Logsdon*
Crazeology: The Autobiography of a Chicago Jazzman *Bud Freeman, as Told to Robert Wolf*
Discoursing Sweet Music: Brass Bands and Community Life in Turn-of-the-Century Pennsylvania *Kenneth Kreitner*
Mormonism and Music: A History *Michael Hicks*
Voices of the Jazz Age: Profiles of Eight Vintage Jazzmen *Chip Deffaa*
Pickin' on Peachtree: A History of Country Music in Atlanta, Georgia *Wayne W. Daniel*
Bitter Music: Collected Journals, Essays, Introductions, and Librettos *Harry Partch; edited by Thomas McGeary*
Ethnic Music on Records: A Discography of Ethnic Recordings Produced in the United States, 1893 to 1942 *Richard K. Spottswood*
Downhome Blues Lyrics: An Anthology from the Post–World War II Era *Jeff Todd Titon*
Ellington: The Early Years *Mark Tucker*
Chicago Soul *Robert Pruter*
That Half-Barbaric Twang: The Banjo in American Popular Culture *Karen Linn*
Hot Man: The Life of Art Hodes *Art Hodes and Chadwick Hansen*
The Erotic Muse: American Bawdy Songs (2d ed.) *Ed Cray*
Barrio Rhythm: Mexican American Music in Los Angeles *Steven Loza*
The Creation of Jazz: Music, Race, and Culture in Urban America *Burton W. Peretti*
Charles Martin Loeffler: A Life Apart in Music *Ellen Knight*
Club Date Musicians: Playing the New York Party Circuit *Bruce A. MacLeod*
Opera on the Road: Traveling Opera Troupes in the United States, 1825–60 *Katherine K. Preston*
The Stonemans: An Appalachian Family and the Music That Shaped Their Lives *Ivan M. Tribe*

Transforming Tradition: Folk Music Revivals Examined
Edited by Neil V. Rosenberg
The Crooked Stovepipe: Athapaskan Fiddle Music and Square Dancing in Northeast Alaska and Northwest Canada *Craig Mishler*
Traveling the High Way Home: Ralph Stanley and the World of Traditional Bluegrass Music *John Wright*
Carl Ruggles: Composer, Painter, and Storyteller *Marilyn Ziffrin*
Never without a Song: The Years and Songs of Jennie Devlin, 1865–1952
Katharine D. Newman
The Hank Snow Story *Hank Snow, with Jack Ownbey and Bob Burris*
Milton Brown and the Founding of Western Swing *Cary Ginell, with special assistance from Roy Lee Brown*
Santiago de Murcia's "Códice Saldívar No. 4": A Treasury of Secular Guitar Music from Baroque Mexico *Craig H. Russell*
The Sound of the Dove: Singing in Appalachian Primitive Baptist Churches
Beverly Bush Patterson
Heartland Excursions: Ethnomusicological Reflections on Schools of Music
Bruno Nettl
Doowop: The Chicago Scene *Robert Pruter*
Blue Rhythms: Six Lives in Rhythm and Blues *Chip Deffaa*
Shoshone Ghost Dance Religion: Poetry Songs and Great Basin Context
Judith Vander
Go Cat Go! Rockabilly Music and Its Makers *Craig Morrison*
'Twas Only an Irishman's Dream: The Image of Ireland and the Irish in American Popular Song Lyrics, 1800–1920 *William H. A. Williams*
Democracy at the Opera: Music, Theater, and Culture in New York City, 1815–60
Karen Ahlquist
Fred Waring and the Pennsylvanians *Virginia Waring*
Woody, Cisco, and Me: Seamen Three in the Merchant Marine *Jim Longhi*
Behind the Burnt Cork Mask: Early Blackface Minstrelsy and Antebellum American Popular Culture *William J. Mahar*
Going to Cincinnati: A History of the Blues in the Queen City *Steven C. Tracy*
Pistol Packin' Mama: Aunt Molly Jackson and the Politics of Folksong
Shelly Romalis
Sixties Rock: Garage, Psychedelic, and Other Satisfactions *Michael Hicks*
The Late Great Johnny Ace and the Transition from R&B to Rock 'n' Roll
James M. Salem
Tito Puente and the Making of Latin Music *Steven Loza*
Juilliard: A History *Andrea Olmstead*
Understanding Charles Seeger, Pioneer in American Musicology
Edited by Bell Yung and Helen Rees
Mountains of Music: West Virginia Traditional Music from *Goldenseal*
Edited by John Lilly

Alice Tully: An Intimate Portrait *Albert Fuller*
A Blues Life *Henry Townsend, as told to Bill Greensmith*
Long Steel Rail: The Railroad in American Folksong (2d ed.) *Norm Cohen*
The Golden Age of Gospel *Text by Horace Clarence Boyer; photography by Lloyd Yearwood*
Aaron Copland: The Life and Work of an Uncommon Man *Howard Pollack*
Louis Moreau Gottschalk *S. Frederick Starr*
Race, Rock, and Elvis *Michael T. Bertrand*
Theremin: Ether Music and Espionage *Albert Glinsky*
Poetry and Violence: The Ballad Tradition of Mexico's Costa Chica *John H. McDowell*
The Bill Monroe Reader *Edited by Tom Ewing*
Music in Lubavitcher Life *Ellen Koskoff*
Zarzuela: Spanish Operetta, American Stage *Janet L. Sturman*
Bluegrass Odyssey: A Documentary in Pictures and Words, 1966–86 *Carl Fleischhauer and Neil V. Rosenberg*
That Old-Time Rock & Roll: A Chronicle of an Era, 1954–63 *Richard Aquila*
Labor's Troubadour *Joe Glazer*
American Opera *Elise K. Kirk*
Don't Get above Your Raisin': Country Music and the Southern Working Class *Bill C. Malone*
John Alden Carpenter: A Chicago Composer *Howard Pollack*
Heartbeat of the People: Music and Dance of the Northern Pow-wow *Tara Browner*
My Lord, What a Morning: An Autobiography *Marian Anderson*
Marian Anderson: A Singer's Journey *Allan Keiler*
Charles Ives Remembered: An Oral History *Vivian Perlis*
Henry Cowell, Bohemian *Michael Hicks*
Rap Music and Street Consciousness *Cheryl L. Keyes*
Louis Prima *Garry Boulard*
Marian McPartland's Jazz World: All in Good Time *Marian McPartland*
Robert Johnson: Lost and Found *Barry Lee Pearson and Bill McCulloch*
Bound for America: Three British Composers *Nicholas Temperley*
Lost Sounds: Blacks and the Birth of the Recording Industry, 1890–1919 *Tim Brooks*
Burn, Baby! BURN! The Autobiography of Magnificent Montague *Magnificent Montague with Bob Baker*
Way Up North in Dixie: A Black Family's Claim to the Confederate Anthem *Howard L. Sacks and Judith Rose Sacks*
The Bluegrass Reader *Edited by Thomas Goldsmith*
Colin McPhee: Composer in Two Worlds *Carol J. Oja*
Robert Johnson, Mythmaking, and Contemporary American Culture *Patricia R. Schroeder*

Composing a World: Lou Harrison, Musical Wayfarer *Leta E. Miller and Fredric Lieberman*
Fritz Reiner, Maestro and Martinet *Kenneth Morgan*
That Toddlin' Town: Chicago's White Dance Bands and Orchestras, 1900–1950 *Charles A. Sengstock Jr.*
Dewey and Elvis: The Life and Times of a Rock 'n' Roll Deejay *Louis Cantor*
Come Hither to Go Yonder: Playing Bluegrass with Bill Monroe *Bob Black*
Chicago Blues: Portraits and Stories *David Whiteis*
The Incredible Band of John Philip Sousa *Paul E. Bierley*
"Maximum Clarity" and Other Writings on Music *Ben Johnston, edited by Bob Gilmore*
Staging Tradition: John Lair and Sarah Gertrude Knott *Michael Ann Williams*
Homegrown Music: Discovering Bluegrass *Stephanie P. Ledgin*
Tales of a Theatrical Guru *Danny Newman*
The Music of Bill Monroe *Neil V. Rosenberg and Charles K. Wolfe*
Pressing On: The Roni Stoneman Story *Roni Stoneman, as told to Ellen Wright*
Together Let Us Sweetly Live *Jonathan C. David, with photographs by Richard Holloway*
Live Fast, Love Hard: The Faron Young Story *Diane Diekman*
Air Castle of the South: WSM Radio and the Making of Music City *Craig P. Havighurst*
Traveling Home: Sacred Harp Singing and American Pluralism *Kiri Miller*
Where Did Our Love Go? The Rise and Fall of the Motown Sound *Nelson George*
Lonesome Cowgirls and Honky-Tonk Angels: The Women of Barn Dance Radio *Kristine M. McCusker*
California Polyphony: Ethnic Voices, Musical Crossroads *Mina Yang*
The Never-Ending Revival: Rounder Records and the Folk Alliance *Michael F. Scully*
Sing It Pretty: A Memoir *Bess Lomax Hawes*
Working Girl Blues: The Life and Music of Hazel Dickens *Hazel Dickens and Bill C. Malone*
Charles Ives Reconsidered *Gayle Sherwood Magee*
The Hayloft Gang: The Story of the National Barn Dance *Edited by Chad Berry*
Country Music Humorists and Comedians *Loyal Jones*
Record Makers and Breakers: Voices of the Independent Rock 'n' Roll Pioneers *John Broven*
Music of the First Nations: Tradition and Innovation in Native North America *Edited by Tara Browner*
Cafe Society: The Wrong Place for the Right People *Barney Josephson, with Terry Trilling-Josephson*
George Gershwin: An Intimate Portrait *Walter Rimler*

Life Flows On in Endless Song: Folk Songs and American History
Robert V. Wells
I Feel a Song Coming On: The Life of Jimmy McHugh *Alyn Shipton*
King of the Queen City: The Story of King Records *Jon Hartley Fox*
Long Lost Blues: Popular Blues in America, 1850–1920 *Peter C. Muir*
Hard Luck Blues: Roots Music Photographs from the Great Depression
Rich Remsberg
Restless Giant: The Life and Times of Jean Aberbach and Hill and Range Songs
Bar Biszick-Lockwood
Champagne Charlie and Pretty Jemima: Variety Theater in the Nineteenth Century *Gillian M. Rodger*
Sacred Steel: Inside an African American Steel Guitar Tradition *Robert L. Stone*
Gone to the Country: The New Lost City Ramblers and the Folk Music Revival
Ray Allen
The Makers of the Sacred Harp *David Warren Steel with Richard H. Hulan*
Woody Guthrie, American Radical *Will Kaufman*
George Szell: A Life of Music *Michael Charry*
Bean Blossom: The Brown County Jamboree and Bill Monroe's Bluegrass Festivals
Thomas A. Adler
Crowe on the Banjo: The Music Life of J. D. Crowe *Marty Godbey*
Twentieth Century Drifter: The Life of Marty Robbins *Diane Diekman*
Henry Mancini: Reinventing Film Music *John Caps*
The Beautiful Music All Around Us: Field Recordings and the American Experience *Stephen Wade*
Then Sings My Soul: The Culture of Southern Gospel Music *Douglas Harrison*
The Accordion in the Americas: Klezmer, Polka, Tango, Zydeco, and More!
Edited by Helena Simonett
Bluegrass Bluesman: A Memoir *Josh Graves, edited by Fred Bartenstein*
One Woman in a Hundred: Edna Phillips and the Philadelphia Orchestra
Mary Sue Welsh
The Great Orchestrator: Arthur Judson and American Arts Management
James M. Doering
Charles Ives in the Mirror: American Histories of an Iconic Composer
David C. Paul
Southern Soul-Blues *David Whiteis*
Sweet Air: Modernism, Regionalism, and American Popular Song
Edward P. Comentale
Pretty Good for a Girl: Women in Bluegrass *Murphy Hicks Henry*
Sweet Dreams: The World of Patsy Cline *Warren R. Hofstra*
William Sidney Mount and the Creolization of American Culture
Christopher J. Smith
Bird: The Life and Music of Charlie Parker *Chuck Haddix*

Making the March King: John Philip Sousa's Washington Years, 1854–1893 *Patrick Warfield*
In It for the Long Run *Jim Rooney*
Pioneers of the Blues Revival *Steve Cushing*
Roots of the Revival: American and British Folk Music in the 1950s *Ronald D. Cohen and Rachel Clare Donaldson*
Blues All Day Long: The Jimmy Rogers Story *Wayne Everett Goins*
Yankee Twang: Country and Western Music in New England *Clifford R. Murphy*
The Music of the Stanley Brothers *Gary B. Reid*
Hawaiian Music in Motion: Mariners, Missionaries, and Minstrels *James Revell Carr*
Sounds of the New Deal: The Federal Music Project in the West *Peter Gough*
The Mormon Tabernacle Choir: A Biography *Michael Hicks*
The Man That Got Away: The Life and Songs of Harold Arlen *Walter Rimler*
A City Called Heaven: Chicago and the Birth of Gospel Music *Robert M. Marovich*
Blues Unlimited: Essential Interviews from the Original Blues Magazine *Edited by Bill Greensmith, Mike Rowe, and Mark Camarigg*
Hoedowns, Reels, and Frolics: Roots and Branches of Southern Appalachian Dance *Phil Jamison*
Fannie Bloomfield-Zeisler: The Life and Times of a Piano Virtuoso *Beth Abelson Macleod*
Cybersonic Arts: Adventures in American New Music *Gordon Mumma, edited with commentary by Michelle Fillion*
The Magic of Beverly Sills *Nancy Guy*
Waiting for Buddy Guy *Alan Harper*
Harry T. Burleigh: From the Spiritual to the Harlem Renaissance *Jean E. Snyder*
Music in the Age of Anxiety: American Music in the Fifties *James Wierzbicki*
Jazzing: New York City's Unseen Scene *Thomas H. Greenland*
A Cole Porter Companion *Edited by Don M. Randel, Matthew Shaftel, and Susan Forscher Weiss*
Foggy Mountain Troubadour: The Life and Music of Curly Seckler *Penny Parsons*
Blue Rhythm Fantasy: Big Band Jazz Arranging in the Swing Era *John Wriggle*
Bill Clifton: America's Bluegrass Ambassador to the World *Bill C. Malone*
Chinatown Opera Theater in North America *Nancy Yunhwa Rao*
The Elocutionists: Women, Music, and the Spoken Word *Marian Wilson Kimber*
May Irwin: Singing, Shouting, and the Shadow of Minstrelsy *Sharon Ammen*
Peggy Seeger: A Life of Music, Love, and Politics *Jean R. Freedman*
Charles Ives's *Concord*: Essays after a Sonata *Kyle Gann*
Don't Give Your Heart to a Rambler: My Life with Jimmy Martin, the King of Bluegrass *Barbara Martin Stephens*

Libby Larsen: Composing an American Life *Denise Von Glahn*
George Szell's Reign: Behind the Scenes with the Cleveland Orchestra *Marcia Hansen Kraus*
Just One of the Boys: Female-to-Male Cross-Dressing on the American Variety Stage *Gillian M. Rodger*
Spirituals and the Birth of a Black Entertainment Industry *Sandra Jean Graham*
Right to the Juke Joint: A Personal History of American Music *Patrick B. Mullen*
Bluegrass Generation: A Memoir *Neil V. Rosenberg*
Pioneers of the Blues Revival, Expanded Second Edition *Steve Cushing*
Banjo Roots and Branches *Edited by Robert Winans*
Bill Monroe: The Life and Music of the Blue Grass Man *Tom Ewing*
Dixie Dewdrop: The Uncle Dave Macon Story *Michael D. Doubler*
Los Romeros: Royal Family of the Spanish Guitar *Walter Aaron Clark*
Transforming Women's Education: Liberal Arts and Music in Female Seminaries *Jewel A. Smith*
Rethinking American Music *Edited by Tara Browner and Thomas L. Riis*
Leonard Bernstein and the Language of Jazz *Katherine Baber*
Dancing Revolution: Bodies, Space, and Sound in American Cultural History *Christopher J. Smith*
Peggy Glanville-Hicks: Composer and Critic *Suzanne Robinson*
Mormons, Musical Theater, and Belonging in America *Jake Johnson*
Blues Legacy: Tradition and Innovation in Chicago *David Whiteis*
Blues Before Sunrise 2: Interviews from the Chicago Scene *Steve Cushing*
The Cashaway Psalmody: Transatlantic Religion and Music in Colonial Carolina *Stephen A. Marini*
Earl Scruggs and Foggy Mountain Breakdown: The Making of an American Classic *Thomas Goldsmith*
A Guru's Journey: Pandit Chitresh Das and Indian Classical Dance in Diaspora *Sarah Morelli*
Unsettled Scores: Politics, Hollywood, and the Film Music of Aaron Copland and Hanns Eisler *Sally Bick*
Hillbilly Maidens, Okies, and Cowgirls: Women's Country Music, 1930–1960 *Stephanie Vander Wel*
Always the Queen: The Denise LaSalle Story *Denise LaSalle with David Whiteis*
Artful Noise: Percussion Literature in the Twentieth Century *Thomas Siwe*
The Heart of a Woman: The Life and Music of Florence B. Price *Rae Linda Brown, edited by Guthrie P. Ramsey Jr.*
When Sunday Comes: Gospel Music in the Soul and Hip-Hop Eras *Claudrena N. Harold*
The Lady Swings: Memoirs of a Jazz Drummer *Dottie Dodgion and Wayne Enstice*
Industrial Strength Bluegrass: Southwestern Ohio's Musical Legacy *Edited by Fred Bartenstein and Curtis W. Ellison*

Soul on Soul: The Life and Music of Mary Lou Williams *Tammy L. Kernodle*
Unbinding Gentility: Women Making Music in the Nineteenth-Century South *Candace Bailey*
Punks in Peoria: Making a Scene in the American Heartland *Jonathan Wright and Dawson Barrett*
Homer Rodeheaver and the Rise of the Gospel Music Industry *Kevin Mungons and Douglas Yeo*
Americanaland: Where Country & Western Met Rock 'n' Roll *John Milward, with Portraits by Margie Greve*
Listening to Bob Dylan *Larry Starr*
Lying in the Middle: Musical Theater and Belief at the Heart of America *Jake Johnson*
The Sounds of Place: Music and the American Cultural Landscape *Denise Von Glahn*
Peace Be Still: How James Cleveland and the Angelic Choir Created a Gospel Classic *Robert M. Marovich*
Politics as Sound: The Washington, DC, Hardcore Scene, 1978–1983 *Shayna L. Maskell*
Tania León's Stride: A Polyrhythmic Life *Alejandro L. Madrid*
Elliott Carter Speaks: Unpublished Lectures *Edited by Laura Emmery*
Interviews with American Composers: Barney Childs in Conversation *Edited by Virginia Anderson*
Queer Country *Shana Goldin-Perschbacher*
On the Bus with Bill Monroe: My Five-Year Ride with the Father of Blue Grass *Mark Hembree*
Mandolin Man: The Bluegrass Life of Roland White *Bob Black*
Music and Mystique in Muscle Shoals *Christopher M. Reali*
Buddy Emmons: Steel Guitar Icon *Steve Fishell*
Music in Black American Life, 1600–1945: A University of Illinois Press Anthology *Compiled by Laurie Matheson*
Music in Black American Life, 1945–2020: A University of Illinois Press Anthology *Compiled by Laurie Matheson*
Ballad Hunting with Max Hunter: Stories of an Ozark Folksong Collector *Sarah Jane Nelson*
Play Like a Man: My Life in Poster Children *Rose Marshack*
Samuel Barber: His Life and Legacy *Howard Pollack*
Aaron Copland in Latin America: Music and Cultural Politics *Carol A. Hess*
Stringbean: The Life and Murder of a Country Music Legend *Taylor Hagood*
Danzón Days: Age, Race, and Romance in Mexico *Hettie Malcomson*
Flaco's Legacy: The Globalization of Conjunto *Erin E. Bauer*

The University of Illinois Press
is a founding member of the
Association of University Presses.

University of Illinois Press
1325 South Oak Street
Champaign, IL 61820-6903
www.press.uillinois.edu